# INTIMACY
# DESIRE

# INTIMACY & DESIRE

## AWAKEN THE PASSION IN YOUR RELATIONSHIP

Dr. David Schnarch

BEAUFORT BOOKS
New York

The information contained herein is provided for informational purposes, and not intended as a substitute for advice or treatment that may or should be prescribed by a physician or therapist. Some sexual difficulties may be caused by medical problems. A thorough medical examination is always wise, and if you believe you have a medical problem, consult a doctor promptly. Before adhering to any information or recommendations given here you should consult your physician or therapist.

Case examples are composites of cases from clinical practice.

"Crucible®", "Sexual Crucible®", "Sexual Crucible Approach™", "Crucible Approach™", "Passionate Marriage®", "Passionate Couples®", "Four Points of Balance™", "Solid Flexible Self™", "Quiet Mind–Calm Heart™", "Grounded Responding™", "Meaningful Endurance™", and "Resurrecting Sex™" are trademarks owned and pending by David Schnarch, Ph.D. Programs, trainings, services, and materials using these trademarks can only be provided by the Crucible Institute of Evergreen, Colorado and its authorized designates. Website: www.DesireBook.com

First Paperpack Edition

Quotation from *The Self-Organizing Universe* by Erich Jantsch copyright Pergamon Press. Used with permission.

Lyric to "Eyes of the World" by Robert Hunter copyright Ice Nine Publishing Company. Used with permission.

Interior design: Neuwirth & Associates, Inc.

Library of Congress Cataloging-in-Publication Data
Schnarch, David Morris, 1946
  Intimacy & desire : awaken the passion in Your Relationship. / David Schnarch.
    p. cm.
Includes bibliographical references and index.
  ISBN 978-0-8253-0567-2 (alk. paper)
  1. Intimacy (Psychology) 2. Desire. 3. Interpersonal relations. I. Title. II. Title: Intimacy and desire.

BF575.I5S36 2009
306.7—dc22

                                        2009022161


3  4  5  6  7  8  9  10

This book is dedicated to five important people in my life:

### Dr. Ruth Morehouse

*The nicest woman I know. My wife.*
*The central blessing in my life.*

### Steve Schnarch

*The nicest man I know. I am lucky to have him as my friend.*
*I am blessed he is my brother.*

### Dr. Barry Lester

*My oldest friend. Child researcher extraordinaire.*
*Friend to babies around the world.*

### Dr. James Maddock

*Brilliant theoretician. Wonderful man.*
*His passing leaves a void in the field of sex & marital therapy.*

### The Man Whose Impeccable Integrity Won't Allow Me to Mention His Name

*In memory of a man who brought out the best in me.*

# ACKNOWLEDGMENTS

This book is about desire, and desire is about wanting. Many people have made me want to do better, and helped me do better:

My parents, Stan and Rose Schnarch, have given me so much, just by being the good people they are. They are decent people of integrity and good will. My work helps me appreciate just how lucky I am to be able to say that about my parents.

My wife, Ruth Morehouse, has walked with me through the crucible of marriage and never let go. Together we've learned a lot about sexual desire. She has mapped my mind and, somehow, still chooses to live with me. She lives inside me in ways that bring out the best in me.

My daughter, Sarah Morehouse, has done her job well, making me live what I say about the Four Points of Balance. She has helped me develop a Herculean ability to hold on to myself, or so it seems at my worst times. She makes me want to do better, and make the world better, because beauty and goodness gush out of her eyes when she smiles.

My brother, Steve Schnarch, holds me to high standards of integrity through personal example and helpful scrutiny. Whether we're in the desert or the mountains, or dealing with everyday problems, Steve is often a step ahead of me. Excellence for its own sake is a good way of describing how he conducts himself as a carpenter and a human being.

My friends, Barry Lester, Lynn Legasse, Jim Maddock, Susan Regas,

Josh and Peggy Golden, and Resmaa Menachim have pushed, pulled, dragged, and supported me to function at a higher level. They open my horizons of what is possible and then they help me go there.

My clients lead me to new ways of seeing things through their refusals to grow, finally confronting themselves, and their successes. Students keep me on my toes "looking for the holes" and push me to find better ways to teach them. Professional colleagues and audiences around the world encourage me to make this approach more widely available. It's fine with me if you consider this book an act of "pass it forward."

Grateful thanks to my dear friend Carol Gable for introducing me to public relations maven, publishing veteran, and all-around good guy, Michael Wright, of Garson-Wright, who helped bring together the team of talented people (besides himself) who produced this book. These include Eric Kampmann, Margot Atwell, and Erin Smith at Beaufort Books, who immediately believed in this project. Trish Hoard, who's a delight to work with, did a great job of polish editing the final manuscript. Jay Boggis and Oriana Leckert did the proofing. Melody Englund (Songbird Indexing) produced this book's wonderful index, making its contents readily accessible. Amy King produced this book's lovely cover on short notice.

My attorneys Marc Reisler (Holland & Knight) and Amy Berge (Greenbaum Doll & McDonald) do a wonderful job of looking out for my entertainment interests and intellectual property rights, respectively.

My hope, my wish, my desire is that you read this book, take action, and make your marriage and family (and community) a place of peace and joy. This is what you can do to revolutionize how we understand sexual desire. That is what I *want*. That is my heart's desire.

*Evolution is self-realization through self-transcendence*
Erich Jantsch

*Wake up to find out that you are the eyes of the world*
Grateful Dead

# CONTENTS

# INTRODUCTION

Thirty years ago I developed a completely new approach to sexual and marital therapy.[1] You can learn a lot about desire as couples skid toward divorce. One thing I really focused on was sexual desire problems. It revolutionized my understanding of love relationships and at times left me astonished. I certainly didn't expect sexual desire problems to teach me what they did about intimacy and love. This book is my best effort to pass it on to you.

People shop around for perspectives they prefer. So if you want a book that says your sexual desire basically runs on hormones and biological drives, this one isn't for you. If you want to be told, "Just do it!" don't waste your time here. If you're invested in the idea that desire dies and never returns, read something else.

But if you want to *feel* more desire, or increase the depth and meaningfulness of your desire, you're holding a goldmine. This book will not only change how you think and feel about yourself, it will change how you think and feel—period. It may even change how your brain works. It's hard to imagine how all this comes from dealing with a sexual desire problem, particularly one you haven't been able to solve at this point. That's because you haven't read this truly revolutionary approach. If you want a completely new understanding of desire, love, intimacy, and sex in emotionally committed relationships, read on.

### • *A new approach offering new opportunities*

Anthropologist Stephanie Coontz writes that throughout recorded history couples have married people they didn't know in order to fulfill the financial, political, and kinship agendas of parents and kin. Husbands and wives had little or no say in who they married. However, in the last *two hundred* years, marriage has ceased to revolve around political and economic alliances. People have started picking their own marriage partners. And now, for the first time in history, *marriage hinges on love, desire, intimacy, and sex.* It seems absolutely reasonable to expect these things. And yet, sexual desire problems are a common cause of divorce today. But the solution isn't staying together and giving up sex, or settling for lousy sex. The solution is working together to turn your sexual desire problems into a passion beyond your wildest imaginings.

Generally, you learn five views of sexual desire growing up: There's sexual desire as genetic programming for reproduction, driven by genes and hormones. There's the Freudian "libido" view of desire, in which sexual impulses forever try to pop out and get you into trouble. There's the romantic view, proposing that desire is a natural expression of true love. And the horniness (blue balls) model of desire, centered on "doing what comes naturally." Finally, there's the view that equates sexual desire with biological hungers for food and water. Before I developed my new approach, conventional sexual desire therapy referred to low sexual desire as a kind of "sexual anorexia."

Unfortunately, all these views presume—if you're a healthy person in a healthy relationship—that you *have* sexual desire. And, according to these views, if you have sexual desire problems, there's something wrong with you, your partner, or your relationship. You sure don't want to have low sexual desire, because you would be *abnormal.*

This book offers a different view. It shows *why* normal healthy couples have sexual desire problems. It explains why you and your partner will have sexual desire problems sooner or later, regardless of your love, communication skills, or Tantra workshops.

Research indicates sexual desire problems are so widespread they are *normal* rather than abnormal. A 1994 study of 3,432 randomly selected

Americans found sexual desire was the number one sexual problem. Thirty-three percent of women and 16 percent of men reported sexual desire problems *in the past year.*[2]

In 2006 I developed an online survey for NBC TV's *Dateline.* About 27,500 people participated over four days: 22 percent said they were in the "sex is alive and well" category, and another 10 percent said their sex is "robust, erotic, and passionate." However, *68 percent* had sexual desire problems. That's two out of every three people! Thirteen percent said their "sex life is dead," and 22 percent said it is "comatose and in danger of dying." Thirty-three percent said their sex is "asleep and needing a wake-up call." This came on the heels of *Dateline* running a one-hour program showing two sexless couples going through therapy with me. After the show aired, I received over two thousand requests for help.

Looking at this survey through conventional views of sexual desire, you'd have to conclude people are pretty messed up. This book says just the opposite: It means these people are *normal.* I'll show you, in detail, how normal healthy growth makes sexual desire problems common. Understanding why *normal* couples have sexual desire problems is entirely new.

This book shows you how to create the intimacy, desire, love, and sex that modern couples expect and demand. The kind of desire that makes you want to stay with your partner and be happy you did. The kind of life-giving desire that spreads through your life like wildfire.

## WHAT LIES AHEAD

This book has four sections.

Part One, "Why Normal People Have Sexual Desire Problems," will revolutionize your understanding of human sexual desire and sexual desire problems. These chapters explain how it is possible—and likely—that when you have sexual desire problems nothing is going wrong. You'll get new perspectives on your situation and what may be causing it, as well as what to do about it. Part One provides the framework for the three sections that follow.

Part Two, "How We Co-Evolve Through Sexual Desire Problems," shows how partners push each other to grow through sexual desire problems. You'll learn about the Four Points of Balance™, which will help you in every aspect of your life. (You'll probably wish you knew these facts of life before you started dating.) These chapters explore how partners grow through four conflict areas involving differences in desire, problems with intimacy, questions on monogamy, and sexual boredom.

Part Three, "Sexual Desire Problems: How Your Personal Life Fits In," explores how your particular life experiences, whether from childhood or yesterday, affect your sexual desire problems. You'll learn how to harness this knowledge into powerful forces for personal growth. These chapters cover volatile sexual desire issues, such as not wanting to want, normal marital sadism, and safety and security issues.

Part Four, "Using Your Body, Rewiring Your Brain, and Co-Evolving in Bed," shows you how to kick the people-growing process into high gear by getting your body involved. This part is more sexually explicit, detailing physical things you can do with your partner to enhance desire and create better sex. Four chapters offer time-tested ways of resolving sexual desire problems (including one that hasn't failed in over twenty years). We explore how to create sex worth wanting, and how to change your situation and become the person you want to be. Two chapters show you how to do this without even taking your clothes off. The two remaining chapters are better attempted with them off. You'll find a passionate, tender, loving sex that can fill your soul and maybe change your brain, and a mind-blowing, sizzling eroticism that can do the same. Bring with you a sense of humor, a good grip on yourself, and a spirit of adventure.

(If you're interested in interpersonal neurobiology and the latest cutting-edge brain science, you'll find it referenced and documented in Part One and Four's extensive end notes. *Intimacy & Desire* is written so you don't have to read a word of science, but if you want to follow the underlying facts and research, it's all there.)

## • *Relationship to prior books*

If you've read my prior books, *Passionate Marriage* and *Resurrecting Sex,* this one will fit right in. *Passionate Marriage* contains the most in-depth coverage of marriage's core dynamics. *Resurrecting Sex* focuses on sexual dysfunctions (like arousal, lubrication, erection, and orgasm problems). It covers sexual desire problems from medical causes. But if you're having sexual desire problems, the book you're holding is meant for you.

## • *Suggestions for reading this book*

While reading *Intimacy & Desire,* forget any presumption you have that something must be wrong with you, your partner, or your relationship. Read from a non-defensive position. Try to leave what you already know behind. *Your brain will try to grasp new things by using past experience as a frame of reference. That makes it hard to see things differently. Put your assumptions aside as best you can. Don't get crazy when your usual ways of seeing things are challenged.*

You're going to meet couples struggling with sexual desire problems. Don't focus on how they differ from you. Read with an inclusive attitude. Focus on things that apply to you, even if some aspects differ. You'll find something relevant in every case. Here's the important part: Visualize in your mind what's happening to these people, and what they're feeling and thinking, even if they are your complete opposite. Let yourself imagine what's going through these people's minds. It's easier for your brain to comprehend interactions between people than to work from abstract principles. The intuitive understanding you'll develop by putting yourself in each person's situation will help organize the novel concepts and ideas you'll find here. Also, I alternate using "he" and "she" throughout the book whenever giving generic examples, instead of using "he or she" in every instance.

Summary points appear at the end of each chapter to help you organize and retain what you've read. They delineate an incredible natural system of human development. These are the basic principles of human sexual desire. Ponder these points rather than trying to memorize them: It's more important that you see how they work together as a system than to recite them. Apply them to the couple in each chapter. Apply them to yourself. You're better off this way than trying to remember an abstract idea.

• *Get the most from your efforts*

I encourage you and your partner to have your own separate copies of this book. Many couples have said this really helped them with my other books. Read to each other if you like, but to paraphrase poet-philosopher Khalil Gibran, read to each other from your own book, rather than from a single book. Underline or highlight whatever speaks to you. Use a different marker on your second reading. See which points continue to be important to you. What new things grab your attention because you've grown? Don't bother underlining things for your partner to read. It will just make him or her defensive and less willing to consider your point.

If you want this book to change your life, put what you read into action. Just visualizing and thinking won't be enough. Only by taking action will you and your situation change. According to emerging neuroscience, doing something also changes your brain and mind. So, literally, *do* yourself a favor.

One more point to note: This book considers who controls sex in a relationship. There are many times and places in the world where women do not control their bodies. Opportunistic or systematic rape occurs worldwide. In some cultures, women's bodies are men's property. In these situations the low sexual desire partner (a term I use throughout the book) does not control sex. Women who are systematically battered do not control sex. The same holds true for refugees, prison inmates, torture victims, illegal immigrants who are part of worldwide sex trafficking, and in cultures where women lack equal opportunity for education, voting, or owning property. The list is long and their treatment horribly unjust. They are invariably the low desire partner, but they don't control sex.

Finally, I really enjoyed writing this book. It took me five years. I hope it brings you as much joy as it has me. I will be greatly pleased if facing your sexual desire problems becomes a turning point in your life.

David Schnarch, Ph.D.
Evergreen, Colorado

# PART ONE

# Why Normal People Have Sexual Desire Problems

# 1

## There Is Always
## a Low Desire Partner
## and the Low Desire Partner
## Always Controls Sex

*A*re you having sexual desire problems? Sooner or later most couples do. Desire problems are couples' most common sexual complaint. Couples around the world struggle with them, and it's been happening since the dawn of recorded history—and presumably long before that.

Did you ever think this would happen to you? Most people don't. How can you be having sexual desire problems, particularly if you started off hardly being able to keep your hands off each other? How can this happen when you are (feeling) relatively young? Why are desire problems so common? Why are they so difficult to change? Why does everyone end up with a problem no one thinks will happen to them?! Is this the inevitable price of a long-term relationship? Does this mean humans weren't meant to be monogamous?

If you're up to your eyeballs in questions and problems, and short on answers and solutions, you've got lots of company.

• *Brett and Connie's Story*

Couples like Connie and Brett are often brokenhearted, demoralized, and hopeless when they come for treatment. Brett was the partner with higher desire. According to Brett, Connie didn't want sex. Connie was the partner with less desire. According to Connie, Brett was oversexed.

Brett and Connie's positions had become polarized as tensions between them escalated over time. Brett bitterly complained about "not being allowed to touch his beautiful wife." He said it was unfair that they only had sex when *she* wanted it. What about what he wanted? Brett felt Connie was withholding sex, and that she was doing this to control him. He said they always had to do things her way, and this wasn't just with sex.

Connie countered that Brett was inconsiderate. He was always pressuring her for sex. His complaint about her dominating the relationship was nonsense. If they always did things her way, how come she felt constant pressure to do things his way? According to Connie, Brett was like many men: All he wanted was sex.

Brett and Connie's prior attempt in counseling failed to solve their problem. They feared they would fail again with me. Connie worried I would think there was something wrong with her. Brett scrutinized me for signs he wouldn't get a fair hearing. It's hard not to be defensive when you anticipate being told you are sexually inadequate or a sex fiend.

## SEX IS NOT A "NATURAL FUNCTION"

It's natural to feel bad about having sexual desire problems. You probably believe sex is a natural function. Most people believe sexual desire is automatic in healthy people who love each other. At first glance, this seems like a healthy, enlightened attitude—common sense.

But once you believe sexual desire comes "naturally," you're in for load of problems: You're going to feel pressured to have unflagging sexual desire and perfect performance all the time. You're going to be defensive and despondent when sexual desire problems surface. You're going to feel screwed up, defective, even "pathological." In turn, you'll be less likely to address sexual desire problems and less likely to succeed when you do.

When you believe sex is a natural function, it's no fun to be the low desire partner (also referred to as the LDP). You see yourself as "the one with the problem." Your partner, the high desire partner (also referred to as the HDP), usually sees you that way too. You feel defective and inadequate. No one wants to be the low desire partner.

Unfortunately, it's no fun being the high desire partner, either. On the surface, the higher desire partner is the "healthy partner" and the de facto "sex expert" in the relationship. Supposedly, the HDP "doesn't have a problem." The low desire partner is so busy feeling inadequate, he or she has no idea the high desire partner often feels the same way: If you are lovable, attractive, and sexy, wouldn't your partner naturally want you?

Approaching sexual desire as a natural biological drive creates another big problem: It is hard to be eager for sex when it feels like your partner just wants to "relieve his physical needs," like scratching an itch. Believing "sex is a natural function" does more than make it harder to solve sexual desire problems. It *creates* low sexual desire because it makes sexual desire *impersonal*.

### • *Don't "Just do it!"*

Another theory that messes things up is the exhortation "Just do it!" Brett (the HDP) told Connie (the LDP) to "Just do it!" all the time, but it didn't help. Connie often told herself "Just do it!" and that didn't help either. So when experts encourage "Just do it!"—as they often do—it's not surprising therapy often fails.

Connie and Brett's prior therapist assigned them "touch exercises" to do as homework. Connie didn't like the exercises, and she didn't like being told what to do. When she objected, Connie was told to do it anyway, even if she didn't want to. Maybe she'd desire sex once she got turned on. The therapist said research showed having sex stimulates hormones and brain chemistry that makes you want to have sex. If Connie would just do it, this cycle would start, and she wouldn't have to force herself anymore. The therapist encouraged frequent sex for two weeks, even if

Connie didn't want to. She might surprise herself and like it, the therapist proposed, and she might feel better about herself for being considerate of Brett.

Connie let me know up front that she didn't like this approach. It hadn't helped her, and she wouldn't "Just do it!" if I told her to. I reassured Connie that I recognized the problem with the "Just do it!" approach thirty years ago. "Just do it!" was part of physicians' and therapists' earliest attempts to treat sexual desire problems. The many clients who didn't like the touching exercises therapists prescribed were told to "Just do it!" anyway. Clinicians didn't think twice about encouraging the LDP to have sex she didn't want—to the point of encouraging sex with a spouse she didn't like! The low desire partner was told to focus on her sexual sensations and fantasize about someone else.[3]

I explained to Connie that therapists, physicians, and religious clergy hit upon the "Just do it!" approach long before it became an advertising slogan for Nike shoes. But research indicated that at the end of therapy many couples showed no improvement. Some briefly had sex more frequently, but with no more desire. Within two years, most were back where they started.[4] I had this very much in mind when I designed the Crucible® Approach three decades ago. I go into detail on this approach later in this book.

I gave Connie additional reasons why I wouldn't pressure her to "Just do it!" First, I didn't want to trigger her basic human reaction: *Don't tell me what to do!* Second, I didn't presume anything was wrong with her or her current level of desire. I said, "Many low desire partners hate the 'Just do it!' approach because it promotes impersonal sex. If lack of intimacy is the source of your low desire, this makes it worse. Either way, you get a clear message: *'Do whatever it takes to get turned on. You must have more sex whether you want it or not.'*" As Connie realized I was serious, she relaxed and become less defensive.

"Brett probably got the same message too," I suggested. "Something like, *'Have sex the way the low desire partner wants, even if it's not your preference. Be considerate. She is going out of her way for you. Don't make things more difficult. Settle for less than you want and we'll work out the details later. Any improvement is better than nothing.'*"

"You got that straight," Brett said angrily. "That's exactly the message I got."

Connie looked at Brett and pointed at me. "I think he understands my position. Maybe he can help us." Brett nodded in agreement.

### • *Don't "Just do it!" to make your partner happy*

Is there *any* place for a "Just do it!" approach? Perhaps, if you like sex when you have it, but it never occurs to you to propose it. However, let's say you're never in the mood in advance, and on top of that, your relationship is contentious. Maybe the two of you are arguing over sex. Maybe your partner takes you for granted, or talks down to you, or undercuts you in front of the children. If you have *negative* anticipations of sex, or you're unhappy with yourself, or feel alienated or angry with your mate, you're not a candidate for "Just do it!"

It turned out Connie didn't have problems being in the mood in advance. "When I'm interested in sex with Brett, sometimes I daydream about it beforehand. But I'm usually not interested in sex with Brett, because I don't like the way he treats me. He keeps saying my personal problems screwed up our sex life and our prior therapy. He said I should have done what the therapist told us to do. He keeps telling me I'm selfish."

In self-defense, Brett asked, "Well, what's wrong with just doing it to make your partner happy? What ever happened to old-fashioned compassion? "

"Well, if you're the high desire partner this sounds good," I replied. "But you're probably not going to like the sex you get. Some low desire partners seem to be saying during sex, 'I'm *just* doing this to please you!'"

"You're describing Connie perfectly," Brett murmured. "She doesn't want me to enjoy it even when we're doing it."

"He mopes about, feeling deprived," Connie countered, "trying to raise my guilt so I'll have sex with him. Preaching generosity and consideration is just another way Brett tries to manipulate me to do what he wants. This doesn't get me sexually aroused, it makes me furious!"

Brett flared. "I'm the one who gets manipulated. I get manipulated into only having sex when you want it. What I want doesn't count. I always have to do it your way, or you stop. Our other therapist pissed me off, telling me I should have sex with you however you want it. That's what I've been doing for years. The therapist acted like that would be something new."

Brett turned to me. "Doc, the way Connie acts drives me nuts. I feel like we're in kindergarten, playing 'Simon says do this and don't do that.' We do everything on her terms. If I want her to touch me, the answer is no. If I want to kiss her, the answer is no. It doesn't matter if I do the dishes, talk nicely to her, or we go out on dates. When it comes to sex, she freezes up and I have to take it or leave it on her terms. And if you tell me to just do it her way, I'm walking out of here!"

I waited several moments to let things quiet down. "Then you probably don't need to leave. I'm not going to tell you or Connie to 'Just do it.' One reason I won't do that is because I'm not going to ruin your chance to feel *wanted*. If Connie just did it, you still wouldn't be *wanted*. And as much as I'm hearing you'd like to have sex, it looks to me like you'd like Connie to want you too." Brett looked down at his shoes. When he looked at me again he nodded, and his mood was more subdued.

"My clients *do* get to the point where they can 'just do it' to accommodate their partners, and it *enhances* their feelings of self-worth, rather than *diminishing* them. But that occurs at the *end* of treatment, not the beginning. If I told them to 'Just do it!' at the outset, I'd be encouraging them to ignore their own feelings—which I never do. Getting to the point where you *can* be generous, flexible, and considerate with each other involves a natural process of personal growth. Shortcuts and sermons about being considerate don't work."

Both partners saw I wouldn't make either one of them "Just do it!" Each saw I wouldn't encourage him or her to defer to the other. What I said made sense to both of them.

"So why do I have low desire?" Connie asked.

"I don't know that you actually do have low desire. But it's clear you're the lower desire partner in your relationship."

With that question I knew things were about to take off.

# THERE IS ALWAYS A "LOW DESIRE PARTNER" AND A "HIGH DESIRE PARTNER"

Let me offer you a singular truth about sexual desire that transcends time, culture, and personal circumstance: There is *always* a low desire partner, just as there is *always* a high desire partner—and there is one of each in *every* relationship. This is a profound paradigm shift, like changing from believing the world is flat to believing it is round. It is a shift in viewpoint that creates a totally different picture of yourself and your partner.

This new picture can completely change how you feel, whether you are the low desire partner or the high desire partner. It allows you to stop being defensive or feeling inadequate or "different." It is a *nonpathological* view of how desire problems occur: *The LDP and HDP are positions in a relationship.*

To be precise, the two positions in a relationship are the low*er* desire partner and the high*er* desire partner. In practice, it's easier to talk about the low desire partner and the high desire partner once we're clear about what we mean.

There is a low desire partner and a high desire partner on virtually every issue and decision in your relationship. One partner wants to do something (the HDP) that the other doesn't (the LDP), or wants to do it less. Even if you and your partner both want the same thing, one of you will want it more. At every point of contention, "high desire" and "low desire" are positions (stances) partners take relative to each other. And once there is conflict (which isn't necessarily about sex), it's clear who fills which position.

No one is the LDP—or HDP—on everything. Positions shift on different issues. You may be the HDP for sex, but your partner could be the HDP for intimacy. You may be the HDP for sex or intimacy and the LDP for having a baby or being monogamous. Whether it's having sex, moving in together, disciplining your kids—or not having kids— or visiting your friends or your in-laws, you're going to be either the HDP or the LDP.

- *"Low desire" and "high desire" are relative positions in a relationship*

Being the low sexual desire partner doesn't mean you have no (or almost no) desire. Let's say on average you like sex once a week. That would make you the LDP if your partner wanted sex twice a week. If he or she didn't want sex at all, you'd be the HDP. The same level of desire that makes you the HDP in one relationship could make you the LDP in another. You could want sex every day and still be the LDP if you're paired with someone who wants it twice daily. You'd be the HDP if you wanted sex bi-monthly and your spouse didn't want it at all. What makes your sexual desire "high" or "low" isn't just biological drive, or your past, or how much you like sex. It always involves some standard of comparison. Usually it's your partner!

There is no "correct" frequency of sexual encounters. Realizing that "low desire" and "high desire" are always relative positions stops arguments over how much desire is normal or healthy. This should clarify what frequency of sex I think you should have: If you and your partner are happy with whatever you're doing, I'm happy too.

My HDP/LDP distinction may seem like an obvious and logical way of distinguishing who's who in a relationship, now that I've made the point, but this conceptualization didn't exist before I developed my approach. To do this I had to get beyond conventional ways of understanding sexual desire. Therapists traditionally looked for the causes of sexual desire problems "inside" people. Nothing like the low desire / high desire theory appeared in anything I was taught as a therapist.[5] This new way of thinking changed how I treated sexual desire problems, and my clients' outcomes improved dramatically.

You have to change your viewpoint, too. For instance, you have to stop thinking of low sexual desire as a personality trait. It's not uncommon for the HDP at the outset of the relationship to become the LDP later on (and vice versa). Getting clear that "high desire" and "low desire" are not character traits makes you less defensive about your level of sexual desire, whatever it is. LDPs, in particular, stop feeling inadequate and defective. It gives you and your partner equal standing for dealing with each other.

For Connie and Brett, my LDP/HDP distinction was a wake-up call. They stopped overreacting to each other, and the emotional pushing and shoving between them decreased. They were able to make rapid improvement when their views changed. They were open to the possibility that sexual desire problems are part of a *healthy* sexual relationship.

## THE LOW DESIRE PARTNER ALWAYS CONTROLS SEX

Some couples divorce over sexual desire problems because they don't understand how love relationships operate. Realizing relationships are driven by more than your feelings—and that your feelings aren't always accurate—will help you stop taking things so personally. But when you're bruised by interactions with your mate, it's hard to abandon the thought that you've been wronged. So, just when things seemed to be settling down, Brett unveiled a litany of complaints about Connie controlling him through sex.

"Okay, Doctor. So there's always a low desire partner. And Connie shouldn't feel bad about being it. But there must be something wrong with Connie that makes her dislike sex. I'm sure it has something to do with her childhood. Her parents got divorced when she was young, and her mother didn't particularly like men. I think Connie is as controlling as her mother. Connie tries to control me by withholding sex."

I replied, "You just told your wife she's screwed up, she's just like her mother, and her main goal in life is to deprive you of sex. That wouldn't encourage most women to be interested in sex, let alone to be nice to you. Whether or not what you say about your wife is true, your own complaints are a self-fulfilling prophecy."

Brett thought about this for a moment. "I see your point, Doctor. But I still feel like Connie controls our sex life. I'm just being honest. That's the way I feel."

"I *know* Connie controls your sex life," I replied. "I'm absolutely certain of it." Both Brett and Connie looked at me strangely.

"Maybe this has something to do with Connie's childhood, but maybe it doesn't. Maybe she is withholding from you, and maybe she's not. Maybe the problem isn't Connie at all. Maybe you're banging your head against a truth about intimate relationships and blaming Connie for it. Of course Connie controls when and how sex happens. *She is the low desire partner!*"

This was so outside anything Brett had anticipated, he didn't know what to do. Nobody spoke for a few moments, but I felt the antagonism between them diminish. I had Brett's undivided attention.

"Brett, you might think the low desire partner controls sex when a relationship is in trouble, and that things won't be like this when your relationship gets better. The truth is, *the low desire partner controls sex whether things are going great or not.* It never changes, even when your relationship improves. Happy couples simply handle this better." Brett looked puzzled, and I continued.

"Once I realized there is a low desire partner in every relationship, I discovered a second rule of human sexual desire: *The low desire partner always controls sex.*"[6]

Brett challenged me, "Well, what if I don't like this rule?"

"This is the rule whether you like it or not. You can attempt to get around it by coercing your partner to have sex. Begging, cajoling, criticizing, demanding, and withdrawing are standard methods. But you're here because you've tried and failed. You may pressure Connie into having sex, but you can't pressure her into wanting you or being passionate ... so maybe there isn't something wrong with Connie, or you, or your marriage. Maybe you're dealing with something bigger than how you feel about each other, or your childhoods. All around the world, the low desire partner in a relationship always controls sex. And in your relationship, Connie is the low desire partner."

Brett became less adversarial. Realizing he was "banging his head against the wall" quelled his anger, and made it easier for him to not take things so personally. "I guess it's true, even if I don't like it. But how come no one ever tells you important stuff like this?"

"The idea that marriage has its own ecology is relatively new. Therapists never considered this possibility, but they still had to deal with the problem. That's why they came up with 'Just do it!'"

The reality that the low desire partner *always* controls sex put Brett and Connie on equal footing. They realized I wasn't blaming or making excuses for either of them. I was simply describing the way relationships operate. Connie and Brett settled down, but I could see their minds working.

Brett waded in. "So how am I supposed to handle the fact that the low desire partner always controls sex? Am I supposed to be happy about this?"

"Feel anything you like. It won't change things. You're not the only person to struggle with this. It has sent generations of high desire partners searching for aphrodisiacs for their mate in hope of improving their situation."

Brett laughed. "Don't think I haven't considered that."

## • *The rule applies to more than sex*

Seeing that there's *always* a low desire partner, and that the low desire partner controls sex in *every* relationship, calmed Brett and Connie. They stopped bickering long enough in our session to think anew about what was happening between them. But it wasn't long before Brett started complaining about not getting enough sex. Connie, in turn, harangued Brett about not doing his share of household chores. I cut them both off.

"Complaining about how Brett does and doesn't do housework is no different than Brett complaining about how you approach sex. You can nag Brett to get some control over household tasks. But if you want him to participate, the partner with the least desire for household chores controls when, how, and if they get done. You can stop buying food and let the garbage and dirty clothes pile up to push him to take more responsibility around the house. But he completely controls whether things get handled *fairly and collaboratively*. It doesn't matter whether we're talking about household chores, sex, or raising the kids. The rule holds true in any undertaking that one partner cannot or doesn't want to accomplish alone. It's particularly true when a sense of collaboration is important. The partner with the least desire holds the decisive vote."

Connie didn't say anything for several seconds. She was shocked to realize she was up against the same thing as Brett. In an instant, she had an entirely new picture of her situation and their interactions. Instead of her usual thoughts of Brett's behavior and feelings, she thought of possibilities she'd never considered before. She applied it to other relationships and saw how it held true.

"I can see it now that you point this out. My sister Sally doesn't like getting together for family gatherings and reunions, so events get scheduled around her whims. She always shows up in a bad mood, and everyone accommodates her because they don't want to set her off."

I nodded, acknowledging she understood what I'd said. "You're talking as if Sally enjoys the control this gives her. Maybe she does. Lots of people do. But in lots of couples, the low sexual desire partner doesn't want control over sex—often times she or he feels burdened by it."

Connie nodded. "I know I feel that way about sex. Sally says she feels tremendous pressure around family holidays, like she's spoiling everyone's good time if she doesn't show up. "

Brett interjected, "I think Connie was right the first time, Doc. Sally likes having that control. I think Connie does too. All the women in her family are like that, even her mother!" Brett was angry about feeling controlled by Connie, and he expected her to apologize. This is a common problem for people who approach relationships primarily through their feelings. Brett had a hard time giving up the idea that Connie was "doing this to him" to control him because it went against his feelings. There was no doubt in his mind. If he felt it, it must be true. If Connie created an outcome, this must reflect her motivation.

I said, "If you're the high desire partner, it's bewildering to think that the low desire partner always controls sex. You *feel* controlled, so it's hard to get beyond the picture that your partner is controlling you—and wants to. It's easy to attribute this to personality traits and motivations you think your mate possesses.

"But it's no picnic for the low desire partner. You wonder how you can end up with so much control and responsibility, when you don't want it.

You feel terribly burdened, and you want to be rid of it. How can you be so powerful and destructive *and* so defective or inadequate at the same time? How can you do such terrible things to your partner?!"

Connie started crying. "That's right. That's how I feel. I feel so mean and withholding, when sometimes all I want is to feel like I belong to *me*!"

• *Cutting through psychobabble*

Contrary to stereotypes that low desire partners are "controlling bitches"—or "controlling bastards"—who love every minute of it, many LDPs are bewildered and beleaguered by their inevitable control. After all, you control sex. You must be getting something out of it, since you're doing it. Right?

Wrong. The misguided psychobabble—"If it's happening you must secretly want it or be getting something out of it"—will drive you nuts. Get it straight: The LDP controls sex, *whether he or she likes it or not*! The fact that many LDPs eventually *want* to withhold and punish is not necessarily why it starts in the first place. Sometimes it's the end result rather than the cause of the situation.

Brett challenged me: "Are you telling me I should see things from Connie's perspective?"

"No. See things from your own perspective; just get your perspective straight. Seeing things from your partner's perspective is no magic solution. If you look at yourself through Connie's eyes, what do you see?"

"I'm oversexed."

"Are you?"

"No."

"So much for the virtue of seeing things from your partner's perspective."

Brett laughed, breaking the tension in the room.

"There's also no virtue in approaching your feelings like infallible truths. You may feel controlled, but that doesn't mean Connie wants or tries to control you."

Brett laughed again, his temper now in check. "Well, if I'm not the sex addict she thinks I am, then maybe Connie isn't the controlling bitch I keep telling her she is."

This was a turning point in our session. Brett and Connie became less defensive and looked at their predicament in a new light: The low desire partner controls sex whether she or he knows it—or wants it—or not.

## HOW THE LOW DESIRE PARTNER CONTROLS SEX

But why does the low desire partner inevitably control sex? How could this happen if neither partner wants it? Why can't you stop this, even if you read this book? How come this happens all around the world?

Here's how this works:

1. The high desire partner makes most of, if not all of, the initiations for sex.
2. The low desire partner decides which sexual overtures she or he will respond to.
3. This determines when sex happens. This gives the LDP de facto control of sex, whether she or he wants this or not.

It's shockingly simple and blatantly obvious once you see it, but completely invisible until you do. It operates in every single relationship. Its effects are progressive: The LDP's control extends to where, how, and why sex occurs as well, whether she or he likes it or not. If the HDP proposes changing the frequency, timing, or style of sex, usually all the LDP has to do is hesitate. The HDP backs off, fearing he or she won't get sex at all.

This fact of life drives couples wild. When Connie got defensive or anxious—which was often—she adopted a "my way or the highway" attitude. This gave her insecurities and anxieties a stranglehold on their sex life. Connie had tremendous control and at the same time she felt Brett was trying to control her.

Connie didn't accept what I was saying at first. Her subjective experience was that she was *not* in control. She felt pressured and powerless. Sometimes she had sex when she didn't want it. How could she be the one with so much control? If she was so powerful, why couldn't she get

Brett to stop badgering her for sex? Connie finally got my point when she realized two important things.

First, the LDP controls sex because his or her response determines when sex occurs. Over time, this control grows. How you experience this, and handle this, says a lot about you, whether you're the LDP or the HDP. But it's true whether you know it, or experience it, or like it, or not.

Second, Connie finally realized I wasn't going to turn on her and blame her for their sexual desire problems. She didn't believe it at first because she felt guilty, and looked upon herself as a sexually defective person. Connie *did* look at herself through Brett's eyes. This made it harder for her to believe she wasn't ultimately going to be found at fault.

### • *Something doesn't always have to be going wrong*

As our session progressed, Brett and Connie became less adversarial. But they still figured something must be going wrong if they had sexual desire problems. Connie said, "Maybe no one is going to be blamed for being 'bad,' but I'm still afraid this whole thing will get pinned on me. Something must be going wrong for our sex life to be in shambles."

"What makes you think something's going wrong?" I asked. Brett and Connie both looked at me as though I was out of my mind.

"How about the fact we haven't had sex in six months, for starters. Marriage isn't supposed to be like this. It isn't right for a husband and wife to live together without sex. It's not normal." Brett's tone lacked the blame and condemnation usually directed at Connie. It was more shock and embarrassment.

Connie asked hesitantly, "Can we fix our relationship?"

I paused for effect. "No … because it's not broken. From what you've told me so far, nothing's going wrong."

"Nothing's going wrong, he says. My wife doesn't want to have sex with me, and nothing's going wrong!" Brett was mocking me, but his tone was more ironic than hostile.

"That's right. For starters, things going wrong and things not going the way you want are two different things."

"Oh." Brett had never considered this possibility.

"Secondly, you can probably turn things around—and make them more to your liking—because nothing's going wrong. If something odd or unusual was happening, it might be impossible to change your marriage. But your relationship seems to be working properly: It's doing what relationships do when partners do what you two are doing. When you start functioning differently, your relationship will operate differently, too."

Connie said, "You're telling us there's nothing the matter with our 'car,' the problem is how we're driving it?" I nodded.

Brett had a curious smile. "My wife says she won't have sex with me because I'm a selfish, insensitive lout. I'm telling her she's a controlling manipulative bitch. We fight about this all the time. We don't know if we'll stay together. We already flunked therapy once. And you're telling us nothing is going wrong?"

"Yep."

"On what planet did you get your degree?" It sounded like, *"You're pretty good, Doc!"*

I smiled back. "The planet you're currently visiting. It's hard to get over the assumption that sexual desire problems mean something's going wrong. That's how desire problems have been seen throughout history—and probably before that. But shifting your perspective changes everything. It's helped lots of couples, and it can help the two of you."

Connie looked truly relieved. "You really think nothing's going wrong? I've felt inadequate for such a long time. It's hard to believe it's not true."

"Maybe something is wrong, I don't know. But sexual desire problems often indicate everything's happening as it should." Connie and Brett looked at each other.

"I'm not telling you to *ignore* sexual desire problems, or that they're fun to go through. I am saying that since sexual desire problems are inevitable, you ought to use them *productively*. Desire problems can be *useful* to people and relationships. They push us to become more solid within ourselves. Sexual desire problems aren't a *problem* in your marriage. Sexual desire problems are part of the normal, healthy *processes* of marriage."

Brett and Connie fell silent on my couch, alert, watching me, entranced. They had decided what they were learning was important. This was a whole lot to take in, and they didn't want to miss any of it. Brett smiled. "This is some planet you practice on, Doc. It's different from our first therapy."

Connie chimed in, "It sure is."

A little more respect and consideration flowed between them, making it easier for us to talk about many important things. By the time they left our first session, they looked me in the eye, shook my hand, and smiled.

## WHERE WE'RE HEADED

Throughout this book we'll talk about incredible interactions around sexual desire that foster personal growth. People-growing processes are elegantly simple and tenaciously reliable. The low desire partner always controlling sex is one of the "people-growing processes" of love relationships. We'll focus on your most enlightened human capacities, rather than "doing what comes naturally" or "Just do it!" Yes, we are biologically and psychologically programmed to procreate and perpetuate our species. Like all animals, we have physical sexual tensions, and we seek pleasure and avoid pain. But your brain—not your hormones or genitals—makes you capable of profound desire and transcendent sex. What makes human sexual desire *human* is your brain's unique capacity to bring *meaning* to sex. Your desire greatly impacts your partner and your relationship, and vice versa. It's an amazing system.

How you feel about your partner, yourself, and your relationship is critical to robust desire. Enhancing desire requires more than breaking sexual routines. It involves intimacy, passion, eroticism, respecting yourself, and liking your partner—and being mature enough to be more capable of all these things.

Low desire can be caused by problems with hormones, neurochemicals, and a long list of medical problems. (It always pays to get a complete physical checkup.) But these cases still have everything to do with the desire dynamics and people-growing processes described throughout this book.

While they may not have caused the problem to start with, they most certainly come into play. When you have a medically based desire problem, you are the low desire partner who controls sex, whether you like it or not.

Desire problems often involve more than sexual inhibitions, lack of fantasies, and difficulty getting started. The ebb and flow of sexual desire is human nature at its best and worst. What you'll discover about sexual desire problems coincides with the growing science of resilience and positive psychology.[7] They can develop your capacity to cope with stress and catastrophe, your emotional resilience, and your resourcefulness. You can use them to develop the strengths and virtues that make life more fulfilling and enable you to thrive. It's not about curing mental illness.

Can you fan the flames of sexual desire once they have gone out (or never ignited)? Yes, you most certainly can. The point is: Everyone has to! It's a natural process of personal growth.

Brett and Connie went on to turn things around, more quickly and with better results than they imagined. They settled down and applied the same things you'll learn here. I suggest you do the same.

Stop blaming yourself because you have sexual desire problems. Something bigger than your feelings—or your past—is at work. Stop taking things so personally. Be less defensive and more curious. Pay more attention to what's going on. This makes it easier to turn things around. If you're reading this, you've already started.

─────────── IDEAS TO PONDER ───────────

- Normal people have sexual desire problems.
- There is always a low desire partner and a high desire partner. They are positions partners take in every relationship, whether about sex, intimacy, doing household chores, or visiting relatives.
- The low desire partner always controls sex.

# 2

## Since Your "Self" Showed Up, Sexual Desire Hasn't Been the Same

*I*n Chapter 1 we discovered there's always a low desire partner (and a high desire partner), and the low desire partner always controls sex. Why and how did humans evolve this curious trait, giving the low desire partner control? By the end of this chapter we'll answer this question and consider what it means for your relationship.

• *Doreen and Adam*

To get us started, let me introduce you to a couple that, like many couples, had fallen out of love. Sitting in my office, Doreen lamented, "Adam says he has no romantic feelings or sexual desire for me anymore. He doesn't think they can be rekindled. We love each other, but there's no passion. We used to have sex twice a week. Now we have sex once a month—and only when I initiate it. I miss the way things used to be at the start of our relationship."

Adam defended himself. "We used to have good sex, but the chemistry is gone. I can't make myself feel what I don't feel any more. I love Doreen, but I'm not in love with her."

I said, "I can't count the times I've heard this from couples. Like them, this upsets you. It makes sense that it would. At least you feel you have something to rekindle. People who never had it to begin with think they're worse off."

"Well, that's not much solace," Doreen replied. "I don't feel important to Adam. Besides, he's the man. He's supposed to have the higher desire and initiate sex. This isn't normal." Adam bristled but said nothing. He felt outgunned in their arguments.

"In half the couples who seek my help, the man is the low desire partner, so you look pretty normal to me. But regardless of who the low desire partner is, couples fear that once passion and desire die it is gone forever. Most clients are pleased to find out they were wrong."

Adam perked up. "How did you help them?"

"I helped them approach sexual desire problems with an entirely new picture about how things work. You and Doreen think this shouldn't be happening. But sexual desire problems are natural and inevitable."

Doreen was primed for verbal combat. "If sexual problems were natural and inevitable," she crowed, "the human race would have died out." I paused and gentled my tone, signaling that I would work with her, but I would not argue with her.

"You're thinking of sexual desire as mating and procreating. It takes a while to get over that. You need patience to stay open and alert to a new way of seeing things. I've found sexual desire problems can be the *midpoint* rather than the *end* of a relationship. When you understand this, you'll stop feeling unloved, and you'll watch your interactions with Adam differently."

Doreen eased off, and she and Adam settled down.

"You *can't* go back to the romantic love you shared early in your relationship." I continued, "But that's not the problem. You need to *go forward*. That's what everyone needs to do: Your sexual desire has to come from an entirely new source. Lots of people find this more satisfying than what they had before."

This possibility had never occurred to Doreen. "Well, why can't we rekindle what we had at the start of our relationship? I read 'rekindling' articles all the time. If Adam spent more time with me—and we had more sex—maybe that would be enough."

Adam asked, "What do you mean by a new source of sexual desire?"

I could see from their questions that the process of resolving their sexual desire problems had begun.

## THREE DRIVES OF SEXUAL DESIRE AND LOVE

Helen Fisher is a celebrated anthropologist and author of wonderful books, including *The Sex Contract* and *Anatomy of Love*. Recently, in *Why We Love,* Helen documented the brain circuitry and chemistry of romantic love and desire.[8] Using the latest brain-scanning technology, Helen studied the brain activity of women and men who had recently fallen madly in love. A region deep near the center of the brain lit up when lovers gazed at a photo of their sweetheart.[9] This region is located in the most primitive (reptilian) part of your brain (which evolved over 65 million years ago), and produces the natural stimulant dopamine.[10] The more active this part was, the more madly in love the people were.[11] Another part of the brain lit up as well, which also produces dopamine.[12]

In other words, the initial madness and irrationality we feel in romantic love comes from the primitive emotional centers of your brain.[13] Romantic love involves the brain's self-reward system, which is why we like to be in love.[14] We feel energized, aroused, elated, and focused on our new beloved.[15] Initially, we're preoccupied with our own feelings, reactions, desires, and insecurities. We feel in love and alive, but we really don't know this other person. As romantic love progresses, we start to see our partner as a separate person, with thoughts and feelings of their own.[16] All this corresponds to what is happening in your brain. Helen Fisher discovered that as love relationships lengthen, your brain responds in new ways: People in love for longer periods of time showed brain activity in parts that map other people's thoughts (mind-mapping) and emotions.[17] The brains of people who had recently fallen in love did not.

The parts of your brain that *don't* light up are particularly interesting. Both maternal attachment and romantic love *deactivate* regions in your brain associated with negative emotions, assessing social situations, and mapping out other people's intentions and emotions. Human attachment employs a "push–pull mechanism" that deactivates your discerning social judgment and negative emotions, while gluing you to a partner through your brain's reward circuitry.[18]

Romantic love is more than a feeling. Helen concluded that it is a fundamental human *drive*.[19] "Like the craving for food and water, and maternal instinct, it is physiological need, a profound urge. Romantic love is the instinct to court and win a particular mating partner."[20] This is why romantic love seems to be universal.[21]

According to Helen, romantic love is one of three basic drives of human love and desire:

1. *Lust* (craving for sexual gratification, biological horniness)
2. *Romantic love* (infatuation with a particular partner)
3. *Attachment* (a calm, secure union with a long-term partner, including pair-bonding, monogamy, parenthood, and kinship)[22]

Each drive instructs sexual desire and mating differently. Lust is animal attraction, your desire to have sex with any semi-appropriate partner. Romantic love makes you focus on one particular partner. Attachment makes you want to live with a partner long enough to raise a child through infancy (presuming you have a child).

Each drive involves different neurochemicals in your brain. Lust is associated with testosterone and estrogen in both men and women.[23] Romantic love involves dopamine, norepinephrine, and serotonin. Attachment involves oxytocin and vasopressin. Because of how dopamine, norepinephrine, and testosterone mutually interact, romance can trigger lust and vice-versa.[24] However, testosterone can play havoc with attachment. And attachment's brain chemistry can suppress sexual lust and romantic love.[25] It's one reason why lust and romantic love are relatively short-term cycles.

Helen came to a conclusion you probably don't want to hear: Romantic love is time-limited and doomed to fade. Your brain cannot maintain this revved-up state for long. "Many of us would die of sexual exhaustion if romantic love flourished endlessly in a relationship. We wouldn't get to work on time or concentrate on anything except 'him' or 'her.' ... Romantic love did not evolve to help us maintain a stable, enduring partnership. It evolved for different purposes: to drive ancestral men and women to prefer, choose, and pursue specific mating partners, then start the mating process and remain sexually faithful to 'him' or 'her' long enough to conceive a child."[26]

## A FOURTH SEXUAL DRIVE: DEVELOPING AND MAINTAINING A SELF

Having long admired Helen Fisher's work, I met with her in 2002. Needless to say, we had an incredibly exciting conversation. We spent a delightful afternoon at the restaurant on the lake in New York's Central Park. I proposed to Helen that humans had developed a fourth "evolutionary strategy" that now drives desire: *Our drive to develop and preserve a self.* When the human self emerged millions of years ago, we embarked on an uncharted path no animal's sexual desire had ever taken before.

• *Your sense of self: A core part of your sexual desire*

In my clinical experience, issues of selfhood control sexual desire as much as (and probably more than) lust, romantic love, and attachment. How you see yourself, how your partner treats you, and how you think your partner sees you profoundly shape your sexual desire. Struggles over sexual desire and struggles of selfhood go hand in hand in love relationships.

Your sense of self permeates your sexual desire. When, where, how, and why you have sex in an ongoing relationship is determined by more than lust, romance, and attachment. "Self" issues shape sexual desire as much (or more) than testosterone, oxytocin, and vasopressin.[27] Your hormones may be pumping, and you can be horny as hell, but one sharp put-down from your partner can bring things to a screeching halt.

There's more to romantic love than a dopamine rush from the reward centers in your brain. Loads of selfhood processes are involved. We love being in love because it makes us *self*-aware. We feel tremendously alive in the whirlwind of infatuation.[28] One moment we're flying high, and the next moment we're crashing. Our sense of self inflates and deflates in response to a look or a word from our partner. This emotional roller coaster, itself, motivates us to develop a more solid sense of self. And after lust, romantic love, and attachment have run their course, this solid sense of self provides stability in long-term relationships. (We do miss the intensity and emotional excitement nonetheless, and Part Four will show you how to get it.)

- *Selfhood is a drive. We are driven to develop a self*

Maintaining your sense of self is a need, a profound urge, a motivational system that propels you toward (and away from) an intimate relationship with your partner. Just like with lust, romantic love, and attachment, self-preservation, preserving our psychological "self," is a driving force in human nature. But it is a force that is tenacious and difficult to control.

This is all possible because your brain has the physical capacity to support a complex sense of self. Your self even has a definable pattern of brain activity! The self possesses an incredible drive to preserve and expand itself. At times this dominates all other drives, superseding even our urge for biological preservation. Some people choose to die physically in order to preserve their psychological integrity. (Some lie to themselves to maintain a deluded sense of internal consistency.) For better and for worse, we are driven to preserve our self.

That's why your ability to maintain your sense of self in your relationship plays a pivotal role in your sexual desire, your emotional functioning, and your connection with your partner.

- *Where does your "self" reside?*

Just like lust, infatuation, and attachment, the human self has its own underlying brain real estate. Part of it is located in your prefrontal neocortex (your forebrain), the most recently evolved and unique aspect of the human brain.[29]

In three separate tests, researchers scanned people's brains while they had them think about themselves, other people, and different situations. They found that when you're thinking about yourself or others (as compared to thinking about situations), two parts of your brain light up.[30] But an additional separate region turns on when you're thinking about yourself—one that doesn't turn on in either of the other two instances.[31] Thoughts pertaining to your "self" are discernable in your brain from your thoughts about other people. Thinking about your self is so special it occupies a unique place in your head.[32]

As I mentioned earlier, Helen Fisher found that over time, romantic love engages parts of your brain that map other people's thoughts and emotions. Well, these parts map your own feelings, too. They are central to self-awareness and your sense of having a "self." In other words, the same neurons that let your partner become a real person in your mind also support your sense of self. This leads to inevitable battles of identity, autonomy, and togetherness.

## • *Two kinds of consciousness*

Your self doesn't simply reside in an identifiable pattern of neurons and neurochemicals inside your skull. Your mind is the mental space in which your self resides. Stick with me for a few paragraphs while I explain this.

Your sense of self has both a primitive and complex level, just like your sexual desire. Your most basic sense of self comes from your body.[33] This "primary consciousness" arises from bodily cues. This is your sense of where you physically end and other things begin. Your "body self" comes from your brain's ability to distinguish self-generated movement versus motion and sensations induced by outside sources.[34]

Any creature has primary consciousness if it establishes a connection between what happens in the world and how its body feels, so it can take actions that create pleasure and avoid pain.[35] Your cat or dog—like most animals—has primary (primitive) consciousness.[36]

You have this sense of self because your brain constantly maps the state of your body.[37] Nature built upon these stable gangs of neurons to create your "mental self." Your mental self is anchored in this continuous sense of physical being, the reference point for organizing your actions.[38]

Your self also involves "higher-order consciousness," which stems from more sophisticated discriminations than "this is me" vs. "this is not me." Two facets of higher-order consciousness are consciousness of being conscious (self-awareness), and reading the minds of other self-aware beings (mind-mapping, which we'll cover next chapter).[39]

Your forebrain (prefrontal neocortex) holds the "hardware" for your complex sense of self and highly nuanced sexual desire. But higher-order consciousness is not reducible to brain neurons firing.[40] The "software" of consciousness is created through our interactions with other people.[41] That's why your sexual desire is greatly influenced by what's happening in your relationship.

Your brain, your self, and your sexual desire are fundamentally social entities. Humans, who possess language and true linguistic capability, have the most complex self—and the most sexual desire problems—on the planet.[42] And if the foregoing doesn't convince you that your brain is a social organ, perhaps this will: Your brain perpetually rewires itself in response to interpersonal contact throughout your lifetime.[43]

### • Body, brain, mind, and relationship

You have a socially defined nameable self, a mental construct replete with a past and biographical details ("autobiographical memory"). Your self is not a static image. It is a constant *process*, an identity that is both stable and changeable over time. Your self is a constant barrage of images, feelings, memories, pleasures and pains, beliefs, and moods.

Your self allows you to project yourself into the future and organize your intentions. But it also brings trials and tribulations. For example, feeling put down by your partner involves a symbolic interaction with another self that greatly changes your desire. In the same way, your sense of how your body looks, feels, and functions shapes your interest in sex and your desire. Feeling competent and desirable can rise and fall on your (or your partners') sexual performance. Your sexual desire is inextricably tethered to your complex sense of self, which exists in your brain, your mind, and the mental space between you and your partner.

### • *When did our sense of self emerge?*

When did our lovely complex sense of self first emerge? When did it hijack human sexual desire?[44] It's hard to say because your earliest ancestors looked quite human. "By 600,000 years ago everyone had a big brain, and by 200,000 years ago people in Africa looked like modern humans."[45] At what point shall we draw the line and say the human self arrived? No one knows.[46]

Helen Fisher told me anthropologists would guess the human self arrived about 1.6 million years ago. That's when our cerebral cortex exploded in size and when humans first developed language (required for higher order consciousness). Paleoneurologists also believe this may be when our brain's oxytocin production changed, enabling relationships based on enduring social bonds.[47] Scientists think this is about the time humans and chimpanzees went down different evolutionary paths.

The important thing is that our complex self *did* arise. And you and I have to deal with it. Ever since a complex self appeared in your great ancestors' minds, sexual desire hasn't been the same.

Given that complex consciousness is socially embedded, it's probable that when the human self first emerged, it was a "reflected sense of self." A reflected sense of self is one that is reliant on feedback from others; and it has controlled sexual selection since it first appeared on the scene. We are more likely to have sex with people who make us feel good about ourselves (read: inflate our ego). This irrevocable development in human sexual desire, like walking upright, fundamentally changed human existence.

Selfhood issues started playing a central role in sexual selection. People mated, fell in love, became families, struggled to stay together, and fought about sex and breaking up. Maintaining a sense of self, and especially their *reflected sense of self*, increasingly shaped the choices people made about why and with whom they had sex.

## BIOLOGY, ENVIRONMENT, CULTURE, AND MIND IN THE EVOLUTION OF DESIRE AND LOVE

No gene by itself made your ancestors leave the trees of Africa and set off across the savanna. It involved some measure of choice.[48] Your fore-bears made a self-determining act, an irrevocable decision that had far-reaching impacts: Humans began walking upright and women's pelvises narrowed. This, combined with our rapidly increasing brain size, led to women giving birth sooner during pregnancy, to pass their babies' larger heads through their smaller birth canals. Consequently, humans joined a small group of animals that give birth to exceedingly helpless ("atricial") babies. This, in turn, required forming families and kinship relationships to care for them.

Humans have accomplished a lot through co-evolution: Bipedal pos-ture liberated our forelimbs for communicative gestures and freed us to regulate our breathing and develop a vocal tract that made speech pos-sible. Our forefeet became hands capable of making and using tools. Our teeth stopped being our primary weapon, and our mouths became more refined. Our growing brain supported more sophisticated communica-tion through co-articulated sounds. Human speech and the intricacies of the human kiss came into being.

Human sexual desire changed because what men and women found attractive changed. Unlike other primates, we walk upright and mate face to face. Upright posture changed what people saw in each other, literally and figuratively. It changed what we found sexy and how we signaled sexual interest. But when our reflected sense of self evolved, the *impor-tance* of being attractive and sexy skyrocketed. Your ancestor's sexual de-sire and daily life was as irrevocably changed as when they developed hands with opposing thumbs.[49]

Anthropologist Stephanie Coontz documents how marriage has changed more in the last two hundred years than throughout recorded history. This reflects shifts from agrarian and hunter-gatherer societies to industrialization, voluntary control of conception, and women's rights to education, to vote, and to own property. But it also reflects millions of years spent developing a complex sense of self. In most modern societies, desire, sex, intimacy, and love have become accepted reasons for getting married, staying married, and getting divorced. In the process, our sense of self has taken over marriage.

In that light, marriage's recent dramatic changes are not surprising. Culture amplifies our ability to modify our environment and influence evolutionary natural selection.[50] Contraception and Viagra are good examples. What do contraception, Viagra, and mature adult love all have in common? They are examples of our brain bucking its own biology and influencing sexuality and sexual desire.[51]

### • *Building your personal niche: Developing a self*

Accelerating changes in marriage reflect the exponential impact of culture and selfhood. We want to control what happens to us by controlling what's happening around us. We like to carve out personal space in our environment, bend things to suit us, and construct our own little niche. Niche construction goes on constantly in relationships. Culture is the long-term result of niche construction by large groups of people trying to shape their immediate environment.

We all want to carve out a personal niche, a situation suited to our abilities, temperament, and shortcomings.[52] We renovate our homes or move to new quarters. We create a niche in society through our careers and social activities. We create an emotional niche by pressuring others to adapt our interests, values, temperament, and limitations. In marriage, both partners try to carve out personal space in their relationship. These interactions greatly shape their sexual desire.

For better and worse, we develop some sense of self by successfully modifying the space—and the people—around us to suit ourselves. In the long run this influences how your brain forms and your genes express themselves. Efforts to construct your niche in your relationship greatly shape your life experiences and how your brain (re)wires itself.

This is co-evolution: Your and your partner's efforts to shape your relationship—and each other—create your selves. Here's where conflict comes in: One partner's attempt to establish his niche and maintain his self collides with the other partner's similar efforts. That's why couples fight about the frequency and depth of sex and intimacy, furnishing their home, relationships with extended family and friends, and proper work-leisure balance. It's why healthy couples with good relationships have sexual desire problems. It's why these conflicts are important.

My friend, psychiatrist Dr. Jürg Willi, is well-known in Europe for studying partners' reciprocal criticisms of each other (what he calls "reproaches") as attempts to construct their "personal niche" within their relationship. He believes criticisms have four important unappreciated aspects: First, your partner's criticisms of you are her attempts at niche construction. Second, what you criticize in your partner are her attempts to construct her personal niche. Third, partners' criticisms are often accurate about each other. Fourth, although not always well-intended, criticism is how partners in normal relationships push each other to grow.[53]

## CO-EVOLUTION: MIND, BRAIN, BODY, AND RELATIONSHIP ARE ONE WHOLE

Your sense of self evolves through your lifetime in the same way the human self evolved. You and your partner impact each other, day in and day out, shaping each other's personal development through the problems you develop and resolve (or don't). This is co-evolution.

This is why sexual desire problems, like Doreen and Adam's, often are signs that everything is going *right*. Co-evolution occurs when you and your partner interact. It occurs big time when you cohabitate, and goes into overdrive when you have sexual desire problems. You and your partner shape your own and each other's reality and personality through your interactions.[54]

You develop different abilities and characteristics from coping with the people around you. This was true with your family growing up. It is true with your partner now. Throughout your lifetime, you create your personality, reality, and destiny—and wire the neurons in your head accordingly.

## • *Why the low desire partner controls sex: Co-evolution*

So, now let's reconsider the fundamental aspect of sexual desire we encountered in Chapter 1: There's always a low desire partner, and the low desire partner always controls sex. But *why* does the LDP always control sex? Why has this come to pass? Why didn't humans work it out so the *high desire partner* controls sex, and the *LDP* has the temperament to go along with it?

After helping couples with sexual desire problems for over thirty years, here's what I've concluded: Mother Nature (natural selection) gave the low desire partner control of sex because the resulting complex interactions caused our self to grow. The verbal arguments, mind-games, monitoring, strategizing, and self-control issues made our brains develop. We had to learn to tolerate inner tension and interpersonal anxiety as the price of having an ongoing love relationship. Countless couples have participated in this development by falling in love, having sex, raising families, and struggling to stay together. This shaped our psychology, our physiology, and marriage as we know it. It's made us the most resilient and adaptable animal on the planet.

The low desire partner always controlling sex helped us develop a brain capable of bringing profound meaning to sex. It made human sexual desire the most complex desire on the planet. It fostered the birth of the sense of self and the possibility of mature adult love. Because love relationships are difficult, we developed a resilient and indomitable spirit. It strengthened our species. Now it challenges you to develop your self, too.

This is why normal healthy couples have sexual desire problems. It's not a sign of something going wrong. It's the culmination of millions of years of human evolution. Through sexual desire problems we became incredibly adaptive and resilient animals. Once we possessed a brain capable of autonomy and selfhood, as well as attachment, love relationships more strongly propelled human evolution. That's how we became artful and adventurous. The low desire partner always controlling sex contributed to human *fortitude*.

From this perspective, the old argument about whether sex is for reproduction or pleasure or love looks terribly misguided. *Sex is for self-development*. Developing and maintaining your self shapes your (and your partner's) sexual desire as much as hormones, horniness, lust, infatuation, craving for closeness and bonding, and the urge to distribute your genes. The ebb and flow of your sexual desire is greatly controlled by the battles of selfhood that inevitably surface in love relationships.

## THE CRUCIBLE® APPROACH TO CO-EVOLUTION THROUGH LOVE RELATIONSHIPS

Love relationships still harness our sense of self, propelling us to grow. Importantly, challenge and conflict hammer our more primitive reflected sense of self into a more advanced solid flexible self, bringing forth the best in us. Unfortunately, the worst in us shows up as well.

Love relationships are part of Darwinian natural selection and evolution. They helped your ancestors evolve a brain capable of compassion, generosity, and mutuality (and cruelty). You can experience this in your relationship. When you're struggling with the fact that the low desire partner controls sex, remember these problems gave rise to humankind's steadfast refusal to submit to tyranny and nurtured our capacity to truly love.

Your two most basic drives, your twin desires for autonomy *and* connection, permeate your sexual desire. We want to feel we belong to ourselves *and* have profound connection with our partner. The mark of a solid flexible self is being able to do both. Sexual desire problems develop your ability to do this, but the process is neither easy nor comfortable.

Sexual desire problems are co-constructed dilemmas, but I'm not referring to mutual fault. There is no fault. Sexual desire problems make us grow. They are one of many co-constructed "people-growing processes" of marriage. So instead of feeling abnormal, take your place among countless generations who preceded you. Pay your dues. There's a good chance you'll experience one of the greatest and simplest sexual pleasures: being self-aware, in the presence of another self-aware person, aware of (but not prisoner to) the fact that she is aware of you. That's an important part of my Crucible® Approach to resolving sexual desire problems.

Crucible® Therapy harnesses the natural growth processes that permeate love relationships to resolve sexual desire problems (and lots of other things). Events and situations in committed relationships inevitably come together in ways that push you to the limits of your abilities— and beyond. They take you outside your comfort zone. Sexual desire problems are just one example. Crucible Therapy helps you use these difficult-but-predictable developments to grow and become capable of handling your problems. A crucible is a difficult challenge or trial, arising from a confluence of factors that test and change you. That's why I named my approach as I did.

A crucible is also a metal or porcelain container that can withstand extreme heat and not react to what's placed in it. Crucibles are used to refine metals or hold powerful chemical reactions. This describes Crucible Therapy, too. Marriage's people-growing processes turn up the heat of their own accord. When you and your partner are in the midst of them, things can get pretty heated. This often happens with desire problems. Crucible Therapy helps you use these situations, including emotional meltdowns, to change and grow.

### • *An ecological approach for love relationships*

The "rules" of world ecology are built into our ecosystem. They pre-exist of their own accord. When not subject to our preferences and prejudices, they reflect a greater wisdom. When we don't respect the rules, living things start dying, species become extinct, and ultimately we jeopardize our own survival. Hopefully we will learn this before it's too late.

Similarly, it's in your best interests to understand how love relationships really operate. The rules of love relationships pre-exist of their own accord: Your sexual desire, interaction patterns, and sense of self are inseparably entwined. They are as much determined by millions of years of evolution as by things you experienced during childhood or things that happen during sex. The way your brain is wired comes from prehistoric times, recent generations of your family, and your particular life experiences.[55]

Understanding your sexual desire means understanding the natural ecology of love relationships. The rules of love relationships often differ from what you want to believe. Throughout history, laws have surfaced giving men legal control of their wives' bodies. These laws document how patriarchal societies attempt to overcome the way sexual desire operates in emotionally committed relationships. Today, the man is the LDP in half the cases I see. But the rule still holds true: The low desire partner always controls sex.

My approach will help you get it right: It embraces a unique view of love, sexual desire, and relationships. It is an *ecological* approach. An ecological approach says that the rules of love relationships already exist in your marriage. When you live according to how things work, rather than how you want them to be, relationships become more productive and gratifying.

Ignore the rules of love relationships at your own peril. These rules exist within even the most destructive relationships—the reason they're so destructive is because no one heeds them or acts accordingly. You are more likely to stay together, and be happy that you did, if you heed the rules of how relationships really work.

This is a huge shift if you're indoctrinated with the modern mantra, "Work on your relationship!" In many ways you *can't* work on your relationship, any more than you can work on the environment. You can support the environment doing what it does naturally, instead of interfering with it. But you can't improve the way it functions as an elegant, interdependent whole. If you understand and respect how love relationships operate (relationship ecology) and how people operate (individual ecology), your life will be healthier and happier.[56]

• *Sexual desire problems: Learning to take care of your self*

It's easier to resolve sexual desire problems if you see how they involve your brain, mind, body, and relationship. There's a lot more involved than doing what comes naturally. Resolving sexual desire problems can create powerful personal development that ripples through your life.

We've laid a scientific basis for what I'm telling you: Sexual desire problems are a normal and healthy midpoint in the evolution of a relationship and the people in it. They don't necessarily mean something is going wrong. Sexual desire problems replay epic sagas of human evolution. Now it's your turn to go through it. Don't waste your time perfecting your sexual techniques.

Nature is clever: The relationship in which you seek refuge pushes you to develop a more solid self, like pushing toothpaste out of a tube by progressively winding the other end. The love relationship you thought would make you feel safe and secure pounds your fragile reflected sense of self into something solid and lasting.

It sounds weird to think of sexual desire problems as naturally occurring growth processes, but that's how I've come to see them. That's the way my clients come to see them too. Like Doreen and Adam, many folks come to look upon their desire problem as one of the best things that ever happened to them. If you handle your opportunity wisely, there's a good chance you'll end up feeling that way, too.

## • *Back to Doreen and Adam*

Adam said, "I don't like Doreen thinking I owe her sex. She makes me feel like my body doesn't belong to me. She doesn't see me as a separate person. She doesn't respect my boundaries. She's constantly telling me what to do, down to the clothes I wear. I don't belong to her, I belong to me."

Doreen retorted, "When we first got together you liked us belonging to each other. I know you felt supported and encouraged by me, and I felt important and needed in your life. Now the idea of belonging to each other makes you furious. I think you have a problem with commitment. It comes out by you withholding sex."

Doreen looked at me and said, "Why does something so natural have to be so complex and difficult?" Her tone sounded like she was saying, *Adam is making this difficult! He's the problem.*

Adam scowled, clearly feeling criticized. Doreen barked, *"Can't I even ask a question!"* Adam's head snapped back as though he'd just been slapped.

"Things shouldn't be this difficult," Doreen repeated. "Sex and desire are natural functions. They're built in. If we love each other, we should have sexual desire for each other." She turned to Adam. "Maybe you don't love me at all!" The tension in the room rose.

To head off the looming disaster, I steered our attention in a different direction. I said to Doreen. "I've learned that the exact opposite of what you believe is true. If you love each other and stay together, you can count on sexual desire problems."

"Why do you say that?" she challenged. "Are you saying there's a flaw built into long-term relationships?"

"No, I mean the exact opposite. You can count on sexual desire problems if you love each other and stay together, because long-term emotionally committed relationships are that *perfect*."

"*Perfect?*" Doreen said. "How could relationships be perfect if they have sexual desire problems! Adam and I don't have sex. Our relationship is falling apart. We're talking about splitting up. He doesn't love me anymore. He says I pressure him for sex all the time. I feel unattractive. I have a hard time accepting what you're saying, Doctor. You make it sound like it's okay to have sexual desire problems, like it's normal."

"That's exactly what I'm saying."

"How could that be true? If every couple has sexual desire problems, we'd all be divorced."

"You mean people wouldn't go through the kinds of problems you're having?"

"Right! It would be easier to just find a new partner who wanted to have sex. I've certainly thought about that option."

"But have you done that yet?"

"No."

"So you endured the tensions, you didn't take the easy way out, and you hung in there."

"Yes."

"Why'd you do that?"

Doreen stopped and thought for several seconds. Then she spoke slowly and thoughtfully. "Because my relationship with Adam is important to me."

"Then you operated differently than your own picture of people. Your sexual desire problem hasn't ended your relationship—yet. You can use it to help the two of you grow as individuals and as a couple. It comes down to how you go about solving your desire problem. I can show you how to do that if you like."

Doreen looked at me and nodded. She was demonstrating an important and often unappreciated aspect of love relationships: they push the best in us to stand up.

---

### IDEAS TO PONDER

* Your brain, body, mind, and relationship are one whole system in which sexual desire plays a key role. Problems with sexual desire and struggles of selfhood go hand in hand in love relationships.
* Developing and maintaining a solid sense of self greatly shapes your sexual desire. Your reflected sense of self and solid self often outweigh horniness, hormones, or your desire for intimacy and attachment.
* Love relationships have people-growing processes that call for the best in you to come forward to endure and cope with them. Doing that makes us creative and resilient.

# 3

## The Low Desire Partner Usually Controls the High Desire Partner's Adequacy

*I*n Chapter 1 we began to explore what happens to the low desire partner when there are sexual desire problems. We saw through Connie that your reflected sense of self really takes a beating. But what if you're the high desire partner? In Chapter 2 we started to see in Doreen that your reflected sense of self also gets bruised, because you take your mate's lower desire personally, too. Some HDPs don't feel rejected, inadequate, or undesirable, but they are the exception. Lots of them *say* they don't take it as a negative reflection on themselves, but a good percentage of them march around the house shouting, "It's not me who is the problem, it's *you!*"

• *Sally and Robert*

Like many LDPs, Sally frequently heard these kinds of comments. Her partner Robert, the HDP, often felt compelled to share his feelings, specifically that she was hung up about sex. When Sally and Robert first came to see me, Robert said he felt good about himself and deserved more than what he was getting in his marriage. If I hadn't listened carefully, what he was saying would have made perfect sense. As I learned more, however, I saw a different picture: Sally, the LDP, indeed controlled when sex occurred. But how and why Robert pictured this control happening said a lot about him and his sense of self.

Robert blamed Sally and made her feel defective because his own reflected sense of self was crumbling. Robert took Sally's lack of desire as a criticism of his desirability and adequacy as a lover. Sally controlled Robert's self-worth simply by choosing when to have sex or not. Robert's reflected sense of self hinged on having sex. She controlled Robert's adequacy whether she liked it or not.

Sally intuitively knew this. She knew how Robert's mind worked. Robert made himself less sexually appealing by acting like he didn't take it personally. Sally knew Robert's self-image relied on her responding *enthusiastically* the moment he made an overture. The pressure made her even less desirous.

Last chapter we saw how your sense of self is woven into your sexual desire, and previously we learned that the LDP always controls sex. What happens when this combines with the fact that most of us depend on a positive reflected sense of self, *especially* when it comes to sex? Sally and Robert illustrate what this looks like in daily life: In addition to controlling sex, *the LDP controls the HDP's sense of adequacy, too.*

This starts long before any hint of sexual problems. This is how things are in love relationships from the outset: (Women, in particular, are taught to be acutely aware of protecting their partner's "sexual ego.") When desire problems or sexual dysfunctions show up, *the LDP controls the HDP's adequacy whether she likes it (or knows it) or not.* When the HDP takes steps to bolster his sagging self-worth, it usually further affects the LDP's already-diminished sense of self. And thus, the age-old cycle of sexual desire and human development begins anew.

## IT STARTS AT THE BEGINNING: BEING NORMAL

Like many couples, Robert and Sally had problems from the start. The second time they had sex, Robert asked if she had problems having orgasms. Sally said she didn't think so. It just took her longer with a new partner to really relax and get into it. Robert said this was fine with him, but Sally felt he wasn't being honest. Thereafter, Sally made more signs of pleasure—even when she wasn't feeling it—because Robert seemed to need this. He certainly seemed happier when she moaned and groaned. Sally also did this because she felt unsure of herself, and she wanted Robert to like her.

What I'm describing is normal stuff. It transcends gender, sexual orientation, and culture. I've worked with other couples like Sally and Robert except their genders are reversed. Gay and lesbian couples do this too. We all want other people to like, accept, and admire us. But like many people, Robert *depended* on Sally (and other people) to help him feel good about himself.[57] He didn't have much solid self, but instead relied on his reflected sense of self. Although he never saw it, Robert wanted Sally to accommodate and defer to him. This made him feel important, loved, respected, and cherished.

Sally did this early on in their marriage. She felt it her responsibility to make Robert happy. His unhappiness meant she was failing as a wife. Satisfying Robert propped up Sally's own reflected sense of self—for a while. This was her response whenever important people in her life got nervous or unhappy.

Now, after twenty years of marriage, Sally refused to do this anymore. It wasn't just stubbornness. It was beyond feeling frustrated that she never made Robert happy for long. Years of *success* in accommodating Robert and supporting his reflected sense of self finally caught up with her.

The more Sally supported Robert's needy reflected sense of self, the more he came to expect it, and the more loudly he complained when he didn't get it. The more Sally had sex and feigned enthusiasm, the less she wanted to do it. As Robert increasingly expected it and demanded it, her desire waned further. Robert's attitude impinged on her sense of autonomy and triggered the human impulse to tell one's partner, "Enough is enough."

• *Propping up your partner's reflected sense of self*

It didn't surprise me that Sally and Robert had sexual desire problems. They were gridlocked over sex and they didn't like each other very much. In bed, their sexual encounters often collapsed in the opening moments.

Their initial visit with me wasn't much different. Robert complained that Sally didn't want sex very often, and she didn't take his needs into consideration. Sally got defensive and reeled off a long list of things she did for him, sex being one of them. Sally acknowledged she often didn't have desire, but for years she went along and did it anyway.

Robert countered that this was the problem: Sally always seemed to be doing him a favor. She never wanted sex for herself. According to Robert, Sally had some kind of problem because she never seemed interested in sex like normal people. He alternately criticized her for years of just going through the motions, and then for not being willing to continue doing that. I could see that Robert's emotional whiplash of Sally was completely beyond his awareness.

Robert pretty much did the same thing at home: He initiated sex several times a week and blew up if Sally wasn't perky and raring to go. Then he sulked for days, breaking his deafening silences with curt responses that were punitive and withholding. Robert wanted her to know he was unhappy. If Sally didn't pay enough attention to his obvious displeasure, his litany would start: "It's not me, it's *you* who has a problem!"

For years, Sally apologized to Robert and said she was sorry. Robert usually accepted Sally's apology if it was followed by sex. All was forgiven—until next time. But if Robert was really hurt and angry, they went through a second level: When Sally apologized, Robert responded with, "You don't mean it." Sally was supposed to cajole him into believing she cared. She was also expected to be particularly enthusiastic in the sex that inevitably followed. This was how Sally propped up Robert's reflected sense of self—and sex wasn't the only way they played this out.

Sally "slid underneath" Robert, gave in to him, about disciplining their teenage son Jason. Robert was generally punitive with the boy. He demanded unquestioned obedience and deference from Jason, even more than he did from Sally. Robert's reflected sense of self was piqued if Jason hesitated to follow his dictates. Day by day Robert squeezed the life out of Jason.

Sally knew this wasn't right. But saying anything to Robert about it invariably triggered accusations of betrayal and undermining. As far as he was concerned, she was presenting a divided front to Jason, or aligning with Jason against him. So Sally usually kept silent. Until recently, Sally's reflected sense of self prevailed whenever Robert was angry. Sally felt calmer, and things felt more stable if she gave in to whatever Robert wanted.

## BORROWED FUNCTIONING

Robert and Sally illustrate what I call *borrowed functioning*. Borrowed functioning is a way people cope with the fact that our first self is a reflected sense of self. We depend on a reflected sense of self because of how human beings develop. From infancy, our mind looks to other minds for help supporting our own self-awareness. You see yourself through the eyes of people important to you. You internalize how others see you and treat you as indications of who you are.

Our first realization of being a "self" elicits anger and frustration rather than joy and relief. It starts the moment you realize you and Mommy are not a single entity. Suddenly, there is "I" and "Thou." (According to theologian Martin Buber, this relationship is initially "I" and "It."[58]) Your initial experience of selfhood comes when your parent or care-giver *isn't* doing what you want. When you're feeling comfortable and nurtured, you're not aware there are two of you. I'm not describing life's initial "trauma." It's just the nature of things to come.

Borrowed functioning is "borrowed" because it doesn't give you a solid sense of self or the ability to function in lasting ways. It's like your self is a balloon your partner inflates. While you're inflated, things seem better. You may look better, feel better, and even act better briefly, but these transfusions of "pseudo-self" don't hold up. Even if your partner doesn't deflate you, you "leak" enough to require further inflation before long.

Borrowed functioning is also "borrowed" in the sense that it *diminishes* the donor's (your partner's) functioning, resilience, and reflected sense of self. This may not show at first, because even though it's illusory, borrowed functioning can enhance both people's functioning. But inevitably, as the LDP eventually descends into insecurity (and smoldering defiance), the HDP, having borrowed functioning, magnificently ascends on the wings of self-righteousness. In relationships where partners truly help each other, the hallmark of a healthy love is that a couple's functioning improves together over time. The difference between real love and caring, and what Robert and Sally were doing, is that Sally was being emotionally depleted and Robert was only artificially holding himself up.

Just because Robert and Sally engaged in borrowed functioning doesn't mean they didn't have a real relationship. Borrowed functioning *is* a relationship—it is *most* relationships. Whenever partners depend on each other for a positive reflected sense of self, they have an *emotional fusion*. (True interdependence requires a solid sense of self.) An emotional fusion means people are regulating their emotions (and reflected sense of self) through their interactions with their partner, rather than handling them internally, with a solid sense of self, on their own. The partner borrowing the function can change depending on the circumstances. But borrowed functioning can't occur without a real relationship, because there's no way for the borrowing to take place. Borrowed functioning and emotional fusion are powerful forms of relatedness, arguably the most common type. But as normal as this is, you need to grow beyond this.

Robert felt better when Sally humbled herself and apologized, even if she had done nothing wrong. Robert was less belligerent and dogmatic when his son deferred to his authority. When everything went his way, Robert felt life was as it should be. He couldn't see why Sally seemed so unhappy. They lived a good life. Robert figured it must be something in her past. But things between Sally and Robert weren't happening simply because of their childhoods. They were in the groove of a love relationship, laid down millions of years ago when the human self emerged.

- *Do you depend on your partner for validation and reassurance?*

Normal people depend on others for their sense of identity, self-worth, and security. We do so because we are generally at a common modest level of personal development. A reflected self is the first self we have. Many people never develop much of a solid self and engage in borrowed functioning all their lives.

Most of us take our partner's desire personally, be it high or low. We depend on a positive reflected sense of self from others about highly sensitive issues like sex. We feel attractive when others find us attractive. We feel desirable and desirous because someone desires us. When you're getting the positive reflected sense of self you need, you're unaware of the process. As far as you're concerned, everything's going fine. You're in love. When people speak of rekindling romance in their marriage, what they really want is the euphoria of borrowed functioning and a positive reflected sense of self.[59]

But the price of feeling good about yourself because others approve of you—or want to have sex with you—is feeling bad about yourself when they don't.

## DEVELOPING A SOLID FLEXIBLE SELF

Isn't it perfectly normal to take it personally when your partner doesn't want to have sex with you? Likewise, wouldn't you feel bad if you don't desire your partner and he tells you you're screwed up? Of course! That's the point: Most people rely on a reflected sense of self from others.

This doesn't result from childhood trauma, like not getting enough praise or unconditional acceptance when you were young. Constant criticism and rejection during childhood gives you a particularly *negative* reflected sense of self. Parental neglect makes you believe you're unimportant and unworthy. But inexhaustible positive reinforcement won't solve the basic issue, *because you still depend on others to make you feel okay about yourself.* Even if you were the gleam in your parents' eyes, you may still demand constant attention, support, and reassurance from your partner. No amount of praise gives you a *solid* sense of self.

*A solid sense of self develops from confronting yourself, challenging yourself to do what's right, and earning your own self-respect.* It develops from inside you, rather than from internalizing what's around you.

It takes much longer to develop a really solid sense of self (i.e., reach adulthood) than many people think. So, when we marry we usually still depend on others for a positive self-reflection. We bring our reflected sense of self into our marriage, because it got us there. Meanwhile, the lust, romantic love, and attachment circuits in our heads are working overtime. What happens next is a no-brainer: We become a "couple." Marriage is an ecosystem designed to help you become an adult, by making your reflected sense of self incredibly vulnerable and finally untenable.

## • *What happens to the low desire partner?*

Like most LDPs, Sally believed sexual desire is a natural function. This put her in a weak position in her own mind. Robert believed this, too, which diminished Sally's status in their marriage. Robert's desire became the standard by which Sally's desire and adequacy were measured. Since Sally measured herself by Robert's dissatisfaction, she readily assumed the lesser position in their sex life.

In our initial session Sally complained that Robert frequently beat her down emotionally, telling her she had a sex problem. I said this was *his* reflected sense of self talking.

"It's pretty common for the high desire partner to rescue his drowning sense of self by saying, 'It's you, not me, that's the problem.' The more you depend on a reflected sense of self, the less you can handle being seen as less than perfect. When your flaws emerge, your picture of yourself cracks, and you crash emotionally. If you depend on a reflected sense of self, blaming someone else makes you feel better. So lots of low desire partners frequently hear, 'I'm not the problem. It's *you!*'"

Sally complained, "I feel so bad when he says this to me. I'm depressed all day. I keep replaying our interaction in my head. I keep seeing myself disappointing Robert."

"That's what happens when your reflected sense of self [pointing to Robert] is having a bad day." Sally and Robert laughed. The tension in the room lessened.

"It's hard to hang on to yourself when you're getting *two* simultaneous messages: One is, *You're no good, you're defective and inadequate, and you don't have what it takes.*' The other is, *You're the one with the resources, and only you can feed my physical and emotional needs. You have no right to withhold this, because I need it.* The emotional whiplash leaves the low desire partner wondering who she really is."

My description started to trigger Robert's reflected sense of self. "So why doesn't Sally ever initiate?"

"You and Sally go through a typical pattern. You are the high desire partner, and like most high desire partners, you try to instill desire in Sally. Sally is the low desire partner, and like most low desire partners, she knows you need her to validate you as a lover. She's supposed to do that by having sexual desire. The only problem is that having to validate you makes her feel less desire and more pressured. Sally knows you feel rejected when she doesn't want sex—and this, in turn, makes it harder for her to enjoy having sex with you. The low desire partner's sexual desire goes down, and the high desire partner's reflected sense of self goes with it.

"That's where you come in." As I said this Robert sat up in his chair. "The high desire partner starts feeling undesirable, unattractive, and unloved. He tries to make the low desire partner more desirous, to shore up his sagging sense of self. The low desire partner sees this and gets turned off by the high desire partner's insecurity. So the cycle gets worse.

"Next, the high desire partner adopts a seemingly enlightened attitude: The low desire partner has a treatable problem, and the high desire partner wants to help her fix it. The high desire partner offers to 'accompany' the low desire partner to treatment. The low desire partner bristles at the high desire partner's patronizing attitude, and the cycle gets worse." Robert smiled. Sally was so relieved he didn't explode, she giggled.

"When the high desire partner blames the low desire partner, any fledgling desire evaporates, and the low desire partner becomes resentful, defensive, and unmotivated. The high desire partner takes this personally too. So, the cycle worsens."

"Sounds familiar," Robert said.

"The high desire partner's reflected sense of self takes a beating with each experience of rejection—meaning any time the low desire partner doesn't want sex—and a deep withdrawal follows. As time passes, the withdrawal deepens into an emotional deep-freeze. As the cycle worsens, the high desire partner pushes harder for sex, trying frantically to instill desire in the low desire partner, while alternately pulling away more violently."

Robert and Sally exchanged knowing looks. Robert's demeanor continued to soften. "So why doesn't the low desire partner get off her ass and do something?"

"Why should she? The low desire partner has nowhere to go. If she doesn't develop more desire, she gets the blame. If she does, the high desire partner gets the credit. You supposedly created the desire in her. With nothing to gain and nothing to lose, the low desire partner isn't highly motivated to make things better. She's more prepared for rebellion and passive-aggression." Sally smiled self-consciously and blushed.

## • *Are you and your partner emotional Siamese twins?*

Robert had to smile. "Okay. I'm impressed. I get the idea that Sally and I are interacting largely because we are the high desire or the low desire partner, and that this determines what we're going through. It sounds like we're completely on auto-pilot."

"Like most couples, the two of you are *emotionally fused*, like Siamese twins. Every move one of you makes upsets the other's emotional balance. One's efforts to control or mobilize herself deeply perturbs the other. Sexual desire problems don't require anger, a vendetta, or malevolent intent. You want to control your own life. When you are as tightly fused and emotionally entangled as the two of you, any move—or lack of movement—from one partner deeply impacts the other."

Robert nodded. "Is that sick? I thought we had grown apart."

"If you're normal, you are emotionally fused. The problem isn't that you're 'too close.' It's that you are too dependent on each other for your emotional balance. When you rely on a reflected sense of self, you have *no choice* but to attach to someone else. Emotional fusion becomes an overriding necessity and a forgone conclusion.

"You and Sally are like two businessmen in intense negotiations. When one is satisfied with the deal, the other feels he hasn't bargained hard enough. One's satisfaction makes the other think he could have gotten more in the trade. He begins to think he cheated himself—or was swindled. Each needs the other to be unhappy in order to feel that he did well in the competition. You and Sally talk about win-win solutions, but your reflected sense of self makes that impossible."

Sally spoke up. "I know that's true: Even when I push myself to please Robert in bed, a part of me knows I'm withholding at the same time. I'm constantly watching him to see if he can tell. I'm at war with myself when we have sex. I'm driving myself nuts!"

"You are both highly accomplished at tracking each other's minds, which I call mind-mapping." Sally and Robert gave each other suspicious looks. Then, they broke into nervous laughter. The intimacy was so intense, they looked at the floor. When Sally and Robert walked out of my office, they watched each other from the corner of their eyes.

## MAPPING YOUR PARTNER'S MIND

If you have a reflected sense of self, being able to read other peoples' minds is all-important. You do it constantly, vigilantly searching for clues about how others think and feel about you. You have to know what other people are thinking to make sure you look good in their eyes. That's what a reflected sense of self is all about, and you can't be sure you've got other people's approval if you can't map their minds.

Actually you are *hyper*-vigilant, scanning for advance warning of the rejection you anticipate. You play three moves ahead. You become expert at it. It's a full-time job. You don't want to be caught off guard or look like a fool.

You couldn't do this if your brain couldn't figure out another person's mind. Mind-reading plays a critical role in successful social interactions and manipulating other people (e.g., to get them to like you). It can be used negatively or positively. Mind-mapping is an incredible process, but sometimes it's no fun. You can learn more than you really want to know. Many times you have disappointing or scary realizations. Shortly, I'll introduce you to the Four Points of Balance, which will help you keep your mind-mapping on track.

## • *Mind-mapping*

Reading someone's mind means understanding his thoughts, feelings, and motivations by studying his reactions and behavior. Mind-mapping arises from awareness that (a) other people have their own minds, replete with perceptions, beliefs, and desires, and that (b) other people's behavior can be explained and predicted by deducing the content of their mind. Scientists refer to everyday mind-mapping as folk psychology or "mentalizing."[60]

Mind-mapping begins in childhood as you study the people in your family. You behave in particular ways because you recognize their emotions, desires, and thoughts; you understand their distortions, moods, personalities, and past histories. Mind-mapping occurs in every culture, in every aspect of life, during every waking moment.

Mind-mapping lies at the heart of *all* social interactions. Manipulating the mental states of others to alter their behavior is a sign of social intelligence. Successful social interactions, straightforward or manipulative, come from recognizing who the players are and what makes them tick. There are usually loads of mind-mapping going on in unpleasant and unsatisfying interactions too, it's just more likely to be inaccurate.

Mind-mapping plays a critical role in maintaining your reflected sense of self. If you can't figure out how someone feels about you, you don't know where you stand. Not knowing makes you anxious, so you want to figure it out. Mind-mapping allows you to present yourself in such a way as to get the acceptance and validation you need from others.

For example, Sally and Robert were unaware they were mind-mapping each other every night as they went to bed. Sally would pretend she was oblivious, but she monitored Robert for signs he might initiate sex. Robert scrutinized Sally for clues that she might be "in the mood."

• *Your brain is built to map other minds*

In the last decade researchers have focused on how your brain accomplishes mind-mapping. They have identified a vast and diverse neural network involving specific cells in different parts of your brain that work together in a sophisticated system. Mind-mapping involves three main parts of your brain: Cells in the back of your brain detect other people's motor behavior. Cells in the middle part of your brain read other people's emotions, to which you add your own emotional response, and then integrate the data. Cells in your forebrain take the result and execute it. This greatly oversimplifies how your neocortex negotiates with the emotional centers in your brain and tries to organize them. But for our purpose, this lets you know the part of your brain that determines the meaning of things isn't necessarily the more rational part.[61]

Mind-mapping arises from reliable and powerful mechanisms pre-existing in the reptilian part of your brain, the most archaic part, which distinguishes between animate and inanimate objects, and between human and nonhuman animals. This part of your brain distinguishes your own actions from those of others.[62]

Other parts of your brain build on this by "sharing attention," focusing on what other people focus on. By following other people's gaze, and perceiving their emotions, you can deduce their goals. You figure out what they want (desire). This lets you anticipate their future course of action, and organize your own goal-directed actions accordingly.[63]

Reptiles do this on a rudimentary level.[64] But your mammalian brain adds meaning and emotion to the data. This non-rational, emotionally reactive part of your brain largely shapes what you're going to do about what you're mapping. Your prefrontal neocortex adds details to your mental map of the other person's mind, negotiates with your mammalian brain about your course of action, and implements it.[65]

Earlier I told you Helen Fisher found that certain parts of the brain light up in romantic love, and new parts light up when you've been in love longer. These latter parts play a key role in mapping someone else's mind, as well as your own mind (self-awareness).[66]

• *Why did humans develop mind-mapping?*

Why did people develop the ability to map each other's minds? Two zoologists independently came to the same conclusion: Coping with the "hostile forces of nature" (i.e., Darwinian natural selection) wasn't enough to necessitate mind-mapping. The necessary stimulus and reward was increased contact with other human beings.[67] Your higher consciousness is largely occupied with mapping the thoughts and feelings underlying other people's actions.[68]

Before this theory, scientists approached communication like naïve marital therapists: They thought the purpose of communication was transferring information. They pictured the sender and the receiver both benefiting from clear, accurate, and honest messages. However, scientists finally realized many animals use communication to manipulate each other rather than to transmit information. All the great apes have the ability to imagine alternative worlds, as is evident in their deceptions. Calculated intelligent deception occurs occasionally in chimpanzees, rarely but existent in baboons, but commonly among humans. Mind-mapping greatly facilitates building alliances, and alliance building ("salesmanship") is a key to success among human beings. But deceiving others and detecting deception may also be a primary reason humans developed mind-mapping.[69] Deception plays such an important role in human communication that your brain is hot-wired to detect it.[70]

• *Mind-mapping starts young*

The rudiments of mind-mapping show up as soon as you're born. During your first year of life, you're already tracking other people's attention and intention.[71] You orient toward what other people focus on and point out objects of their interest. You seek "moments of meeting" in which you share "joint attention" with someone else.[72] By twelve months old, you also draw your parents' attention to objects or events that interest you by pointing. You look toward their faces when you are uncertain, trying to read their expression.

By eighteen months you can track someone else's gaze into space hidden from your view, and recognize that he or she sees an object you cannot see.[73] You understand that when someone looks or points at an object, or focuses attention on an event, he or she becomes mentally connected to it. You know from personal experience that two people become connected when they focus attention on the same thing or event.[74] These joint-attention behaviors are your very first experience of intimacy.

When you are eighteen to twenty-four months old, your ability to make distinctions between yourself and others marks the passing from infancy to early childhood. You recognize yourself in the mirror and engage in fantasy play in your mind. You play cooperatively with other children and do simple acts of altruism. You imitate and complete an action you've seen someone else attempt but fail to finish.[75] You smile when you succeed at a task, cry when you fail, and loudly signal your desires.[76] Most importantly, you understand *pretence*, which requires understanding other people's intentions.[77] (Yes, this means your children have mapped your mind, too.)

By the time you are two, you're preoccupied with your emotions and desires, babbling incessantly about your wishes, wants, and hopes. You know pain comes with wanting something but not having it. When you're three, you've learned that if you figure out what someone wants, you can accurately predict what that person will do.[78]

In other words, mind-mapping greatly focuses around *desire*.

It's much easier for children to understand other people's desires than their own. Figuring out what someone wants (or doesn't want) uses the primitive parts of your brain. Mapping out your own motivations—and other people's knowledge and beliefs—comes later as your brain and social intelligence mature.[79]

By age five you arrive at a critical turning point: You understand someone's mind can have a false belief.[80] As a child you first encounter alternative mental worlds and the possibility of deception by mapping out inaccuracies and self-deceptions in your parents' minds. For instance, the first time you do something wrong, tell a lie, and get away with it, you realize your parents don't have an all-knowing, perfect picture of the truth. When they give you ice cream instead of punishing you, you discover they can make inaccurate presumptions.

At that point you start engaging in deliberate acts of deception. Lying (deliberately implanting false beliefs) is positive proof of mind-mapping ability.[81] To be a good liar you have to read other people's minds, because that's the only way you know when you've been successful. Like sharpening a knife, lying hones your ability to map out other people's minds.[82] Your mind-mapping ability becomes more sophisticated around age eleven, and during adolescence it goes through another revolution.[83]

I'm telling you this because you and your partner are mapping each other's minds all the time—even when it doesn't look like it. Lots of people *pretend* they're not. Some of the shrewdest mind-mappers I've ever met look as though they are not doing anything and have no idea what's going on.

So, are you a mind-mapper? I know you are. The question is: How accurate are you? Do you let yourself know what you see, or do you blind yourself? Do you let your partner (and other people) map your mind?

### • *Mind-mapping in sexual desire problems*

Mind-mapping plays many critical roles in sexual desire. Once couples have sexual desire problems, mind-mapping runs amok. No doubt you use mapping to figure out whether or not your partner desires you.

The politics of mind-mapping shift as relationships evolve: Early on, you usually *want* your partner to know whether or not you want him—because you probably do. (If you don't desire him, you mask this if you want the relationship to continue.) Later on, when you're sexually bored, you probably mask your mind from being mapped about your level of desire.

If you don't want your partner, you usually don't want him mapping your mind. It may destabilize your relationship, or shift it into an undesirable balance. At the same time, when desire fades in one partner (or both), both partners begin mind-mapping sorties, gathering information about the other's thoughts, feelings, and motivations. This squirrel cage of contradictory agendas underlies what most couples refer to as "growing apart." (But from this perspective you can see it's a kind of emotional fusion. Each partner's emotional equilibrium rests on what he or she thinks is going on in the other's mind.)

The politics of mind-mapping also play out differently depending on who's involved. For instance, you might *want* to hurt your partner's feelings, or tamper with her reflected sense of self, or shift the balance of power in the relationship. In that case, you'll go out of your way to make it easy for her to read that you don't desire her.

### • *Mind-mapping: With or without empathy?*

If we can read each other's minds, why don't we use this to be more considerate of each other? How can people with highly developed ability to intuit another being's mind use it in such self-preoccupied and insensitive ways? This is easier to understand when you know how your brain got organized into a mind-mapping machine.

According to some experts, mind-mapping involves developing and applying general principles about human behavior and human nature. We deduce other people's inner reality by cross-referencing what they say, what they do, and what their behavior suggests they want, analyzing this through prior social learning. (This is the "theory" aspect of mind-mapping).[84] Children show remarkable ability to approach situations with powerful deductive logic that quickly zeros in on their parents.

Other scientists say we map someone's mind by mentally simulating his thoughts and feelings, using our own mental state as a model of what's happening inside him.[85] (This is the "simulation" aspect of mind-mapping.) We do this by role-taking and dramatic impersonation, imaginatively putting ourselves in the other's place, and assessing our own emotions and physical sensations. We can either assume he or she will respond as we do, or we adopt alternative character traits and do a mental recalibration. Our goal is to figure out what they find attractive or unattractive, what they wish to pursue or avoid.

Research suggests that "simulation" occurs directly from seeing other people's faces and bodies. Neuroscientists discovered we have automatic and unconscious neural responses when we observe someone else doing something. We feel visceral responses and "gut feelings" when we see another person's face express an emotion.[86] When you see someone grasp an object, it triggers "mirror" neurons in your premotor cortex as if you were grasping it. When you see someone eating an apple, or being hit with a stick, motor neurons fire as if you were doing the movements yourself or it was happening to you. This gives you the same motor, visceral, and psychological pain responses as the person you're observing. Your brain uses this to infer what's happening in another person's mind and body.[87]

Highly accurate mind-mapping probably uses all these sources. If someone's behavior is predictable you use mental simulation. When he doesn't act the way you expect, you shift to "collect and analyze data." Your visceral reactions from watching his face and body cue you to his state of mind.[88]

A large part of mind-mapping has nothing to do with empathizing or identifying with other people.[89] That's why sociopaths and con artists, lacking any empathy and compassion, can be stunningly good mind-mappers. They are trackers. They deduce your beliefs, desires, and intentions from their understanding of human nature and watching what you do. They put themselves in your place, figure out what you think and feel, and use this to manipulate you with lies. Mind-mapping is the human refinement of prehistoric social intelligence that keeps animals alive.[90] Mind-mapping doesn't primarily derive from your neocortex. Making meaning of what you've mapped out primarily goes on in your limbic system—the less rational, highly emotionally reactive, "non-thinking" part of your brain. The raw data comes from an even more primitive part called your *reptilian brain*, which you have in common with reptiles.

I believe you *can* get your neocortex in charge of your mind-mapping. When you do, your mind-mapping improves. Your perceptions and judgment will be less shaded by emotional distortions. You *can* direct your mind-mapping efforts toward your partner's happiness, but doing so involves more than improved accuracy. If you lack a solid self, you're not likely to do this, because it means potentially giving up something else you want. It's easier to act as though you're clueless while tracking your partner's every move.

Mind-mapping accuracy and benevolence improve when you're willing and able to tolerate uncomfortable feelings, including confronting yourself and mapping your own mind. When you're not willing to look at yourself or be truly known, or the most important thing to you is having things your way, you'll map your partner constantly, but it won't involve empathy.

It's hard to get the best in you orchestrating your mind-mapping. It takes a fair amount of solid self for true empathy and caring to be your motive. If you're like most people, you need help becoming a more solid person. So to improve your mind-mapping—and *many* other things in your life—in the next chapter I'll introduce you to my Four Points of Balance™ program. The Four Points of Balance will help you develop a solid self. If you want the best in you doing your mapping so you can resolve your sexual desire problems, then embrace the Four Points of Balance. This will ripple throughout your life.

## PEOPLE WHO CAN'T CONTROL THEMSELVES CONTROL THE PEOPLE AROUND THEM

We'll talk about mind-mapping throughout the remaining chapters of this book. Mind-mapping shapes human nature, love relationships, and your sexual desire. If you and your partner depend on a reflected sense of self, you are constantly mind-mapping each other, manipulating each other's minds through your interactions, and trying to get the positive reflected sense of self you want. *When you rely on someone for a positive reflected sense of self, you invariably try to control him or her.* You don't want your emotional "drug supply" going away.

• *Regulating the one you love*

People who can't maintain their own sense of self squeeze the life out of the people around them—whether they know it, or like it, or not. Earlier we saw how Robert tried to control Sally when he couldn't control himself. He badgered her with the idea she was sexually defective. He tried harder to turn her on to rescue his sinking reflected sense of self.

The same holds true if you can't calm your own anxieties. If you can't regulate your own emotional temperature, you'll regulate everyone around you to keep yourself comfortable. Think of a parent who can't control her temper or anxieties. Everyone else in the family has to act accordingly to keep her calm and stable.

Your inability to hold on to yourself upsets your partner's emotional balance. The more your reflected sense of self drives you, and the more you look to others, the more your partner will feel oppressed and controlled. The more you try to regulate yourself through your partner, the more you trigger her refusal to submit to tyranny, which is part of human nature. This is why *normal* people have sexual desire problems.

This is why I no longer preach compromise, negotiation, and consideration. Instead, I help people hold on to themselves. I've learned there's more than enough power and control to go around, when you empower and control *yourself*. When clients first realize this, as you are now, they stop bickering, and pay more attention to what's going on.

## • *Moments of Meeting*

Mind-mapping can create a powerful psychological encounter known as an "intersubjective state." It happens when you stop using mind-mapping to figure out how to present yourself, and instead allow yourself to be known. When you let your mind be accurately mapped, your partner can map that you are doing this. It creates the intersubjective state—something like "I'm seeing you, and you are seeing me, and we know we are being seen by each other, because we are both letting this happen."

In *The Present Moment in Psychotherapy and Everyday Life*, Daniel Stern describes intersubjective states as socially based co-created experiences of great overlap in partners' phenomenological consciousness. Each person has a similar experience. Each is acutely aware of the other's experience, and aware that the other is aware of having a concordant experience.[91] Stern says we are capable of intersubjective states by the age of nine to twelve months old.

Intersubjective experiences with a partner are special moments of intense interaction, engraved in your mind. You often think back to them after they are over. They are shared events, something you've gone through together, which impact you as an individual and briefly define you as part of a "unit." Co-created experiences. *Moments of meeting.* Experts believe intersubjective states play a pivotal role in how your brain wires itself, and continually rewires itself, throughout your life.

Here's why *moments of meeting* are special: Not all mind-mapping (sometimes called tracking) creates a profound intersubjective experience. Trackers often *mask* the fact they're tracking the people around them, to *minimize* the possibility of an intersubjective experience. Perhaps the sweetest and most profound aspect—if not the essence—of sex, intimacy, and eroticism is two people openly mind-mapping each other and allowing themselves to mapped.

You may have moments of meeting every day with people you barely know. But moments of meeting between lovers during sex have a special place in human existence. The same is true between parents and children. It always involves two people mapping each other's minds, and allowing their own mind to be mapped.

### • *Sometimes the best in you uses mind-mapping*

The following week Robert and Sally reported that they'd played out their pattern again. Robert made sexual overtures, and Sally was willing but unenthusiastic. Robert exploded, and Sally backed down one more time. They had sex, but the next day Robert was still in a black funk. Before long, Robert and Jason were at each other again. Robert lost his temper and called Jason "worthless" several times.

Sally spent several days berating herself for not speaking up. Fearing she was losing any vestige of self-respect, Sally asked Robert to come to their bedroom. There she took a stand: There would be no further belittling comments from Robert. Not to Jason, and not to her. "When we start treating ourselves and each other with a little respect, then maybe Jason will have some for us."

"How dare you talk to me this way?!" Robert flared.

"Dare? What happens if I don't dare?" Sally said firmly. "Jason can't stand us, and he's right. I can't stand myself. And I can't stand you. You're angry all the time, and I'm always apologizing. I have sex to pacify you.

You make Jason obey you because you're afraid he won't respect you. We'll he doesn't, and neither do I! I don't even respect myself! This whole thing is so unappealing and unattractive, why on earth would I want sex? The three of us are going down the toilet. And you can forget sex until we get out."

This was a powerful "moment of meeting." Robert mapped out Sally's mind and knew this wasn't bluster. She wasn't kidding. Sally wasn't looking down apologetically; she looked him squarely in the eye. She seemed scared but determined. Her voice wasn't shrill or tremulous, which unsettled him. Robert said they would talk about this after he had a chance to think about it.

For several days Robert didn't say much, but his withdrawal was different. He wasn't pounding on Sally emotionally. He seemed preoccupied with his thoughts, considering what to do next. Sally let him stew.

Four days later Robert came to Sally. He said he'd thought about what she said about not respecting him or herself. His tone was somber and introspective. "I've needed you to make me feel like a man, the same way I've needed Jason to respect me as a man. I guess I'm needier than I realized. I never imagined it was so obvious." Robert looked down at the floor. There was clearly more on his mind, but once he stopped he couldn't bring himself to say anything else. He looked up at Sally, smiled weakly, and quietly said goodnight.

The next morning, as they ate breakfast, Robert and Jason had another incident. Jason spilled milk on the table. Expecting to be called names, he prepared to spar with Robert. Instead of being concerned with his own feelings, Robert let himself map Jason's mind. Robert saw his son wasn't being disrespectful. He just felt stupid in front of his father.

Robert suddenly saw the situation in an entirely new way. He moved to defuse the situation. He took his toast, mopped up the milk, and ate it. Jason stared in disbelief. For a moment he wasn't sure if his father was mocking him. Jason kept staring at Robert, trying to map his mind.

After a moment, Robert said, "It's not good without milk. It's too dry." Then he smiled at Jason.

• *Mind-mapping never ends*

In the days that followed, Robert acted better than he usually did when he and Sally didn't have sex. He didn't initiate, and she didn't either. He could have locked in to Jason any number of times, but he didn't. Robert didn't push Jason to defer to his authority. To his credit, Jason wasn't quite so defiant.

Needless to say, Sally was impressed. She respected Robert for taking a hard look at himself. This, in itself, didn't resolve things. But Robert didn't look as weak and small as he had for so long. Sally found herself more interested in sex, and more interested in having it with Robert.

Ever-vigilant about Sally's perceptions of him, Robert mapped this. He felt better about himself because Sally seemed to like him. But more importantly, Robert thought he handled himself with Jason pretty well. He chuckled every time he thought back to eating the toast. It helped him stop overreacting to Jason and give more measured responses. He became less worried about whether Jason respected him or not.

Robert and Sally made love a few weeks after their big encounter. The important thing was how they got there. It felt different because it had a brand new meaning: Sally wasn't doing it to placate Robert, and Robert hadn't demanded it. During sex, they created another new meaning: Robert and Sally stopped trying to bring each other to orgasm to quiet and calm their reflected sense of self. This allowed them to have their first positive moment of meeting during sex: Sally and Robert opened their eyes and looked into each other for several minutes. Neither said a word. They were open with each other in a way they never were.

This episode didn't resolve all of Sally and Robert's difficulties. But it was certainly a powerful beginning. At least now they had hope. They had a glimpse of a different way of living. If you appreciate the elegance of love relationships, you can have hope, too. Marriage is driven by people simply being people. A love relationship is a path to becoming more of a person.

# THE ANSWER TO THE AGE-OLD QUESTION: DOES MARRIAGE KILL SEX?

Does marriage destroy sexual desire? This question has haunted lovers for ages. People have suspected emotionally committed relationships kill sex at least as far back as two thousand years ago, when the poet Ovid wrote in *The Art of Love,* "Quarrels are the dowry married folk bring one another."[92] And in more recent times, Oscar Wilde quipped, "Bigamy is having one wife too many. Monogamy is the same."[93]

We've covered a lot of ground in Part One to prove what these authors feared is true! Marriage *does* kill desire! But that answer means something different than they or you might have thought. Sexual desire problems are part of the middle phase of marriage. They are how love relationships grow. They are normal evolutionary developments in the life cycle of a relationship.

What you're going through feels painful, heartbreaking, frightening, and demoralizing. I've been there too, so I speak from personal experience: Realizing you're going through one of marriage's processes gives you hope and helps you make the most of it. Understanding what you're going through makes you more resilient and less defensive, and speeds your progress. *How* you go through desire problems makes a huge difference in how you come out—including whether your relationship comes out intact.

• *Welcome to the club: Where we're headed*

When you started reading *Intimacy & Desire,* perhaps you wanted tips and tricks to get your partner hot or ignite your own rocket. You probably never thought the ebb and flow of sexual desire, and the resultant conflicts, are part of the natural growth processes of love relationships. You probably never imagined you'd be reading about sexual desire, the human self, and mind-mapping co-evolving over millions of years.

Where does love fit in the picture? Not romantic love, driven by your reptilian and mammalian dopamine-laced brain, but mature adult love, driven by your prefrontal neocortex and your solid sense of self. Love and desire that involve your most uniquely human capacities, like eroticism, intimacy, compassion, and commitment. That kind of adult love and mature desire is exactly where we're headed.

Since your ancestors hatched the human self, we have all had the potential for exquisite sexual desire and mature adult love. Mastering your sexual desire doesn't mean conquering your animal nature. It means developing the highly tuned sense of self necessary to explore your sexual potential. This always involves a stretch. Sexual desire problems will stretch your reflected sense of self as taut as a drumhead. Guaranteed.

A more solid sense of self gives you more *capacity* for desire. It may sound strange to think of sexual desire as a capacity you can develop. But think about it in terms of your capacity to love. You wouldn't think twice if I said your self-development greatly determines your capacity to love. Until you have some degree of solid flexible self, your capacity to love someone—including yourself—is severely limited, as is your tolerance for profound desire. The rigors of mature adult love require an accurate and resilient sense of self, if love is to last. Love, desire, and selfhood are innate human abilities we all need to develop.

In Part Two, I'll show you how to use your desire problems to develop a more solid flexible self. We'll uncover things that control your capacity for profound sexual desire and mature adult love. I'll introduce you to the incredible Four Points of Balance™ and a process called *differentiation*. These are core pieces of my approach. The Four Points of Balance are the best way to resolve sexual desire problems because they also reduce emotional fusion, borrowed functioning, and emotional tyranny. Best of all, they increase your dignity and self-respect, and that's always the best aphrodisiac.

---

## IDEAS TO PONDER

---

- A solid sense of self develops from confronting yourself, challenging yourself to do what's right, and earning your own self-respect.
- Partners are always mapping each other's minds.
- People who can't control themselves control the people around them. When you rely on someone for a positive reflected sense of self, you invariably try to control him.
- Mind-mapping never ends. However, the politics of mind-mapping can shift as a relationship evolves.

# PART TWO

# How We Co-Evolve Through Sexual Desire Problems

# 4

# Holding On to Your Self

*R*eady to stretch your appreciation of sexual desire further? In Part One, we focused on the nature of human sexual desire and the role your sense of self plays in its ebb and flow. We saw how the common tendency to depend on your partner for a positive reflected sense of self creates normal sexual desire problems. This is not "stunted growth" or "arrested development." Think of it as untapped potential. Your reflected sense of self is an early stage of the most sophisticated self on the planet!

The human self is a pretty miraculous thing. You are capable of developing an internalized solid self that does not hinge on validation from others. A self that remains resilient in the face of challenges from life and other people. But a more solid self is not a static, rigid self-image. It is stable and flexible at the same time. (That's pretty amazing in itself.) You can stretch it and bring out new facets, and prune old aspects that no longer fit you. You can change a solid sense of self when you want to, but retain your shape when others try to make you into who or what they want you to be. Flexibility and resilience are two basic and important characteristics of a solid sense of self.

A solid flexible self is also a "clear" sense of self, meaning clearly defined. A clear sense of self comes from developing an accurate identity, intrinsic self-worth, and lasting values and goals (ones that don't arise from other people validating you).

A solid flexible self is arguably humankind's most unique evolutionary achievement: It makes freedom, autonomy, choice, and self-determination possible. Developing a solid flexible self makes love relationships meaningful and long-term passionate marriage achievable.

### • Sexual desire: The bigger picture

The balance between your reflected sense of self and your solid flexible sense of self determines whether you experience desire or not. It determines when, where, and why you have desire (or don't), and whether you miss it or not. But this is only the tip of the iceberg.

The really amazing part is that a solid flexible sense of self is just one of *four* powerful human abilities that shape your sexual desire, your marriage, and your life. There are three other unique human abilities (which I'll discuss shortly) that you can develop to support and develop your self. In other words, there's more to developing your self than staying clear about (or changing) who you are and staying true to your values and goals. You may be a sweet person with fine values and good intent. But if your anxieties drive you to avoid things or act impulsively, you'll do things that violate your integrity, ideals, and goals, and diminish your self-worth. This often has a whopping impact on your sexual desire.

### • Carol and Randall: Trouble from the outset

Carol and Randall were middle-aged folks who came to see me for their desire problems and marital difficulties. They were desperately seeking a new solution. Minutes into our first session, they locked into their typical interaction.

According to Carol, Randall wasn't interested in having sex very often. "It's like we're brother and sister, rather than husband and wife. He forgets that I'm a woman. It shouldn't be my job to remind him to act like a man."

Randall retorted, "I know who I am. I don't need you to tell me." Carol rolled her eyes in contempt. Randall threw up his hands in disgust. "I'm not putting up with your crapola any more, Carol! I'm done. I'm really done. I've had it!"

Carol didn't miss a beat. "You're not the one who's done here. *I'm* done! I can't put up with you any more. We should get a divorce!"

Then, Randall and Carol said nothing. After insisting (once again) that they wanted nothing more to do with each other, what else was there to say? Neither one had any intention of leaving, and they both knew it. We sat in silence for several minutes. Their secret had been exposed: They had frequent nasty outbursts like this at home.

"I understand you're both done. Now that we've established that, let me ask you something else: How long has it actually been since you've done each other?"

For a moment, Randall and Carol didn't know what to say. Then they both broke into laughter. As they did, I mapped them out: They were smart. They had quick minds. They could change their frame of reference. They didn't seem too terribly upset about threats of divorce. They'd done this many times. They lost themselves quickly and severely, but they also could recover fast with help.

Carol said, "It's been six months—way too long."

Randall immediately reacted. "You're wrong. It's only been four months. Don't tell me it been six months. I know it's not. I can count!"

I turned to Randall, waited a moment, and then slowly asked my question. I wanted him to map my thoughts and be clear this wasn't a rhetorical question. I was really interested in his answer.

"If you know who you are … and you know you can count … then why do you take offense and get upset when you think Carol suggests otherwise?"

Randall's immediate impulse was to get defensive and prepare for battle. Thankfully, he read me accurately and realized I wasn't attacking him. He settled down and took a moment to actually think about my question.

"I guess I don't have to be offended," Randall said. "I know who I am. Pretty much." The tension lessened, and he seemed more at ease and less agitated. This wasn't happening because what Randall said was true. It was happening because I'd helped him support his reflected sense of self and momentarily disengage from his emotional fusion with Carol.

## THE FOUR POINTS OF BALANCE™

Let me tell you about four amazing human abilities that evolved over millions of years. Just like your solid flexible self, the origins of the other three abilities lie in the earliest days of the human race, and yet they surface in your lifetime only as you evolve and mature. They are as central to being a mature adult—and as woven into your sexual desire—as a solid flexible self. These abilities control more than your sexual desire: They determine how *all* desires in your life play out. Much like your solid (or reflected) sense of self, they control interactions with your children, parents, friends, and co-workers. So you can bet these four abilities are pretty powerful.

Like most people, Randall and Carol had difficulty in four key areas crucial to maintaining one's emotional balance. I call these the Four Points of Balance. They are:

1. Solid Flexible Self™—the ability to be clear about who you are and what you're about, especially when your partner pressures you to adapt and conform.
2. Quiet Mind–Calm Heart™—being able to calm yourself down, soothe your own hurts, and regulate your own anxieties.
3. Grounded Responding™—the ability to stay calm and not overreact, rather than creating distance or running away when your partner gets anxious or upset.
4. Meaningful Endurance™—being able to step up and face the issues that bedevil you and your relationship, and the ability to tolerate discomfort for the sake of growth.

The First Point of Balance, when you have a *solid flexible* self as opposed to a reflected sense of self, lets you maintain your own psychological "shape" in *close* proximity to *important* partners who pressure you to accommodate them. You don't have to keep distance (physically or emotionally) to stay clear about who you are. The more solid your sense of self, the more important you can let your partner be to you, and the more you can let yourself be truly known. You can seek advice and let yourself be influenced by others. You can change your mind when warranted. You can be flexible without losing your identity.

The Second Point of Balance—having a quiet mind and calm heart—allows you to regulate your own emotions, feelings, and anxieties. If you can't soothe and comfort yourself, then your desires and life's frustrations will pull you apart. Self-soothing is your ability to calm yourself down, soothe your own hurt feelings, and keep your fears and anxieties under control. A Quiet Mind–Calm Heart plays a critical role in mature adult love. It is central to our being the most adaptable, resilient animal on the planet.

The Third Point of Balance involves making grounded responses to the people and events around you. It means not overreacting in response to your partner's anxiety. Grounded Responding plays a big role in mind-mapping: You have to buffer what you learn when you map the minds of the people you love. If you're like most people, your ability to mind-map far exceeds your ability to remain calm and grounded. Mapping your partner's mind can make you upset and highly reactive.

The Fourth Point of Balance lets you endure discomfort for growth. All animals seek pleasure and avoid pain. But what makes humans adaptive and successful is our capacity to forego immediate gratification and endure hardship. This allows us to pursue long-term goals and values we hold dear. Being able to endure the pain and heartache of relationships makes marriage, families, parenting, and caring for others possible. That's not easy. But it's easier to tolerate when your pain and heartache is meaningful, when it serves some purpose you value or something good might come out of it. Purposeless, wasteful, stubborn, or foolish pain and suffering is much harder to tolerate and accomplishes virtually nothing.

All Four Points of Balance are involved in maintaining, caring for, and developing your self. These four abilities are the pillars undergirding your sense of self. These four capacities will help you keep your emotional balance when things get rough.

Do you stay clear about who you are when someone tampers with your sense of self? Or do you fall apart? Can you calm yourself when you're upset or hurt, or do you need someone else to comfort you? When your relationship is struggling, do you overreact and run away from (or cling to) your partner? Do you accomplish those difficult things that need to be done to meet your goals, or do you give up, bail out, or goof off? These Four Points of Balance determine the strength or weakness of your sense of self.

### • *More about Carol and Randall*

Carol and Randall had sex about every third week, but they fought several times a week about whose fault it was that it wasn't more often. They were emotionally brittle, and the intermittent cease-fires between them didn't last. Neither could handle being wrong or imperfect. Usually one—and often both—would crash emotionally after an argument. They were quick to take offense and slow to heal. They often felt depressed. They could dish out abuse, but they couldn't take it.

Carol and Randall argued about who was responsible for their marriage being in shambles. In truth, both of them felt bad about it—which was why they blamed the other. They took each other's accusations personally, got their feelings hurt, and withdrew for days on end. Both Carol and Randall were hesitant to reach out to the other. This was why they rarely had sex, and things broke down in bed at the first sign of trouble.

Carol and Randall's difficulties with their Four Points of Balance (Solid Flexible Self, Quiet Mind–Calm Heart, Grounded Responding, Meaningful Endurance) permeated their lives. Outside the bedroom, things also rapidly deteriorated. Their children witnessed their nasty tirades and name-calling. Relationships with friends and co-workers were somewhat better, because these people were less important. But Randall had few friends, if any, and Carol had a long history of difficulty at work.

In our initial session Carol pushed Randall to talk about his childhood. Randall's blank stare told me he didn't want to talk about it. So she started to tell me his history herself. "Randall was sent to boarding school, and he has never talked about it. I think this has something to do with why he doesn't like sex. He needs to talk about this and get this off his chest." Carol picked at this emotional scab, like she was trying to open Randall up so he could "heal." She took Randall's defensiveness and silence as proof this was necessary. Randall was the low desire partner for sex, for therapy, and for talking about the past.

Months after therapy ended, Randall confirmed he had indeed been sent off to boarding school. He didn't want to face how easily his father and mother had sent him away, ostensibly to get a better education. Randall wanted to blind himself to what he had mapped out about his parents: They treated him like a pet. He could stay as long as he made them look good and didn't disrupt things or make a mess. But Randall got into trouble at school, and, on one occasion, with the police. That's when his parents "became concerned for his education" and sent him to boarding school.

However, in our session Carol wouldn't stop pushing Randall to talk about this. If Randall closed off the topic one way, she found another way to bring it back up. Emotionally, she was all over him. Just as we saw with Connie in Chapter 1, it wasn't surprising Randall wasn't interested in sex.

Carol was emotionally consuming. She engaged in borrowed functioning without any self-awareness of the toll on herself or Randall. In fact, she was much like her intrusive mother, who controlled Carol's childhood, monopolized Carol's wedding, and still tried to manipulate her. But Randall knew better than to say this—Carol became enraged at any mention of her mother. Given how Carol zeroed in on Randall's childhood, you might think she had scrutinized her relationship with her own parents. But, like many people, Carol had all of her mind-mapping radar trained on Randall. She remained quite blind to herself.

Randall and Carol had previously seen a therapist who agreed Randall should talk about his childhood, since he seemed so defensive about it. The therapist suggested Randall's low sexual desire might stem from getting his feelings hurt back then. But Randall refused. Eventually they stopped treatment because they were getting nowhere. The topic always seemed to get back to why Randall didn't want to talk about his past.

Carol had co-constructed Randall as the stereotypical man who wouldn't deal with his feelings. When she picked on that scab, he became defensive, and it made him look as though he was "protesting too much." Carol decided what the big issues in their relationship were going to be, and Randall got to decide what position he took on them. She determined when they bought a new house, or took a vacation, or ate out at a restaurant. Randall fought for the style of house, or the vacation location, or the type of restaurant they went to. But Randall's refusal to discuss his childhood was not the step toward autonomy that it might have looked like on the surface. He depended on Carol for a positive reflected sense of self, which made him overreact to her intrusions.

You might think someone with Randall's background would be so emotionally calloused and withdrawn that he wouldn't care about what other people thought about him. That's what it looked like on the surface. But underneath, Randall needed Carol's approval. He needed her to make him feel like he was worthwhile, that his parents had made a mistake when they gave up on him. Carol's opinion meant so much, he acted as if he didn't care—just as he did when his parents sent him away. As long as he and Carol argued, it meant she hadn't given up. Arguing also kept Carol at arm's length. Randall was afraid Carol would control him, see who he really was, and that would be the end.

When Carol and Randall weren't fighting over sex, they battled over talking. Eventually she said she would leave if he didn't try therapy again and "deal with it." Randall replied she could leave if she wanted, but he wouldn't talk about his childhood, even if his life—or his marriage—depended on it. Carol backed down about divorce, but insisted they try therapy one more time. That's when they came to see me.[94]

Although Randall refused to talk about his childhood, he was also afraid treatment would fail because it seemed that this was such a critical ingredient. Being afraid to talk about the past, and also being afraid if he didn't, was not a good way for Randall to start therapy. In short, he had trouble with his Four Points of Balance. He had difficulty quieting and calming himself, and this made him emotionally prickly and combative in our initial session.

Randall also wasn't prepared for the meaningful endurance required for growth. He gave up quickly and looked like he didn't care. He was afraid of really trying and being found inadequate. He ducked their sexual desire problems for years, even though he knew Carol was unhappy with their situation. This created fights with Carol, but all things considered, he could live with it.

Carol was as emotionally brittle as Randall. She had very little solid flexible self: She couldn't stand looking imperfect in any way. Reflexively, she presumed she was right and put the other person on the defensive. In our session, when Randall stopped bickering, Carol felt she looked worse by comparison. Instinctively, she took another crack at Randall to elevate her reflected sense of self. She went after him, saying he didn't have to argue because he knew who he was.

"You may think you know who you are, but you don't. You may think you can count how long it's been since we had sex, but you can't. It's been five months and twenty-one days. You are so damn self-righteous, but you won't do anything about your problem. The problem *you* created for us."

Having briefly emerged from their emotional soup, Randall dove back in. "This is not *my* problem! This is *our* problem! That's what the other therapist said."

"The other therapist with whom you wouldn't talk about your childhood?"

Carol acted like she had checkmated Randall in their emotional chess game. But I saw it as evidence of difficulty with her Four Points of Balance. She was unsure of her identity because Randall no longer desired her, and being unsure of her own adequacy led her to attack Randall's competency. Like Randall, she had difficulty calming her anxieties and soothing her own heartache. Carol had difficulty making well-grounded, measured responses. She overreacted when Randall momentarily functioned better. She wanted to blame their problems on him rather than endure the discomfort of looking at herself.

### • *Difficulties with the Four Points of Balance*

Carol had the same difficulties holding on to her self that Randall did. She needed Randall to be attracted to her in order to feel good about herself. When he avoided sex, she looked to men who paid attention to her. This frightened and angered her because she didn't want to have an affair.

When Carol got anxious, insecure, and angry enough, she said things like, "Maybe we should just get divorced! You'd be happier with someone who doesn't want sex. I'd find someone what wants to have sex with me. We'd both probably be better off apart." Secretly, Carol wanted Randall to convince her to stay.

Predictably, however, Randall took offense and picked up the challenge. "You want a divorce? Good. Let's get a divorce. You tell the kids. Tell them you're going to break up our home because you're so horny."

Terrible things would be said in the ensuing arguments, leaving Carol and Randall emotionally bruised—and somewhat tender. Often they had sex within twenty-four hours, exchanged promises to try harder, and took back the hateful things they said—until next time. Carol went along with this because she feared what would happen if she didn't. Besides being emotionally dependent, she loved Randall, and she didn't want to face having to leave if their sex life didn't improve.

Carol and Randall often argued about sex, but they never addressed their sexual desire problems seriously and directly. That was too personal and painful. Randall's reflected sense of self caved in. He felt crushed whenever Carol brought up the topic. Randall, literally, wouldn't talk about it. He wouldn't endure the pain of facing his sexual problem, his marriage, and his life because he didn't believe he'd succeed. Likewise, the meanings he saw weren't worth going through hard times to come out better. To Randall, everything said his parents were right, he was incompetent. He couldn't imagine that facing up and working things through could mean his parents were wrong. The meanings you hang on things greatly affect your determination and resilience.

As I learned more about Carol and Randall, everywhere I looked I found difficulties with their Four Points of Balance. They had:

1. Difficulty staying clear about their value and worth in the face of criticism from their partner.
2. Difficulty calming their anxieties and soothing their emotional bruises.
3. Difficulty staying grounded and not overreacting when their partner was anxious or on edge. Attempts to calm themselves down consisted of avoiding conversations, or clinging and arguing.
4. Difficulty confronting themselves about what they were doing or not doing. They wouldn't tolerate frustrations or put forth the sustained effort required to achieve their goals.

Your Four Points of Balance shape the course of your life. Difficulty with one Point usually goes hand in hand with difficulties in the others, although sometimes one ability is stronger than the rest. Either way, it's normal to have difficulty in the Four Points of Balance—which makes sexual desire problems normal, too. But resolving any imbalance by strengthening all four Points resolves the problems.

Randall and Carol's marriage was a constant uphill battle, especially when it came to sex. Actually, Carol wasn't as comfortable with sex as she thought she was. They both thought it was Randall's responsibility to get her relaxed and turned on. When she had difficulty getting aroused, Carol critiqued his technique. Randall got reactive and defensive. Carol reacted in kind. Randall's sexual interest evaporated on the spot.

Carol couldn't hold on to the idea that she was desirable without Randall's sexual interest. And when she couldn't, her impulse to have an affair increased. Carol's reflected sense of self soared when she received sexual vibes from men she met in the course of her day. This made her nervous she might have an affair, and when Carol got nervous she invariably overreacted: She'd threaten Randall and issue ultimatums, trying to shake him into action. Carol was actually really afraid they might get divorced. Sometimes when she threw out, "Why are we even married?" she wasn't just trying to hurt him. She was mapping his mind to see if he wanted to break up.

Randall and Carol's respective difficulties left them completely gridlocked. Randall didn't have much sexual desire for Carol. Carol needed him to want her. Each looked to the other for emotional calm and safety and security. Neither could offer these to the other. Both overreacted and took personally what their partner said in anger. Each wanted a commitment from the other, when in fact, they both often gave up and didn't really try.

Like many gridlocked couples, Randall and Carol didn't have sex together for months at a time. Struggles to maintain their sense of self took precedence over horniness. They took care of any horniness by themselves. They weren't choosing autonomy over attachment, or taking better care of themselves. They were emotionally fused and withholding from each other, and when they masturbated they didn't really enjoy it.

## EMOTIONAL GRIDLOCK

In our session, Carol said, "I don't know what to do anymore. We argue all the time. Sometimes I don't even finish my sentence before Randall is angry. I feel like I can't talk to him about anything!"

Randall responded without missing a beat. "That's right. We're at each other's throats all the time. She never says she's sorry, and I'm tired of saying it. We don't see eye to eye on things. But Carol always has to be right!"

Carol was furious. "No I don't! You hurt my feelings all the time, and you don't care about my sexual needs at all! You used to say you're sorry, but not anymore. We never resolve anything. We have irreconcilable differences. If I don't initiate sex, we never have it. I can see we're not going to resolve this. We might as well get divorced!" Randall shook his head in dismay and disgust.

I said, "You don't have irreconcilable differences. You and Randall are *emotionally gridlocked*!"

Carol and Randall stopped their bickering. Randall couldn't figure out if I was aligned with Carol against him. He wasn't sure what I meant by emotional gridlock, but the picture of two cars blocking each other at an intersection seemed even-handed. "How are we gridlocked?" he asked. "What's emotional gridlock?"

"Emotional gridlock is when what you want to do blocks what your partner wants to do, and vice versa. Marriage has lots of forced-choice decisions, when you can't agree to disagree—like having sex. You can't compromise, negotiate, or communicate your way through gridlock. That's why you think your differences are irreconcilable. Gridlock *can* be resolved, but it takes different strategies. You and Carol are gridlocked up to your eyeballs. This is one reason you don't have much desire for sex with her."

- *So you're gridlocked!*

Carol and Randall had all the classic signs of emotional gridlock:

- Constant, repetitive arguments.
- You can't agree to disagree about the issue.
- Increased communication provides no solution, and often makes things worse.
- You feel like you have no room for compromise or negotiation because your integrity is on the line.
- Apologies or "repair attempts" cease or are unsuccessful.
- You and your partner frequently have angry hurt feelings.
- You feel alienated and cut off from each other.

Conflict in love relationships is inevitable. You can't avoid it with premarital education, communication skills training, psychotherapy, or this book. (I'll explain this in a moment.) Mind-mapping limits the utility of communication skills and empathy training, because no matter how nicely you say something, your partner is tracking your thoughts, emotions, and motivations. Gridlock comes from *good* communication: successful mind-mapping. Your partner usually knows what you really want (or don't want).

Conflict is inevitable because of inherent dynamics in love relationships: You can agree to disagree about intangibles like emotions, perceptions, and values. You can debate political issues throughout your marriage without a problem. But this doesn't work when it comes to *behavior* that dramatically impacts your partner as well as yourself. Try agreeing to disagree about whether your partner has an affair. This is why the four most common areas of emotional gridlock are sex, money, kids, and in-laws. You can't agree to disagree about these things and go along your merry way.

### • *The midpoint of marriage*

Gridlock is not an inherent weakness in love relationships. Gridlock is testimony to their elegant design. Emotional gridlock is a normal and natural development in the evolution of a relationship and the people within it. Going through emotional gridlock creates anxiety, anger, frustration, feelings of rejection, and emotional pressure. This is difficult but it isn't a flaw: it enhances human resilience. Gridlock is Nature's survival boot-camp for adult-wanabees.

When misunderstood and mishandled, gridlock leads to divorce. Given that gridlock *is* usually misunderstood and mishandled, it is arguably the greatest single cause of divorce around the world. It is commonly misunderstood as irreconcilable differences, or communication problems, or falling out of love. But gridlock isn't caused by a lack of communication, so more communication won't resolve it. When people are unable to resolve gridlock with a communication-based approach, they wrongly convince themselves their problems are irreconcilable. If they depend on a reflected sense of self, they feel unloved and become unloving.

### • *Co-constructing emotional gridlock*

There are better ways to resolve gridlock than by talking about your feelings and emotions. There's a science of love relationships that revolves around emotional gridlock and the Four Points of Balance. Although I didn't use the term "gridlock" in Part One, we talked about how the low desire partner always controls sex, and often controls the high desire partner's feelings of adequacy. This is a quintessential gridlock of love relationships.

Many other things cause emotional gridlock, and they're as shockingly simple and powerful as the fact that the LDP always controls sex. That's why gridlock is unavoidable. For instance, another primary cause of gridlock is the *process of elimination*. This means each time an event occurs it removes subsequent options, and the pool of remaining possibilities grows smaller.

Emotional gridlock comes from you and your partner doing what everyone does to build a good relationship: You regulate each other's anxieties by accommodating and bolstering each other's reflected sense of self. You give in to your partner on one issue, and then your partner gives in to you on another. This keeps everyone's anxiety down and makes you feel loved and wanted.

However, each adaptation brings you one step closer to the critical point where you can't or won't adapt any longer. In theory you can compromise and negotiate forever, but in practice you won't. That's not human nature. Moreover, love relationships offer a finite set of options. And if your Four Points of Balance are weak, this further limits your adaptability and increases your need for accommodation.

Emotional gridlock happens in six neat steps:

1. During the lust, infatuation, and attachment phases occurring in your brain, you and your partner are validating, reassuring, and accommodating each other in whatever ways you can.

2. Difficult, contentious interactions arise between you. You both are frustrated about not getting the validation, accommodation, and soothing you want. You're also frustrated about being unable to satisfy your partner's complaints.

3. Your limited ability to hold on to your self (limited Four Points of Balance), plus your unresolved personal issues, create an upper limit to how much you can accommodate, validate, and regulate your partner before your *own* functioning deteriorates. The same holds true for your partner. Even the most patient and giving people can only go so far.

4. Your unwillingness to violate what remains of your integrity shows up. Your drive to preserve your tenuous sense of self becomes tenacious. You can't accommodate your partner without violating your integrity, and you refuse to adapt.

5. Eventually you *don't* want to adapt to your partner. Your battered reflected sense of self ushers in willful refusal, stubbornness, and defiance.

6. Your partner accommodates you as much as she can or wants to, and eventually stops. You do the same. You both have no room to back up or go forward. At that point, you're gridlocked. You have no good solution in sight and no prospect of resolution. Things look pretty bleak.

The areas of gridlock in your relationship are those where you and your partner have the least flexibility. Gridlock occurs when and where your and your partner's limitations collide, leaving you no further room to accommodate each other. You cannot give your partner what she wants. *Through the process of elimination you have stretched yourself as far as you can go without (a) experiencing more anxiety or (b) violating your integrity.* You stop accommodating when your anxiety reaches unacceptable levels—especially if you have difficulty calming and soothing yourself.

Emotional gridlock sounds *simple* but usually involves unimaginably *complex* entanglements. Gridlock is *universal,* occurring all around the world. But gridlock is always *custom tailored* because you and your partner co-construct it. Your pattern of gridlock says a lot about who you and your partner really are.

Gridlock shows up differently in different relationships, depending with whom you're paired. If you married a neat-freak and you're cleaning style is "relaxed," you'll be gridlocked over household chores (and this will affect your sexual desire). If you're both either neat-freaks or slobs, you'll be gridlocked about something else (and you'll still have sexual desire problems). Even if initially you have sex three times a day, eventually you'll struggle over when to have sex and how often to have it. If you both like sex at the same time of day, but one of you doesn't feel appreciated, sexual desire issues will still come up.

## • *Gridlock: A profound shift in perspective*

Understanding emotional gridlock allows you to handle sexual desire problems in a completely new way, even if you've been gridlocked for decades. It's hard to appreciate the elegance at first—particularly when you're in the thick of it. It's hard to see past your fears and insecurities. You can't see that the things that threaten your relationship and your sense of self will actually strengthen both—if you can endure the pain of growth.

Resolving gridlock (especially around sexual desire problems) is how you and your partner co-evolve. This is part of the people-growing machinery of love relationships. Of this I have no doubt. Moreover, some experts believe your brain is made flexible by stressful and highly meaningful events, facilitating brain rewiring. Nature depends on something far more reliable than your unconscious to drive the evolution of the human race. Is gridlock Nature's way of creating neural plasticity and opportunities for brain repair?

Here's more good news: Partners play "leap-frog" with their personal development. Each partner's growth in the Four Points of Balance (Solid Flexible Self, Quiet Mind–Calm Heart, Grounded Responding, Meaningful Endurance) provokes the other's growth. One partner's increased functioning greatly impacts the other when you're gridlocked and emotionally fused. That's a good thing, because resolving gridlock requires (at least) one of you to increase your Four Points of Balance.

Unfortunately, this is not what you usually want to do. You usually want your partner to make you feel better. This response is so instinctive it's difficult to see how this could be problematic. We all want someone else to comfort us, ever since we were children.

In Part One I encouraged you to jettison the idea that "sex is a natural function." Now I'm encouraging something similar: Stop picturing interactions between infants and mothers as the appropriate model for adult love relationships. Forget the idea that unmet "attachment needs" are the primary source of your problems. This distortion intensifies emotional gridlock, makes sexual desire problems harder to deal with, and makes you more likely to get divorced.

## DIFFERENTIATION

The process I described for developing your Four Points of Balance is called *differentiation*. Although we didn't label it, we actually discussed two forms of differentiation in Part One: One form was *species* differentiation—an evolutionary process spread across generations of a life form. The other form was your *personal* differentiation—your need to develop and preserve a solid sense of self that will help you get closer to others. *Think of differentiation as your ability to keep your emotional balance while interacting in important relationships. In practice, this is using your Four Points of Balance. The stronger your Four Points of Balance, the more differentiated you are (and vice versa).*

Differentiation is about how life forms evolve and gain new abilities, sometimes giving rise to whole new species. When we discussed humans taking a different evolutionary path from chimpanzees and gorillas, we were talking about differentiation. When we explored how our changing brain evolved complex selfhood and mind-mapping, we were seeing the results of (brain cell) differentiation. When I described three different couples reacting differently to the low desire partner always controlling sex, I was highlighting their personal differentiation (their lack of it). You saw how they struggled with (a) reflected sense of self, (b) difficulty controlling their anxiety and soothing their emotional bruises, (c) overreacting to each other's anxieties and tension by withdrawing or attacking, and (d) avoiding what needed to be done to grow in the relationship. Having well developed Four Points of Balance is synonymous with a high level of differentiation. Your level of differentiation shows how far you've evolved as a human being.

### • *Differentiation: The big and small pictures*

Differentiation is a more powerful force than you can imagine: Differentiation *is* evolution. When I say differentiation is your ability to hold on to your self and maintain your emotional balance in a relationship, I'm talking about your evolution as a person. Multiply that by millions of people over millions of years and you have human evolution.

Differentiation affects all living things, in every moment, and has done so since life began on Earth. Species differentiation is about how life forms get along: How members of a species (e.g., plants, insects, and animals) interact with others of their kind and with other species.

Differentiation occurs when members of a species stay in contact with each other. Your great ancestors formed relationships and stayed together long enough for our species to evolve. It changed our physiology and psychology. The end result was a human self with the ability to map other minds and achieve the Four Points of Balance. We developed the brain we have today from your forebears interacting in increasingly sophisticated ways.

Developing and maintaining your Four Points of Balance in relationships with others raises your personal level of differentiation. Human differentiation takes a tiny step forward through your relationships with other people. Your interactions with others make you *more unique* rather than just like everyone else. (Isn't that amazing?!) Interacting and facing new challenges produces more evolved members of a species, and eventually, a more evolved species. This cycle of being heir to our past and creator of our future goes round and round without end.

Dating, mating, and marriage largely revolve around dramas of personal evolution (differentiation). Your Four Points of Balance greatly determine when, where, and with whom you copulate. Your genes are along for the ride. Your sexual desire is more determined by your self-development (differentiation) than your urge to spread your genes.

Millions of years of human differentiation drive today's love relationships. It surfaces through you and your partner co-constructing emotional gridlock, and co-evolving by resolving it. Emotional gridlock is Nature's attempt to trigger differentiation in you, your partner, and your relationship. Failure to differentiate (reduce emotional fusion, get rid of borrowed functioning, and undo gridlock) is a major cause of divorce.

Let's put this together with what you learned in Part One: Your brain function shifts from infatuation and romantic love to attachment, where your sexual desire drowns in pools of vasopressin or oxytocin. But many couples don't last long enough to have this problem. Very poorly differentiated people (who have very weak Four Points of Balance) don't make it past infatuation without breaking up. Your differentiation determines whether your brain gets the opportunity to shift over into attachment or not. If you get that far, your level of differentiation plays a key role in keeping sexual desire alive in a long-term marriage. Differentiation

operates concurrently with the lust, romantic love, and attachment processes in your brain.

### • *Differentiation: Your Four Points of Balance*

Differentiation takes different forms in different species. For humans,
differentiation boils down to your Four Points of Balance, the four abilities that support and develop your sense of self: Holding on to your self
while your partner pressures you to adapt; regulating your own anxiety;
staying non-reactive *and* engaged; and tolerating discomfort so you can
grow. These four abilities, or lack thereof, shape your destiny and your
sexual desire.

These four incredible human adaptations work together, creating a
larger and more wondrous process that happens inside you, and goes on
between you and other people. Understanding why and how this happens
can radically change your desire, your sex, your marriage, and your life.

### • *How to think about differentiation*

Differentiation is a tangible *interpersonal* process that goes on between
you and other people moment-to-moment. It is also a powerful *individual* process that shapes your thoughts, feelings, and behavior throughout
the course of your life. "Differentiation of self" is the technical phrase,
but "holding on to your self" describes what it feels like in practice.

In my own mind, I use "differentiation," "maintaining balance," "Four
Points of Balance," and "holding on to your self" interchangeably.[95] Differentiation is your ability to maintain your emotional balance. You can
substitute the word "balance" for "differentiation" at any point, and you'll
be right on track.

When I refer to your "level of differentiation," I'm referring to the strength
of your Four Points of Balance. Sometimes when I use the word "differentiation," I suggest you stop and apply the Four Points of Balance before you
read further. Each Point plays a role in holding on to your self: Keeping
clear about your goals and self-worth in the face of adversity, soothing your
heartache and licking your emotional wounds, not over-reacting when

your partner acts crazy, and tolerating hard times and doing difficult things to get where you want to go. After a while, you'll think of differentiation as a "whole" (a process) and as "parts" (Four Points of Balance), and as something inside you and between you and your partner.

This gives you a "one-two-three-four" strategy for handling difficult situations in your relationship: First, identify your situation as a differentiation process. (I'll show you how to do this shortly.) Second, recognize you are losing your emotional balance. Third, break down your problem in terms of your Four Points of Balance. This shows you where you're having difficulty and what you need to do. Fourth, use your mantra to keep yourself focused when things get tough: "Hold on to your self!"

## FOUR POINTS OF BALANCE: BALANCING ATTACHMENT & AUTONOMY

As I talked with Randall and Carol about emotional gridlock, Randall was alert and attentive. No longer defensive, he was encouraged by the idea that he and Carol were going through a process he never imagined. What he didn't know—and what he still worried about—were the implications.

"So what does this all boil down to, Doctor? Are you giving us a fancy label and a scientific explanation for why we're screwed? Is gridlock hopeless?"

"No, you're not screwed. That's your problem, not your prognosis."

It took a moment. Then they started laughing.

"Gridlock is resolvable—if you do the hard work of getting a better grip on yourself. It's not impossible, but it isn't easy. Gridlock isn't hopeless. *You feel* hopeless, because you've gotten nowhere solving a problem you didn't know you had. Fortunately, your feelings are not the final authority about what's going on."

"I am pretty hopeless about fixing this, Doctor. We are constantly at each other's throats. Sometimes I wish I was single. Other times I can't stand to be away from Carol, and the thought of divorce breaks me up. I'm like that old phrase, 'Can't live with 'em, and can't live without 'em.'"

Carol felt as if she had just been put down. "I feel the same way about Randall, too!" Fortunately, Randall didn't react.

"There's a reason for that old phrase, and you both are living proof of it."

Randall ventured, "You mean we're competitive and ambivalent about each other?" Randall was smarter than he came across. I saw he could be thoughtful, observant, and collaborative.

"Yes, you're ambivalent about each other and very competitive, but there's a lot more going on. You are playing out humankind's two most basic drives. You want a relationship, and you want to chart your own destiny and control your own life. At your stage of development, it feels like 'Can't live with 'em, and can't live without 'em.' If you stay together and work through gridlock productively, this will change."

Perhaps you've heard the idea that people get divorced for the same reason they got married. Poorly developed Four Points of Balance drive you into and then out of love relationships. Your Four Points of Balance are as critical to stabilizing and developing a relationship as they are to developing and maintaining your self. Without these four abilities, it's difficult to survive and thrive through the rigors of marriage.

It's hard to keep your emotional balance when you're juggling two fundamental human drives: We want closeness and connection *and* freedom and self-direction. Imbalance either way causes our self to feel impinged upon. (The lower your level of differentiation, the less it takes to perturb you.) When relationships feel confining and your partner seems demanding, your refusal to submit to tyranny kicks in and low sexual desire is the result. When your relationships feel distant (even when you're emotionally fused), sexual desire is often similarly diminished.

Strengthening your Four Points of Balance makes it easier to balance these two fundamental biological drives. I drew a diagram like this for Carol and Randall to help them get the picture:

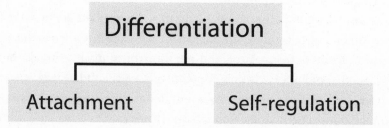

Notice I called one side *self-regulation* instead of autonomy. I wanted to make clear that autonomy doesn't mean you do whatever you want and to heck with anyone else. You have no autonomy and no self-direction if you can't control your fears and soothe your emotions, or give measured responses, or make yourself do what you need to do. When your Four Points of Balance are weak, you have no freedom, nor do those around you. In the last chapter we discussed that people who can't control themselves control the people around them.

Autonomy promotes stable attachments. When you'd like to unload your frustrations on your partner, and he or she deserves it—but you don't do it—that is real autonomy. That is also incredibly hard to do.

In lectures around the world, I ask, "Does anyone in the auditorium not understand about 'refusal to submit to tyranny' in marriage?" The response is always belly laughter and knowing nods.

In Part One, we saw how the LDP understands tyranny: He feels oppressed, pressured to want sex and have sex, badgered by his mate's higher desire. The HDP understands tyranny too: She feels pressured to have sex when and how it's available, because opportunities may be few and far between. She has to settle for "getting lucky" instead of being wanted, and act grateful for mediocre sex. But on top of this, add in the many people who lack Solid Flexible Self, Quiet Mind–Calm Heart, Grounded Responding, and Meaningful Endurance. This is why the *Devil's Dictionary* defined marriage as a state of slavery involving two masters and two slaves.[96]

• *Love relationships: Learning to stand on your own two feet*

What if humans only had one leg and crawled to get around?[97] It wouldn't be long before people figured out they could put their arms around each other and stand up. As animal adaptation goes, this would be a pretty neat achievement. But, being who we are, it wouldn't be long before one wanted to walk somewhere the other didn't, and the other would complain, *"Why are you trying to control me? Don't tell me what to do!"* Still, going it alone wouldn't be satisfying, because it would mean giving up a higher level of functioning. The resulting tension is the hu-man condition, especially for poorly differentiated people who have a weak sense of self.

Difficulty maintaining your own balance makes you feel oppressed by others. (Your narcissism turns them into oppressors in your mind.) That's another reason why love relationships turn into tyranny and op-pression. It's a low level of differentiation that makes it happen.

Looking for someone who has the leg we need, and needs the leg we have, doesn't work because the balance has to come from your self not from the relationship. Yes, holding on to your partner lets you stand taller (function at a higher level) than you can alone. But your partner's life is no longer her own if you won't give up standing tall, or learn to maintain your own balance. You'll demand she be there to support you, and this is borrowed functioning and emotional fusion.

Now imagine two people trying to become whole individuals. Each tries to balance his attachment and autonomy needs within himself. Pic-ture each one standing alone, wobbling as he learns to balance and coor-dinate his legs. This is probably what you and your partner look like at this point, trying to get your autonomy and attachment needs into better balance.

Then take the next step: Visualize what happens when these two peo-ple get together. Barely able to maintain their own balance, they put their arms around each other for support. They try to keep themselves and each other from falling down, wobbling all the while from their own lack of balance. Both partners greatly disturb and upset each other as they sway back and forth, unwilling to let go and find their own balance. As clumsy and inept as this may seem, I'm describing an elegant process: This is how we co-construct each other. This is how we co-evolve.

From what I've said, you might picture us forever at war with our attachment and autonomy drives. When you're not very differentiated, that's the way it feels: Attachment and autonomy seem mutually in-compatible and impossible to reconcile. Your need for others, and your drive to belong to yourself, seem like opposites tearing you apart. But attachment and autonomy are two sides of the same coin (differentia-tion). Each needs the other in order to exist. Attachment and autonomy are actually two forms of one incredible biological drive to evolve a personal self.

As you strengthen your Four Points of Balance, your need for others and your need for solitude feel less at odds with each other. (*Both* needs actually increase.) It's easier to tolerate the inevitable tensions, deprivations, and conflicts of marriage when you stop seeing them as conflicts with your partner. They arise from two different sides of your self. The tensions within you, and between the two of you, drive you to develop your Solid Flexible Self, to have a Quiet Mind–Calm Heart, to achieve Grounded Responding, and to put forth Meaningful Endurance.

### • *Back to Carol and Randall*

Like most poorly differentiated people, Carol and Randall were emotionally brittle. Things often broke down between them. When they did, their reflected sense of self cratered, and their anxieties went sky-high. Because they were emotionally fused, they overreacted to what the other one did or said.

Differentiation is the opposite of emotional fusion. Emotional fusion is togetherness (attachment) *without* separateness (autonomy). Differentiation is togetherness *with* separateness. The lower your Four Points of Balance, the greater the emotional fusion and borrowed functioning with your partner.

Your personal differentiation goes hand in hand with emotional gridlock. The speed and intensity of your gridlock is related to your Four Points of Balance. A lower level of differentiation means:

1. Gridlock shows up quicker.
2. Gridlock is more intense and pervasive.
3. Gridlock is more complex and harder to resolve.
4. Gridlock is harder to tolerate.

Seeing this tight connection may help you accept that emotional gridlock is not a sign of something going wrong. Gridlock is the ripened fruit of emotional fusion. Gridlock is a natural development, a hallmark of (limited) differentiation in human relationships.

Randall said, "I've had serious concerns that our relationship is messed up. Carol and I argue all the time. You're saying we're going through something that makes everyone argue. But we get so out of control sometimes, and our shouting matches go on and on. We've never hit each other, but it gets pretty bad." Randall wasn't complaining about Carol. Now that their arguments were out in the open, he wanted my professional opinion.

"Here's what I can tell you: Intense pervasive conflict does not automatically mean your relationship is unhealthy. It's all in how you handle it. But here's a rule of thumb: Your gridlock is inversely proportional to the strength of your Four Points of Balance. When you can't tolerate internal conflict, you direct it outwardly and interpersonally, so poorly differentiated couples have very intense gridlock. It gets less intense and pervasive as you grow."

Carol joked, "Are you saying we're healthy because we can fight openly?"

"No. Understanding that conflict is normal, inevitable, and healthy does *not* mean anything goes. Fighting openly is not the issue. Domestic violence is a serious widespread problem. You have to *use* conflict productively, not indulge in it. You lock horns because you don't have much internal emotional buffer. You get stuck on just a few topics because of the process of elimination. You and Randall don't really talk—or fight—about the bigger issues between you. That's why you keep pushing Randall to talk about going to boarding school."

## THE CURE FOR EMOTIONAL GRIDLOCK

As it turned out, Randall never talked about his childhood throughout their treatment. He was relieved we had something else to talk about, and he really learned about gridlock and the Four Points of Balance. This allowed him to be in therapy without capitulating to Carol's efforts to make him talk about his past. We dealt with things that were more directly controlling their sexual desire problems. This allowed them to turn things around.

As he built a more Solid Flexible Self, Randall liked not having to see things Carol's way. He also found it fascinating to think about himself, Carol, and their desire problem in entirely new ways. Between sessions, he thought about our discussions and applied them to his life. Had he simply refused to talk about his childhood and done nothing else, it would just have been defiance, not better balance. But getting a better grip on his self was something else again.

## • *The turning point*

Emotional gridlock is inevitable but resolvable. You resolve it by increasing your Four Points of Balance: Developing a more solid flexible self, getting better at quieting your mind and calming your heart, staying grounded and making more modulated responses, and enduring hard times because you're emotionally invested will all open up new solutions you weren't capable of seeing before.

Carol and Randall understood their Four Points of Balance were poorly developed. The result had been constant arguments, blaming each other, guardedness, taking things personally, being highly reactive, easily hurt, and slow to heal. Finding method in the madness calmed Carol and Randall down. It gave them hope, direction, and purpose. This allowed them to turn situations that usually went bad into incredibly good things. Let me tell you about their landmark interaction.

After several sessions, Carol had worked up the nerve to talk with Randall about their sexual desire problems. Randall was reading his paper, oblivious to the battle in Carol's mind. She started getting angry with him for seeming to lack any awareness of what was going on. But this time Carol thought, *This is nuts! I'm starting to get angry with Randall because I don't have the guts to speak up. I need to soothe myself and open my mouth—but not shoot it off.* She took a deep breath.

Carol spoke forthrightly and non-defensively. She didn't use the sheepish and hesitant delivery that irritated Randall. This time, Carol broached the topic of sex clearly and directly. She didn't have to say much. Carol said evenly, "I want you to talk with me about our sexual problem. I'm not going to avoid this anymore."

Randall looked up and didn't say anything for a moment. It seemed like eternity to Carol, but she held on to her self and didn't overreact. Immediately, she saw something different in Randall's eyes. He wasn't glaring at her or freezing her out. He was mapping her mind, taking in how and why she was doing this. He saw she wasn't driven by her anxieties the way she usually was.

Randall thought to himself, *We're gridlocked!* instead of his usual thought, *She's pushing me!* Randall was less defensive because he saw new meaning that increased his endurance. He understood his desire was as much or more about what happened during sex, and things like emotional gridlock and differentiation, than it was about his childhood. He stopped focusing on shielding information from Carol and tried to get through the gridlock. Once relieved of defending his past, he was a fast learner. He started focusing on what really happened between Carol and himself, analyzing their interactions through the lens of the Four Points of Balance. And all this happened in real time.

Randall realized his heart was racing. He took a deep breath to calm himself. He knew this was a big moment. He didn't want to overreact and set Carol off. He talked to himself about meaningful endurance for growth, and then he spoke before he had the opportunity to change his mind.

"I really don't know how to say this, but here goes … I am between a rock and a hard place. You want me to want you, but I feel like you're always interfering or telling me what to do. I know you often mean well, but you drive me nuts … If I express dissatisfaction with anything you do, like pushing me to talk about my childhood, you either blow up or get hurt—usually both."

Randall paused to see if Carol exploded. When she didn't, he continued:

"I, myself, am no gem … I'm so poorly balanced I can't stand it. I don't feel very good about myself. When you're not screaming, I usually am—no, correct that: When you're screaming, I'm usually screaming too … But I can take all the Viagra I want and all I get is a good erection. It doesn't make me eager to get together with you."

Carol mapped Randall's mind: He was more focused on what he wanted to say and less focused on her reaction. He wasn't taking a shot at her in the name of speaking his truth. He was confronting himself and telling the truth. Carol saw Randall putting the Four Points of Balance into action.

Carol and Randall looked at each other. Their moment of meeting lasted for almost a minute. Randall mapped Carol's mind and saw this was not countdown to an explosion. Carol's face was relaxed, her eyes were alert, but not filled with hurt.

"Well, you're right," Carol said slowly. "Normally, I'd be bouncing off the ceiling about now ... But I'm calming myself down and trying not to overreact ... This is a special moment for us, and I don't want to blow it."

For a minute, neither knew what to say or do. Randall walked over and gave Carol a kiss that probably lasted half a minute. "My word," Carol said, "that sure beats blowing up." Randall smiled back at her. Then they ambled off to make lunch.

That afternoon Carol and Randall made love without an argument appetizer. It wasn't just that they actually did something new. Carol stopped taking Randall's hesitancies so personally. Watching him confront himself and master his insecurities made her realize Randall needed room to have his own difficulties.

### • *Reality looks different*

Randall and Carol came to their next session filled with their success. "I told myself to calm down," Randall said, "and I made myself repeat the Four Points of Balance. I do it like a mantra. I tell myself: *Hold on to your self and stay clear about what's important. Quiet your mind. Don't overreact. Stay grounded. Meaningful endurance will get you what you want.* This helps at work, too. The other day I almost blew up at a coworker, who's a real sweet guy. I talked to myself. I didn't react to something careless he had done. I didn't take it so personally."

Carol said, "It works for me too. It makes it easier when you're gridlocked. At least I know what's going on, and I'm not so terrified that everything's going wrong. And the Four Points of Balance tell me what

I need to do—even if I can't always do it." Randall laughed and nodded in agreement.

I added, "The important thing is doing them, not just saying them."

Carol nodded. "I can see the difference in Randall. I see him trying to calm himself down. I've never seen that before. I like it. Just seeing his effort makes a difference, even if we're not great at it. At least I know where his head is at."

I said, "Lots of people ask me, 'How do I learn to self-soothe? How do I become more differentiated? Is there a book I can read or some skills I can practice?' My response is, 'Just get married. You'll get all the practice you need.'"

Randall and Carol smiled and nodded their heads in agreement.


• *How things turned out*

Randall and Carol resolved their sexual desire problems. No longer feeling that he had something to hide, Randall let me see more of what really happened between him and Carol. They had common problems with intimacy (like the ones we'll discuss next chapter). Resolving them made Randall more interested in sex. Intimacy was another area where Carol picked at his shortcomings. That's where Carol made the most progress. By working with intimacy, Carol learned to calm herself down. She no longer gave off what Randall called "an electric hum of anxiety."

Carol and Randall developed a resilient collaborative alliance (discussed in Part Four) and used it to explore their sexual potential for eroticism. During the next several months sex became more frequent, daring, and intimate. On average they had sex once or twice a week, which was fine for both of them. Carol and Randall developed mutual respect out of the sexual desire problems that earlier had them screaming for divorce.

Several months later, Carol contacted me to let me know things were going well. She told me Randall had talked to her about being sent off to school. She had finally gotten what she wanted so badly, and she realized why she wanted it: Her reflected sense of self took it as proof she was a "safe person" for someone to go to. To Carol this meant, *I'm not like my mother.*

Randall's and Carol's Four Points of Balance gave them more room to accommodate each other, and room to move forward, which allowed them to resolve their gridlock. In the end Carol finally got what she wanted, but not the way she'd anticipated: When Carol backed off from Randall and learned to regulate herself, she stopped tampering with Randall's sense of self. He, in turn, was more eager to have sex and be open with her. But everything didn't hinge on Carol making the first move; Randall's sexual interest grew as he developed greater emotional independence.

## • *Differentiation throughout our lives*

Carol and Randall discovered that as you strengthen your Four Points of Balance, the best in you, rather than your reflected sense of self, drives your quest for growth. You start seeking happiness and fuller meanings in life. It's not always fun: You will experience difficult soul-searching and have to go through self-confrontation. But it's the pathway to enlightenment, wisdom, and compassion.

A robust sexual relationship requires holding on to your self. It comes from the Four Points of Balance. So if you want to lend your partner a helping hand in bed, hold on to your self first.

Sexual desire problems aren't particularly unique. All life crises demand of us similar growth, be they medical illness, injury, personal trauma, money problems, or difficulty with kids and in-laws. When the best in you stands up and faces the realities of your life, it produces intimacy, passion, and commitment. When the worst in you reigns, what might have been a manageable problem becomes a long-term disaster.

It's dismaying to watch desire and passion die. But a bad time gets a little better if you know nothing is necessarily wrong with you or your relationship. Remember, low desire and sexual boredom are often signs you're right on track.

The ebb and flow of desire in love relationships is natural, healthy, and purposeful. The same forces that have driven millions of years of evolution control your desire. These forces are now driving you to grow as a person and as a partner in your relationship. Handled properly, your desire, your overall relationship, and how you and your partner feel about yourself and each other, can markedly improve. Your Four

Points of Balance shape your *capacity* for desire, the *depth* of your desire, and the *resilience* of your desire. I'll tell you more about this in the
next chapter.

---

―――――――――― **IDEAS TO PONDER** ――――――――――

- Your Four Points of Balance are (1) Solid Flexible Self, (2)
  Quiet Mind–Calm Heart, (3) Grounded Responding, and
  (4) Meaningful Endurance.
- Understanding emotional gridlock allows you and your
  partner to co-evolve and leap-frog together toward personal growth. Resolving sexual desire problems stretches
  your Four Points of Balance.
- A high level of differentiation—your Four Points of Balance—controls the depth of your desire, intimacy, sexuality, and love.

# 5

## Intimacy Shapes Your Sexual Desire

*I*f there's an area of marriage as misunderstood as sexual desire, it has to be intimacy. Emotional intimacy plays an amazing role in stabilizing love relationships. However, intimacy creates stability in long-term relationships in ways you never imagined. How this works will seem as striking as anything you've read thus far.

Intimacy is a complex system, just like sexual desire. It is another drive-wheel of marriage's people-growing machinery. Intimacy and sexual desire push you to develop a more solid flexible self. The strengthened Four Points of Balance you gain by properly handling intimacy problems creates long-term stability and lasting sexual desire in love relationships.

Couples who seek my help have no knowledge of this miracle. For instance, Sharon and Thomas had no notion that their frustration, angst, and heartache were elements that would help them build a stronger relationship with greater intimacy. All they saw was a growing gulf between them that could end their marriage.

Sharon and Thomas illustrate how you can be the high desire partner for one thing and the low desire partner for something else. Sharon was the HDP for intimacy and the LDP for sex. Thomas was the LDP for intimacy and the HDP for sex.

Sharon complained Thomas never talked to her about their relationship. He never shared his feelings or asked her about hers. She felt he never listened to her and wasn't supportive about troubles at her job. She didn't feel seen or heard by Thomas. Sharon said she often felt invisible.

Thomas said he was okay with talking, but Sharon was always trying to get into his head. She always wanted to know what he was thinking and feeling. Besides, Thomas felt Sharon had no business acting like some Intimacy Queen because she never wanted to have sex. He summed up the situation this way: "Here's what it boils down to, Doctor. Sharon doesn't want to screw, and I don't want to talk."

"You don't want Sharon in your head, and she doesn't want you in her body?"

Thomas smiled. "That's right."

I turned to Sharon. "Are you familiar with Thomas's wife? Do you happen to know if and why she doesn't want sex?"

Sharon was equally emphatic. "I don't feel seen. I don't feel heard. I feel like I don't exist for him. Why would I want to have sex with him?!"

"You mean you don't feel like you exist *within* him?"

"Yes, that's what I mean." Sharon stopped and thought about the difference. She immediately mapped out that I knew what she was saying, and calmed down. "I'm *not* in his mind. He never thinks about me—even when he's with me. His mind is always somewhere else. Sometimes I think he does that on purpose. I feel like he doesn't accept me. I'm unimportant to him. It's like I don't exist."

Thomas snarled, "You're hung up about sex."

Sharon flared, "You have problems with intimacy."

## • *Intimacy: Marriage's second-biggest pitfall*

After a moment I asked Sharon, "Do you think Thomas shows good judgment or bad judgment in not listening to you?"

"*Bad* judgment." Her response was instantaneous and emphatic.

"Then why would you take your husband's bad judgment personally?"

"I … don't know … I just feel like I don't exist for him."

"Are you going to cease to exist every time Thomas has bad judgment? He has a bad day, and poof, you disappear?"

Sharon frowned. "… I never looked at it that way … I don't know … I want him to understand me. I need to know I'm important to him."

Thomas spoke up. "I get defensive when I hear Sharon talk about me never thinking about her, "I'm *always* thinking about her: Is what I'm doing going to make Sharon mad? Or will she be mad at what I'm not doing? Am I going to come up short again?" He was embarrassed revealing that he often worried about how Sharon felt about him.

"How come you never share this with me? I didn't know you felt that way."

"I feel like I'm not allowed to have a private thought. Everything I'm feeling and thinking I'm supposed to report to you."

## • *Intimacy and desire in poorly differentiated couples*

As in many couples, Sharon pressured Thomas for intimacy because she needed a positive reflected sense of self, and talking with Thomas about her feelings gave it to her. It calmed her anxieties and insecurities. Sharon said she wanted intimacy, but she really wanted validation, empathy, and acceptance. She regulated her anxiety through Thomas.

In this way, actually, Sharon was much like Thomas. Thomas got his positive reflected sense of self from Sharon through sex. He pressured Sharon for sex the same way she pressured him to share his feelings. Thomas said he wanted to be physically intimate and make love to his wife, but what he really wanted was tension release and reassurance he was desirable and a good lover.

Sharon talked a lot about the importance of "being emotionally open." But what she really wanted was to feel good about herself by mapping Thomas's mind. Her insecurities took over when he wouldn't share his thoughts. Sometimes she worried about what he was hiding from her. She was infuriated that he wanted to keep her out. She didn't like seeing herself as someone who needed to be fended off. That's what she saw when she looked at herself through his eyes.

When Sharon and Thomas talked about their feelings, she was more willing to have sex. Her reflected sense of self felt understood, accepted, and validated. Sharon called this "feeling taken in" (in the positive sense). When she felt this, she had more sexual desire. Sharon wasn't unique this way. This is one way intimacy can impact your sexual desire.

It wasn't surprising Sharon was more sexually receptive if they were intimate before they started. Nor that Thomas fought Sharon from probing his mind. They were a typical couple, gridlocked over intimacy and sex. To resolve their situation they needed a new picture of intimacy and how it operates.

## OTHER-VALIDATED INTIMACY AND SELF-VALIDATED INTIMACY

When I started studying emotional gridlock in the 1980s, I had to coin two other terms: *other-validated intimacy* and *self-validated intimacy.* I needed these terms, together with *emotional gridlock*, to describe what I saw clients going through. Other-validated intimacy and self-validated intimacy are not (just) theoretical constructs. They are two kinds of intimacy, two parts of one amazing process.

Like most people, you probably focus on *other*-validated intimacy. My exhaustive review of professional literature on intimacy revealed that therapists invariably focus on other-validated intimacy, too.[98] Other-validated intimacy is our first experience of intimacy as children. Other-validated intimacy involves one partner disclosing feelings, perceptions, doubts, fears, and inner truths, and the other partner (a) accepting, validating, and empathizing, and/or (b) disclosing in kind. Other-validated intimacy hinges on reciprocity. The listener is supposed to reciprocate by self-disclosing or just validating, both of which shore up the speaker's reflected sense of self. When you think of intimacy, this is what you probably envision.

When people say they want deep and profound intimacy, they usually envision a bottomless pool of unconditional positive regard, trust, security and acceptance—in other words, other-validated intimacy. When Sharon complained of lack of intimacy with Thomas, other-validated intimacy was what she wanted. She wanted to talk about her feelings, and Thomas was supposed to reciprocate by validating her and making disclosures of his own.

Sharon openly stated that she wanted "emotional support." But what she really wanted was an emotional fusion of selfhood using borrowed functioning. Other-validated intimacy appeals to your reflected sense of self. But as you'll see, self-validated intimacy hinges on having a solid flexible self.

The distinction between other-validated intimacy and self-validated intimacy aligns with how your brain is organized. Different cells are involved in making basic distinctions between "self" and "other" in the most archaic parts of your brain.[99] Research indicates mapping out other people's mind involves different locations in different brain lobes (with some overlap) than mapping your own. These differences in sensory processing and complex cognition further suggest that mapping someone by developing a model of her mind involves different cognitive processes than imagining yourself in her place ("simulation").[100]

The "self-oriented" and "other-oriented" parts of your brain involved in mind-mapping others and yourself also play a critical role in intimacy. You take in how much your partner is truly confronting and disclosing himself, as well as the level of your own self-confrontation and self-disclosure. Both dramatically impact how intense intimacy feels. Other-validated intimacy can't exist without mapping your partner's mind and assessing his actual empathy, validation, and acceptance of you. Likewise, self-validated intimacy couldn't exist if you couldn't map your own mental states.

## • *A broader view of intimacy*

Here's a hard thing to get straight in your mind: *Being intimate with your partner doesn't mean you get the response you want.* Granted, we all want to be accepted, and we don't want to feel rejected. We all want to feel safe and secure. But relationships that rely on other-validated intimacy go downhill when either partner has a bad day. Marriage is an interdependent relationship; its resilience lies in both partners' abilities to function independently. If marriage over the millennia relied on other-validated intimacy, fortitude would not be a dominant human characteristic.

Intimacy is an interpersonal process, involving confronting yourself and disclosing yourself in your partner's presence. *Intimacy involves mapping your own mind in front of your partner, and letting your partner map your mind, too.* Sometimes your partner accepts and validates you, and sometimes she doesn't.

Unfortunately, intimacy is often not like mother's milk. Intimacy can be hard to digest and leave you choking and gasping. In moments when you are open, revealed, and exposed, your partner might offer you empathy, validation, acceptance, and support—or look bored, make a hostile remark, or say nothing at all.

When your partner doesn't accept or validate you, *but you can validate and calm yourself* you experience *self*-validated intimacy. Self-validated intimacy generally emerges later in life, often as a matter of necessity. It is the bedrock of love relationships.[101]

Self-validated intimacy hinges on your Four Points of Balance. It requires Grounded Responding and Meaningful Endurance when your partner doesn't accept what you say, openly criticizes you, or doesn't pay attention to you. Other-validated intimacy revolves around your reflected sense of self.

### • *Intimacy in marriage*

Dating couples and newlyweds thrive on other-validated intimacy. Most people seek intimacy for a sense of closeness, togetherness, *we-ness*. Sharon wanted to feel oneness with Thomas, with no boundaries between them.

Unfortunately, long-term relationships require *self*-validated intimacy. Marriage operates in ways that stretch you. That's why intimacy often doesn't feel good. Intimacy is not designed to make you feel one particular way; it's designed to make you grow. This happens in a variety of ways.

First off, other-validated intimacy—the intimacy that supports your reflected sense of self—is definitely time-limited in marriage. This is caused by the process of elimination. Eventually you have to talk about things you know your partner won't like. He or she won't validate you when you bring up topics that make him or her anxious or angry. At this inevitable point, other-validated intimacy stops, and emotional gridlock sets in.

Second, being honest about who you are without guaranteed validation creates a mini identity crisis. If you can digest this challenge to your self in front of your partner, you become a more solid person. Your Four Points of Balance get stretched by mapping out your own mind and letting your partner map your mind while you do it. That's intimacy.

Third, intimacy involves being *accurately* known by your partner. This, in itself, will make you feel insecure. If you've depended on a reflected sense of self, you're not sure you're okay as you are. It's hard to believe you'll be loved if you are truly known. It's hard to allow yourself to be accurately mapped, particularly if you delude yourself about who you really are. But until you finally let yourself be known, you'll never feel secure.

Fourth, difficult important things often need to be said. You can't do this if you depend on other-validated intimacy. But with self-validated intimacy you can. This kind of intimacy doesn't make you feel secure, safe, accepted, cuddly, warm, or close. You have to hold on to your self while you do it, because your partner may not want to hear what you have to say and vice versa. In fact, it is often the accumulation of unsaid things that prompt people to shift to self-validated intimacy.

Struggles over intimacy, and the ensuing emotional gridlock, helped your forebears develop the best brain on the planet. That's why you'll go through them, too. It's normal! Knowing this can help you not take things quite so personally.

Sharon didn't know this. She and Thomas came to their next therapy session having had yet another argument over sex and intimacy. That was three days ago, and Sharon was still on the warpath.

"I told Thomas, 'I have no desire to have sex with someone who shuts me out.'"

This time Thomas worked at not defending himself and managed to keep his mouth shut. When their typical bitter exchange didn't occur, the tension in the room diminished. Sharon didn't quite know what to do.

"See, you're not saying anything," she said. Thomas waited a moment.

"I'm not saying anything because I'm trying to make things better." His voice lacked its typical cutting and condescending tone. Only later did I learn what prompted Thomas's shift: He had found out his best friend was getting divorced.

I turned to Sharon. "You want to map his mind. That's why you want Thomas to share his thoughts and feelings."

"That right." Sharon calmed down.

"But you don't want him mapping *your* mind—particularly during sex. You want to limit the intimacy to talking. You want him only to see what you want to show him. This keeps you and Thomas from experiencing anything approximating peace and serenity when you are physically or emotionally intimate." Sharon nodded. She was taking in what I was saying.

"This is why you freeze up during sex when Thomas asks you what you like. You want to follow his lead—and then complain about it afterward. You don't want to do what *you* want. That would require self-validated intimacy. Even if Thomas likes what you want, you're still revealing yourself through your preferences."

Sharon looked at me seriously. "What if I don't know what I like?"

"Are you saying you have no idea what you like sexually?"

Sharon paused for a moment and smiled. "I have a vague idea."

"That's enough. That's all you need. If you pursue your vague idea with Thomas and approach it like a team, I'm sure you'll clarify what you like."

Sharon giggled, "What if I'm not comfortable with what I like?"

Obviously Sharon knew more about her sexuality than she could validate. I looked her in the eye and thought, *I know you know more than you're acknowledging. You're hiding the erotic part of you!* Sharon kept my gaze, read my mind, and blushed.

- *Mind-mapping in self-validated and
  other-validated intimacy*

Intimacy inherently involves mind-mapping. Mapping out that your partner is deeply involved in the moment with you, that you have his undivided attention, contributes to the feeling of "togetherness." Likewise, realizing there are parts of your partner's mind you *don't* know is also part of intimacy. That same moment in which you recognize something previously unseen in your partner's mind confronts you with the fact that there are parts of your partner you *still* don't know.

Intense intimate experiences are "moments of meeting." Moments of meeting are invariably electric, but not always soothing. In moments of meeting, people map out each other's minds. You *know* each other. Keep in mind what I told you earlier about scientists thinking your brain (re)wires itself in moments of meeting (intersubjective states) throughout your life. You'll start to recognize a utility to intimacy you never imagined.

Reciprocal mind-mapping fits most people's picture of intimacy. This is popularly referred to as "being open with each other." It speaks of our highest aspirations, but it also greatly inflates our reflected sense of self. What if your partner doesn't reciprocate in kind? Intimacy doesn't always involve permission to map someone's mind, or reciprocal disclosure, or even a kind word.

Thomas didn't want Sharon in his head. He wouldn't talk about his feelings or encourage her to disclose hers. However, Thomas couldn't stop Sharon from mapping that he didn't want her reading him. Sharon could tell he was shielding his thoughts, even if she didn't know exactly what he was thinking. Sometimes Thomas tried to mask that he was hiding. Other times he wanted Sharon to know he locked her out, because he knew it hurt her feelings.

This kind of moment arose as they ate breakfast one morning. Sharon tried to engage Thomas in conversation. Thomas made a big show of reading his newspaper. When she persevered, Thomas looked Sharon in the eye and screamed, "Stop trying to pick my brain. *Leave me alone!*"

This intimate moment—two selves knowing each other—felt terrible to Sharon. Thomas didn't want her to know him, and he wanted her to know that. Thomas knew she'd be hurt, and he watched her reflected sense of self crumble. In that moment, Sharon saw the side of Thomas she hated. She knew Thomas knew she would be hurt by this, and yet he did it anyway. Sharon took it personally that Thomas wanted her to hurt. It crushed her. This intersubjective experience diminished Sharon's ability to function.

## INTIMACY IS A SYSTEM, JUST LIKE SEXUAL DESIRE

In Part One, we said sexual desire is more than a feeling. It's a sophisticated system permeating love relationships. The same is true of intimacy.

Intimacy evolved along with humankind's emerging sense of self. Your forebears learned through trial and error that exchanges of factual and emotional information created an intersubjective state that made them feel better. Given that we start life with a reflected sense of self, it was virtually guaranteed humans would develop other-validated intimacy. Just as being LDPs and HDPs led to a people-growing process, so did other-validated intimacy and self-validated intimacy. You'll discover other important similarities and differences when you consider who controls intimacy.

- *The low desire partner for other-validated intimacy
  always controls it*

In Chapter 1 you learned the low desire partner always controls sex. Intimacy operates much the same way: *The LDP for intimacy always controls it—as long as partners don't develop their Four Points of Balance and remain dependent on other-validated intimacy.*

Let me explain how the low desire partner for other-validated intimacy always controls it. Once again, this arises from the process of elimination: As you and your partner become a couple, you disclose things you have in common, plus things your mind-mapping suggests your partner will accept. Eventually these disclosures are "used up." Redisclosing them doesn't create the feeling of intimacy. Intimacy requires disclosing new information as your relationship progresses.

In due course, you and your partner are faced with disclosing information and confronting issues where your partner's acceptance and validation is not guaranteed. You reach a fateful point when the low desire partner for other-validated intimacy doesn't want to go further. He doesn't want to hear the things his partner has to say. He stops disclosing and won't validate his partner's disclosures. This is how the low desire partner controls the level of intimacy.

Now we've arrived at the point where sexual desire and intimacy operate differently. With sex, the LDP always controls it. As partners develop their Four Points of Balance they handle this much better. But whether you are highly differentiated or still emotionally fused, the LDP always controls sex.

Intimacy operates differently because the dynamics of other-validated intimacy and self-validated intimacy differ. Your level of differentiation changes how your relationship operates. For *other*-validated intimacy, the LDP always controls the level of intimacy. But as partners develop their Four Points of Balance, they begin to explore *self*-validated intimacy and everything changes: The partner with the greater desire for *self*-validated intimacy, the HDP, controls its timing, frequency, and depth.

In other words, *other*-validated intimacy operates just like sex: The partner with the least desire always runs the show. But *self*-validated intimacy gives control to the partner who wants it the most. When you have a solid flexible self and can soothe yourself, you are able to validate your own disclosures and can say anything you need to. Your partner no longer controls you or the level of intimacy in your marriage.

Yes, the LDP for intimacy can always get up and walk away, just as the low sexual desire partner can always stop having sex. But in both cases, there's a limit to how far you play that card if you want to stay married—particularly happily married.

### • *Intimacy and adequacy*

In Chapter 3, we discussed how, besides controlling sex, the low sexual desire partner usually controls the HDP's adequacy too. This stems from the HDP's sense of self being based on having sex and being desired.

Well, when it comes to intimacy, the low desire partner controls their partner's adequacy, too—for similar reasons.

If you depend on other-validated intimacy, your self-esteem craters when your partner won't talk. It's just like when the high sexual desire partner crashes because his mate won't make whoopee. Sharon felt good when Thomas revealed his feelings and thoughts, and let her read his mind. She felt rejected when he stopped. Thomas stopped because he didn't want her to ferret out things that might offend her.

Of course, Sharon didn't see it this way. She believed Thomas had problems with intimacy. She just wanted to be close with him. In her mind, Thomas focused on sex to keep from being intimate.

This created serious gridlock. When your Four Points of Balance aren't well developed, there are real limits to how much intimacy you can handle. As much as Sharon complained about Thomas being incapable of intimacy, when he was intimate she didn't want to hear things that weren't flattering and reassuring. She also hung back when Thomas wanted to be sexually intimate.

In truth, Sharon was uncomfortable being known sexually. She attributed this to needing to feel more secure with Thomas. (Read: *Thomas was supposed to make her feel more secure.*) Sharon hid during sex because it was too revealing, too intimate. This was beyond the limits of her Four Points of Balance. Sharon fended off Thomas's attempts to map out her secret wishes and sexual fantasies. It was the same as Thomas fending off her prying into his feelings.

Sharon was able to control their sex because she controlled Thomas's feelings of adequacy, too. But eventually this caught up with her when Thomas finally took hold of himself. There came a time when instead of getting loud and counterattacking, Thomas just looked at his shoes. Then, with a sad and somber face, he quietly said, "You know, I just don't have the heart to fight about sex—or talking—anymore."

Sharon had never seen him act like this before. She watched a stranger slowly rise from Thomas's chair and go to bed. She read his mind: He was telling the truth, and he wanted her to know it. She could feel she was losing control of him. That frightened her. In both intimacy and sex, the LDP loses control of the relationship as the HDP develops a more solid flexible self.

# DEPENDENCE ON OTHER-VALIDATED INTIMACY CREATES EMOTIONAL GRIDLOCK

There isn't something inherently wrong with other-validated intimacy, or the fact that Sharon wanted it. Given her reflected sense of self, it made perfect sense. The rub is that after a while the well runs dry. Your partner fights to keep his own autonomy, and that shows up as refusing to validate and soothe you whenever you want. That's how marriage works.

You probably love the fantasy of losing yourself in a love relationship. It sounds so romantic at first. But if your Four Points of Balance aren't well developed, the stage is set for a battle between autonomy and attachment. Your own dependency and autonomy needs trigger the differentiation process. Your or your partner's need for separateness surfaces when dependence on other-validated intimacy runs its course.

- *Other-validated intimacy is inherently time-limited*

Your dependence on acceptance, validation, and empathy from your partner—and feeling entitled to it—cause emotional gridlock. In long-term love relationships, other-validated intimacy is inherently time-limited.

Reciprocity is a beautiful thing. But if your relationship hinges on it, you're in trouble. Many couples temporarily establish a high level of intimacy through reciprocal validation and disclosure, but invariably they can't maintain this level once borrowed functioning collapses. Relationships built on other-validated intimacy crater when one partner won't accept and validate the other or disclose in kind.

Sharon demanded reciprocal acceptance from Thomas before she revealed her sexual self. But she couldn't get acceptance *before* revealing herself. The feeling she wanted required Thomas's *knowledgeable* acceptance. Countless couples hit this inherent paradox, and the weaker your Four Points of Balance (Solid Flexible Self, Quiet Mind–Calm Heart, Grounded Responding, Meaningful Endurance) the sooner it happens. The real question is, do you keep insisting on the impossible or do you grow up? By "grow up" I mean relinquishing unrealistic expectations and having the guts to show your erotic persona. That's easier said than done, but by exercising your Four Points of Balance you can do it. It's hard to keep your mind from spinning off when putting your ass on the line (literally). But taking those risks provoked your ancestors to evolve a more sophisticated brain. If you handle it right, it can do the same for you.

At first, Sharon felt entitled to what she expected and expected no less. "What's so wrong with wanting acceptance? Doctor, I don't know what kind of screwed up marriage *you* have, but I want Thomas to accept me! Who wants to live with someone who rejects you?"

I waited a second, softened my voice, and spoke slowly. "You're more interested in being accepted and validated than being truly known. You demand acceptance before you reveal yourself. You think the problem is with Thomas. But the problem is, you're creating a logical conundrum and driving both of you nuts.

"No matter how much Thomas accepts and validates you, you're never going to feel secure and accepted until you lay the whole picture out, warts and all. No spin on the delivery, and nothing held back. I don't know if he's going to applaud or run screaming out the door. But you're both keeping your self from being seen and known. Guaranteed upfront unconditional acceptance from Thomas isn't possible. If you want profound intimacy, it's right in front of you. All you have to do is step up and show yourself."

In the time it took to say this, Sharon pulled herself together. She was settled enough to see she couldn't beat the system. She mapped out my commitment to really work with her. Sharon nodded and said, "I hear what you're saying." Her eyes said, *I see what you are doing. Thank you.*

- *Other ways couples reach gridlock over intimacy*

It's just a matter of time before you are gridlocked over intimacy. Nature has developed redundant mechanisms to insure this. If your Four Points of Balance are weak, it happens quickly. Here are other ways this gridlock occurs:

1. You and your partner lay the groundwork for later intimacy problems *by* first creating other-validated intimacy. Success increases your
   emotional dependence on each other, and reinforces expectations.
2. When your disclosure makes your partner nervous or angry (even
   when you're right), acceptance and validation will not be offered.
   Your partner won't be encouraging and accepting when you broach
   a topic she wants to dodge. She can't accommodate you without
   confronting her own limitations.
3. Because of the process of elimination you've reached a sensitive issue. Gridlock in intimacy arises when you demand validation from
   your partner in areas where you are emotionally blind, and have a
   distorted or incomplete picture of who you really are.

Partners who initially accept and validate everything eventually stop
when they feel like they've compromised themselves, sold themselves
out, and violated their integrity. The way we blunder through love relationships seeking other-validated intimacy unerringly creates emotional
gridlock.


## GRIDLOCK OVER INTIMACY CREATES LOW DESIRE

Problems with intimacy cause sexual desire problems, and sexual desire
problems cause problems with intimacy. Once intimacy problems arise,
regardless of their cause, poorly differentiated people handle them in
ways that kill desire. If you depend on your partner for empathy, understanding, acceptance, and validation, you can count on desire problems
in your marriage.

In some couples, the LDP for intimacy is also the LDP for sex. (Next
chapter's couple is like this.) When this happens, the low desire partners wield tremendous control. They have a stranglehold on physical
*and* emotional intimacy and can play havoc on the high desire partner's
reflected sense of self.

However, things line up differently for couples like Sharon and
Thomas, where they both have the LDP role. Sharon controlled Thomas's

adequacy when it came to sex. Thomas controlled Sharon's self-worth when it came to intimacy. Both felt rejected, controlled, and emotionally insignificant. Each angrily and resentfully withheld what the other wanted. But even when they stopped withholding from each other, they were still gridlocked over intimacy and desire.

Thomas wouldn't talk with Sharon in ways that reflected that she had special status in his life. He couldn't give Sharon that acknowledgement because he felt as though she already had too much control. Subjectively, he felt he was being asked to pay for sex with conversation and opening up.

Sharon was jealous of Thomas's best friend, Phil. She wanted to be Thomas's closest confidant. She believed Thomas talked to Phil about her, and she worried what Phil thought of her. Thomas knew she overestimated his openness with Phil, but he liked her distortion and the fact that it upset her. She was withholding sex from him, and he was retaliating by not opening up with her. People who depend on a reflected sense feel the need to get even.

### • *We don't desire partners we constantly have to validate*

There was another deep and profound reason for Sharon and Thomas's desire problems: People don't desire partners they constantly have to validate—at least not as long-term partners. Reciprocal validation is a big part of dating but not long-term marriage: You lose desire and respect for each other if the other's need for acceptance and validation dominates the relationship.

Your response to the pressure is to comply or defy. Either move intensifies gridlock. The pressure to validate and accept your partner triggers your refusal to submit to tyranny. The demand to "be there for each other" feels suffocating. Sexual desire fades as your urge to escape grows.

The rule that we don't desire partners we continually have to validate fit Sharon and Thomas. Thomas's neediness turned Sharon off. It's harder to see how Thomas fit the rule. He was pressing for sex but had no desire for Sharon. Obviously, he didn't want to talk with her. He didn't find her emotionally attractive or desirable, and in truth, many times she wasn't. Thomas was the high sexual desire partner in their marriage because he wasn't willing to give up having sex altogether. It wasn't because Thomas really wanted her. This deepened their gridlock because Sharon was an excellent mind-mapper.

Sharon didn't want sex because she felt taken for granted. She was tired of propping up Thomas's feelings of adequacy. She felt controlled—and, in truth, she often was controlled—by her dependence on Thomas. She felt restricted, constrained, and obligated to go along.

Early in their relationship Thomas's desire for sex *increased* Sharon's desire because she felt valued and necessary. Sometimes they had sex three or four times a week. After the first year, Sharon's ardor cooled. Thomas started trying to make her feel guilty and responsible for his satisfaction. Sharon started "giving in." After fifteen years of giving in to his neediness, Sharon no longer respected Thomas.

Thomas's reactions were similar. Initially, he liked Sharon because she was so self-disclosing. She drew him out, and he shared more about himself than he had with anyone. He liked Sharon thinking he was interesting. She was a good listener. She caused him to think more about himself and his life. He liked that Sharon was getting more adventurous in bed. Thomas thought she'd show more eroticism if he could just make her feel more secure. He sensed that could be very interesting.

However, with each step towards becoming a couple, Thomas felt increasingly suffocated. It started with their engagement. Thomas didn't want to get engaged, and this hurt her. This was repeated when they got married. Both times he felt obligated to swallow his doubts and reassure Sharon that he wanted her. Thomas saw Sharon as incredibly emotionally dependent. He didn't want to talk because she expected him to "dump his guts out on the table." And he didn't like Sharon saying he had a problem showing emotions.

### • Could this be how your brain rewires?

It's hard to imagine something productive at work in the midst of this. But Nature has created a human brain capable of coping with life's traumas. Brain research documents the neurobiological damage done by trauma. But a million years ago, things were *far more* traumatic than they are now. Without our resilience, our brain would have *devolved* rather than evolved. For the human race to get where we are now, we had to evolve naturally occurring systems by which our brains could self-repair. Maybe there's more to gridlock than Nature pushing your self to grow.

Scientists know your brain sloughs off old dominant ("grooved") neural pathways and creates new ones all through life. This changes how your mind works, down to the thoughts you think, the emotions you feel, and the behaviors you do (and don't do). It changes your perceptions of yourself and the people and world around you. I've come to believe resolving gridlock plays a key role in this process. I think gridlock is the way Nature spontaneously creates "neural plasticity." Gridlock heats up your situation and your brain with acute meaning and anxiety, especially when it involves desire. These conditions may displease you, but they probably facilitate brain rewiring if you use them wisely.

We are not simply expressions of our biological heritage. We have become co-creators of our own brains and minds. We increasingly control our biology rather than the other way around.[102] Seeing love relationships as simple expressions of our genes, or our childhoods, truly misses what we are about.

## SHIFTING TO SELF-CONFRONTATION AND SELF-VALIDATED INTIMACY

Until they came to see me, Sharon and Thomas were sure they knew the problem in their relationship: They thought they were completely out of sync, on two different wavelengths. Sharon complained they weren't connecting and she wasn't getting the "mirroring" she needed. This was a term she read in a book that expressed what she wanted: she and Thomas interacting as though they were one person.

But Sharon's notion of "mirroring" really meant having her reflected sense of self inflated and her image of herself (distorted as it was) fed back to her. What she got back instead was an accurate picture of herself as a controlling person—which she didn't perceive herself to be.

Actually, Sharon and Thomas were *too much* in sync. Perhaps you've already picked this up. Interlocking layers of gridlock, withholding wars, reflected sense of self, and dependence on other-validated intimacy create an undesirable *synchrony*. Contrary to Sharon and Thomas's subjective experience, they were like two Siamese twins, joined through their reflected sense of self, dependence on other-validated intimacy, difficulty regulating their emotions, overreactions to each other, and unwillingness to venture into the unknown. They *felt* out of sync because they were so thoroughly emotionally *fused*.

## • *The importance of getting out of sync*

Other-validated intimacy is synchrony personified, the Holy Grail in our never-ending quest to find our perfect soul mate. Synchrony means one partner discloses and the other accepts and validates and/or discloses in kind. The importance of emotional synchrony is well known: Potential partners court through synchronized behaviors, mirroring each other deliberately or unconsciously. In dating situations, when one partner crosses his legs, the other crosses hers. When one leans inward, the other does too. When one tells a joke, the other laughs. Research indicates dating couples are less likely to have sex if they don't establish high levels of synchrony.[103]

Seventy years ago, mother-infant synchrony was the dominant focus of child psychology. Did Mother feed her baby when he cried in hunger? Did she look at him when he tried to engage her attention? Did she comfort him when he became upset or irritable? Professional wisdom has long held that the greater the synchrony, the better the attachment bonding and the better the baby.

However, in the last several decades child development experts have studied what happens when infants and mothers get out of sync. Scientists no longer view "time out of sync" as lost time for attachment and bonding. "Time out of sync" is just as important as "time in sync." They are two different halves of a whole relationship.

Babies are wired from birth to cope with getting out of sync with caregivers. *Babies deliberately break synchrony several times each minute.*

They do it to regulate their heart rate and their relationship when they become over-stimulated. Time out of sync prepares the baby for positive re-engagement with his caregiver.[104]

Sharon and Thomas often got stuck in downward spirals, sending each other "disqualifying messages." Eventually they learned that getting out of sync when things were bad was just as crucial as getting in sync in positive ways. They needed to function more independently, break out of their pattern, and send a different message. This was the path to a new synchrony involving deeper, more resilient, and more pleasant intimacy. They had to use their Four Points of Balance to get there.

So getting out of sync isn't necessarily a bad thing. Sometimes it's *important*: To resolve gridlock, you have to deliberately get out of step and dampen negative reverberations in you relationship. You have to stop responding in kind and author new behaviors. That's "all" you need to do to resolve gridlock over intimacy and sexual desire. This can be exceedingly hard to do. That's where your Four Points of Balance come in.

## • *Resolving gridlock: Shifting to self-validated intimacy*

This is also where self-validated intimacy comes in: Other-validated intimacy requires partners to be in sync; self-validated intimacy doesn't. Self-validated intimacy often occurs when partners are out of sync. In fact, if you want to get out of sync with your partner in positive ways, self-validated intimacy is your ticket.

Self-validated intimacy is a positive "out of sync" experience. It's positive for you, positive for your relationship, and positive for your mate (who may not appreciate it at the time). Self-validated intimacy breaks the tyranny of lock-step reciprocity and stops the volleys of negative emotional reactivity. Screaming and shouting typically diminish because you stop feeling controlled by your partner.

Earlier we discussed how your partner controls the level of intimacy *only* as long as you rely on other-validated intimacy. As long as you depend on your partner for your emotional balance, there is no escape from gridlock. However, when you shift to self-validated intimacy, *you* control the level of intimacy because you can increase it unilaterally. Self-validated intimacy involves validating, accepting, and soothing *yourself*. Self-validated intimacy gives you the freedom to say what needs to be said. Breaking free of gridlock involves holding on to your self and taking a leap of faith: Self-validated intimacy challenges your identity and self-worth. It asks, *"Who do you think you are?!"*

Self-validated intimacy isn't telling your partner how much you loathe him, spewing your venom in the guise of honesty. Self-validated intimacy strengthens your Four Points of Balance (Solid Flexible Self, Quiet Mind–Calm Heart, Grounded Responding, Meaningful Endurance). It involves confronting *yourself* and addressing things you've avoided up to now. It requires calming yourself down, validating yourself enough to look at the truth, and being willing to be wrong. You have to stay non-reactive, because your partner usually reacts when you make this differentiating move.

When you initiate a productive out-of-sync experience, your partner will immediately try to map your mind, because your actions are inconsistent with his picture of you. Realizing you are functioning independently often elicits an immediate response (although sometimes not a positive one). Your partner can *feel* changes in emotional fusion as you unhook from his responses, even if he's never heard of self-validated intimacy.

### • *Back to Sharon and Thomas*

Sharon and Thomas came into their next session still reeling from a recent argument. I decided it was finally time to confront both of them. "You both know your partner has a soft emotional underbelly. Why do you keep acting like that's not the case?"

Awkward silence filled the room. After several seconds, Sharon and Thomas realized this wasn't a rhetorical question. I expected an answer. No one said anything for almost a minute. Then, speaking slowly, Thomas went first.

"Sharon acts like she's always ready to talk, but she runs away when I try to discuss difficult things with her. She covers her own insecurities by telling me I have problems with intimacy ... I know what she's doing. I act like I don't because I'm hurt. I act like I don't know she's covering up because I'm insecure too. I know she has a soft emotional underbelly. It's easier to respond to her hard shell because that way I get to express my anger ... I'm not sure I can control my temper, actually ..."

Sharon was shocked. This was a real demonstration of self-validated intimacy. It signaled Thomas was taking a different stance and trying harder. He wasn't accusatory. He spoke matter-of-factly, and his voice was calm. Thomas was finally willing to confront himself and his life.

But that wasn't the only reason Sharon was shocked. Thomas obviously understood feelings and how people's minds work. It took several minutes for her to realize he had been tracking her all along. She looked at Thomas the entire time. When she finally spoke, her words came slowly, as if she was speaking her thoughts as they came to her.

"I do it ... I do it too ... I pretend I don't see Thomas's sensitive side ... because ... because I'm afraid ... that deep down ... he is more sensitive than I am."

"What?!" Thomas's eyes grew wide with amazement.

"I'm afraid you are more sensitive than I am." This was self-validated intimacy. Sharon said it as a fact. She wasn't looking for reassurance.

All rancor in the room evaporated. Two instances of self-validated intimacy created hope. This was the first positive synchrony between them in a long time.

"I didn't know you felt that!" Thomas's tone said, *It must be awful to feel that!*

"I don't let you see that." This was more self-validated intimacy from Sharon. To me it sounded like, *I'm not looking for sympathy. This is difficult for me, but I'm anteing up. You may track me, and you may think you can read me like a book, but you don't. There are still some things about me you don't know.*

Sharon followed Thomas's lead by openly confronting herself. They were in sync. Their previous banter and repartee was typically negative and disconfirming. Their competitive sides usually surfaced. This response and counter-response using self-validated intimacy was completely new. This felt a lot better.

Thomas said, "I can understand why you wouldn't let me see that. I'd probably use it to pressure you for sex."

Sharon responded, "I understand why you'd do that. I make you pressure me to have sex because that's the only time we have it. I don't initiate."

"I always initiate, you never get a chance."

"Forget it. I never initiate. You'd have a better chance winning the lottery!" Thomas and Sharon laughed.

It was time for me to speak up. "You two are very competitive. Is the new competition going to be more honest and self-confronting? Is this going to fall apart when you leave?"

Sharon looked at Thomas. Thomas looked at the floor. Sharon said, "This isn't like winning the lottery, but I feel better than before. I feel freer and lighter ... I need to do this for myself. I have to stop treating you like you're a jerk, because I know you're not. And I need to stop withholding sex because I'm only hurting myself."

Thomas looked up. He waited a moment to make clear he wasn't responding reflexively. "At the risk of sounding like a copycat, I have to say, 'Me too!' ... I need to stand on my own two feet and talk straight, even when you don't ... I need to stop withholding from you, too ... And if that's competing with you, well, then screw me!"

"I just might!" she laughed. Thomas was taken aback. He looked at Sharon from the corner of his eye and laughed a little, half afraid to believe it.

Sharon and Thomas left our session feeling better but unsettled. Self-validated intimacy creates intense moments of meeting, profound intersubjective experiences. Operating on this level, they were virtual strangers to themselves and each other. They left with the awkwardness of two people just starting to date.

## CREATING INTERSUBJECTIVE EXPERIENCES

On the way home Sharon and Thomas were friendly toward each other. Each was lost in thought, reflecting on what had just happened. They left my office feeling like *a couple*. It happened by functioning *more independently as individuals.* They felt more together and more free. It developed quickly, and it could disappear just as fast. They had something positive going between them, and neither one wanted to drop it. The overriding sense of anger between them was replaced by hope.

When Sharon and Thomas went to bed that night, the question of sex hung in the air. Thomas wanted to, but he didn't want to ruin things. He was sort of impressed with himself, and with her, too. Sharon looked more sexually appealing.

Thomas decided to go for it. He asked Sharon if she wanted to have sex. For his efforts he received an immediate, reflexive "No." Sharon's response was more modulated than usual, but she regretted it as soon as she said it. She hadn't considered for a moment whether she wanted to or not. She was shocked by her own reaction. On the way home she had actually thought it might be nice to have sex.

Thomas saw both sides of Sharon's response. He got her automatic negative answer, but saw some effort on her part to modulate it. Her tone didn't have its typical message: *You're making me angry! Stop badgering me!* But for Thomas, it was rejection nonetheless.

Thomas sagged. Sharon braced for his impending emotional barrage. This was usually enough to set him off. But this time, instead of raging at Sharon, Thomas kept himself under control. This time his disappointment was more than just a punctured reflected sense of self. The better part of Thomas was hurt too. His hopes from the therapy session crashed. He was angry with himself for initiating so soon, and not just because Sharon said "No." Thomas thought he had blown his alliance with her, and she'd think he'd never change.

Typically, this would have launched Thomas into another emotional nosedive. He usually felt the impulse to lash out at Sharon. But Thomas didn't indulge himself in it the way he usually did. He didn't say anything at first. Then he said softly:

"It's okay. I had my own ambivalence about asking. I thought it was probably premature, but I haven't felt this good about you in a long time."

Sharon heard, *I'm okay. This is just hard to swallow. I'll take care of my feelings. I'm disappointed, but you're not doing something wrong. I'm not going to let this ruin things between us.*

Time stopped. This was a *huge* intersubjective moment. Sharon watched Thomas confront, calm, and master his feelings. She watched him go through a whole range of reactions, then sag and struggle, and emerge more solid on the other side, albeit a bit shaky. He went through this in a matter of minutes instead of days or weeks or months. Sharon was impressed.

"Thank you," she said. Thomas knew she meant it.

"No problem," Thomas said. It was clearly a *big* problem, but Thomas handled it. He wasn't denying his feelings. He was trying to be kind. He was putting all his effort into maintaining his emotional balance.

"I really mean it." Sharon's earnestness drew Thomas to look at her. Their eyes met, and they *saw* each other. Sharon wanted Thomas to map her mind. They were acutely aware of the significance of what was happening, and the positive change in their alliance. Thomas knew Sharon was watching him confront himself and keep himself under control.

"I know you do," said Thomas. Sharon saw that his words and his mind lined up, and her face and body relaxed. This interaction felt incredibly different. They weren't stroking and reinforcing each other as usual, they were standing on their own two feet. Each one's behavior brought out the best in the other, but they didn't get there by trying to accept and validate each other. They were speaking for themselves, trying to be honest, rather than trying to ingratiate themselves by saying what the other wanted to hear. This was self-validated intimacy.

Sharon regretted having said "No" even more. She decided this wasn't the time to mention it. She didn't want to interfere with what Thomas was doing. He didn't need to be propped up with sex, and she didn't want to look like she was paying him off. She also wasn't over being stunned by her "hardwired" refusal.

By the time they went to bed, Thomas felt good about himself. He slept more peacefully than usual. Sharon hardly slept a wink. She was upset—frightened actually—by how automatically she had turned Thomas down. It didn't have anything to do with what she was feeling at the time. It just came out of her, like a grooved response in her brain. Sharon replayed the countless times she'd made that response. She gasped when she saw how awful this must have been for Thomas. Instead of feeling pressured *by* him, she felt compassion *for* him. Far from feeling self-righteousness, Sharon felt *awful*.

In the wee hours of the morning, Sharon initiated sex. Thomas awoke at 2 a.m. to find Sharon fondling him. "Am I dreaming?" Thomas said groggily. He was clearly pleased. He wasn't being sarcastic.

"No, you're not dreaming. I'm just waking up." Thomas realized this had different meanings. He needed to be sure.

"Couldn't you sleep?"

"I've been asleep a long time," Sharon said, as she straddled him and took him inside her. It wasn't like Sharon to get on top. Self-validated intimacy wasn't Sharon's preferred sexual style. Sharon looked down at Thomas and smiled. "I'm sorry I said 'no' when you initiated before. I don't know why I did that. It was completely automatic. It must be hard for you when I do that."

Thomas smiled back. Sharon responded by grinding her pelvis. A smile grew across her face as Thomas's eyes began to bulge.

### • *Intersubjective experiences and personal reality*

Self-validated intimacy isn't always contentious. Some of the best self-validated intimacy is carnal. Moments of meeting like these can change your life. They can lead to profound desire, intense intimacy, and pretty incredible sex. Just bring along your Four Points of Balance.

Scientists believe interpersonal encounters shape the neurobiology of your brain. As experiences go, few are better than sexual self-validated intimacy. (Right up with going through childbirth together.) If you picture Sharon and Thomas's intense moment of meeting, it won't surprise you when science demonstrates you can rewire your head this way. It contained many conditions thought to expedite the process.

First, the sex Sharon and Thomas had was moderately stressful and highly emotional, against a background of peace and calm—perfect conditions for creating brain plasticity. Second, both their "body self" and complex self were involved. Third, the new information and experience they gained required their minds to integrate their thoughts, emotions, sensations, and behavior. Presumably this forced the right and left halves of their brains to interact in new patterns.

Perhaps this explains why couples find such events truly transformative. Sharon and Thomas's sexual encounter didn't change everything, but it gave them a solid start. If you string together a whole bunch of similar transformative experiences, you'll think and feel differently, one way or another. If that's what you want to do, pay attention to two things that determine the intensity of an encounter:

*The importance of your partner.* The more important your partner is to you, the greater the challenge to your selfhood, especially if her immediate response is not warm and fuzzy. This vulnerability increases your sense of intimacy. Openly acknowledging caring for your partner also increases the intensity.

*Depth of self-confrontation.* Self-confrontation is a core part of intimacy. The more you reveal to your partner who you really are, without masking or misrepresentation, the greater your experience of intimacy will be. Conversely, the more your disclosures involve self-presentation, rather than self-confrontation, the more intimacy will seem superficial. If you want to increase the meaningfulness of intimacy, let your partner map your mind while you take a good look at yourself.

Here's one final related point: Just because intimacy is an intersubjective state, that doesn't mean both people feel it equally. If you heed these guidelines, and your partner doesn't, then you will have a profound experience, and your partner won't. This will involve more self-validated intimacy for you, because you'll have to validate your experience when it differs from your partner's. It takes two to create intimacy, but only one partner may feel it.

Sharon and Thomas went through difficult experiences of self-validated intimacy on their way to getting the marriage they wanted. Sometimes one confronted and revealed himself, but the other didn't move forward. Sometimes it took five or six exchanges before the other came around. Occasionally it took days. But now they knew the benefits of self-validated intimacy. They knew it could get them out of gridlock, and it made them more willing to persevere.

# ADULT INTIMACY HARNESSES THE BEST IN YOU

The process of knowing yourself and letting your self be truly known, without demanding acceptance, involves powerful self-confrontations. Mastering these challenges strengthens your Four Points of Balance. A solid sense of self is a more flexible self. You have more room to compromise because you're clear about who you are. This creates new options for resolving gridlock.

- *Self-confrontation drives you and your relationship forward*

Why does self-confrontation develop your sense of self? Challenge strengthens your self, like lifting weights challenges and strengthens your muscles. Questioning your behavior or motives, instead of justifying them, challenges your picture of who you are.

This involves asking yourself tough questions like *Was I really correct about what I told my partner?* or *Am I really as patient (or considerate, etc.) as I think I am or think I should be?* or *What am I dodging?* Answering these kinds of questions involves difficult soul-searching and not settling for easy answers.

Self-confrontation lies at the heart of self-validated intimacy. Self-confrontation is a vital part of developing a solid flexible self, because a solid self develops from self-confrontation rather than internalizing validation from others. If you won't confront yourself about who you really are, you'll stay dependent on how you think you look to other people (reflected sense of self).

Self-validated intimacy often happens outside your comfort zone, far beyond the boundaries of warm "closeness," "togetherness," and "we-ness." Adult intimacy smacks you with the reality that you and your partner are separate beings. You become acutely aware of yourself, your partner, and your relationship.

Intimacy satisfies your attachment needs but it can stomp on them as well (and often does). You can end up being known by your partner in ways that make you uncomfortable. You can become more self-aware than you really want to be. Intimacy in love relationships requires meaningful endurance. Sometimes that means controlling mammalian fight-or-flight responses, and muzzling the reptile in you that wants to bite your spouse.

### • *Intimacy and sexual desire*

Intimacy and sexual desire don't necessarily go hand in hand. There are people who find intimacy diminishes their desire. For some, intimacy diminishes focus on sheer eroticism, and this is the only level on which they want to connect. Others can't share intimate sex with someone they love. Some people's desire evaporates once they are in a relationship and intimacy deepens.

But lots of people find increased intimacy during sex (and outside the bedroom) creates a potent cocktail of other-validated and self-validated intimacy that ignites desire. A mix of both types of intimacy works best in long-term relationships. If you're only capable of other-validated intimacy, your desire and your intimacy will fade away. Self-validated intimacy is crucial for curing sexual boredom and keeping desire alive, because this is how you introduce new behaviors. However, other-validated intimacy endows sex with *we*-ness, romance, and nurturance, and many people's sexual desire withers without this.

Intimacy during sex combines two of humankind's most powerful intersubjective experiences. It's no wonder profoundly intimate sex impacts us so greatly. This doesn't always have to involve tender loving sex. Quickies and raunchy sex can be intimate too, if this isn't all you ever do.

Intimacy during sex can make *you* more interesting, more desirable, and more desirous. That's because intimacy makes us grow in ways that make us beautiful. There is no inherent beauty in sex. The beauty comes from the people involved. You have to bring beauty to sex if you want it to be beautiful. You have to find that beauty within your self. Daring to let your self be truly known, warts and all, is one big way to do this.

Intimacy leaves an indelible impression in your mind and brain, which you carry for the rest of your life. It's where your partner lives, long after he or she is gone. Some of intimacy's power comes from accepting this.

One night, as Sharon and Thomas started to make love, this thought arose between them. They were lying on their sides, looking into each other's eyes. Thomas's fingertips brushed Sharon's cheek. Thomas saw she was letting herself appreciate him, at the same moment he appreciated her.

"I don't want to lose you," Thomas croaked, his voice thick with emotion and his eyes brimming with tears.

The synchrony staggered Sharon's brain. The thought went through her mind: *We're thinking the same thought at the same time!*

## IDEAS TO PONDER

- Intimacy is a system, just like sexual desire. *Intimacy involves mapping your own mind in front of your partner, and letting your partner map your mind too.* Your Four Points of Balance determine your tolerance of profound intimacy.
- Intimacy problems create low sexual desire, and gridlock over intimacy is virtually inevitable. Other-validated intimacy is time-limited in love relationships. Self-validated intimacy hinges on the strength of your Four Points of Balance.
- To resolve gridlock, you have to deliberately get out of step and dampen negative reverberations in you relationship. You have to stop responding in kind and author new behaviors.
- Realizing there are parts of your partner's mind you *don't* know is also part of intimacy.

# 6

## Changing Monogamy from Martyrdom to Freedom

*K*aren spat the words at Julian: "Did you think I would wait forever?"

"I thought we had an agreement to be monogamous," Julian countered.

"*I* thought we had an agreement to work on having sex five years ago!" Karen retorted.

Julian and Karen were so locked into each other they were almost oblivious of me. He was on the attack, and she was defensive. They had obviously been over this many times. It was a great demonstration of gridlock, but they were both too far gone to notice it.

"I can't believe you'd do this!" Julian thundered.

"It's natural to want to have sex," Karen parried. "And I've heard monogamy may be contrary to our basic nature. Everyone screws around. Get over it."

"I can't get over it. I didn't screw around. You did!"

"That's because you wouldn't screw me!!"

Julian turned to me. "You tell her, Doc. Tell her that not everyone screws around."

Karen picked up Julian's challenge. "No, Doc. Tell him that monogamy isn't natural. Tell him it's not natural to never make love to your wife!"

I didn't say anything for a moment to cool things off. "You two don't want to mess up your fight with facts, do you?" I replied. "There's a whole lot of human nature going on between you, but you seem more interested in pounding on each other than studying it as it plays out between you."

There was no point in going into detail while Karen and Julian's emotions were out of control. Their emotional intensity, coupled with what they were saying, screamed that they were living with emotional fusion and borrowed functioning. At least one of the three of us was learning something in their therapy.

### • *Karen and Julian's story*

Karen, the high desire partner, was a star employee selling business machines to large corporations. Julian, the low desire partner, taught mathematics at a private high school. Julian had been the major bread-winner until Karen went back to work after their two children entered high school. Karen's success had surprised them both.

Karen had always been the more sexually eager of the two, but she hung back in fear of intimidating Julian or embarrassing herself. Julian had long-term difficulty reaching orgasm too rapidly (within two min-utes) when they had intercourse. Julian steadfastly avoided dealing with this problem, and after ten years of gentle prodding Karen finally con-fronted him head-on and told him she wanted a divorce. At that point Julian said he would go for treatment. However, when Karen made the appointment, Julian made excuses, and they never went. That was five years ago, and at that point their marriage collapsed. Karen lost desire for sex with Julian, and they basically became celibate. They'd had sex a couple of times a year since then.

Karen stayed with Julian because she loved him and their two children, but she hated sex with him. She hated how his rapid orgasms dominated their sex. More than that, Karen hated the way Julian used sex like a prize. If she pressed him on other issues in their relationship, she knew sex was off the table for a good long time.

Although in her marriage Karen looked sexually uninterested, sex was very much on her mind. Since early adolescence, she had masturbated four or five times a week. She'd had sex with many men before she met Julian. Men she met at work found her attractive and frequently propositioned her. A year ago she'd had a six-month affair. Julian found out while she was breaking it off. In the six months since then, Julian and Karen had had no sex. Karen recently told Julian she was thinking of leaving. That's how they came to be sitting in my office, Julian raging that Karen had wronged him, and Karen saying her affair was both natural and his own fault.

## MONOGAMY, ADULTERY, AND HUMAN NATURE

Many clients have questioned me about monogamy, adultery, and human nature, so I educated myself a little about what science has to say. I learned that originally, humans were probably promiscuous, like the sexually active Bonobo monkeys. But as "human nature" developed some 350,000 years ago, things changed. Sexual patterns probably shifted back and forth between promiscuity and monogamy as living conditions went from good to bad and back again. Anthropologist Helen Fisher says, "Modern human sexual anatomy and the human sexual emotions evolved in conjunction with the evolution of the reproductive strategy of serial monogamy and clandestine adultery."[105]

Hunting-gathering societies are more tolerant of infidelity than industrial societies, but your hunter-gathering ancestor's reflected sense of self was there to take it personally. Social rules prescribed a beating, an argument, or public ridicule. They had a conscience and a sense of right and wrong. "Should" and "shouldn't" existed by this time. So did, "I know I shouldn't, but maybe I can get away with it."

### • *Monogamy*

Many animal species form harems, but humans pair off. Pair-bonding is a peculiar human trademark. Monogamy is the rule (with a few exceptions). The vast majority of people only marry one person at a time. Of 853 cultures on record with the United Nations, 84 percent permit a man to take more than one wife at a time (polygyny). Only 16 percent prescribe monogamy (one wife at a time). *But only 5 to 10 percent of men actually have several wives simultaneously where polygyny is permitted.*[106] Women around the world marry only one man at once. Another study of 250 societies concluded that every known human society is, in practice, monogamous.[107]

However, *monogamy and fidelity are not the same thing.* Strictly speaking, monogamy is being married to only one person at a time. It is essentially an exclusive relationship, but covert mating outside the pair bond occurs in all monogamous species. "Cheating" has been observed in over one hundred species of monogamous birds and monogamous mammals including monkeys. From a Darwinian perspective, adultery "improves" monogamy. [108]

Despite social rules, moral precepts, and our ability to anticipate emotional and social consequences (including punishment with death), no culture exists in which adultery is unknown. Alfred Kinsey found over a third of six thousand married men in his sample from the 1940s had affairs; he figured the real figure was closer to half. One out of four women had affairs by age forty. Forty-one percent had one affair, 40 percent had two to five, and 19 percent had more than five.[109] In 1970, a survey of *Psychology Today* readers revealed 40 percent of husbands and 36 percent of wives reported extramarital affairs. A 1974 *Playboy* magazine survey found roughly 40 percent of men in their sample had affairs.[110] A *Redbook* poll from 1975 found almost 40 percent of married women had an extramarital affair.[111] In the early 1980s, a *Cosmopolitan* magazine survey found 54 percent of married women had at least one affair. Another poll found 72 percent of men married for over two years had affairs.[112] While these results suggest more men than women have affairs, estimates from cultures around the world generally suggest women have extramarital affairs as often as men do—if she wants to, and if her society says she has an equal right to do so. (This last "if" is the rub.)

Bonding with a single mate (monogamy) *and* extramarital affairs seem to be part of our evolutionary pair-bonding strategy. We like devotion *and* philandering.[113] That's where your ability to map other minds comes in: To have an affair you have to use your ability to deceive (implant false beliefs in another person's mind). Mind-mapping makes clandestine affairs possible.

## • *Do you belong to your mate?*

Karen and Julian were in no shape to contemplate such things. They couldn't appreciate how their reflected sense of self did the talking in their shouting matches.

"You made a fool out of me in front of our entire community."

"Why are you the fool? I had the affair."

"You're my wife."

"I don't belong to you!"

"Don't give me that crap. You know what I mean. What you do reflects on me."

"All you care about is how you look to other people."

"That's not true. I care about you. I want you to make a commitment this won't happen again. Why can't you commit?!"

"Why didn't you commit to working on our sex? You said you would five years ago, and then you did nothing. Why should I commit when you don't?"

"I don't know if I can have sex with you now. I don't trust you."

"Well I don't want sex with you, either!"

Until now Karen managed to keep up with Julian, parrying his thrusts. But Julian's reflected sense of self really wanted Karen punctured. He wasn't about to have her come out intact. He needed her reduced to tears, and he knew how to do it.

"No, we've got to have sex now, whether we like it or not. Because if we don't, you'll end up screwing someone else!" Julian's move was cold and calculated.

Karen mapped Julian's mind. He was saying this to hurt her. What punctured her was the calculated violence. Julian wasn't just expressing his feeling or venting his anger. He was pounding on her emotionally, and eventually she burst into tears.

### • *Propping yourself up by not having sex*

This was Karen's first extramarital affair. But she and Julian exhibited the long-term effects of borrowed functioning and subjugation to tyranny. It happened when Julian insisted that they not talk about sex. Avoiding his problem with rapid orgasm kept his anxiety down, his self-esteem up, and his feelings of inadequacy at bay. Julian subjugated Karen by withdrawing sex, intimacy, and approval, and making her feel cheap and slutty. The only reason he could get away with it was because they had a monogamous relationship (or so he thought).

Why did Julian do this? He said the most immediate reason was he was threatened by Karen's success. She wanted to have more influence in family decisions because she contributed a growing percentage of their income. Julian feared Karen would eventually dominate him. At the same time, he feared she would leave him. Maybe she'd find someone else more successful and dynamic than him.

Their script was as old as the human race. Conflict over personal development and monogamy shaped how the human race turned out.

### • *Monogamy in prehistory*

Ten thousand years ago, men apparently engaged in the greatest act of borrowed functioning ever: men began subjugating women. This continues to shape marriages and societies around the world.

*Homo sapiens* apparently came out of the Stone Age different from how they went in. As far as we know, men and women were equal in status in hunter/scavenger–farmer/gatherer societies.[114] But by the end of the Stone Age, man was the master and the woman was his property.

What caused this huge shift? This might have been early man's solution to emotional gridlock. It could have been his response to woman's request for (other-validated) intimacy. Some evidence suggests it came from man's needy reflected sense of self. No one knows for sure why it happened, but there's no question that it did. Some authorities say it came when hunter-gatherer cultures shifted to agrarian societies, with the domestication of animals and the invention of the plow. Men took over farming and caring for livestock, and women's status sank because they didn't put food on the table; they cooked it.

Apparently, this gave man's reflected sense of self delusions of grandeur. Earliest records indicate it clearly got out of hand. By 3000 B.C., women had become chattel, and double standards for sexual conduct were well in place. The male-dominated society was born.[115] No doubt man's ageless quest for aphrodisiacs was a matter of necessity. It is easy to imagine your female ancestor's low desire and sexual withholding when she shifted from being a partner to being property.

Because people were tied to the land, agrarian life demanded permanent monogamy. As industrial societies became the dominant economic and social force, women regained some measure of equality. Today we are freer to play out our primordial sex, love, and marriage dynamics as equals. The most recent trends of human differentiation have shown women gaining *choice*—cognitively, socially, and reproductively. Increasingly, women around the world refuse to submit to tyranny.

### • *Discovery of man's role in reproduction*

In *The History of Sex*, Reay Tannahill blames the subjugation of women on man's reflected sense of self. She thinks around the Stone Age, men figured out their sperm played a crucial role in women's pregnancies and ensuing children. Until this point (and still today in some remote native cultures), sex was thought of as something couples did, but insemination was between women and the gods. When man's reflected sense of self realized *he* was the baby-maker, Tannahill proposes, women's role in procreation shifted from central to peripheral. Rather than men and women being equal partners, each contributing something, women became the "earth" in which men planted a complete "seed."[116] Man's reflected sense of self basked in the glory of *my* wife and *my* child.[117]

Unfortunately, about the time "my son" came into being, so did "cuck-old." Men started to control women's sexuality because she could not only tamper with spreading his DNA, she could tamper with the inside of his head.

• *Paternity*

Paternity is the other side of what Helen Fisher called the "sex contract": Women became multiply orgasmic and interested in sex throughout the year, and they used it, through sexual selection, to breed with men willing to pair-bond and help with the kids. "Dad" emerged on the *Homo sapiens* scene, and thousands of years later we celebrate Father's Day.

Unfortunately, Dad's reflected sense of self turned paternity into patriarchy. This is how we got the sexual double standard that still exists today.

• *Borrowed functioning*

The subjugation of women illustrates borrowed functioning. Man's sense of self was artificially enhanced, and woman's was correspondingly suppressed. Women's chastity became important because sex with other men upset man's reflected sense of self and made paternity uncertain. The sexual double standard gave man what many people want: sexual variety for themselves and sexual exclusivity for their partner.

Women have been bred to support men's reflected sense of self for at least ten thousand years. (Odds are its closer to millions.) It shows up as women "sliding under" men to prop up their ego and feelings of adequacy. It occurs around the world. Although they've been doing it a long time, women have not learned to like it. Their instinct to refuse to submit to tyranny always seems to come up.

Women engage in borrowed functioning too. Women tend to marry—and have affairs with—men of status, power, wealth, and influence. In Darwinian terms, this gives her genes the greatest chance of surviving into subsequent generations. In reality, however, women have affairs because they *like* them, and they prefer rich influential men who inflate their reflected sense of self in many ways.

# MONOGAMY IS NOT A PROMISE, IT'S A SYSTEM!

In Chapter 5 you learned that intimacy is a powerful system at work in your marriage that dramatically affects desire. Now let's consider monogamy the same way. Monogamy is another opportunity for personal growth. Let's approach this with an eye toward sexual desire, commitment, and refusal to submit to tyranny.

Monogamy is not simply a promise or a commitment. It is a *system,* just like intimacy. And since all systems change depending on who's inside the system, monogamy operates differently depending on the strength of a couple's Four Points of Balance (Solid Flexible Self, Quiet Mind–Calm Heart, Grounded Responding, Meaningful Endurance). Monogamy among well-differentiated couples feels, looks, and operates differently than in poorly differentiated couples.

Monogamy in well-differentiated couples encourages high desire. For instance, you're more likely to want sex with a partner who has a strong sense of self. But monogamy in poorly differentiated couples encourages low desire. As we've seen, desire evaporates when someone feels claustrophobic from emotional fusion and borrowed functioning. The good news is that if handled right, the sexual problems caused by monogamy can strengthen your Four Points of Balance and lead to profound desire.

It can be shocking to realize monogamy is not a static commitment, but actually a dynamic system. Not only is monogamy a system that changes over time, the nature of monogamous commitment changes also. Connecting this with the Four Points of Balance can be a bit much to take in. So let's slow down and take a look at how this all happens.

- *Monogamy works off Your Four Points of Balance*

Monogamy creates a monopoly in the same way the LDP always controls sex. This is true in all couples. But couples respond to this differently, depending on their Four Points of Balance. Well-differentiated couples heed and respect the fact that monogamy gives the LDP a monopoly on sex. Poorly differentiated couples act variously with ignorance, negligent heedlessness, and belligerent exploitation of this fact.

### • Monogamy for Karen and Julian

Monogamy created a "closed system" that gave Julian (the LDP) a monopoly on sex. There was no one else Karen could turn to, so she had to deal with Julian if she wanted sex. However, they weren't negotiating from equal positions because he controlled when, where, and how sex happened. Emotionally speaking, he could name his price, and sometimes the price of sex was that Karen had to make Julian feel "special." Sometimes the price was kissing his ass. Sometimes it was staying quiet when she might rightly confront him about something.

Like all monopolies, Julian limited the supply of "goods and services" (sex). He did this for many reasons: Sometimes he felt intimidated by Karen earning more money than he did. Withholding sex increased his control in their relationship. Sometimes he was angry about something Karen did or didn't do. Sometimes he restricted sex to increase his bargaining power on other issues. Sometimes he did this to push Karen away or draw her closer. Sometimes he liked the way he felt powerful to influence her so greatly.

Frequently, Julian withheld simply out of his own anxieties about sex, and his insecurities about being "used." He didn't want Karen to use him in the sense his mother used men. His mother used his father as a stepping stone to "more important" partners. She used flattery, seductiveness, and sex to attract a progression of wealthy men. As a teenager Julian was nauseated watching her in action, sucking up to men at the same time she looked down on them. His mother excused her behavior by saying she was lonely, but Julian saw she was manipulative and exploitive, and used anyone to get what she wanted.

### • The dating marketplace vs. the marital bedroom

Monogamy allowed Julian to get away with limiting supply in ways he never could if he and Karen had an "open relationship." If they were just dating, or if Karen was free to have sex with other men, she could simply turn to another partner to fill the disparity in their sexual desire. But, like most couples (and unlike most primates), they wanted the sexual exclusivity of monogamy and fidelity. And this set monopoly dynamics in place, which Julian's reflected sense of self then exploited.

Bargaining differs in monopolistic and free market economies, and this showed up in Karen and Julian's interactions. In free market systems, like dating, people are courteous of each other while presenting themselves most advantageously. Monopolies, however, flaunt their power by inflating prices and insulting customers with a "take it or leave it" attitude. This shows up in dowry negotiations in arranged marriages where families differ greatly in wealth. In Julian and Karen's case, he acted like she had to wait until he felt like having sex, and there was nothing she could do about it. The "nothing she could do about it" was her promise to be faithful.

In open relationships, the HDP simply takes her sexual interests elsewhere. But, human nature being what it is, the LDP usually doesn't want this to happen. Among many reasons, this would shatter his reflected sense of self. He attempts to forestall this shattering by invoking fidelity agreements. This is how monogamy stops being virtuous or wholesome. Monogamy is how the LDP manages two anxieties at once: He forces the HDP to accept sex in accordance with his insecurities and immaturities, and he keeps his partner from seeking other partners she might prefer.

Like many LDPs, Julian knew this intuitively and exploited it. Julian had sex when, where, and how *he* wanted it. All of Karen's initiations and suggested variations were rejected. He saw them as her attempts to control or criticize him.

Through the system of monogamy, Julian created other things that he himself didn't appreciate. He didn't realize the more he limited sex, the more it exacerbated his fears the next time he got into bed. When sex happened rarely, there was more performance pressure on him. He increased his own fear that Karen might have an affair. He couldn't see he was also increasing her motivation to have one. He tortured himself by picturing her having sex with someone else, her *wanting* other men, and berated himself for his sexual inadequacies. This increased his fears that Karen secretly wished to be "free." Unfortunately, but predictably, this made Julian less interested in sex, in part, because he had the security that Karen still wanted him.

## • Foreplay: Negotiating intimacy, eroticism, and meaning

Foreplay is a negotiation for the level of intimacy, eroticism, and meaning in the sex that follows. Poorly differentiated folks get their feelings hurt in the process of foreplay and lose desire.

Julian used his monopoly every time they had (and didn't have) sex. His preferences and shortcomings dominated who did what to whom, and the order and meaning of what happened.

Julian's rapid orgasms controlled their sexual behavior. He wouldn't let Karen touch his penis during foreplay because this made him climax more quickly. They didn't have oral sex because Julian wasn't comfortable going down on Karen. Karen had encouraged him to do it, but Julian always demurred. She didn't push this, given her fear that Julian would start restricting sex again if she pissed him off. Karen didn't do oral sex for Julian because this made him climax quicker, too. Julian said if sex was going to be brief, he wanted to be inside Karen when it happened.

Not only did Julian control how they had sex, he also controlled the level of intimacy and eroticism between them. He controlled the meaning of the sex they were having and the messages they sent each other. This went on through the mind-mapping of subtle behavioral cues partners always communicate.

It happens in something as seemingly simple as a kiss. Julian didn't like to smooch. Karen got her feelings hurt and backed off when he turned his head. Karen got the message loud and clear that Julian didn't want to do it. They had sex in the dark because Julian "thought it was more romantic." Actually, Julian was uncomfortable really being intimate. He liked the dark because he felt less exposed. Several times Karen suggested they watch a porno flick, and Julian said he was interested. But he never acted upon her suggestion, so she surmised he was uncomfortable with it. Karen constantly monitored Julian for how forward she could be about sex without intimidating or angering him.

For his part, Julian constantly gauged Karen's reactions. He knew from past experience Karen wanted more kissing, but he also knew she wouldn't push this any further than she pushed for sex. All he had to do was hesitate, whether during kissing or having sex, and Karen would get the hint and back off. Mind-mapping was the medium of Julian and Karen's negotiations for intimacy, eroticism, and meaning during foreplay.

This sufficed most of the time, but eventually she put a different strategy in play: Julian overestimated how captive Karen was by her own promise of fidelity. He was shocked when she had her affair because he had read her incorrectly.

Partly this happened because Julian didn't appreciate how angry Karen was and how controlled she felt. Partly he misjudged her because Karen went to great lengths to keep Julian from reading her mind. Karen didn't want Julian accurately mapping her because he'd discover she was having an affair.

• *Affairs are not acts of autonomy or differentiation*

In the last several years, Karen developed low desire for sex with Julian. But while they were basically celibate, Karen had lots of desire for sex. She struggled with a strong desire to have an affair. She watched porn on the Internet, joined in sexually tinged chats, and eventually started a physical affair with someone she met online.

Affairs are pseudo-differentiation—masquerading as standing on your own two feet, when in fact you're not. Karen's affair had an element of monopoly-busting, and a refusal to submit to tyranny. But both were nothing more than dressed-up defiance. Thumbing your nose at your partner does not strengthen your Four Points of Balance.

Defiance is not autonomy because the locus of control still resides with your partner rather than yourself. The best way to "resolve tyranny" is by getting a better grip on yourself. Autonomy and independence involve taking care of yourself—not doing things that diminish you. Karen could have broken Julian's monopoly by taking an open stand of no longer tolerating the status quo, and not allowing her promise of monogamy and fidelity to be misused to perpetuate it. Emancipating herself didn't have to involve violating her own beliefs. "All" she had to do was deal with Julian directly, risk his wrath, and handle his attempts to punish her.

## MONOGAMY CREATES LOW DESIRE IN POORLY DIFFERENTIATED COUPLES

Monogamy isn't easy for anyone. It's particularly difficult for poorly differentiated people. It's hard to resist the inflated self and dopamine rush of an extramarital affair. That same reflected sense of self makes desire problems virtually certain in your marriage. This deadly combination creates lots of affairs in folks lacking in the Four Points of Balance.

I'm not a critic of monogamy. I'm providing the argument for it. Monogamy is poorly understood and poorly used. If you were Mother Nature, and you wanted to encourage human psychological development, you'd be pretty clever if you made the things humans do to avoid growth the very things that make them grow. Monogamy is where poorly differentiated people run for safety (read: avoid growing).[118] But you need to develop stronger Four Points of Balance, or your marriage—or your sexual relationship within it—doesn't survive.

There are other ways monogamy functions like a gear in the people-growing machinery of marriage. Monogamy involves an implicit sense of ownership or property rights in your partner, and a basic sense of territoriality regarding potential interlopers. When your Four Points of Balance are weak, this takes on greater importance. Monogamy gratifies your reflected sense of self (at least initially) when someone turns to the world and declares, "Stay back! He's *mine!*" It makes you feel valued and chosen. You feel the same during courtship when your partner looks you in the eye and says, "Your mine!" Either expression of possessiveness is often rewarded with sex, but only if your partner maps your mind and reads that you mean it.

Expressing ownership of your partner once you're married introduces you to celibacy. Being taken for granted violates your dignity, autonomy, and reflected sense of self. It makes you angry, rebellious, and withholding. There's nothing like your partner thinking she owns your genitals to kill your ardor. Everyone has this reaction. If your Four Points of Balance are lacking, it triggers the War of Independence.

All this over things that exist only in your partner's head! Possessiveness, ownership, and entitlement. You can't feel taken for granted if you can't map your partner's mind. Just another way mind-mapping shapes your monogamy.

Innumerable iterations of *If you love me you will* and *If you love me you won't ask* enshrine our expectations that our partner should do whatever it takes to makes us happy. It inflates your reflected sense of self when she does something for you that she doesn't really want to do, or gives up something she really wants. In truth, you probably expect her to sacrifice *her* self to support *your* self. This interaction drives poorly differentiated people's relationships. We take this for granted as human nature, but it's what makes human sexual desire incredibly unique.

- ## *Communal genitals: Emotional fusion and borrowed functioning*

"Communal genitals" is my term for partners acting as though they have rights to their partner's body for sexual purposes. It describes how people feel and act. Communal genitals sounds like, *If I'm not going to have access to other partners, your genitals half belong to me. Keep them clean and ready to go, and make them available when I want them.*[119]

Some religions promote the notion of a marital "sexual debt," which doesn't help.[120] When sexual obligations surface, so does low desire. At first, it sounds simple that sex is something you expect in marriage, but it creates trouble if your Four Points of Balance are weak. The standard monogamy/fidelity agreement creates low desire because it violates someone's wobbly reflected sense of self.

Communal genitals only exist because we're able to map out our partner's mind. We read each other's expectations and attitudes. After a while, you get the feeling your mate believes he jointly owns you, if not out of entitlement then out of need. Here's where your Four Points of Balance come in. The weaker they are, the quicker you get this feeling. And since your partner's Four Points of Balance are probably similarly undevel-

146 INTIMACY & DESIRE

oped, the more likely she will manifest this usury attitude. Whether it starts with her or your wobbly sense of self, the weaker your Four Points of Balance (Solid Flexible Self, Quiet Mind–Calm Heart, Grounded Responding, Meaningful Endurance), the more monogamy triggers feeling of tyranny and loss of autonomy in one or both of you. This creates low desire, even in people who really love sex. Battles of selfhood far outweigh hormonal drive in determining your sexual desire.

When I describe communal genitals, you might picture someone who is selfish, immature, and a high-desire slob. He complains about his physical needs not being met and acts like his wife's vagina belongs to him. Even if she isn't interested, he wants to use her body to bring himself to orgasm.

But, like many HDPs, Karen didn't fit this mold. She wanted to be with Julian. It was Julian who introduced the "all you want is my body" mind-set. Julian had no idea he was doing this. He was terribly insecure since he learned of Karen's affair. He thought a monogamy agreement would make him feel more secure. But this agreement put pressure on him to have sex with her.

Mother Nature generates increasingly sophisticated adaptations of the most primitive parts of your brain. It happened by countless couples confronting these kinds of mind-boggling dynamics, day after day, for millions of years. Your forebears developed a prefrontal neocortex in self-defense.

• *The worst in us loves monogamy too*

Sometimes it's the worst in us that wants monogamy (just like the worst in you could want an open marriage). That's why the first chapter of my book *Passionate Marriage* is entitled "Nobody's Ready for Marriage; Marriage Makes You Ready for Marriage." I wrote that people invariably marry for "wrong reasons" because the right reasons don't exist yet. The purpose of marriage is to make you capable of good reasons to be married. The worst in us sometimes wants monogamy because the weakness of our Four Points of Balance drives us into and out of relationships.

Sometimes we demand exclusivity because we fear our partner will find someone "better." We want protection from our own feelings of being unattractive, unworthy, and undesirable. Sometimes we want "commitment" to calm our fears of getting old and less appealing, or to make it safe to get fat and sloppy. Sometimes we want our partner to promise to be there forever—*before* he finds out too much about us. We want to hold him to his blind choice, because we don't figure he'd pick us once he knew us.

It's important to say that highly differentiated people often want monogamy too. However, they want monogamy for different reasons. And their monogamy operates differently.

### • *When you can't hold on to your Self, monogamy creates low sexual desire*

Monogamy turns sexual desire problems into gridlock because there aren't alternative sources for sex. And if you lack in Four Points of Balance, you handle this poorly. Monogamy reinforces the "togetherness pressure" that exists between emotionally fused couples. You're also more likely to reach gridlock over other issues in your relationship. And since emotional gridlock (from any source) increases desire disparity, you're particularly prone to desire problems.

Lots of couples start out this way and remain so throughout their relationship. Karen and Julian started with this typical pattern, but at some point Karen's response "flipped" into another common scenario: Instead of making her more needy and solicitous for sex, her reflected sense of self made her refuse sex altogether. When she stopped pursuing Julian, she was saying, *Keep your damn sex!* Karen was fed up with humbling herself, and now she wanted to one-up him. Some of the best in her was standing up and saying, *I'm not going along with this anymore!* But a lot of it said, *I'm not going along with this, but I'm not leaving either. If you want a war, buddy, you got one. And it's going to be one long, cold war.*

How do you reduce this emotional fusion? Not with an affair or an "open relationship." Hold on to your Four Points of Balance. Stay clear about what's really important to you. Quiet your mind, calm your heart, and soothe your own anger. Keep your responses measured and grounded. Don't act impulsively or vindictively. Stronger Four Points of Balance increases your capacity for healthy desire and diminishes neediness and emotional dependency. Reducing emotional fusion, and rescuing desire from annihilation, always involves a leap of faith: Confront yourself about what you're really doing—to yourself and to your partner.

## THINGS REACH CRITICAL MASS

In prehistoric times, there were the first man and the first woman to figure out that the other was deliberately tampering with his or her reflected sense of self in order to inflict pain. They probably put up with this for a while, thinking the other didn't understand how hurtful he or she was being. They preferred to think the other was insensitive or emotionally blind. But mapping your partner's mind and realizing his or her behavior is deliberate usually creates a turning point. It did for Karen and Julian.

Julian and Karen's fateful conversation started in my office with Julian's familiar, *"How could you have an affair?"* Karen would typically respond, "THAT'S BULLSHIT! You're just saying that to back me off." However, this time it didn't come out as an accusation. She said it flatly, like she finally accepted a matter of fact. "You won't deal with sex."

"You won't deal with your affair." Julian was testing to see if he could still hook her.

"Bullshit, Julian. You won't deal with sex."

I motioned to Karen. "You're not listening to yourself."

Julian used my comment to swipe at her. "She doesn't listen to me either, Doc."

I continued speaking to Karen. "Why won't you pay attention to what you're telling Julian? You're saying he's using the fact that you had an affair to avoid confronting himself about his own difficulties."

"That's right."

"Well, you allow him to do that as long as you avoid dealing with your affair. You're saying he's trying to back you off by throwing your affair at you. So why don't you take that weapon away from him?"

"You mean confront myself about my affair?"

"Yes."

There's something about realizing your partner deliberately tampers with your reflected sense of self that makes a person willing to make a move. Things reach critical mass right then and there. Maybe your reflected sense of self is just so pissed. Maybe it feels imperative to free yourself from your partner's grasp. But, for one reason or another, many of us mobilize to do things we wouldn't otherwise do.

However, it is possible to free yourself from your partner's grasp *and* strengthen your relationship with yourself in the process. This was the point of my comment to Karen: When you confront yourself, your partner can no longer control you through your shortcomings. You have to do four things: Confront yourself and heed your own counsel, soothe your own heart, emotionally unhook from your partner, and stand up and face the music. These are your Four Points of Balance. This is the process of differentiation.

## GOING THROUGH THE CRUCIBLE

Karen thought for several seconds. "Okay Julian, you want me to confront myself about the affair? Well here goes. I had an affair. I lied to you ... I broke my vow ..."

Karen's words slowed as she listened to herself as she spoke. She shifted from confessing sins to thinking about what she was saying. Her tone wasn't defiant, it said, *I'm ready to finally deal with this and accept what comes of it. I'm afraid, but I am not doing this to myself anymore.* Julian sensed now was not the time to take a shot at her.

"You have no reason to ever trust me again ... I have no integrity ... I lost most of that trying to stay married to you ... and the rest I threw away ... I cheated on you ... I know to you I'm no different than your mother." There was no malice in Karen's voice. She was being brutally honest but she wasn't slamming him. She paused a moment to think of what else she needed to say.

"... I cheated on my vows ... I've cheated myself ... out of having some integrity ... cheated myself out of having someone who wants me ... I ... guess ... I'm ... just ... a ... cheater!" Karen convulsed into sobs.

Afterward, it wasn't hard for Karen to understand her earlier state of mind. If Julian was going to withhold sex and affirmation, and make her "crawl," she would go around him and find someone who wanted her. She didn't think of it as finding someone to pump up her reflected sense of self, or of being so emotionally fused with Julian she'd be willing to throw herself away to get back at him. She told herself she needed someone to care about her. Setting up her first meeting with the guy from the Internet Karen thought, *I'm going to violate my marriage vows. I'm a liar and a deceiver. So is this guy. Whoever he is, I know I won't leave Julian for him. I can never trust this guy because he's doing the same thing as me.*

Karen was shocked to see how she was able to stop listening to herself. She ignored her own thoughts. She just clicked off her mind and went to sleep. Here she was ready to get divorced because Julian wouldn't listen to her. She had an affair so some guy would give her some attention. And yet she didn't listen to herself. She threw herself away to get someone to validate her.

Confronting herself about the affair and her Internet activities helped Karen begin to repair her integrity. She also refused to push Julian for sex any longer. She wasn't willing to accept more "mercy sex." Karen was anxious because there was no way to know how Julian would handle himself. But she operated in ways that have made human beings the wonderful creatures we are: Her desire for integrity caused her to stand up to her fears in ways that busted Julian's monopoly on sex. She refused to have sex on his terms, and she wouldn't settle for lousy sex either. This is how Karen balanced humankind's two most powerful drives, her desire to preserve her marriage and her desire to preserve her self.

Karen's monopoly-busting move made Julian anxious, even though she was ostensibly doing what he demanded (no affairs, no porno). What she was doing took guts, which made her more attractive to him—at the same time it frightened him. Now that she was worth keeping, he was more afraid of losing her. Now she was acting in ways many men would find attractive. He thought it wouldn't be long after they divorced that other men would seek her out. Julian could have escalated an argument, but with Karen acting more solid, he decided to confront himself instead.

## STRONGER FOUR POINTS OF BALANCE MAKES MONOGAMY OPERATE DIFFERENTLY

Julian went through his own crucible over the next several weeks. Karen continued to confront herself about her affair, and the benefits to her were tangible. She looked better and seemed calmer and more solid. She didn't push Julian to confront himself in kind. He knew she was watching to see what he would do, and she had taken away his excuse that she wasn't confronting herself.

At our next session, Julian said to Karen, "I know you're waiting to see if I'm going to address my part in our mess. I've been thinking about this for over a week, so here goes … I felt like you betrayed me. I'm still troubled by the pictures in my head of you having sex with someone else. Maybe my reflected sense of self will get over it. But what else can I expect if I don't have sex with you and the sex we do have is pretty bad? I haven't left you much choice. I guess, in a sense, I've been unfaithful, too. I don't have much room to talk about unfaithfulness." Karen nodded in appreciation but didn't say anything.

"I'm ready to commit that I'll work with Dr. Schnarch on my rapid orgasms and developing more desire. Can you commit to me that you won't have any more affairs?"

Karen thought for a long moment and looked him square in the eye. "No, I can't, Julian."

• *Self-directed rather than controlled*

Julian started to get reactive. "What do you mean?"

Karen stayed calm and steady. "I'm not going to have any more affairs. But I'm not going to promise that to you. It's a commitment I'm making to *me*. I don't want to feel like I have been feeling anymore." Karen paused for a moment. "And I don't want you promising me that you're going to work on the sex. I'm not running after you anymore to make you fulfill your commitments. So if you're going to commit, commit to yourself. I'm not interested in promises, I'm only interested in what you're going to *do*. I'm clear I want to have a sex life. If I'm celibate because I'm so angry with you, I still lose. You aren't going to control me anymore by not having sex. I'm prepared to get divorced if need be."

Karen was defining herself right in front of Julian. She was determined but not belligerent. It helped him keep his reactivity under control. Julian took a long deep breath and replied, "I haven't been a man of my word until now. And you're right, that's really about my lack of commitment to myself. So I guess there's no reason for you to trust me either, although I've complained about not being able to trust you. And you've stuck with me in a way my mother never did with any of her men. Maybe we can work together to earn each other's trust."

"I don't mean to hurt your feelings, Julian, but I'm not interested in earning your trust anymore. I want to earn my own trust."

"I see," said Julian, shocked and disappointed. "I can appreciate what you're saying ... although this isn't what I imagined the path forward would look like."

### • *Monogamy: Commitment to yourself rather than a promise to your partner*

Most couples struggle with commitment at some point, whether it's about sexual exclusivity, moving in together, getting legally married, or having children. It's common to hear, *"Why won't you make a commitment?"* as couples struggle to balance attachment and autonomy. When your mate is taking your lack of commitment personally and his reflected sense of self is wounded, few of us have the presence of mind to ask, *"Commitment to whom? Commitment about what?"*

I've said monogamy is a system and not a promise. But to the degree that monogamy *is* a commitment, the "to whom?" and "about what?" parts are often poorly understood. Karen never gave Julian the commitment he wanted. Karen said she wouldn't have sex with someone else, but she made this vow to *herself* because it was what *she* wanted. She wasn't willing to violate her integrity again to get back at him. Julian was welcome to count on this or not. Whether he trusted her was his problem. *Her* problem was being someone *she* could trust.

### • *Monogamy: Socially imposed or individually determined*

Some experts believe we humans learned to control our sexual impulses because our survival depended on it. Adolescents had to handle themselves around older and more powerful males to advance up the dominance hierarchy. Other experts propose our brain's capacity to preserve peace and order expanded as societies became more complex. Those who couldn't control their sexual impulses were socially ostracized and reduced in number by sexual selection.[121]

One way to think of monogamy is as a social institution, a socially enforced way of behaving. "Society" is social rules enforced by social pressure. Social pressure is group control of your reflected sense of self. Social pressure harnesses your ability to map other people's thoughts about you, and reward-centers in the human brain release dopamine when social rule-breakers are punished![122]

In other words, aspects of this highly sophisticated monogamy system are rooted in interpersonal neurobiology and the operation of your brain. This monogamy system turned your savage forebears into human beings and gave rise to human culture. The kind of monogamy most of us know is externally enforced, whether we feel the pressure to conform coming from our spouse or society at large. This kind of monogamy derives from limited Four Points of Balance, which in turn generates the problems and conundrums we've discussed thus far.

### • *Generosity rather than withholding*

There is a second kind of monogamy based on self-confrontation, self-soothing, non-reactivity, and frustration tolerance. It comes from Solid Flexible Self, Quiet Mind–Calm Heart, Grounded Responding, and Meaningful Endurance. It is something you do for yourself. This kind of monogamy is internally imposed, and operates differently from externally-imposed monogamy. This monogamy prompts generosity rather than withholding, and generates freedom rather than tyranny.

Julian and Karen started having sex more frequently—and better sex, too. She started initiating sex again, and Julian struggled more with himself before he said no. Julian didn't just blow off Karen's initiations or treat her dismissively. When they had sex he was more present, instead of going through the motions. Karen was more accepting and less reactive when Julian didn't want to get together.

Julian also initiated sex more often. He wasn't done with his issues about women, his tendency to be derisive, or his proclivity to feel controlled. But he began to realize his urge to withhold sex was as much about himself as about Karen.

One time Julian found himself thinking about Karen always demanding sex and exploiting him. He realized he was having these thoughts—but he knew they weren't true! He promptly walked over to Karen and initiated sex. Much to his surprise and delight, it was a lovely sexual encounter. This was the beginning of Julian getting a grip on his thoughts and feelings. He developed more self-respect and more sexual desire, which made him more eager to please Karen and be generous with her. Watching him go through this process made Karen respect him and desire him, too.

Their foreplay became more varied and detailed. Often it was slower, less rushed, and more tender, with both partners taking time to pleasure the other. Other times it was playful, or raucous, or daring. Through it all, the intimacy and the meanings were deeper and richer than before. Their foreplay carried the message, *What should we do today?* Rather than *How little can I get away with giving you?*

Well-differentiated monogamy increases your sexual desire. It makes you want to give your partner your sexual best. You still have to struggle with your own laziness and selfishness. There's a mercenary aspect that helps you do this: You realize your partner is a gem—someone other people would snatch up in a moment if your partner entered the dating market. He will be a valuable commodity, sought after by many of your friends, who will be eager to have sex. Keeping your partner sexually happy is simple self-interest. Deliberately withholding sex is self-destructive. It isn't safe to withhold from a partner who makes a monogamy commitment to herself. If she isn't going to put up with nonsense from herself, it's a mistake to think she will put up with it from you.

For sound and logical reasons, monogamy operates differently when driven by your Four Points of Balance. Different things push you to be sexually generous and interested. Karen and Julian no longer felt controlled by each other. Julian no longer felt pressured by Karen's sexual desire. Karen didn't pressure him for sex. It wasn't smart, and she didn't have to: Julian was starting to initiate more, and getting creative with how he did it.

## • *The best in you wants monogamy too*

The best in us wants monogamy for good reasons. Many of us prefer to have sex with just one person we love, particularly if this doesn't involve sexual martyrdom. If we have a choice about having great sex and intimacy, we'd rather stay home than go out. A lot of time and energy is wasted looking for clandestine romance, and many of us don't need the extra complexity. Intimacy is difficult at best. We don't want any additional things standing in the way of the deepest possible connection with our spouse. We don't want the distraction of worrying about passed-on diseases. The romantic in us can like sexual exclusivity, without thinking of our partner as chattel. From what I've seen, as people strengthen their Four Points of Balance (Solid Flexible Self, Quiet Mind–Calm Heart, Grounded Responding, Meaningful Endurance) they decide extramarital affairs aren't worth it.

Notice I didn't say they lose their desire to have sex with new partners. Your Four Points of Balance don't blind you to attractive people who catch your eye. Because of our origins, even the most highly differentiated person will be sexually attracted to others. Becoming well-differentiated doesn't eliminate the inner tensions this creates. Your Four Points of Balance help you tolerate the sexual tension *and handle it cleanly*. It helps you soothe the disappointment, and not blame your partner for it. You keep your reflected sense of self on a tight leash. The same solid sense of self that lets you do this also gives you the backbone to deal with sexual problems and expand your sexual relationship.

• *How do you create a state of blessed monogamy?*

Karen and Julian went through their crucible and emerged more capable of solid desire for each other and for sex. The tyranny of monogamy drives you, your partner, and your family to evolve. It can be another miracle of co-evolution in marriage.

Maybe monogamy is Nature's way of getting you to have a better relationship with yourself. Handled properly, you end up clearer about your own desirability, better able to maintain yourself when your partner pressures you to conform, better able to quiet your disappointments and anxieties, less reactive to your partner, and better able to endure difficult episodes without giving up.

Maybe that's the best way to summarize this chapter: Monogamy is about meaningful endurance, tolerating discomfort for growth. So is real love.

---

### IDEAS TO PONDER

◆ Monogamy is not a promise; it's a *system* involving your Four Points of Balance. Monogamy creates a sexual monopoly, and monopolies control supply. But to the degree that monogamy *is* a commitment, the "to whom?" and "about what?" parts are often poorly understood.

◆ When your Four Points of Balance are weak, monogamy creates low desire. But there is a kind of monogamy that prompts generosity rather than withholding, and generates freedom rather than tyranny.

◆ Turning monogamy from martyrdom into freedom strengthens your Four Points of Balance and enhances desire.

# 7

# Desire
# Fades When
# You
# Stop Growing

*T*o conclude Part Two, I want to tell you about a wonderful couple who came for therapy. Regina and Ellen were a high-functioning dual-income middle-age couple. Regina was a TV producer and Ellen was a successful attorney. Together they raised Ellen's children from her first marriage, who now had families of their own.

Regina and Ellen came for therapy because their sexual frequency was declining and marital discord was growing. Although unusually talented and accomplished in many ways, they were a typical conflict-avoidant couple that "never fought." Their increasing arguments upset them greatly.

Regina was the low desire partner, who initially thought her declining desire was due to menopause (it turned out it wasn't). Regina and Ellen's story illustrates normal desire problems that develop so gradually you don't see them coming.

## • *Regina and Ellen's problem*

Regina and Ellen had desire problems triggered by shifting circumstances in and around their relationship. Approaching retirement age, they were contemplating moving to an exclusive community in another part of the country, where Regina had grown up. Heretofore Regina and Ellen maintained their emotional balance by having separate careers, friends, and money. However the proposed move involved Ellen giving up her law practice and her professional identity and colleagues. Regina planned to work part-time at the TV station where she started her career. She was returning to a town full of former business associates and friends. Ellen wouldn't know anyone there except Regina.

The proposed move unbalanced their relationship, triggering issues that had been situationally held at bay. Regina and Ellen had kept their competitiveness in check by having separate but relatively equal situations. Competitive conflict-avoidant couples often keep everything rigidly equal to prop up their reflected sense of selves. Highly talented couples can maintain this precarious balance for long periods. Now Regina and Ellen were in crisis because circumstances were about to change all that.

## • *Too busy for sex? No time for love?*

Ellen was anxious and somewhat miffed to start with. "This is a much bigger move for me than it is for Regina. I'm not eager to relocate when Regina never wants to have sex with me. I know I'm a little insecure about her being back with all her buddies, but I think I'd be a fool if I presumed everything will get better once we relocate."

Regina deflected her comment gracefully. "Well, I think maybe some of our problem is that we don't have time for each other. I'm on the go most of the time, and Ellen is either in court or preparing to be. We really don't have that much time together. Maybe if we had more time for each other, we'd have more sex."

"I don't think it's a matter of time," Ellen replied.

I said, "I don't think so, either."

Regina turned to me. "What makes you say that?"

"I've never seen a couple whose business responsibilities and out-side activities presented an intractable impediment to resolving desire problems or marital difficulties. I've also never seen a couple where this was the main cause of those difficulties. I remember lots of cases where couples *thought* this was their problem and went on to realize they were wrong. Would you let your job stop you from getting one of the best things in your life, if the sex you were having was that good?"

"How do you know sex between us is not great?" Regina picked up my implication. She was good at mapping minds. She wasn't disputing what I said. She wanted to know how I knew.

"If sex between you was great, I don't think you'd let your busy life-styles stand in the way. You're a pretty determined woman. I presume that's gotten you where you are today. People spend their time where they get the most rewards. Lots of people prefer going to work over going to bed, because that's where they feel they get the most strokes. If sex and intimacy were so rewarding, they might feel torn about the time apart. But, for lots of folks, it's no contest. We like the fairy tale that we just don't have time for each other, and it's just these gosh darn obligations that are in the way."

Regina smiled at me like I had just passed her test. I wasn't settling for superficial answers. It's too easy to dismiss difficult issues by mislabeling them as "hectic lifestyle," "modern life is too complex," and "my demand-ing career leaves no time for us."

Ellen said, "That's what I meant before, when I said I didn't think solv-ing our sexual problem was simply a matter of more time together. Sex doesn't happen very often, and when it does it's not very good."

## • *Regina and Ellen argue about sex*

Competitiveness between spouses is a given. Competition between partners lacking Four Points of Balance becomes a problem. It leads to constant bickering, which can get pretty vicious and mean-spirited. Re-gina and Ellen were better off than some couples I've seen. Their ar-guments weren't really nasty or vituperative. They were more like two highly competitive, talented women, ready to spar with each other at the first sign of trouble.

Regina smoothly fended Ellen off. "It's not my job to script every time we have sex, or do it to your liking. You could propose something new if you wanted to."

Ellen got defensive and turned to me and said, "I'm the one who proposes new things in our relationship. Regina generally doesn't say anything about our sex life, and when I do, it seems like I'm blamed for it. I'm not the only one responsible for making sex interesting. Why doesn't Regina ever suggest something new?"

"Why don't *you* do something new?" Regina countered.

"When I do, you don't seem interested, or you go back to doing what we usually do. I feel rejected and unheard."

"I feel rejected and unheard, too," said Regina.

"Well, you do agree on some things," I said and paused. "You agree you're both feeling rejected and unheard. You agree that something is going wrong, and you agree that someone is to blame. You just disagree about whose fault it is." They both laughed. I had successfully interrupted the cadence of their cycle. "So when you have sex, how do you have it? What do the two of you actually do?"

Neither woman said a word, clearly embarrassed and hoping the other would speak. Regina and Ellen looked at each other and still neither one said anything. Then Regina said, "We grind against each other, pelvis to pelvis, until one of us comes, or we do each other with our fingers. Sometimes we use a vibrator. Sometimes we bring ourselves to orgasm in front of each other."

Without a pause, Ellen said, "Yes, that's right. That's what we do." Then she added, "And I'm sick of it. It's boring!" Regina and Ellen started arguing about who was responsible for sex being boring. I had to wave my hand to catch their attention.

"Of course the two of you are bored. What else could you be? You're normal!" Regina and Ellen looked at me. Regina said, "If you're saying that for effect, Doctor, it's very effective. Telling us we're normal so we'll stop fighting, that's very clever."

"I'm telling you you're normal if you're bored senseless because it's true!"

## SEXUAL BOREDOM IS NORMAL

Ellen and Regina had a normal sexual relationship. At the outset, Regina ruled out sexual behaviors that made her uncomfortable or anxious. Ellen did the same. They did this by dodging anxiety-provoking sexual topics, tracking each other's hesitations, and following each other's lead in bed. Regina and Ellen went along with what the other wanted to do—until someone got nervous or awkward. When that happened, they switched to something else and rarely tried that again. This had nothing to do with being a same-sex couple. Heterosexual couples usually follow this exact same pattern, even if preferred sexual behaviors differ.

Ellen wanted to experiment with a dildo in their lovemaking (they already used a vibrator), but she sensed that made Regina uncomfortable. She had brought the topic up several times in their early years together, but Regina never picked up on it. Actually, Ellen never brought up the topic directly. That was too much self-validated intimacy for Ellen. After several oblique references to dildos, she dropped it.

Ellen also wanted to receive oral sex, and she was quite willing to offer Regina the same. Regina was resistant. The negotiation mostly consisted of mind-mapping, like Ellen positioning her crotch close to Regina's head and Regina going passive or quickly shifting positions.

Like all couples of all sexual persuasions, Regina and Ellen co-created a mental world of sex. The sexual landscape included "the way we make love," "off limits," "way off limits," and the "skirmish area." The dildo was presently off limits. Oral sex was the current controversy and skirmish area for Regina and Ellen.

Oral sex was easier for Ellen to accept than the dildo. She felt this was more mainstream and less kinky, something lots of people did. It was easier for her to validate having this desire. Ellen had brought up oral sex intermittently during their ten years together. They'd squabbled openly about this over the last year and a half. Regina said she wasn't comfortable with it for some reason, she didn't know why. Ellen was tired of waiting for her to figure it out.

Actually, what Ellen really wanted was for Regina to do her with a dildo. She was happy to reciprocate if Regina wanted the same. Specifically,

Ellen wanted to have a particular experience when she climaxed while she and Regina made love. Ellen didn't miss her ex-husband or his penis. Ellen just liked something inside her when she climaxed. Ellen wanted to share this experience with Regina. She was willing to settle for Regina going down on her. That was the point at which they were stuck: For the last two years, when they started talking about moving, the topic of oral sex was also on the table. Nothing ever happened because Regina wasn't comfortable with it. The topic just sat there.

Regina had been lesbian since her adolescence, but she'd never performed oral sex on anyone, woman or man. She'd never done it; she figured she wouldn't like it, and she didn't want to have a bad experience. Aside from potential discomfort with the taste and smell, she was afraid of getting "claustrophobic" with her head between Ellen's legs. Regina's embarrassment about this hesitancy only made things worse.

### • *Off in a new direction*

Regina didn't address oral sex unless Ellen brought it up. When Ellen broached the topic in our session, Regina complained, *"Why do we always have to talk about oral sex?"* Ellen folded and dropped the topic. Regina was taken aback when I took her question seriously.

"You act as if you're asking a question, but do you really want an answer?"

"Answer to what?" she asked guardedly.

"Your question. 'Why do we always have to talk about oral sex?' There's an answer to your question."

"There is?" Regina couldn't figure out where I was headed.

"Yes. And it isn't that Ellen is an oral sex fiend!" Ellen realized I wasn't against her. She relaxed and smiled.

"So tell me. Why do we always have to talk about oral sex?" Regina's tone sounded challenging and demanding.

"Because that's the way marriage works. It's part of all that's left to talk about. Topics vary from couple to couple, but the process is the same. You've talked about all the things you both want to talk about. All that's left to talk about is the stuff you don't want coming up."

Regina realized I wasn't trying to undercut her defenses. I was talking seriously to her. Turning her attack into a serious question presented Regina at her best instead of her worst. "It is?" Regina asked shakily.

"Yes. Every couple has a 'Do we always have to talk about that?' topic. Yours just happens to be oral sex."

"Well, why does ours have to be oral sex?" Regina seemed genuinely interested.

"Because that topic fits the two of you."

"Meaning, we're the kind of people who have difficulty with oral sex?"

"No. You're people who *do* have difficulty dealing with oral sex. That's why it's your 'Why do we have to talk about that?' topic. Topics you can talk about and accommodate each other on are the ones you *don't* have to keep talking about. You talk through them, and you're done with them."

"So why do we keep talking about topics I don't want to talk about?"

"It's the process of elimination."

"What the hell does the process of elimination have to do with why I have to deal with oral sex?"

"The process of elimination is how normal sexual relationships develop."

## • *Sexual relationships always consist of "leftovers"*

Some sexual desire problems occur through the simple process of elimination. In a normal sexual relationship, you get to decide what makes you uncomfortable, which you then rule "off limits." In the name of equality and fairness, your partner gets to do the same. Then, you and your partner do whatever sexual behaviors are left. Regina and Ellen had sex in ways they were comfortable with, and they avoided ways that make them nervous. This is why I say sexual relationships always consist of leftovers. (Later on I'll show you how to turn leftovers into a banquet of delights.)

This is a lot more complex than two people and their hang-ups. The solution isn't as simple as reading *Joy of Sex,* or giving Regina and Ellen permission or instructions to do new things. The process of elimination works slowly and imperceptibly, but it's as unstoppable and as powerful as an ice glacier flowing downhill. The people-growing machinery of marriage is at work. And Nature doesn't build flimsy mechanisms.

## • *People have sex up to the limits of their development*

Normal sexual relationships develop invisibly to most of us, but they work simply and elegantly. You and your partner explore all the mutually acceptable sexual things you are comfortable doing, and through the process of elimination they all lose their novelty. You continue having sex within the boundaries of your current sexual development. Over time, boredom is guaranteed. *Boredom is a given in normal sexual relationships, and not because something is going wrong.*

This is why I say people have sex up to the limits of their sexual development. It's an outgrowth of the normal process of partners eliminating behaviors that make them nervous. Having sex beyond your sexual development means you'll feel uncomfortable. This is how we grow sexually, from your first kiss to whatever else you do now. Growing sexually means tolerating anxiety. Becoming a sexually mature adult involves converting things you initially thought were disgusting and perverted into the way you now make love.

Realizing people have sex up to their level of development helps you understand why couples fight about sexual behaviors. Going forward always creates some level of anxiety. Regina said Ellen needed to respect her sexual preferences and boundaries (in this case, about oral sex). The truth was Regina expected Ellen to live within her sexual limitations.[123] No matter how understanding Ellen was of Regina's feelings, she couldn't change something Regina wouldn't accept about love relationships: They don't always make you feel safe and secure. And you can't postpone some parts until they no longer make you nervous. Repeated experiences of tolerating anxiety and going into the unknown are built into becoming a sexually mature human being. There is no way around this.

Are you having sex beyond *your* development? It's virtually certain you're not. Not if you're having trouble with sexual boredom. The only solution to sexual boredom involves stepping outside your familiar repertoire and creating novelty. This raises your anxiety, challenges your identity, and shakes up your relationship. This calls into play your Four Points of Balance: You have to hold on to your self, calm yourself down, soothe your own feelings, not overreact, and tolerate discomfort for growth.

Novelty is more than new sexual behaviors. It is the opportunity to map out a different part of your partner's sexual mind, her eroticism, or reveal a previously hidden part of yourself. When you realize novelty is mostly mental, you see that couples fighting over *doing* something new are really fighting about *revealing* something new.

### • *Our craving for sexual novelty drives the process*

An essential part of this people-growing process comes from the evolution of our species: In human prehistory, your forebears desired sexual novelty and multiple partners. Anthropologist Helen Fisher suggests our craving for "fresh features" and sexual variety arises from parts of our brain that emerged when humankind first appeared. The tension between our urge for sexual novelty and our desire for pair-bonding drove the evolution of our prefrontal cortex. And because of your prefrontal cortex, it's possible for you to have sexual novelty *and* pair-bonding with a single partner in a long-term relationship. To accomplish this, you have to go through the sexual growth processes that stretch your mind and regulate your brain. Our inherent desire for sexual novelty creates a sexual tension for growth within monogamous relationships.

Some time ago anthropologist Donald Symons proposed that men are more interested in sexual variety than women, due to differences in male and female sexual psychology evolved during hunter-gatherer times. Symons proposed that men who liked sexual variety did a better job of spreading their genes, and over time it evolved that men liked sexual variety more than women.

Helen Fisher doesn't buy this.[124] Helen proposes that "women's biological drive to acquire resources, to obtain an insurance policy, and to secure better or more varied DNA, the potentially intense and long female sexual response, and the high incidence of female adultery in societies where there is no sexual double standard, all suggest that women seek sexual variety regularly, perhaps as regularly as men."[125] She suggests women are just as interested in sexual variety and just as adulterous as men, but for different reasons.

Since the dawn of humankind, women have slept around for fun as well as for goods and services. Sex researcher Alfred Kinsey found that women have extramarital affairs with some regularity, even in cultures which rigorously attempt to control this. Other research indicates women have affairs as often as do the men in societies that have no double standard and permit multiple liaisons.[126]

In other words, the sexual tension created by our desire for sexual novelty does not have its origins in gender differences. That is why it surfaces in lesbian and gay couples, too. The tension between our desire for sexual variety and our desire for pair-bonding and sexual exclusivity arises in all of us, regardless of gender.

So if you were thinking Regina and Ellen's sexual desire problems stemmed from the fact they were lesbian, think again. Gay and lesbian couples have problems with sexual desire just like heterosexual couples. They have many of the same problems for the same reasons. Sexual desire problems stem from the fact you're *human*.

## WHEN YOUR PARTNER BECOMES TOO IMPORTANT TO YOU, DESIRE PROBLEMS SURFACE

Our cunning personal growth system is incredible. Sexual boredom is inevitable because sexual relationships always consist of leftovers, and the only way to resolve boredom is to step outside your comfort zone. There's a second process operating in tandem that also hastens sexual boredom. This equally elegant level kicks into gear from sheer passage of time. It isn't driven by the limits of your sexual development. It's driven by *caring*. In Regina and Ellen's case, it wasn't long before this topic came up. Ellen said, "I don't feel very cared about by you."

Regina replied, "I don't feel very cared about, either. I don't feel very important in your life."

I spoke up. "I know you think both of you are entitled to your feelings, but I don't think they're good indicators of what's going on. I think one problem is you're *too* important to each other. You're more important to each other than you are to yourselves. Your partner is preoccupied with what you think about her, and afraid and intolerant of your disapproval. Feeling unimportant is just your reflected sense of self complaining."

Ellen was triggered. "How on earth can we be too important to each other? How can *anyone* be too important? It's good to feel other people care about you."

"That's true. But being important to someone who can't stand on her own two feet doesn't feel as good as you think."

### • *You can't innovate*

Everyone believes caring about your partner is important in a good relationship. Everyone wants to be cared for. No one realizes how your level of emotional development makes this play out. When you care for your partner but her importance to you exceeds the strength of your Four Points of Balance, it creates desire problems.

As your partner becomes more important to you, sexual boredom becomes more likely. It's harder to innovate sexually, because as her opinion grows more important to you than your own, you won't risk her rejection. Sooner or later you reach a point where you won't take off your sexual mask. The weaker your Four Points of Balance are, the quicker you reach that fateful point when you won't reveal hidden sides of yourself by proposing something new.

Ellen and Regina struggled with this inevitable tyranny of perpetual accommodation. Ellen was afraid of upsetting Regina by letting Regina see what her eroticism was really like. She envisioned a lengthy cross-examination from Regina about "where has this been hiding?" Ellen didn't want to risk disrupting the relationship—or being worked over by Regina. She was stuck in her false persona because she didn't show her eroticism to Regina at the outset of relationship.

Lots of low-desire women are actually incredibly *carnal*. They are the end result of millions of years of women being bred for sex through sexual selection. These are women—more common than you might think—who love sex, thrill to it, and "want to be rode hard and put away wet," as my Texan client says. These women hide this (and past experiences with other partners) at the outset of the relationship, reinforcing a false persona in their partners' mind. Years later, they follow their partner's lead through sex, bored out of their minds and frustrated with their sex lives. They have little desire for sex because the sex they're having isn't worth wanting.

### • Sexual novelty is always introduced unilaterally

Sexual novelty is always introduced unilaterally. You and your partner are already doing everything sexual that is mutually agreeable, which has left you with leftovers. Your partner probably doesn't want to do anything new you propose, because it is beyond her current sexual development. (Unless you're proposing what your partner wants that you've previously refused to do.)

This means your partner isn't likely to applaud your new sexual proposals. You're more likely to hear, "You want to do *what*?" than "Thanks for sharing!" And count on having to make your proposal more than once.

Our discussion about intimacy (Chapter 6) applies here: Sexual boredom results from dependence on other-validated intimacy. Depending on your partner for validation, as opposed to being able to validate yourself, makes you unable to innovate or create sexual novelty. With weak Four Points of Balance, you won't propose something new and daring like oral sex (or using a dildo). It's easier to just let things be boring.

### • Introducing novelty reveals your erotic mind

Sex gets boring because it's hard to let your partner map parts of your mind that you've previously shielded. It reveals a heretofore undisclosed part of your psyche. The big hurdle in sex isn't letting your partner see your body. Saying, "Why don't we do *this*!" reveals your erotic mind. Letting your partner get a fuller picture of you is daunting regardless of the topic. Revealing your eroticism is a particular challenge to your Four Points of Balance. Using self-validated intimacy to show your hidden sexy side builds your Solid Flexible Self, Quiet Mind–Calm Heart, Grounded Responding, and Meaningful Endurance.

What interests you? What do you fantasize about? What really floats your boat? The big hurdle to making sex interesting is letting your partner map your mind where your eroticism lurks.

- *When your partner's importance exceeds your Four Points of Balance, there are limited possibilities*

Poorly balanced people get a reflected sense of self from how they act, including what they do and don't do sexually. When they change their behavior, they lose their identity. They feel as though they have given up who they really are, and given in to their partner, which makes them resentful, rebellious, and indignant. Any request for change is taken as a criticism, insult, and rejection of who they are now, which justifies not changing. The fact that people have sex up to their level of development, and going beyond that raises anxiety, magnifies this reaction to all requests for changing the sexual routine.

Facing the choice between boredom and sexual novelty freaks people out. This occurs in other relationship areas too. It develops anywhere you want your partner's approval, but you don't want to change, and he or she doesn't want to live within your limitations. This can happen when your partner complains, but he or she doesn't have to say a word. If you're desperate for your partner's validation, all it takes is you knowing he or she wants things to be different. When your partner becomes more important than your Four Points of Balance can handle, you are confronted by a set of choices you don't want. The way marriage works, there are four possibilities: (a) dominate your partner, (b) "submit" to your partner, (c) withdraw physically or emotionally from your partner, or (d) strengthen your Four Points of Balance. (One LDP at our Passionate Marriage® Couples Enrichment Weekend described his choices as fight, freeze, flee, or fuck.) Guess what most people choose?

For Regina and Ellen and countless couples, the correct answer is "all of the above." Choosing to strengthen your Four Points of Balance usually comes last. Regina and Ellen had do go through the other options first. First, Regina tried dominating Ellen when she brought up oral sex by refusing to talk about it. When Ellen persisted, Regina shifted to option two: She agreed to talk about it, but acted like this was a huge sacrifice and burden. They had several brief conversations in which she made it clear she wasn't happy doing oral sex, and that was suppose to be the end of that. Regina then moved to option three: She withdrew physically and emotionally for almost a month. However, none of these moves solved Regina's problem. Ellen was still too important. Ellen's mere desire to change their sexual relationship felt to Regina like a demand.

Regina thought a lot about getting out of the relationship, and decided she wanted to stay. Having exhausted her other options, Regina chose to strengthen her Four Points of Balance to counterbalance Ellen's growing importance to her, though she didn't think of it that way at the time. Regina decided she had to step up to the plate and face her sexual anxieties and discomforts.

- *Your partner becomes too important, even if you don't like him or her*

When I say your partner becomes increasingly important to you, that doesn't mean you like or love her more. It simply means your partner becomes more central in your life. Things like joint bank accounts, raising kids, and having mutual friends and linked identities will do it. Co-parenting after divorce still gives your partner a pivotal role in your life (presuming you want to see your children). If you're lucky enough to have a partner you love, the greater and longer your love, the more she becomes irreplaceable.

Sooner or later, depending on your Four Points, your partner becomes *too* important to desire. Low desire surfaces as you attempt to diminish the tremendous impact she has on your life now and the eventual loss you'll feel when she dies. For Regina and Ellen, their impending relocation and alteration of lifestyle, friends, and finances exceeded the strength of their Four Points of Balance. This move was saying they were life-mates.

You don't have to have something going wrong in your relationship to have sexual desire problems. All you need is the mere passage of time. The forces of differentiation will catch up with you. When your partner becomes more important to you than the strength of your Four Points of Balance, you can start kissing sex goodbye. This is often why desire fades in long-term relationships: Maintaining sexual desire requires continued growth. Unfortunately, lots of us think we don't have to grow once we're a couple because our partner has to accept us as we are.

## ANXIETY-REGULATION THROUGH ACCOMMODATION

In the same way things go on between partners that trigger and support growth, there are things that limit it. Our animal nature leads us to avoid discomfort. Mammals evolved group behaviors that reduce anxiety (herding being a prime example). When our reflected sense of self showed up, human interpersonal anxiety regulation became incredibly more sophisticated—and terribly more important. Clever humans evolved interactions that regulate their anxiety but don't involve growth.

People regulate their anxieties by interacting with others, the same way they regulate their reflected sense of self. I call this *anxiety regulation through accommodation.* By giving in, accommodating, and avoiding particular topics, one partner can regulate both partners' anxieties. It also happens by giving up on contentious issues when challenged ("folding"). This pattern is normal, everyone does it—and sometimes it's the best thing to do. However, couples who normally *depend* on anxiety regulation through accommodation have great difficulty curing sexual boredom.

It didn't take much challenge for Ellen to fold. Her fear of upsetting Regina and embarrassing herself was more than enough. Ellen told herself she was being considerate of Regina in not bringing it up. Actually, Ellen couldn't handle her anxiety when Regina got upset or angry—and Regina usually got upset and angry when she was nervous. In fact, Ellen told herself she was virtuous at the very moment she was being irresponsible. This helped her avoid the fact that she was really ducking out.

But folding like this made Ellen more dependent on Regina. Having dodged a clear and accurate presentation of herself, all she could go on was Regina's acceptance. Dependence on anxiety regulation through accommodation and dependence on a reflected sense of self usually go hand in hand, being natural outcomes of weak Four Points of Balance.

Reflexive anxiety regulation through accommodation is the opposite of the Second and Third Points of Balance (Quiet Mind–Calm Heart and Grounded Responding). Trying to regulate the anxiety of the people around you is an indirect way of regulating yourself.

All relationships involve anxiety regulation through accommodation to some degree. But depending on it makes relationships brittle and inflexible because everything focuses on anxiety reduction per se. This rules out sexual novelty and intimacy (because these create anxiety) and promotes sexual boredom.

It's easy to get hooked on anxiety regulation through accommodation because it works so well. It seems like the essence of a loving marriage at the outset. You and your partner both feel better, so you do it repeatedly and come to expect it. You never think you're setting something in motion that will eventually confront you.

### • Sooner or later, the house of cards falls down

Life circumstances impact your sexual desire, especially if they uncork long-standing issues.

On top of issues about commitment, power, and control, and the logistical problems of relocating, Regina and Ellen were experiencing intense identity crises that happen when your reflected sense of self is adrift without moorings.

Regina was undone when Ellen pressed her to retire completely. Because she had a reflected sense of self, the prospect of losing her professional identity meant losing her identity altogether. Regina was incredibly accomplished and talented. She loved the adrenalin-sparked pace, and the status and respect she had from other professionals in the industry. Regina's sense of self was tied up in her work.

Although they wouldn't admit it, Regina and Ellen were extremely status conscious. In their minds, they focused on equality and equity. But once they got triggered about who had the upper hand, or who was looking down on whom, their reflected sense of self ran away with them. They snapped at each other and then fell into cold awkward silences.

Even "high functioning" couples like Regina and Ellen have sexual desire problems. Keeping sex alive in long-term marriage requires continued personal development, greater self-clarity, less reactivity, better self-soothing, and going through tough times: strong Four Points of Balance.

## (LACK OF) DESIRE, INTIMACY, FREEDOM, AND SEXUAL NOVELTY PROMPT YOU TO GROW

Regina and Ellen argued so frequently about sex, their arguments were as predictable as their sexual interactions. Here too, any change in routine had a big impact. In my office Regina said, "I think oral sex is all Ellen thinks about these days." This was a dig, delivered as news.

Instead of launching into her typical self-defense, Ellen looked down for several seconds. "No. Actually I've been thinking about one other thing."

Regina sprang to engage. "What is that?"

"I've been thinking I want you to screw me with a dildo."

"*What?*" Regina was as shocked as Ellen was pleased.

"I've always wanted you to do me with a dildo. I made a few overtures when we first got together, but you never picked up on it, and I took it as a signal you weren't interested. I've never had the nerve to say this the entire time we've been together."

Regina stopped to think about how she wanted to handle this. "Why didn't you say something if it's what you really wanted?" Regina's tone made it sound like she had nothing to do with Ellen not asking.

"I didn't have the nerve. I was embarrassed. I was young and thought it was kinky. I was switching from men to women and I thought that was kinky enough. Asking you to screw me with a dildo was just too much. I thought you'd think of me as a heterosexual woman hooked on having something inside her. Now I'm more sexually mature. I simply see it as being a woman who likes something inside me when I come. Sue me."

Ellen's "sue me" was perfectly delivered as the attorney she was. She was making a declaration of selfhood. Regina said, "Well, faced with the choice of having oral sex or doing you with a dildo ... well, that's a choice I never thought I'd face! Quite honestly, I don't know which I'd choose."

Ellen laughed. "Are you kidding? You're not sure which one you'd choose? I was sure you'd choose oral sex over doing me with a dildo. It's much easier for me to ask you for oral sex."

"That's your hang-ups talking, honey. To me, they'd be the same size step: *Huge!*"

I spoke up. "What kind of huge step?"

Regina paused. "I'd have to confront my eroticism and my hang-ups."

"In what way?"

Again a pause. "I'd have to get past the taste thing with oral sex. I get worried that I'm not going to like the taste. I know I'm not supposed to have this issue because I'm lesbian, but I do."

Ellen spoke up. "I don't think that's a lesbian thing. I had the same thing when I started giving guys blowjobs. It's no fun until you get over that. But I got over it, and you can too. Once I did, I got real good at it. I could show you a good time, if you'll let me."

Regina didn't flatly refuse. "We'll see. I'm not promising anything. Having my head forced down there doesn't do good things for me."

"I understand. I've been there, too."

"Besides the taste thing, I have to get over you seeing me enjoy it."

"You don't want me seeing you enjoying it?" Ellen was amazed.

"I've told you, I like being behind the camera. I don't like being in front of it. I get weird about being seen as being sexual, really getting into things. It's like you know too much of me." Regina paused momentary. "But it may be easier for me to do you with a dildo."

Ellen smiled. "Maybe. We'll see!"

Regina and Ellen shared a moment of mutual appreciation. Their sexual relationship had reached a new level. There was no need to ask the other to confirm it. Everything rang true. Each could read the other's mind.

## • *How do you stand up?*

What makes someone finally stand up and redefine their self? It's not enough to say humans are sexually curious animals who are easily bored. It has to do with what makes us unique. Eventually, your integrity and self-respect kick in. Feeling like you've sold yourself out—and your desire for interesting sex—motivates you to do it.

How can you change without losing your identity? Actually, that's not the way it works. You have to change *and struggle with the feeling of, "Is this really me?"* You're usually not calm, and you don't feel secure in yourself. You have to do something that is "not you yet"—but fits who you want to be—and live through it until it becomes "the new you." Revealing your hidden sexual self often creates a growth-spurt because your Four Points of Balance come into play.

## • *The need to tolerate anxiety is part of the system*

*Anxiety-tolerance*, rather than anxiety reduction, lies at the core of how relationships and sexuality work. Enduring anxiety for growth is built into becoming a sexually mature adult. Each step in development, from French kissing to your first intercourse to your first oral sex, involves doing something you're uncomfortable with until you're not uncomfortable anymore. Every step involves mastering your anxiety rather than having no anxiety at all.

This is possible because we are primarily self-soothing animals, not wounded children. Our primary way of soothing ourselves involves giving our dilemmas meaning. When things become sufficiently meaningful to us—and we become sufficiently anxious about the outcomes—we tolerate pain for growth and face our own anxiety.

What made Regina and Ellen face sensitive issues they'd always dodged in the past? All the structure of their lives was falling away. Ellen decided it was better to face their sexual issues now, when they were setting up their new life together. It was also in her interest to get this cleared up now, before she uprooted herself and moved.

Next session Regina and Ellen told me the details of their sexual encounter. It was clear they'd had a good time. Once Regina relaxed, oral sex wasn't nearly as awkward or unpleasant as she'd imagined. She shifted her focus from avoiding a bad time to focusing on making Ellen moan. Ellen alternated between letting herself luxuriate in the sensations, appreciating the meaningfulness of their interaction, and watching Regina go down on her. She saw a side of Regina that warmed her heart and curled her toes. They shared a powerful moment of meeting that made them hopeful about their future. The combination was more than enough to put her into orbit. Ellen's delicious orgasm put a smile on Regina's face.

## • *Our reluctance to grow*

People like to espouse the desire to grow throughout their lifetimes. Supposedly "it's the journey, not the destination." But the truth is, once we're in an emotionally committed relationship, we think it's safe to slack off. Growing is often a pain in the butt. We don't really want to grow, we just want the benefits of being grown. The growing part we could do without. This is where the Fourth Point of Balance comes in: Meaningful Endurance for growth.

Throughout Part Two we've seen how partners continually—and often unwittingly—push each other to evolve (co-evolution). Human nature is part of an interpersonal system that pushes you to grow. It is normal in sexual relationships to experience sexual boredom, emotional gridlock, and to feel rejected and unwanted. Problems even happen through partners becoming too important to each other. The intricate interplay between differentiation and sexual desire takes many forms. You have to keep growing if you want to keep sexual desire alive.

You can be too important to your partner, too important for your partner to show you her secret sexual side, and reveal the things she really likes to do.[127] The same thing can keep you from going after the sex you really want. We all want to be important to someone, especially the people we love. *But it's no virtue to be important to someone who can't hold on to herself or himself.* It's the reason country-western ballads croon, "She was more important to me than I was to myself," and whine about getting screwed in a divorce instead of having fun in the sack.

—————————— IDEAS TO PONDER ——————————

- Desire problems arise when your partner becomes more important to you than you are to yourself.
- Sexual relationships always consist of "leftovers." People have sex up to the limits of their Four Points of Balance. The solution to sexual boredom involves stepping outside your familiar repertoire and creating novelty. This raises your anxiety, challenges your identity, and shakes up your relationship.
- Sexual novelty is always introduced unilaterally. Couples fighting over *doing* something new are really fighting about *revealing* something new. If your Four Points of Balance are weak, you can't create sexual novelty.

# Sexual Desire Problems: How Your Personal Life Fits In

# 8

# Wanting, Not Wanting to Want, and Two-Choice Dilemmas

hus far we've seen why and how normal healthy people have sexual desire problems. These are universal problems that can lead to personal growth. (I'll show you several more in this chapter.)

In Part Three, we'll focus on how your life experiences influence your sexual desire. We've laid out the relationship context, the interrelatedness, in which our particular experiences play out. The combination of normal relationship processes, idiosyncratic personal experiences, and our response to them, shape our lives and our desire. We experience sexual desire problems against the background of our life, past and present. These experiences can make sexual desire problems more likely to happen, more complex to resolve, and more powerful and impactful on our lives.

How does this actually happen? It stems from the same thing that makes your sexuality special. What makes your desire different from all other species? What makes your sexual desire uniquely *human*? What makes your sex more than barnyard rutting? The answer to all these questions is your capacity to bring meaning to sex, which is rooted in the evolution of the human brain. The meanings you bring to sex can greatly enhance or diminish your sexual relationship.

But how are those meanings determined? I don't mean your sexual values or intellectualizations. I'm referring to how sex, desire, and intimacy are emotionally and physically wired in your brain. The themes that dominate your relationships and sex life are your sexual dynamics, what make you tick. This is largely learned. Experiences with other people greatly influence which meanings dominate your sexuality—for better or worse. To the degree you haven't dealt with negative life experiences, you don't know how they influence the meanings you bring to sex, and you can't do anything about them.

## DESIRE: A CAPACITY YOU CAN DEVELOP

In Part Two we saw how marriage is a people-growing process. In Part Three we'll apply what we've learned to you and help you increase your capacity for desire. *Desire is a capacity you can develop.* It's not simply a biological drive. But it's not as simple as removing sexual hang-ups or increasing your libido. It's about increasing your *capability*.

People are capable of much greater and more meaningful desire than you may realize. This is especially true as we grow older. Your capacity for desire typically increases as you age. Some couples solve desire problems later in life that they simply couldn't handle when they were younger. In reality, aging and sexual potential are highly correlated.

This way of approaching desire might seem odd had we not seen how love relationships are people-growing processes. It should seem intuitive now that stronger Four Points of Balance (Solid Flexible Self, Quiet Mind–Calm Heart, Grounded Responding, Meaningful Endurance) increase your *capacity* for desire. It also changes the *nature* of your desire.

Increasing your sexual desire is not just about wanting sex. If that were the case, desire problems would be simpler. *Human sexual desire is about desiring your partner, and not just desiring sex, per se.*

You can desire your partner but not want sex. You can also desire sex but not desire your partner. That's true for lots of people. It's a common source of low desire in marriage. Sometimes your low desire reflects your partner's undesirable characteristics. But you need to confront yourself: Does it reflect your own limited ability to care for and want another person?

## • *Think of Desire as Wanting*

Desire isn't a biological drive that drags you into bed and takes you along for the ride. Human desire is more active. Think of desire as *wanting*.

Do you hunger for intimacy, love, and profound union? Do you crave sexual desire that borders on spiritual desire? If so, developing your Four Points of Balance will enable you to *want* more deeply. People who have difficulty quieting their mind, soothing their feelings, or handling hard times don't *want* very well. Some find the discomfort of *wanting* so intolerable that they don't let themselves want sex or their partner.

Desire is complicated. You can *want* from the best in you, or from the worst. You can *want* from what is good and solid in you, or what is weak, empty, and covetous. For some HDPs, it's just their reflected sense of self seeking an emotional transfusion. Wanting from neediness is fairly automatic (if you let yourself want at all). Wanting from your solid flexible self takes personal development.

## • *Tom and Helen*

Helen and Tom were a couple in their thirties. When they first came to see me, they had lived together for several years but were not legally married. Both had been legally married once (to other people). Tom and Helen argued over frequency of sex, and whether or not to get married.

Tom was the LDP and Helen was the HDP. Sex was pretty good when they had it. They'd had sex four or five times a week when they first met. But after four years together, they were down to less than every other month. Tom said he wasn't interested in sex because they were always fighting about getting married. Helen said sex dropped to its current level less than a year into their relationship, when getting married wasn't an issue.

Tom said he didn't want to make another mistake, referring to his first marriage. He said his own parents were poor role models, who divorced when he was thirteen. Tom felt he needed to be sure he wanted to get married.

Helen understood Tom's feelings, because she didn't want to make another mistake either. But over the last year she kept asking Tom to decide what he wanted. Did he want to have sex? Did he want to get married? Helen loved Tom, but she was ready to move on, having spent three years on these issues with no end in sight.

Helen felt stuck because Tom couldn't decide. He didn't consider these questions when she didn't push him. When she did, he complained. When Helen said she was losing hope, Tom said she was giving up their relationship prematurely. Why wouldn't she give him a little more time? Tom said he knew what he *didn't* want: He didn't want to have sex, he didn't want to get married and divorce again, and he didn't want to give Helen up.

## • *The strength to want*

Desire has a compelling quality: It's a tremendous motivation. Our desires mobilize us. Desire propels you to alleviate your deprivations. It can make you move mountains to get something you truly want.

But wanting takes energy. It takes effort to get what you want. And there's no guarantee that your wants will be fulfilled. You have to want *first*, before you know how things turn out. In this way sex is no different from marriage, parenthood, or your career. Wanting creates the space in which our highest aspirations come into being.

One poignant part of wanting—the part people strive to avoid—involves deprivation. Desire is the feeling that accompanies an unsatisfied state. Wanting, itself, creates a state of deprivation. Wanting puts you in the condition of being without. In an earlier usage, *to want* means *to be lacking*.

*Wanting* entails wishing, craving, and yearning for someone or something. *Wanting* is about longing, and longing is painful. Longing is persistent desire for something or someone continually unattainable or distant. When you *want* your partner and *want* sex, you've got powerful sexual motivation. But that means you must have the strength to *want*.

*Wanting* differentiates your desire from the sexual desire of other species. It elevates your sexual desire beyond a hormonal rush or reproductive drive.[128] Besides lust, infatuation, and attachment needs, humans have the capacity to cherish another person. This means acting in the best interest of another, even at our own expense, because we want the best for them. Earlier I said your desires don't necessarily arise out of the best in you. So don't confuse *wanting* with these four things:

1. *Wanting* is not about desiring your partner to do something for you. It's not the same as wanting him to pay attention to you, or to make you feel secure and desirable.

2. *Wanting* doesn't make your partner a criminal, the way the police want a fugitive. Wanting doesn't give you permission to make your partner a prisoner.

3. *Wanting* is more than an urge to merge. Wanting your partner is about a desire for *her*. It surfaces as concern for her separate interests, even when they don't line up with yours. Wanting obliges you to act in her best interests, because her welfare and happiness is intrinsic to yours.

4. *Wanting* is not being covetous, possessive, or jealous. Possessiveness and jealousy masquerade as profound desire, but they stem from weakness. True wanting stretches your Four Point of Balance.[129]

## • *Tom and Helen's backgrounds*

I've said desire is a capacity you can develop by expanding the depth and scope of meanings you bring to it. Tom's meanings could be summarized in a single sentence: *If you love me, you will …*

After Tom's parents divorced, he lived with his mother. Times were hard. Mother struggled to keep them fed with a roof over their heads.

She worked hard and expected Tom to help around the house. But more than that, Mother expected Tom to make her life easier since she worked so hard. During his adolescence, it was a rare day that Tom's mother didn't say, *"If you love me, you'll do this for me. Look at all I do for you!"*

Tom hated when his mother said this. When he was younger, he worked hard to appease her. When he got older, he walked out when she harangued him. He'd heard it all before. He became more defiant and reactive to his mother saying, *"If you love me, you will …"*

Tom became a young man who didn't want to want. Wanting produced feelings he didn't handle well. Mother used Tom's desire to please her against him. It made him an easy target for her manipulations. Over time, wanting her to be happy was tantamount to offering himself up to do whatever she wanted.

In our initial session Tom said, "I guess it made me somewhat leery of women. My mother was a pretty controlling and manipulative woman. She had to be. She had to take care of herself and me. She didn't get any help from my Dad. Maybe the reason I hesitate to get married—maybe the reason I don't want to have sex—is because I'm afraid Helen is going to turn into my mother." Tom thought he had made it to safe ground.

I asked, "Is that why you haven't chosen Helen yet?"

Tom looked surprised. "I never thought of myself as not choosing Helen. Maybe that's why I haven't asked her to marry me."

## CHOOSING YOUR PARTNER

Part of *wanting* involves *choosing*. Choosing means selecting one person among the many you could want. Choosing requires making a decision (hopefully involving deliberation) and arriving at a selection. Choosing is a deliberate act of will and judgment. Choosing is the co-evolutionary process of self-definition. Choosing is self-creation. Choosing is how we become the self we want.

Choosing involves selecting some life options and forgoing others. When you choose your partner, you relinquish other possibilities. By making choices and living with them, you become clear about who you are, and more adept at the Four Points of Balance. Part of getting what you *want* involves accepting the loss of paths not taken, in the process of fulfilling your heart's desire.

Lots of people have difficulty with wanting and choosing. Testosterone and estrogen don't choose, and choosing and bonding are different: Mammals mate with the best available partner when their hormones kick in. Highly intelligent animals may have a rudimentary capacity for choosing, but only humans have the degree of choice that we do.

Choice became part of human sexual desire in the sociobiological adaptation that changed your ancestors' bodies and minds millions of years ago, when women's sexual biology changed. Unlike other primates, women shifted to inconspicuous ovulation, which gave them more control of their sexuality. As women had more ability to modulate their sex, they evolved a brain that could control it.[130]

As they developed a mind that could choose, they chose partners whom they wanted. One factor in whom they chose was driven by their reflected sense of self. Humans learned to signal desire through nuances of language and behavior, rather than the appearance of genitals. These same nuances got them the reflected sense of self they wanted.

Choice is how humankind's emerging self shaped the body that housed it. Through millions of years of sexual selection, women probably bred men for two things they liked. One was a man's capacity to engage with women's personal emerging self. This hastened the co-evolution of the prefrontal neocortex. The other, according to some anthropologists, was that women bred men to have long and thick penises.[131] If that doesn't illustrate the power of sexual selection, nothing will.

Women's conscious control of their sexual desire laid the foundation for our ability to bring meaning to sex. Choice is a primary activity of selfhood. It's how we define ourselves.

When humans started having sex for more than lust, infatuation, and attachment, they also *stopped* having sex because of those same reasons. Going at it "self to self," and not just genitals to genitals, took sex to new heights and lows. When our reflected sense of self showed up, issues of power common in all primates took on entirely new proportions. At some point in prehistory, there had to be the first man with a small penis who had the first feelings of sexual inadequacy.

We have the capacity to choose a partner, but that doesn't mean everyone exercises this ability. Not everyone chooses the partner they marry. Many people don't. *In many marriages, one partner chose the other, and the other got married because he didn't have to choose.*

### • *Letting yourself want your partner*

Countless LDPs have told me, "I don't have those kinds of feelings of desire for my partner," making it sound specific to this person. When we looked deeper they often fit this rule: People with weak Four Points of Balance don't want to *want*. *Wanting* makes them nervous. There's anxiety in choosing a partner, so they don't choose. Living with someone doesn't mean you've picked each other. If you lack Four Points of Balance, the vulnerability in choosing is just too much.

In the last chapter we saw that desire problems surface when your partner becomes more important to you than you are to yourself. When you choose someone, her importance grows exponentially. Suddenly you're in a situation that may be more than your Four Points of Balance (Solid Flexible Self, Quiet Mind–Calm Heart, Grounded Responding, Meaningful Endurance) can handle.

This was Tom's situation. Tom didn't want Helen to be more important to him. Tom was too dependent on a reflected sense of self. He couldn't handle the real and imagined vulnerability that came from choosing. By not choosing Helen, Tom kept the emotional maelstrom within him in check. Tom modulated Helen's importance in his life to compensate for his difficulty holding on to himself. As it was, he could barely keep his emotional balance. Choosing Helen would grant her privileged status in his life. Tom couldn't handle her being that important.

In choosing your partner, you bring her inner world into your mental reality. (Accurate mind-mapping is important.) You consider her inner world when you deliberate about your own life, with all its complications, frustrations, and limitations. This invariably limits your choices (which poorly differentiated people experience as being controlled or suffocated).

You can't choose your partner if you can't hold on to your self. That's why Tom couldn't choose Helen: It wasn't that he couldn't make up his mind; he couldn't handle the emotional impact of making a choice.

Why couldn't Tom handle Helen becoming more important to him? This is where Tom's history with his mother comes in: Tom's experiences with his mother's *If you love me, you'll give me what I want …* made him keep his emotional investments in check, lest they be used against him. Helen's growing importance in their first year together triggered his sexual withdrawal. As his caring for her increased and she became a more central figure in his life, this triggered his fears that she would use this to manipulate him.

An inability to maintain your own sense of self makes you afraid the Chosen One will swallow you whole. Without some solid sense of self and the ability to regulate your own anxiety, you don't have much free choice in your life. That includes the ability to choose your partner.

You can see this in how Tom and Helen got together. Tom's first post-divorce girlfriend had just dumped him, and Helen had recently separated from her husband. A few movies and dinners later, things got sexual, and they began to think of themselves as a couple. Because both were on the rebound, they agreed to just date and see what happened. Neither was ready to make a big commitment, and they didn't want to ruin things by discussing it.

As they spent more time together, separate housing became a real bother. After six months, Tom sort of moved in with Helen. In some ways it was no big deal, because half his wardrobe was already at her house. There was never a clear discussion of what this meant between them. Helen didn't want to push Tom, and Tom didn't want to discuss it. He said it was wonderful to be together, and they should just enjoy it and see what happened.

Fast forward three years and things look different. Tom still wanted to live with Helen, but he didn't want sex and he wasn't ready to marry her. And there was Helen, with Tom in her house, without him ever making an active decision to be there. Looking back, she could see how they got from where they started to where they were now: They ignored the difficult questions about what they meant to each other.

- *The importance of being chosen*

Tom didn't want to choose Helen, but he didn't want to lose her, either. To cover up, he fended off Helen's attempts to map his mind. He deliberately said things to implant a false picture in Helen's mind. Perhaps Tom feared Helen would turn into his mother, but Tom was actually the one playing out his mother's dynamic. Tom's message throughout their sexual relationship was *If you really love me, you will stay with me with or without sex and make me happy.*

Then there was the problem of Helen needing to feel chosen. Her reflected sense of self relied on being chosen and wanted. Helen needed to be chosen for the same reasons Tom didn't want to choose: limited Four Points of Balance. This explains why millions of people are like Helen. But it doesn't explain why Helen is one of them.

Helen's family was in shambles growing up. Her father gambled and drank. Her mother ran the house with the money she made. Her father squandered everything else. Helen's parents spent most of their time fighting with her older brother. He was her one ray of hope, running interference for her in their house. But he went to prison for car theft when Helen was fourteen and died in a brawl with other inmates. Helen had a series of fruitless love affairs over the next decade, followed by a brief marriage and a messy divorce. By the time she met Tom, she was ripe for anyone who would be nice to her.

The meaning Helen brought to sex was, *I'm glad just to be allowed to participate, you don't have to pick me.* Her need to be wanted didn't mean she held out for someone who really wanted her. Quite the contrary. She lied to herself about Tom the same way she lied to herself about her parents. Growing up, she had learned the advantages of being helpful and not asking for much. Her parents were nicer when they needed her to do something. If she doted on them, sometimes they would actually be quite pleasant.

- *Do you want to be wanted but need to be needed?*

Helen doted on Tom in bed. She was an attentive and active partner, eager to please. She didn't complain if she didn't orgasm. She made sure Tom had his orgasm. If he didn't feel like reciprocating, that was okay too.

I said to Helen, "It sounds like you do the wanting for both of you."

"I'm better at it than Tom."

I continued. "You make it sound like a virtue. I think you do the wanting for both of you because you think Tom can't do it, and you don't expect him to. But your wanting doesn't come from the best in you. It stems from your neediness, not because you're stronger."

Helen got what I was saying, but it made her defensive. "Well, I think I chose Tom. Tom didn't choose me."

"In many marriages, one partner chooses the other, and the other partner gets married because he doesn't have to choose. Tom never chose you because he didn't have to or want to. You chose him out of your difficulty keeping your emotional balance. He *didn't* choose you, because of his similar difficulty holding on to himself. Lots of couples dodge the thorny question of 'who picked whom?'"

"I want Tom to want *me,* and not just for sex."

"You're understating things. You *need* him to want you."

Helen got defensive. "There's nothing wrong with wanting Tom to need me. It makes me feel important to him."

"Yes, it does. But it interferes with you getting what you say you want."

"How so?"

"You want Tom to want you, to choose you?"

"Yes."

"And you want him to need you?"

"Yes."

"Unfortunately, as long as Tom needs you, he can't really choose you. It's not really much of a choice."

"Ohh …"

"You may want to be wanted, but your shaky reflected sense of self needs the security of being needed. You make yourself indispensable to your partner."

"Ohhhh…" Helen's eyes widened.

"So who keeps you from being chosen? Ultimately, you do—through your need to be needed."

"Ohhhhhhhh …" From that moment, Helen began dealing with never having been chosen. She confronted herself about conveniently ignoring that Tom had never chosen her. From then on, Helen developed a single-minded focus. She wanted to be with someone who had the backbone to choose her.

"I guess I've been tolerated all my life. I've glommed on to anyone who would have me. I know my first husband never choose me. His first choice was to marry another woman, but she married someone else so he married me. I'm clearly not Tom's overwhelming choice. I settle for men who like me to keep them company. They can see I don't expect them to choose me." Helen glanced at Tom and then at me. "Maybe I'm kidding myself. I know I have my shortcomings. But I think I deserve to be with someone who really wants me!" She sounded determined.

## CONSCIOUSLY CHOSEN, FREELY UNDERTAKEN DESIRE

When I said earlier you could expand your desire, I was referring to *consciously chosen, freely undertaken desire*. Choosing and wanting are large parts of your desire.

Another level of desire involves your intentionality. The 1940s singer Al Jolson crooned, "You made me love you! I didn't want to do it! I didn't want to do it! You know you made me love you!" Obviously loving and choosing don't necessarily go hand in hand. You can be in love with someone and wish you weren't. You can have desire for someone and wish you didn't. You can have no desire for someone and be glad you don't. You may not want your partner, but know you should look like you do.

• *Wanting to want*

Pick the mythical quest or romantic love story you find most appealing. Odds are they involve consciously chosen and freely undertaken desire. That's the kind of desire we want to feel within ourselves and emanating from our partner.

Do you really want more desire? Perhaps you don't. Your desire to have desire—and your intent to do something about your situation—controls whether or not you'll be successful. Everyone knows this. That's why Helen closely mind-mapped Tom about his reluctance to have sex or get married.

Tom framed his problem as lacking desire to have sex or get married (i.e., he was unmotivated). The real problem wasn't that he didn't want sex or Helen. Tom didn't want to want, period

Intent is tremendously important in sexual desire problems. Partners dance around this by expressing a wish to have desire (for sex or their partner), misrepresenting themselves as being open to developing desire when in fact they are not. This forestalls the other partner from taking it personally. Misrepresenting your desire to have desire only shores up your partner's reflected sense of self briefly.

### • *Can you want something you never had?*

Tom didn't want to *want* because *wanting* made him feel vulnerable. Experiences with Mother taught him wanting her love made him susceptible to her manipulations. He also couldn't handle the loss of paths not taken. There might be a better partner for him out there. But what Tom really couldn't handle was wanting something or someone and not getting what he wanted. *Wanting* put him in touch with an emptiness he felt inside him. Tom avoided this at all costs.

This played out during one of our sessions. Tom had structured the issue as him not knowing what he wanted. If he knew what he wanted, he maintained, he'd want it. But *wanting, itself,* creates the disquieting state of lacking something.

I asked Tom if this was the best relationship he'd ever had. He thought for a moment and acknowledged that it was. "Perhaps you can't afford to decide about getting married or having sex because you'd be vulnerable to wanting the best relationship you've ever had."

Tom tried to maneuver back to more familiar turf. "I said I haven't had many good relationships. So how can I want what I've never known? What about people who had a crappy childhood? Can they desire something they've never had?" Tom thought he had an irrefutable argument.

Without hesitation I said, "Sure!" trying not to sound combative. Tom was surprised. Tom wasn't my first client to rationalize that he couldn't desire something he never had, like a fruit he'd never tasted. This argument misses the essence of human desire: Desire is *all about* wanting to have what you have never had, desiring to do what you have never done, and desiring to become what you have never been.

Desire mobilizes you to become more than you are, to reach for things beyond your grasp. Human desire took us from hunting and gathering to exploring other planets. Desire for the untasted drives saints of all religions, national heroes of all countries, and couples who visit me for therapy. The solution always involves the strength to want something you've never had or doubt will happen. Your Four Points of Balance (Solid Flexible Self, Quiet Mind–Calm Heart, Grounded Responding, Meaningful Endurance) are called upon to aid you in doing three things:

1. To feel worthy as a person in a way you never have
2. To collaborate with someone you love in ways you couldn't growing up
3. To relax and make contact during sex in ways you have never done

This is what Helen and Tom needed to do. Helen was challenged to believe in herself and act as though she was worthy of being chosen. Tom's challenge was to openly display his desire and caring, but not allow himself to be exploited or manipulated.

### • *It's not safe to want your partner more than she wants you*

After a few sessions, Helen and Tom's issues were more apparent, and she became bolder. She opened one session by asking herself the question she had long avoided: "Maybe Tom isn't strong enough to choose a partner?" This was more of a self-confrontation rather than a question to Tom. She was entertaining a thought she previously dodged, demonstrating her Four Points of Balance were growing stronger.

This threatened Tom and he couldn't leave it alone. He made a move to trigger Helen's insecurities and keep her in her place. "What makes you think it's about me not having the ability to choose? Maybe I don't really desire you."

I stepped in. "That's not a question anymore. You *don't* desire her."

Tom was taken aback. I had taken his emotional club out of his hand. "Maybe I desire her. That's what I'm trying to figure out."

"No. It's clear. The issue isn't do you have any smidgen of desire. It's do you have *loads* of desire for her. Helen doesn't want to marry someone who wants her a little. And you're not dying to have sex with her or marry her."

"Well, maybe I am. I'm not sure."

"We're not talking about repressed feelings. You obviously are not bowled over by Helen."

Tom finally acknowledged my point. "So what are you saying? That I don't love Helen?"

"One possibility is that you don't love Helen." I paused. "Another possibility is that you can't love anybody." Another pause. "A third possibility is that you've made sure you pair up with someone who wants you more than you want her. That's what you've done in all your relationships with women, from what you've told me. You said your last partner complained you never paid attention to her. Finding partners who want you, more than you want them, makes you feel desirable and gives you control in a relationship. It helps you stave off your fears of emotional extortion. You need your partner to defer to you, and when she doesn't, you're out the door."

"But what if I really don't want them?"

"For you, it's not *safe* to want your partner. You get around this by making sure you want her less than she wants you. Helen complains she can't get your attention, but you are constantly monitoring her. You're always mapping her mind, gauging how much she wants you, and ratcheting down your desire so you always want her less."

"Well, what if that's true and I wish I could change? It would be good for both of us if I really wanted Helen."

"You see Helen's frustration over your inability to make a decision about your relationship. When she isn't frustrated, you don't deal with it. When she's frustrated, you still don't deal with it. But today when Helen gets to the point where she's ready to give up, and you think she doesn't want you anymore, *then* you express some wish to have more desire. That's all you have to do. You don't actually need to have sex with her. That's enough to keep Helen wanting you."

Tom smiled. He'd been caught. He glanced at Helen to see her reaction. Helen said, "We are both so pathetic!" I didn't acknowledge what Helen said and continued talking to Tom.

## • *Tom's turning point*

Helen was looking at a corner of the ceiling, trying to keep from crying. She saw herself settling for "possibly" being wanted. Tom sat forward on the edge of the couch to engage me. There was no sarcasm in his voice now. "So what's wrong with me, Doctor?"

"You want to be wanted, but you don't want to want. If you find someone like Helen, you can play this out for a while. But if you pair up with someone like yourself, the relationship would probably be volatile, brief, and end on a bad note."

"You're describing the relationship I had before Helen." Tom was offering me a different kind of alliance. I didn't know if this would last, but at least it was a turning point.

"I saw that in your history. I presumed you picked Helen because you wanted something different."

Tom said, "Yes! I wanted something different."

The room was quiet for few seconds before Helen added, "This is where the fool—meaning me—fits in. I'm humiliated. I'm angry with you, Tom, for manipulating me this way. But I'm angrier at myself for letting you do this to me."

The moment was heavy with meaning. I spoke slowly, drawing our session to a close. "Then, on that note, if the two of you settle down, maybe you can do something about this."

I looked at Tom. "If you want something different badly enough, you'll make the difficult decisions necessary to get what you really *want*."

I turned to Helen. "If you're sufficiently angry and humiliated, ask yourself why you let this happen to you." Helen and Tom left my office with sober looks on their faces.

## DESIRE PROBLEMS INVOLVE
## TWO-CHOICE DILEMMAS

Normal couples have desire problems because of forced-choice decisions built into love relationships. I call these "two-choice dilemmas." A two-choice dilemma is when you want two choices but you only get one. Two-choice dilemmas create a proverbial twist: "wanting to eat your cake and have it later, too." Loads of two-choice dilemmas arise in long-term love relationships. Helen's *I want you to want me, but I need you to need me,* and Tom's *I want you to want me, but I don't want to want* are examples of two-choice dilemmas.

Other examples are:

- *I want to be in a monogamous relationship with you, but you've had repeated extramarital affairs.* (The partner's two-choice dilemma is, *I want to have sex with other people, but I don't want to get divorced.*)
- *I want to spend our money on things I know you don't approve of, but I want you to make me feel okay and tell me I'm not selfish.* (The partner's two-choice dilemma is, *I am tired of being the bad guy around here, but I don't want you spending more money.*)
- *If I tell you how angry I am at you, I'm afraid you'll leave!* (The partner's two-choice dilemma is, *We need to talk more, but I don't want you to hurt my feelings.*)

Two-choice dilemmas permeate sexual desire problems. The classic is the LDP's *I don't want to have sex, but I want to stay married to someone who does.* And the HDP's *I want to have sex, but I'm married to someone who doesn't.* Or, *My partner gives me mercy sex if I beg, but he doesn't really want me.*

Tom's other two-choice dilemma was wanting Helen to stay in the relationship without having sex or getting married. He wanted things to continue as they were until he "figured it out." He didn't want to break up, but Helen was ready to move on. Tom told himself Helen didn't really care about him or their relationship, otherwise she would stick around long enough for him to decide.

Helen had other two-choice dilemmas, too: She wanted to give their relationship every opportunity, but on the other hand, she had pretty much given up. Helen was stymied by Tom's unwillingness to openly define his true position, or to confront his own inability to *want* her.

The generic two-choice dilemma of marriage is: You want two choices but you only get one (at a time). You want two choices because (1) you want the choice to do (or avoid) whatever it is you want, and (2) you don't want to be anxious about your choice. You want to avoid the results of your decision without anxiety or consequences. The only way you can accomplish this is to keep your partner from exercising her own choices.

## • *Stealing your partner's choice*

People often improvise a solution: They steal their partner's choice. This way they get two choices. It's like having an affair but not telling your partner because if you did she would leave. You get two choices (having an affair and having a monogamous partner) and your partner gets none. The same holds true when one partner wants to move forward with having a baby or moving to another city, and after protracted discussion the other "still can't decide." (You get to avoid doing something you don't want to do, and still keep your partner around.)

When people want to dodge their two-choice dilemmas, they talk about high-minded notions like "compromise" and "negotiation," otherwise known as talking your partner out of her choice. That's also when you hear talk of "win-win" solutions, or complaints of "feeling coerced to make a decision." But, in actuality, people who won't face their two-choice dilemmas are the ones doing the coercing.

The emphasis on "win-win" solutions is right-minded but naïve. Two-choice dilemmas involve choosing between mutually exclusive possibilities. Poorly differentiated people don't use "win-win" strategies when facing two-choice dilemmas, because that involves "taking the hit" and giving up something important. It's far more likely they'll steal their partner's choice. The weaker their Four Points of Balance, the more they feel entitled to do it. "Win-win" is simply beyond many people's grasp.

Tom was avoiding his two-choice dilemmas and stealing Helen's opportunities in the process. Instead of letting her move on with her life, Tom tried to make Helen feel guilty about leaving. Instead of confronting himself and making a decision, he kept asking for more time—but never used it.

Dodging your two-choice dilemmas is another example of borrowed functioning that creates emotional gridlock. *The reason Tom couldn't "figure out what he wanted" was because* this *was what he wanted.* He was replaying his childhood dynamics. He expected Helen to give herself up for him, the same way his mother expected him to do it for her.

Some people steal their partner's choice out of spite or malice. In other situations, like Tom's, it's a core part of their emotional dynamics. The most common reason partners steal each other's choice is pragmatic necessity: It's the easiest way around a two-choice dilemma you don't want to face. You could argue that dodging and stalling are different from stealing, but in this case the impacts are no different. Even if it's not your intent to steal your partner's choice, it happens just the same, because dodging two-choice dilemmas steals your partner's *time.*

## DO YOU TREAT YOUR PARTNER
## LIKE A FRIEND?

Tom's new insight into his family of origin didn't help him much. He vented his feelings about Mother. We even heard some anger towards Dad. But Tom didn't really change. He spent more time asking himself what he wanted, but no new answers materialized.

Sometimes it takes real-world conversations to put the people-growing process into action. That's what happened in Tom and Helen's subsequent session. Referring to their weekend together, Tom said, "We're good friends, but not lovers."

Helen was near the end of her rope. "I don't want to break up our friendship, but this is not what I want."

I said, "Let's not assume the two of you are friends. This may fit your notion of love, but it isn't my understanding of friendship."

Tom kept his defensive reaction under control. "Are you saying I don't love Helen?"

"I'm saying you don't treat Helen like a friend. I'm also saying this may be truly how you love." It was hard to say who was more impacted. Helen was drowning again in humiliation. Tom was visibly shaken.

### • Helen faces her two-choice dilemma

How do you develop enough solid flexible self to give up being needed? How do you finally believe you're a person someone could want? You need to make the move while you still doubt yourself. Some clients tell their spouse, *"If you never chose me before, what is your choice now? If you chose me before, you're free to choose again. Do you want me now?"* It's more common to tell your mate, *"You chose once and you're stuck with me. There's no going back, whether you want to or not."*

Helen made her choice: Mercy sex was no longer acceptable. Tom had to do better than agree to marry her. She wanted to marry someone who really wanted her.

Helen let herself see what she already knew: Tom had never chosen her. He just didn't want to give her up. His lack of choice had been there all along; she simply wouldn't deal with it. Had Helen approached this from her reflected sense of self, she would have felt more humiliated. But Helen confronted herself from the best in her, and it had an entirely different impact: She didn't feel humiliated. She felt free in a way she hadn't expected.

Helen still went through lots of emotional ups and downs for several days, but she bounced back brighter than before. She told Tom, "I think I've figured out the solution to 'I want to be wanted, but I need to be needed.' You have to want *yourself*. You have to hold on to your self. No one else can do this for you." That's when Tom started to feel desperate.

- *When one partner controls herself, the other feels controlled*

Two-choice dilemmas exist because choices are finite in love relationships. In emotionally fused relationships, your choices *decrease* as your partner starts to develop a more solid flexible self.

Like many LDPs, Tom felt pressured. But everything was changing. Now this was happening because Helen was holding on to her Four Points of Balance. She saw how she sold herself out by not expecting to be wanted and chosen. Helen stopped pushing Tom because she could never get *wanted* by him that way. If she continued to push for sex or marriage, Tom wouldn't be doing it because he really wanted to, if and when he did it.

Helen was no longer willing to spend the rest of her life begging for sex and begging to be wanted. She wasn't willing to badger Tom for something he didn't want to do. She'd let go of the relationship if need be, but she wasn't willing to let go of herself. Helen stopped accepting sexual handouts. Sex stopped altogether.

- *Freedom in marriage can be tough*

Autonomy is a terribly important part of human sexual desire, and it plays out in complex ways. Choosing is an exercise of autonomy. When we feel we have no choice, desire often fades. But when we won't choose, to avoid responsibility for shaping our lives, this kills desire as well. Tom talked about feeling pressured to make a decision, because Helen might call it quits.

I said, "You want to be wanted, but you don't want to want."

"I feel like you're telling me to have sex with Helen, although I know you're not."

"If I told you to have sex with Helen, she wouldn't get what she wants. You could just have sex with her without wanting her. Helen wants you to want her."

Tom looked grim. "Normally I'd be screaming, 'I feel pressured!' Not that I'm not feeling it, but I don't want to blow this relationship. If I don't get myself together, Helen will leave." This was the first time Tom wanted something he thought was beyond him. He sounded desperate. I nodded. Tom mapped out that I understood his plight.

"Freedom is a bitch, isn't it? Helen may leave if she doesn't like the deal you offer. She can make that choice. If you could abolish freedom, you wouldn't have this problem."

Tom laughed. "It's times like these that make me favor benevolent dictatorships!"

"Unfortunately, we are not a species where one partner decides and the other just goes along. It's taken millions of years to create the conundrums you're facing, and I don't think you're going to beat the system."

Tom looked at Helen. "I don't want to screw this up."

Then Tom turned to me. "I want you to walk me though this. I'm not good at this, and I want this relationship to be different." It was a genuine plea for help.

"You *want* that?"

Tom realized what I was asking. He wasn't saying he wanted Helen or the relationship, he was stipulating his own wanting. Slowly and deliberately Tom said, "Yes. I *want* that!"

## HOLD ON TO YOUR SELF: SELF-CONFRONTATION AND SELF-SOOTHING

"So, what do I do?" Tom asked.

"You don't have to give yourself up, or do whatever Helen wants—in fact, you need to do the exact opposite. Stop operating like you're giving yourself up. Have the courage to choose what's most important to you. Just be straight with Helen. That's what a friend would do."

Together, Tom and I outlined things he could do to arrive at some clarity about himself and his relationship with Helen. This required self-confrontation and lots of self-soothing.

I helped Tom develop *accurate* self-confrontations. Inaccurate self-confrontations offer little benefit. For example, Tom said he was going to confront himself about possibly being angry with women in general, since he had such a bad relationship with his mother. I suggested he confront himself more specifically about things he could be more certain about. For example, that he was playing out the *If you love me, you'll give up what you want and do what I want* dynamic from his childhood. The question wasn't whether or not this was going on, it was what would he do about it?

The other certainty was that Tom's indecision interfered with Helen pursuing what she wanted. Rather than confront himself about his *intent,* Tom could confront himself about his *impact.*

### • *Tips for developing Quiet Mind–Calm Heart*

Needless to say, anyone finds this kind of self-examination difficult and painful. Sometimes Tom became agitated when he allowed himself to think. He asked about better ways of calming himself down and maintaining an even keel. We broke things into simple points to keep his efforts to quiet himself focused:

- *Give your dilemma meaning.* This is humankind's number one self-soothing strategy. Tom could tolerate a lot more pain by focusing on trying to change his life, instead of seeing it as something Helen was doing to him. Approaching this as his opportunity to be different than his mother helped him have Meaningful Endurance.
- *If you can't regulate your emotions, control your behavior.* When you start to lose your emotional balance, get your neocortex back in gear. Stop talking. Focus on your breathing. Catch your breath and slow your heart rate. Lower your volume and unclench your teeth. When you say, "Maybe I shouldn't say this, but . . ." take your own advice.
- *Don't take your partner's behavior (or lack of response) personally.* Use this to let go of your reflected sense of self. Don't make things harder for yourself than they have to be.

This helped Tom for several weeks. But there were times this simply wasn't enough. At times in conversation he felt cornered. He couldn't shake this feeling while they talked, no matter how he tried. So we developed more self-soothing tips for when he was really losing his grip:

- *Self-soothing may require breaking contact with your partner.* Tom made it clear this was "time out" for self-repair and not to avoid Helen. To demonstrate good intent, he offered to schedule time to reconnect.
- *Stop your negative mental tapes.* Tom had to deliberately stop his ruminating thought-patterns. Focusing on the thoughts in his mind, and ceasing to dodge them, really helped.
- *Use time apart effectively.* Take care and replenish yourself: Exercise, read something you like, do something productive. Friends, hobbies, and outside interests can calm and refuel you (depending on how you use them). Commiserating about marital problems with friends isn't really time apart from your spouse.

These self-soothing tips helped Tom function better when he was with Helen, and when they were apart. Self-soothing doesn't take a single form. You can make different self-soothing responses, depending on your functioning at that moment.

When Tom had a better grip on himself, he could calm himself down in the middle of talking with Helen. He didn't blow out of the room or ignore her while they talked. When this wasn't possible, Tom's fallback solution was taking a time-out, which he used to prepare for re-entering the conversation. Avoiding a situation is a terrible form of self-soothing.

### • *Wanting makes you grow*

Tom got better at *wanting* without losing himself in the process. We examined his thoughts and feelings when he really confronted himself. Tom ran into a deep, crushing sense of personal emptiness. He was willing to tolerate this in the hope that he didn't have to live like this. *Wanting* makes you get up and do difficult things.

Human desire is incredible: Our self mobilizes itself by allowing itself to want. What we want eventually involves becoming more than we are. Rather than being driven by discomforts and deprivations, our sense of unfulfilled destiny drives us forward.

Tom went through some acute self-confrontations. Then he took Helen out to dinner in a quiet restaurant, and they had one of their most important conversations. "I'm astonished I could do to you what my mother did to me, and be completely oblivious to it at the same time. I find that hard to deal with. I thought my issue was that I didn't want you to manipulate me. I never saw how manipulative I've been.

"I also have to tell you that I honestly can't say I want to get married. You deserve a clear answer, and so this is it. I'm still not clear about what I want to do, but I don't expect you to wait any longer. I know you want to get married, so I figure we're splitting up. I want you to know, I don't see you as giving up on me. Do what's best for you. You've given me more time than I deserve." Tom was torn, but doing what he thought was right. He wanted Helen to stay. But he was determined to treat her like a friend. Needless to say, this greatly impacted Helen.

Sex was fantastic that night. The difference was dramatic. Tom had desire. Helen felt wanted. They made love like old friends who unexpectedly ran into each other.

Tom and Helen had sex several times a week for more than a month. Then things cooled off to once or twice a week, which became their new norm. They spent more time together enjoying each other, including conversations about what this sex meant. Through his self-confrontations Tom became less afraid of Helen controlling him. He was less fearful of being manipulated through his caring for her.

Three months later Tom asked Helen to legally marry him. Helen took time to confront herself: Was she settling for someone who really didn't want her? Was Tom capable of really wanting anyone? Was she saying yes simply because he asked her?

This triggered a crisis for Tom. He crashed when he didn't get an immediate positive answer. Suddenly, he *wanted* more than he could handle. The thought of Helen saying no put him in a nose-dive. He started worrying this was Helen's turn to play *If you love me you will …*

Looking back, Helen said that if she'd had any doubts about marrying

Tom, they vanished when she saw how he handled himself. Tom didn't say, "*If you love me, you'll marry me.*" Instead he said, "Helen, you have to do what you really want."

This was the antithesis of his mother's response. Tom brought an entirely new meaning to his desire. It was *I care about you.* This epitomized the growth in Tom's Four Points of Balance. It came from a clearer sense of himself, and better ability to handle his own anxiety, stay non-reactive, and hang in to get what he *wanted.* Tom wanted this badly enough to hold on to himself while Helen decided.

### • *Hope: Stick with the process*

The processes of marriage were at work in Tom and Helen's relationship long before their wedding. In prehistory, the people-growing machinery started up when two people decided they were a couple. It's no different today. You could say the process of marriage helped Tom and Helen get legally married, because Helen told him, "Yes!"

By the time Tom and Helen had their wedding, they had been married for some time. They epitomize the way legally married couples become more married. It's not as simple as vow-renewal ceremonies. Tom and Helen's wedding declared their choice. It wasn't about making their relationship "official."[132]

Every couple learns marriage is the triumph of hope over experience by going through emotional gridlock.

Research indicates that couples who nearly split up but stay together are glad they stayed together ten years later because things got better. You've seen why this happens: Marriage is the best marital therapy, perfected on billions of people over millions of years. I encourage you to stick with the process. Don't abandon your efforts prematurely. We construct ourselves through *wanting* and making choices. In this co-evolutionary process, we are the artist *and* the final product.

———————— IDEAS TO PONDER ————————

* 1. Desire is *wanting*. Human sexual desire is about desiring your partner, and not just desiring sex, per se. Poorly differentiated people don't want to *want*, but they want to be wanted.

* 2. Sexual desire problems create (and arise from) two-choice dilemmas. Two-choice dilemmas exist because choices are finite in love relationships. In emotionally fused relationships, your choices decrease as your partner starts to develop a more solid flexible self.

* 3. Human desire is incredible: Our self mobilizes itself by allowing itself to want. What we want eventually involves becoming more than we are. Rather than being driven by discomforts and deprivations, our sense of "unfulfilled destiny" drives us forward.

# 9

# Normal Marital Sadism, the Devil's Pact, and Other Dark Stuff

*I*n this chapter, we'll explore the dark side of sexual relationships. (In Chapter 11 we'll examine the spiritual and enlightened aspects of your sexual desire.) Unfortunately, lots of dark things go on when sexual desire problems show up. There's a reason why someone wrote, "A long association—prolonged human contact, when a man and woman live together—this ends up producing a sort of rot, a poison."[133]

Unkind acts are a fact of life in marriage. Emotional gridlock, emotional fusion, and two-choice dilemmas trigger everyday emotional abuse that leaves no physical evidence. If you want to torture your partner in a monogamous relationship, there's no better or more common way than to use sex and desire. I call this emotional torture "normal marital sadism."

Normal marital sadism shows up in myriad ways, like saying hurtful things or withholding important information. You might be adept at strategic maneuvering or subtly (and not so subtly) coercing, pressuring, manipulating, and demeaning your partner. Everyone-for-himself, bad-faith dealings are common in some marriages.

## • *The "Beautiful Couple"*

Have you and your partner made a deal with the Devil? Do your desire problems stem from a bargain that's come back to haunt you? From their worst instincts, couples make unwholesome emotional bargains. Some deals kill sexual desire, guaranteed: Think of a trophy wife (or husband). Her marriage is based on the art of the deal. Sex is usually an important part of that arrangement. Ironically, the deal itself guarantees sexual desire will fade.

Let me tell you about Barbie and Ken, a couple whose desire problems grew out of this kind of deal. Barbie and Ken were a matched set: Trophy wife and trophy husband. Ken was a successful neurosurgeon, used to people deferring to him. Barbie was a beautiful stay-at-home housewife, used to men chasing after her. Both Ken and Barbie generally got their way with other people. They were acutely vain and insecure, and both distrusted the opposite sex.

Barbie was movie-star-quality attractive, with large breasts, heavy makeup, and big hair; she was flamboyantly sexual and flirtatious. When Barbie was younger, she created a stir when she entered a party. Now, in her late forties, she looked a bit hardened and overdone.

Ken was square-jawed and rugged featured. He was a buffed nails, power-lunch kind of guy. Women swooned over his charm and good looks. Ken had no respect for them. In this way, Ken was much like Barbie: She disrespected men for being "led around by their dicks," but she desperately needed their attention.

Barbie and Ken were the prototypic beautiful couple. In restaurants, people turned to get a better look at them. They had money, wore expensive clothes, drove nice cars, and belonged to the right country club. They took dance lessons and put on torrid displays of sexy moves that other couples applauded. Ken and Barbie thrived on the applause, because they weren't hearing any in their bedroom.[134]

Ken had been a good catch as far as Barbie was concerned. Barbie's mother had pointed Ken out as a suitable marriage candidate, and Barbie had gone after him. Men were easy for Barbie. She knew men thought they were the ones "scoring," but she was using them. Ken had lit up like a Christmas tree when she sent a little sexual energy his way. He came on strong, and Barbie let him sweep her off her feet.

Barbie liked being adored, in and out of bed. When they first had sex, Ken made love to her slowly. Like most men, he was so taken with her beauty, she got to just lay back and receive. She usually climaxed receiving oral sex. Then Ken would enter her and have his orgasm.

Ken loved screwing Barbie. He marveled at how her slim body looked and felt. He liked to put her on her back and watch her while he was in her. Ken watched himself with this beautiful woman, with the feeling of *Oh man, I'm in heaven. Look at what I get to screw!*

While they were dating, Barbie and Ken had sex two or three times a week. Once married, sex quickly decreased to once a month. Barbie liked being seduced. She doled out sex as a reward. However, once she felt she was expected to have sex, that was the end of that. Neither Ken nor Barbie had much solid sense of self or capacity for intimacy. Being seen accurately by someone else was not their thing. Within five years, sex happened once or twice a year. Their twelve-year marriage turned into a war of attrition.

When they came to see me, Barbie was threatening to leave the marriage. She was the LDP, Ken pressured her for sex, and she had just about had it. She felt used by Ken. She said all he wanted from her was sex. She didn't say that physical beauty and sex were all she felt she had to offer.

Ken said Barbie had "lied to him," because she always acted so sexy when they were dating. In truth, Ken felt he had bought Barbie. She had quit her job soon after they married. He supported her, and he felt entitled to the goods. They had made an implicit deal: his money, status, and financial security for her looks and plenty of sex. This originally got them together. Now the deal turned Barbie off and the lack of sex infuriated Ken.

Barbie and Ken had social acquaintances, but neither one had close friendships. Barbie had girlfriends she gossiped with and exchanged advice, but they never talked straight or confronted each other. Neither Barbie nor Ken felt obligated to tell the truth, particularly when it would be personally difficult. Neither one trusted the other, and neither one was trusting or trustworthy.

Acts of unkindness were daily events between Ken and Barbie. As far as they were concerned, if they weren't yelling, they weren't fighting, but emotional torture was standard fare. Ken worked Barbie over by telling her she was frigid. He would ask her if she was lesbian. Barbie accused Ken of being a sex addict. They competed for who was the bigger victim, who had been more duped going into this marriage, and who was more heroic for putting up with the other's shortcomings.

## NORMAL MARITAL SADISM

As I said, if you want to inflict pain within the confines of marriage, torturing your partner around sexual desire is the most common (and effective) way to do it. Sexual relationships are the Devil's playground for normal marital sadism.

*Normal marital sadism* (also known as NMS) involves pleasure derived from inflicting psychological pain or abuse, but stops short of physical domestic violence. Normal marital sadism occurs far more frequently than physical abuse. We torment those we love while feigning unawareness. Many of us do it often and with impunity.

We've talked about functioning from the best in you. That's because the worst in you can (and probably often does) run the show. We *all* have a nasty side. Nasty as in "not a very good person." There's a side to all of us that's primitive, petty, vindictive, and punitive. Evil, actually. The more you and your partner are emotionally fused—the more you depend on your partner for validation and anxiety regulation through accommodation—the more likely you (and your partner) engage in normal marital sadism.

You're a normal marital sadist if you frequently (a) need to "get even," (b) hold grudges, (c) can't control your temper, or (d) feel justified and entitled to attain retribution when your feelings are hurt. Even conflict-avoidant couples who seemingly agree on everything conduct covert warfare at night between the sheets.

You could argue Barbie had low desire because she was angry at Ken, and certainly she was furious with him. But sexual withholding isn't reducible to low desire. Sexual withholding is how you instill feelings in your mate. Barbie withheld sex when she was angry. She didn't want to be a source of pleasure for Ken. Quite the contrary, she wanted to be a source of unhappiness, which is a common stance in NMS. Barbie was angry a lot, and she wanted to make Ken angry or frustrated too.

Sexual withholding is also how you position your mate in particular ways. Sometimes Barbie withheld sex to make Ken defer to her. Sometimes she did it to make him go away. Sometimes she wanted to attack his reflected sense of self. Other times she faked orgasms, and felt contempt for Ken when he took pride in his sexual performance.

Normal marital sadism is as simple as withholding the sweetness of sex, while acting like you want to please. Even when they had sex, there were times Barbie deliberately thought about other things. Barbie and Ken were equally sadistic to each other. Ken hammered Barbie's reflected sense of self by ogling younger women and sending sexual vibes to her girlfriends. Over the years, Barbie accused Ken of having affairs many times. Ken always denied it and told her she was insecure.

• *How common is normal marital sadism?*

The American Psychiatric Association glossary defines *sadism* as "pleasure derived from inflicting physical or psychological pain or abuse on others. The sexual significance of sadistic wishes or behavior may be conscious or unconscious. When necessary for sexual gratification, [it is] classifiable as a sexual deviation." The Association also considered (and then dropped) the diagnostic category of "sadistic personality disorder." The criteria included (a) humiliating and demeaning others, (b) lying to inflict pain, (c) restricting the autonomy of people in close relationships, and (d) forcing compliance through intimidation. Apparently, this diagnostic category considered marital sadism to be normal: The diagnosis wasn't applicable if sadistic behavior was directed toward one person, such as a spouse.[135]

Do normal healthy people really engage in normal marital sadism?

Judging from research I've done and my clinical observations, the answer is resoundingly "Yes!" According to twenty couples attending one of my Passionate Marriage® Couples Retreats, *every one* reported doing things deliberately to hurt their partner. Half the group reported really enjoying it. One woman found NMS sexually arousing. A quarter of the group added mind-twisting torture by denying they were doing it when accused by their partner. Three-quarters reported deliberately procrastinating to infuriate their mate.

This might suggest people attending our Retreat are a highly select group of troubled souls. But another sample I gathered suggests they are just normal people like everyone else. In a sample of one hundred therapists, 88 percent said they engaged in NMS. Moreover, 87 percent estimated their clients did likewise. Here's the really important thing: Therapists who didn't see themselves inflicting NMS also didn't see it in their clients.

Pretty much everyone engages in NMS. Lots of couples—and 12 percent of therapists who don't recognize NMS in themselves—need to wake up: *Marriage is where you realize you are living with a ruthless sadistic terrorist. And then there's your partner to deal with, too!*

### • Torture: A common form of relatedness

Partners harass and annoy each other frequently. The more emotionally fused you are, the more you agitate, pester, and upset each other. When you don't get the positive reflected sense of self you need, you feel entitled (if not obligated) to let your mate know it. The weaker your Four Points of Balance (Solid Flexible Self, Quiet Mind–Calm Heart, Grounded Responding, Meaningful Endurance), the more likely you are to practice NMS.

Long-term relationships have many frustrations. People who don't handle frustrations and disappointments well, or who take things personally, can wreck havoc in the name of self-protection. One partner's attempt to "protect" herself brings maximum misery and anguish to the other.

Love and torture are often unfortunate bedfellows. When people are dodging two-choice dilemmas they often become particularly sadistic.

Lying is a given to cover your tracks. Screwing with your partner's mind is optional. But some of us really enjoy lying and being evasive and developing mind-twisting arguments simply because it's *fun*.

Stubbornness, vindictiveness, vituperativeness, and competitiveness drive lots of couples into celibacy. Marriage is where the lousy blow job is perfected. It doesn't come from ignorance or lack of experience. The sad truth is, if you have a reflected sense of self and enjoy borrowed functioning, it feels good to screw over your partner.

Barbie and Ken had an emotionally abusive relationship. Emotional abuse is the most common form of domestic violence. It's the psychological version of beating someone with a rubber hose: It leaves no marks or fingerprints. No proof of assault or malicious intent. No proof of the recipient's pain and suffering.

Ken and Barbie worked each other over psychologically. They feigned ignorance or innocence when they went after each other. You might think they were completely insensitive, couldn't communicate, and had no idea what they were doing. But you don't get their kind of accuracy or strategic timing in manipulation and deception without the ability to mind-map and communicate. Shutting your partner out and keeping your partner in the dark are art forms. So is using your partner's mind-mapping to play with her mind, as in refusing to acknowledge an affair your partner knows you're having, or denying disdain you know you're displaying.

Like many couples, Barbie and Ken tortured each other with sex. It could happen during initiation or foreplay, or later in an encounter. It could happen after it was over. Barbie ignored Ken's overtures for sex as if she never heard them. By his third or fourth initiation, Ken was plenty steamed. During foreplay, Barbie made it hard for Ken to get to her genitals by keeping her thighs together. She liked to "make him work for it." She was passive, gave the minimum, and did as little as possible.

Ken had his own ways of getting back at Barbie. He'd put his hands on her butt in public, even though he knew she hated this. Ken said he couldn't keep his hands off her because she was such a beautiful women. When they had sex, he'd squeeze her breasts harder than he should, or stick his finger in her vagina prematurely to see if he could get away with it.

# THE PROBLEM ISN'T YOUR LACK OF RELATIONSHIP, IT'S THE RELATIONSHIP YOU HAVE

I'm not describing the *absence* of a relationship. Emotional torture doesn't result from a lack of relatedness. In many cases, it *is* the relationship. It's the kind of attachment many people know best.

Do we torment each other because of what happened in our childhood? Sure. Do we torture each other because of the love we didn't get? Not so fast. The truth is the other way around: People are often driven to do terrible things *by the love they got*. The love you *get* can twist you up much more than the love you never got. When torture is the only kind of relatedness we can get with our parents or our loved one, many of us will take what we can get. For some of us, it's the only kind of relationship we know how to have.

We prefer to think people do terrible things to each other because they're out of touch with each other. We assume torture and bullying arise from people not relating to the victim, or being out of touch with reality. In truth, people do terrible things to each other *because* of the connection between them. People wreak havoc in the midst of emotional fusion.[136]

Masochism is a powerful and common form of attachment and relatedness (emotional fusion). Masochism structures relationships in familiar ways. When it comes to normal marital (or family) sadism, we're discussing the person who does it rather than takes it. But someone has to play the masochist to keep the relationship going. If you're on the receiving end when you're growing up, you get educated in how to do it. You learn how it is dished out—and develop a taste for it. When you get married you're likely to take one role or the other.

### • *Cruelty and hatred in love relationships*

The sad truth is sadistic relationships occur in many families. A shocking number of parents go out of their way to torment their children by disappointing them and breaking their hearts. This was certainly true in Barbie and Ken's families. Barbie mapped her mother's mind long ago.

Status, money, and the trappings of success were all that mattered to her mother. It was bitterly disappointing to see she was so cold and shallow. As a child, Barbie watched her mother "melt down" over small social embarrassments. Being sat at "the wrong table" at a luncheon was enough to set Barbie's mother off. Her mother frequently badmouthed friends behind their backs, but she was saccharine-sweet when she was with that person.

Barbie's mother was a social climber, and her and her family's appearance was important at all times. During high school, she coached Barbie on how to get in with the most popular boys and girls. She entered Barbie in beauty pageants and talent shows. All she wanted from Barbie was help making herself look good. When Barbie was elected HomeComing Queen, her mother acted like she had won the Miss America contest.

Despite all the attention, Barbie was terribly unhappy. She was often depressed when she was alone. She had frequent emotional crashes, and drowned in an ocean of anxiety, insecurities, and self-doubts. She'd be down for weeks, preoccupied with her current boyfriend—or how to get her next one. She was consumed with her appearance and saw other women as competitors for men's attentions. Barbie was emotionally hollow and brittle, without much solid self.

Barbie and her mother continued an emotionally fused love-hate relationship throughout Barbie's adulthood. Her mother's opinion had tremendous impact on her. Barbie tried to earn her mother's praise, but what she mostly got were cutting comments. Barbie thought her mother was insensitive and blind, but in reality she was just plain cruel.

Barbie's mother lectured her about not getting pregnant, but this had nothing to do with concern for Barbie's welfare. Her message was *Don't get pregnant until you find a wealthy guy. Then "accidentally" get pregnant if that's what it takes to hook him. Don't screw around too much because you'll get a bad reputation—so don't screw guys who can't help you get where you want to go.* The impact of this attitude went far beyond Barbie's feeling unloved. It was devastating to see her mother's incapacity to invest in another human being.

Ken's childhood experiences weren't much better. He grew up in a family he described as an "ice box." His parents emphasized formality and proper appearance rather than physical or emotional affection. Ken watched his father and mother interact in extremely denigrating and destructive ways. Both parents were high-functioning alcoholics. His father was vice president of the local bank, and his mother rubbed shoulders with the social elite. Their smiling faces appeared in the society pages, but at home they constantly argued. Once they started drinking, the screaming matches started, furniture got broken, and occasionally punches were thrown.

Ken and his brothers did what they could to keep their parents from getting out of control. The price of peace was appeasement and accommodation, but never from a desire to please them. Ken hated the way they acted so immature and irresponsible. What really gnawed at him was the way they ate each other's hearts out with their bickering. Despite all their trappings of success, and because of all their wasted potential, Ken thought his parents were disgusting.

In many ways, Ken and Barbie believed in nothing and no one. Although it sounds harsh, their basic attitude could be summed up as *Everyone is full of shit.* But rather than see them as villains or victims, I thought about Ken and Barbie's situation and why they were willing to live like this. I saw them having the kind of relationship they knew best, the same kind they had with their parents: Constant chaos and cruelty were the norm.

Sometimes we hate our parents or mate *because* we love them. Beyond our vulnerability to what they can do to us, our love makes us vulnerable to what they do to themselves. What befalls them—and the ways they destroy themselves—impacts us. Watching your parents diminish themselves rips your heart out. And it's not hard to hate someone you love who constantly diminishes you, lies to your face, and treats you badly in other ways. We deny our hatred because it punctures our reflected sense of self, offends our narcissism, and makes us feel unlovable.

Many long-term partners I know hate each other. The ones with good relationships don't let it get in the way. To do that you have to accept your hatred, and your partner's hatred of you. You have to be capable of genuinely loving too, because that's really the focus of the relationship. The big difference between good and bad long term relationships is *not* whether partners hate each other or not. It's how partners handle it, and whether or not they love each other too. Your Four Points of Balance are greatly involved in tolerating extreme ambivalent feelings toward those you love. They make it easier to soothe the tensions of loving and hating your partner, and accepting that your partner probably loves and hates you too.

### • *The more things stay the same, the more things change*

The untoward experiences I just described didn't create all of Barbie and Ken's marital problems. They also had to contend with the same problems and people-growing processes we all do. As all this came together in their daily interactions, Barbie and Ken had co-constructed their current situation.

Barbie and Ken's sexual style hadn't changed much from when they were dating, although to them it felt like night and day. Now that they weren't the gleam in each other's eye, everything seemed different. Twelve years later, Barbie still lay on her back during sex. Never one to be sexually generous, now she was passive-aggressive and withholding. She knew what Ken wanted, and he wasn't going to get it. The only way Ken got to orgasm when they had sex was by bringing himself to climax during intercourse.

Ken tried to position Barbie the ways he liked best. He liked to pick up her legs and roll her knees to her shoulders, so he could ram his penis into her. Most times, Barbie complained this was uncomfortable and she couldn't breathe. She preferred intercourse with her legs straight out, heels on the bed. Because she was the LDP, Barbie controlled how and when they had sex. Coming to orgasm, Ken frequently thought, *What the hell have I gotten myself into with you, Bitch?!* Although you could say Ken was squeezing the life out of Barbie, they were really doing it to each other.

### • *Do you squeeze the life out of your partner?*

Ken and Barbie couldn't control themselves; and remember, people who can't control themselves control the people around them (Chapter 3).

Poorly balanced people take up too much room in their relationship. There's no room left for other people to have a life. But that's not the only reason life-squeezing happens. If your Four Points of Balance are weak, there's a good chance you're squeezing your partner because you *enjoy* it.

Do you squeeze the life out of your partner? If you're the LDP, one way to do it involves looking like you're starting to understand him. You instill hope and caring in your partner. Then you dash his hopes to pieces by finding some reason to throw your "progress" away. Why would someone do this? It buys time and keeps your partner from leaving while you work him over.

Cold-blooded, isn't it? But some LDPs and HDPs do these kinds of things all the time. Another way to cause pain is by going after your partner's happiness. Find out what she cares about and what makes her happy. Get her to talk about it and look interested and supportive. Then, at a strategic time, criticize or belittle it. When she looks shocked and betrayed, say you didn't know that would hurt her (betraying her yet again).

This kind of torment takes a while to set up because it's inflicted over time. But there are many short-term tortures, such as forgetting responsibilities, appointments, or agreements. There are in-the-moment tortures, like sniping at your partner to keep him from talking openly to you. Normal marital sadism knows no boundaries.

## • *Buying time at your partner's expense*

Do you only do what's convenient or comfortable for you? Does your mate do likewise? Living according to your feelings can squeeze the life out of your partner. When Barbie wouldn't confront herself and deal with their sex life, she squeezed out that part of Ken's life.

Not that Ken was a saint. He initiated sex frequently, even when he didn't want it, to hasten Barbie's guilt over not having enough sex. His initiations were crude, especially when he figured she'd say no. *"Come on, babe, let's do it!"* and *"Wanna fuck?!"* made it clear he wasn't offering romance.

When sexual desire problems arose at the outset of their marriage,

Barbie said she thought her problem might be hormonal. But she delayed getting herself checked out for over a year. When she did, her results came back normal. For the next six months Barbie did nothing, and Ken got angry. Barbie said she didn't trust the results and wanted to repeat them. Six months later, further testing came back in the low normal range. Ken said both tests indicated Barbie's hormones were normal. She said this meant her hormones were low.

Barbie spent the next eight years trying various herbal remedies, to no avail. Barbie's stance was it wasn't her fault she didn't have sexual desire. The problem wasn't her, and it wasn't Ken either. It was her hormones. Ken's position was if this was the problem, Barbie should do whatever it took to fix it.

Instead, Barbie mounted a multi-pronged impregnable defense. Early on, she insisted on homeopathic solutions because she didn't want the weight gain hormone replacement therapy might cause. Asking Ken, *"You don't want me to gain weight and look fat, do you?"* was a great strategic move. Ken's narcissism demanded a wife with an incredible body. When Ken eventually got fed up and opted for weight gain, Barbie changed to *"I don't want to put anything unnatural in my body."*

With moves like these, it's not hard to map out your partner's intent. Barbie wanted Ken to feel the impact of her lack of desire. Ken saw this, but he couldn't crack Barbie's back-up defense: When he pointed out her obvious lack of interest in having more sex, Barbie would get wild and scream, "I don't care, I don't care! No one's going to make me do something I don't want to do! You're torturing me! Leave me alone!" Barbie pushed Ken to back down to keep their relationship together. Ken's difficulty holding on to himself helped keep their marriage going.

## • *Did you marry someone you didn't desire?*

Barbie wasn't a terrible person. She was just a little cold. Reptilian. Cold-blooded. Not "frigid" in the traditional sense. She could lubricate and reach orgasm just fine. It was more as though Barbie was missing a few pints of human warmth and kindness. Apparently her mother had sucked it out of her. This made me wonder whether Barbie was willing to go through the pain of becoming warm.

Remember Barbie emphasized what a "good catch" Ken was? She never chose him. She never wanted him. She just wanted to catch him. (This is similar to what we saw last chapter with Tom, but colder and more calculated.) Barbie never found Ken attractive in the first place. His grandiosity, and Barbie's skill at showing men what they wanted to see, kept him from knowing this. Barbie married Ken to reduce her emotional vulnerability: Sometimes people pick partners *because* they don't desire them. Part of Barbie's feelings of "safety" came from *not* desiring him. Barbie had lost sexual desire in prior relationships. She knew her desire evaporated quickly once the relationship developed.

The best way out of this kind of pattern of cruelty involves (a) giving a clear and complete accounting of yourself and what you've been doing and (b) giving your partner a fair shot at his own vision of happiness. But if you're unwilling or unable to hold on to your self and give your partner a chance to leave, then emotional torture and fusion continue until the marriage falls apart.[137]

Barbie wasn't willing to confront herself about how she got into their relationship. Whenever you dodge a two-choice dilemma, screwing with your partner's mind becomes *de rigueur*. Barbie wasn't about to risk her safety and security by getting to the bottom of things.

Ken's egotism—inflated by wealth and status—made him expect the women he dated to "come after him." However, Barbie expected the same thing from the men in her life. When Ken stopped initiating in their marriage, sex dropped from once or twice a month to nothing in the last two years. In session, Barbie said she was too afraid and awkward to make approaches to Ken. She proposed that she would participate if he initiated, but she reserved the right to say no if she didn't want sex.

## THE DEVIL'S PACT: INITIATION DEALS

What finally led Ken and Barbie to see me? They made a deal to work things out, which I call the Devil's Pact. Many couples spontaneously

222 INTIMACY

hit upon this diabolical deal. (Some therapists actually prescribe it in treatment.) The Devil's Pact is ineffective because it's a bad-faith agreement born of emotional combat and normal marital sadism. It creates a marital theatre of the absurd.

- *Scene one: "Why don't you initiate?"*

One night Barbie and Ken were lying in bed. They were arguing. They were angry, exasperated, and defensive. Ken said, "Why don't you ever initiate?"

Barbie replied, "Because you never give me the chance to initiate. You initiate all the time."

Ken railed, "I give you plenty of time. I have to initiate because you never do. We'd never have sex if I left it up to you."

Barbie grabbed the high ground. "You'll never find out because you always initiate first. You never wait. If you're not initiating every five minutes, you're not happy! You do that to make me feel bad. I may not do it often enough to suit your standards, but I initiate enough to suit me."

Ken tried to take the high ground away from her. "We'd have sex every five years if it were up to you. You never initiate!"

"You never give me the chance!"

Scene One repeated *ad nauseam* for a month.

- *Scene two: "You never give me the time to initiate!"*

It was now a month later. Ken and Barbie were arguing again. They were more hurt, frustrated, defensive, and angry. They hated talking about their problem even more. Nothing was changing. Ken felt pressured because time was flying by. Barbie felt Ken always pressured her for sex, and she deserved some time off when this wasn't on her mind. Scene Two started out louder than Scene One:

Ken said, "Why don't you ever initiate?"

Barbie replied, "I do. Just not as much as you."

"That's not true. You never initiate!"

"That's because *you* never give me a chance."

Ken started to lose himself. "I give you all the chances in the world!"

Barbie spat out her words like a machine gun. "You *always* initiate first. Just when I'm getting ready to initiate, *you* do it. You *never* wait. You're *always* pushing me, expecting me to make a move on you!"

"I could wait until hell freezes over and you wouldn't make a move!"

Barbie became superficially calm but holier-than-thou. "Well, if *you* didn't initiate all the time, maybe *I* would do it more."

"It wouldn't make any difference if I initiated less."

Barbie's tone was snotty and belittling. "*You* don't know. *You're* always initiating."

Ken became more incensed. "*Are you telling me it's my fault you don't initiate? Because I initiate all the time? Are you nuts? I can't believe this!!*"

Barbie's pseudo-calmness was dismissive and infuriating. "I'm saying I don't feel like initiating when I feel pressured all the time. And if I didn't feel so pressured by you, I'd probably initiate more often."

Ken was beside himself with anger. "*This is so frustrating.* How can you say this with a straight face?"

"Because it's true. If you'd just back off, so I didn't feel so pressured, things might be different." Barbie's cool demeanor was like a red cape before a bull.

"Prove it! It's a lie!"

"I can't! *You* prove it!"

"Okay!" Ken said the fateful words. "I'm not initiating from here on out. We'll see what happens. I'll prove you won't initiate."

"Okay. We'll see."

"Yes, indeed, we will."

On the surface, the Devil's Pact makes perfect sense: Create a vacuum, and the LDP will fill it because she no longer feels pressured by the HDP. Unfortunately, it doesn't work because it doesn't change the system. It actually reinforces the status quo.

• *Scene three: The Devil's Pact unravels*

Six weeks later, Ken and Barbie had a huge fight. Ken was screaming like a lunatic. Barbie sat quietly. The expression on her face said, *See what*

*I have to put up with? And you expect me to initiate sex with you when you act like this?!*

Ken screamed, "It's been a month and half! You haven't initiated once! You said you'd initiate sex if I backed off! Why haven't you initiated?!"

The dismissive sing-song quality in Barbie's voice said her take on things was unquestionably right. "At first I didn't initiate sex because I was enjoying not feeling pressured. After all, that's why we made this agreement. The whole idea was that I wasn't going to feel pressured for sex. Besides, I want sex to be meaningful when we have it. I didn't want to do it just to do it."

Ken rolled his eyes in disgust. "Okay. Maybe that explains the first night or the first several days. But why didn't you initiate after that?"

"Well, when we didn't do it the first night, I knew you expected it on the second. I started to feel pressured, so I didn't do it, hoping the pressure would go away."

Ken grabbed the high ground: "I was good. I didn't say a word."

Barbie took it away from him. "I felt like you were watching me, waiting to see what I would do. Which you were—don't deny it. I don't feel sexy when you do that!"

*"But it's been six weeks!"*

Barbie snarled, "You don't *need* to say anything. I could tell you were frustrated and expecting me to initiate. You were doing your same old thing, in a different way. I'm not going to have sex when I feel pressured! *You're not going to force me to have sex with you when I don't want to!*"

Ken eased up a notch. "So why didn't you say something about this weeks ago? We had a deal."

Barbie's snarl turned to weariness and fatigue. "I knew we would fight. I'm so tired of this. I just put it off. I needed a break. This whole thing doesn't have to rest on my shoulders, you know!"

Ken was ready to tear his hair out. "That was our agreement!"

Barbie's tone was mocking. "Oh, so now it's all my fault! You expect me to make all the initiations? I never agreed to do all the work. I'm not the only one in this relationship. You didn't bring it up, either. It's your responsibility, too." And with that Barbie walked out of the room.

### • Understanding the Devil's Pact

The Devil's Pact didn't change their system—the Devil's Pact intensified it. Once it was made, Barbie felt increasing pressure to initiate. However, since part of the premise is to reduce pressure on the LDP, Barbie felt entitled to not feel pressured, and to not initiate if she still felt it. Unfortunately, the longer she waited, the more Ken's frustration escalated, and the spiral intensified. At that point, as she saw it, Barbie was standing up for her rights by refusing to initiate. She refused to recognize how she co-produced the pressure she felt.

Here's the key that gets lost in the drama: The point of making this Devil's Pact is to solve a conjoint problem that can only be solved by the low desire partner making initiations. When Barbie turned around and said Ken's reduced initiations were why she *didn't* do it, after she agreed to it, you have a good demonstration of mind-twisting normal marital sadism. Telling him he could have initiated during their pact was more of the same.

The Devil's Pact starts with the LDP avoiding self-confrontation as long as possible. It then shifts to bad faith negotiations, misrepresentations, and attempts to thwart your partner. It ends with recycled arguments, instead of confronting what's going on. If you want to eat someone's heart out, the Devil's Pact is hot sauce.

### • A common but difficult entry into therapy

This was the point at which Ken and Barbie came to see me. Barbie had moved into their spare bedroom "in order to get some sleep." Their relationship was shaky, and divorce was in the air. They were gridlocked and embittered. Barbie seemed ready to leave.

This is a tough place to start therapy from, but couples do it all the time. The important thing is to get a grip, settle down quickly, and demonstrate some interest in saving your marriage. You do this by confronting yourself about your limitations and your role in co-constructing your marriage. You have to look at your situation more objectively. However, if you (or your partner) insist on approaching the situation from your feelings, it doesn't bode well for staying married.

In our first session, Barbie wanted me to tell Ken to stop pressuring her. She cast herself as coerced into sex, and expected me to side with her. When I didn't do that, Barbie saw me as a threat.

I tried to explain that (in monogamous marriage) the LDP *backs herself into a corner* by repeatedly declining to have sex. There is only one good way out of that corner. She has to come forward and initiate sex, which she doesn't really want to do. When she won't, she also paints her partner into a (different) corner. The Devil's Pact supplies more paint: Barbie pressured Ken to give up his desire for sex, so she wouldn't feel pressured. It wasn't enough for him to give up having sex. He had to give up *wanting* it, too.

I said to Barbie, "In your deal, you still felt pressured when Ken didn't initiate. It came from the fact you knew he wanted it."

"That's right."

"Then the only way Ken can take the pressure off you is by giving up his desire for sex, forever. Intentionally or not, this is what you're pressuring Ken to do."

"I don't think Ken has to give up sex forever. I just want him to stop pressuring me." Barbie's message was *I'm not looking at this from any other perspective than my own. You're asking me to look at this from his perspective rather than from mine. I'm entitled to my feelings. You're taking his side.*

"I'm not taking Ken's side. I'm trying to help you get out of a very difficult corner. You see Ken as backing you into this corner, and you want him to back off. But you are backing him into a corner, and only you can get the two of you out of it."

"I'm not pressuring Ken, he's pressuring me!"

"Knowing he wants to have sex pressures you."

"I'm starting to feel pressured by *you*."

Barbie was entering reptile-mode. I paused to cool things off. I wanted to help her see she was up against a system that was bigger than her feelings, and the only good way to handle it was to come to grips with it.

"Would you believe Ken if he told you he would never want sex again?"

"No!"

"And if he did promise this, would you respect him? Would you feel more desire for him?"

"No!"

"Then there is no way Ken can get you out of your dilemma. You problem is you're living with a man who you know wants to have sex. Even if he promises to give up sex forever, you will still feel pressured."

## • *Tyranny of the lowest common denominator*

"Maybe you can't see my position because you're a man."

"I see the exact same situation in couples where the man is in your position—and has your feelings—and the woman is in Ken's role. I also see this in same-sex couples all the time. What you're going through isn't happening because you're a woman and Ken's a man."

Barbie was running out of maneuvering room. She said, "I'm not going to let Ken abuse me." Her message was *I'm not going to look at this any other way. I like my way of looking at things. It's a defensible position.*

"I don't think you should let Ken abuse you, either. But the problem here is that you agreed to monogamy, and now you want switch to celibacy. When Ken wants to stick to the original deal, you call this being pressured."

"I feel abused."

"I have no doubt that sometimes Ken is abusive. My understanding is emotional abuse is standard fare in your house." In spite of herself, Barbie laughed. When she did, Ken laughed with her. This was momentary acknowledgement of them having an emotionally abusive relationship.

"If it's abuse to force someone to do something they don't want to do, is it abuse to force someone to give up sex they'd legitimately like to have?"

All three of us knew the answer to my question. Barbie was bright. Even if she didn't agree, she could follow my logic. The point I laid out was important for her to hear. But beyond that, I wanted to see if she was willing to tolerate discomfort for growth.

Barbie said, "It's different. It's just different. That's all I can say." Her message was *I can see where you're headed, and I'm not going there. I'm not dealing with this.*

I was quiet for a moment. It was my responsibility to make more than a casual effort to help Barbie. I decided to speak more directly to her. I kept my voice soft and focused on giving a grounded response. I leaned forward in my chair, signaling I was reaching out to her.

"I've seen a lot of couples in situations similar to yours. I'd guess you're thinking it's pretty late in the game, and things are hopeless. But I've seen couples take stock of their situation, confront themselves, make difficult changes, and come out farther ahead then they imagined. If you are willing to do what it takes, I'd be glad to help you do that."

"I'm not going to allow myself to be abused." Barbie declined my invitation. I had to try one more time after giving her several seconds.

"There's a lot more going on here than whether you have sex with Ken. If you hold on to your self, you could significantly change your life."

"Nobody's going to make me do what I don't want to do!"

Barbie declined my third bid. Further efforts would only make her feel more pressured. I sat back in my chair.

"Please include me in that group. I'm not going to make you do what you won't do. It wouldn't help you, and besides, I can't." Barbie looked momentarily surprised.

"Your problem is not as simple as Ken pressuring you for sex. Now *your relationship* is pressuring you. Pressuring the best in you to stand up. The part that understands fair play and right and wrong. Mindlessly repeating, 'I don't have to if I don't want to' isn't going to help you. You don't have to confront yourself here, but you don't have infinite choices."

## THE CRUCIBLE OF MARRIAGE

I've said before that how you go into gridlock determines how you come out of it. The responses you make shape your life and the person you become. By confronting yourself through your sexual desire problems, you can become capable of relating on an entirely different basis (Chapter 12). Unfortunately, not everyone moves forward when the situation presents itself. This is where you and your life history interact with the people-growing machinery of marriage. Deals made at the outset come back to haunt you.

Marriage takes your lowest, weakest, and darkest parts and stuffs them up your nose until you can't stand yourself as you are. That's a good thing, because it often takes crises and pain for us to do something about it. The weaker your Four Points of Balance, the more pain and crisis it takes to mobilize you. (Next chapter we'll discuss reaching critical mass for change.)

That's one benefit of accurately labeling normal marital sadism: It hurts to see yourself inflicting pain on others. Hopefully this creates internal conflict and crisis. But if you refuse to confront yourself, then concepts like normal marital sadism are worse than a waste of time. The worst in you will likely misuse this powerful label.

### • *Good-bye and kiss-off*

I've seen people get through similar problems and go on to have a lovely marriage. Unlike Barbie and Ken, they were willing to tolerate discomfort for growth. A *lot* of discomfort. When we first identified normal marital sadism, Barbie and Ken were somewhat embarrassed. Our conversations about torture and cruelty impacted them. This is where your Fourth Point of Balance is incredibly important.

Your willingness to tolerate pain for growth determines whether things change or not. It separates my successful couples from those who don't do well. It's not how many problems they have, how long they've had them, or how bad they've gotten. Meaningful Endurance is the key to moving things forward.

You can stop normal marital sadism and repair your relationship. Normal marital sadism is *normal*, it's not a disease. Human resilience goes hand-in-hand with our propensity to torture each other. Resilience (enduring discomfort for growth) is what you need to get the sadist in you under control.

Having said that, some clients don't stop when confronted with the truth of their lives. Barbie just kept going. Her attitude was, *Well, that's the way the world is. I have to look out for myself.* She also burned her bridges behind her, so she couldn't turn around.

Barbie entered our next session saying, "Ken has ignored me for years.

I'm not going to live with someone who can't be nice to me and then pressures me to have sex." It meant, *The topic of sex is now closed. If you persist I will leave.*

I turned to Ken. "Where does this leave you?"

Ken looked pale and didn't say anything for several seconds. "… I don't know … Maybe I need to give her more time … I need more time … I need to think about this." Barbie needed a way out. Ken backed down and gave it to her.

Barbie said, "We both need time to heal. We've done a lot of damage to ourselves, and I think we need spiritual help. I know I do. I've made an appointment for a spiritual counselor to see us." Meaning: *instead of you.*

I turned to Ken. "Is this what you want to do?"

I thought Ken might hesitate, but he didn't. "Well, maybe this other person can help us. I think we need to find someone Barbie feels she can work with. If she thinks this other person can help her, I owe it to her and our relationship to go along."

I paused to mark this moment. Respecting the co-creative process is not always easy. Ken and Barbie were shaping their lives in that instant. I said, "I see. Then it's not clear whether you will divorce or stay together. But am I correct that you're terminating with me?" Barbie nodded. Ken agreed.

"Well, in therapy, in marriage—or in bed for that matter—*how* you do it makes the critical difference. I suggest, whatever you do, do it straight. Things will turn out better in the long run."

Barbie looked at me with a cold smile. I read it as *You don't get it. You're not going to get through to me. I am not going to acknowledge what I'm doing.*

Barbie put on her sunglasses. "Thank you for all your help, Doctor. Good-bye."

——————— IDEAS TO PONDER ———————

- Sexual desire problems often involve Normal Marital Sadism (NMS) by both the high desire partner and the low desire partner. Your Four Points of Balance are greatly involved in tolerating extreme ambivalent feelings towards those you love. They make it easier to soothe the tensions of loving *and* hating your partner, and accepting that your partner probably loves and hates you too.
- People are often sadistic when dodging their two-choice dilemmas.
- Partners eat each other's hearts. If you want to torture your partner, one of the best ways to do it is around sex. The best way out of this kind of cruelty involves (a) giving a clear and complete accounting of yourself and what you've been doing, and (b) giving your partner a fair shot at his own vision of happiness.

# 10

## What Does It Take to Really Change Things? Safety, Growth, and Critical Mass

*S*ome people don't grow when given the chance. It's hard to make yourself step up and face the issues in your life. You can know what to do and still not make a move, because you're not willing to actually face your fears. It's understandable. Who wants to confront their demons? But that's not the question love relationships pose. Marriage asks, *Are you willing to stand up now, or do things have to get worse?*

All animals avoid pain. We usually avoid what makes us nervous as long as we can. When things aren't so bad, it feels safe to ignore (sexual) problems. As our relationship craters, we stick our heads in the sand and pretend we know nothing. Fortunately, the people-growing machinery of marriage has evolved to take human nature into account. Love relationships prod you to stand up and deal with things that frighten you. They grab hold of everything solid in you, and everything you hold dear, until the essence of your being feels at risk.

What finally makes you take action despite your fears? Ready for a big answer? The backbone of marriage is the ultimate manifestation of the human self: your integrity.

You usually don't hear much about integrity in books on sexual desire. Integrity is about having ethical principles and living up to them. It's the congruity between what we believe and what we do, and the consistency in our behavior over time. It's about being loyal, truthful, and forthright even when it's difficult. Living up to your responsibilities. Not being deterred by your fears and anxieties.

Your desire to maintain your integrity goes back to our discussions in Part One. Integrity is part of your innate desire to develop and maintain a self. It doesn't involve your reflected sense of self. Integrity is part of your solid sense of self and comes out of your relationship with yourself. People who lack integrity lack a clearly defined coherent self. They lack the Four Points of Balance.

Integrity is more than an abstract principle, it is a core human experience. Integrity is your sense of internal consistency. When you violate your integrity and you scrutinize yourself, you feel dishonored, ashamed, and diminished. Self-confrontation obviously plays a critical role. To the degree you are dishonest with yourself and you won't self-confront, you lack integrity because your self is poorly defined. But if you lie to yourself about who you really are, this won't bother you much. Obviously lots of people do terrible things without feeling bad about themselves.

Integrity involves self-imposed mandates and boundaries that define who you are. The goals and values you pursue, the lines you won't cross, and what you won't do, especially when things get hard or difficult. Although it sounds judgmental, scientifically speaking, the lower your differentiation, the more you lack integrity. Your Four Points of Balance control how much integrity you actually have in practice. It's a function of how much solid flexible self you have and how much you aspire to attain. The "flexible" part isn't wishy-washy ethics; it's getting back on track when you've gone off. If you can't quiet your mind or calm your emotions, and you can't make grounded responses, you will do things that violate your integrity. And you can't have much integrity without Meaningful Endurance because you'll abandon your values and take the easy way out.

As I said, you usually don't think about integrity in sexual desire problems. Fears and anxieties are more common topics. If you're like some of
my clients, you think of sexual desire problems more in terms of issues
of safety and security. Many people think they have difficulty allowing
themselves to feel desire, because they don't feel safe with their partner
or secure in their relationship.

In this view there's something lacking, some security not offered,
some commitment not given, that makes a partner unable to feel sexual
desire. When couples adopt this view, their efforts center around one
partner (or both) offering patience, assurance, acceptance, and encour-
agement to make the other feel more secure. Many marital therapy approaches encourage this whole-heartedly. "Safety and security leads to
passion" is a credo among some therapists. Unfortunately, once again
our fondest beliefs don't coincide with the way marriage really works.
As we saw in Part One, attachment and lust involve different neurobiological systems. And once hormone-driven lust has run its course, keeping sexual desire alive more likely involves developing and maintaining
your self.

## • Sue and Joe

In Sue and Joe's house, "safety" was a daily topic of discussion. They
had been married fourteen years and had two children, a boy and a
girl, ages twelve and ten. Sue had always been extremely insecure, ever
since her parents divorced when she was nine. Sue's mother struggled
to feed her family, and she constantly let Sue and her younger brother
know it.

Sue grew up in constant fear and insecurity. Sue's mother took out her
many frustrations on the kids, while also leaning on them for support.
Mother would withdraw to her bed for days with serious depressions.
She often suddenly lost her temper with a frightening fury. It was Sue's
job to keep her calm, happy, and functional.

Mother exploited Sue and her brother. She had enough time and energy to talk with her friends on the phone for hours, but the house was

always in shambles, since keeping the house clean fell to the children. Sue's brother left home as soon as he could enlist in the army and never returned. Sue lived at home and attended a local college so she could take care of her mother. She dated some in high school, nothing serious, and she had several relationships in college that lasted a few months.

Sue was still living at home when she married Joe. She was twenty-five and he was twenty-six. They met through a mutual friend and married after dating for a year. It was a big adjustment for her mother when Sue left, although Sue and Joe lived in the same town. Sue visited or spoke to her mother by phone several times a week.

By the time they married, Joe was well aware of Sue's difficult childhood, and he was well trained to accommodate her insecurities. Sue's two prior love relationships broke up because the men finally refused to live with Sue's fears and anxieties. By the process of elimination, Sue ended up with a husband who would.

Joe was accommodating to a fault—his first wife told him he had no backbone. With one failed marriage behind him, Joe was generally willing go along with whatever Sue wanted. He was eager to please and pliable as putty. If your childhood had been like Joe's, you might be too.

Joe's parents argued constantly. As a child, Joe wondered why they didn't get divorced. Then they did when he was ten. Apparently, they were as miserable apart as they were together, because they remarried eighteen months later. Joe didn't know what to feel about this. He was happy, embarrassed, angry, and confused. Before long the fighting resumed, and Joe thought he was going to lose his mind. After two years of remarriage, his parents divorced again when Joe was fourteen. Joe lived with his mother until he left home to go to college. Since that time he had had little contact with his parents.

Sue saw her role in life as a "care-taker." Her mother still demanded a great deal of time and attention. But Sue carried deep resentments about her childhood. The possibility she was replicating similar dynamics in her own home never occurred to her. People around her had to accommodate to keep her quiet. Sue and Jim's relationship largely revolved around Sue's anxieties. Sue hated the thought she was anything like her mother, but it was true in more ways then she could handle. Any hint of this from Joe triggered an explosion.

Sue's fears and insecurities limited her own life and the lives of the people around her. When her children were younger, they couldn't play at their friends' houses because Sue was afraid something might happen to them while they were there. Family vacations always involved driving because Sue was afraid to fly. The trips were often unhappy ones filled with Sue's complaints about Joe's driving and her yelling at the kids to stop bickering.

Sue's insecurities reigned supreme in bed, too. They had sex about every other month, and both agreed sex was good when they had it. Joe wanted to have sex once a week, but Sue would let months go by without it. Over time, Joe learned he wasn't supposed to make sexual overtures because they made Sue feel like a bad wife and an inadequate woman. Sue said Joe's initiations made it harder for her to get turned on to begin with.

When they had sex, it was always in the missionary position with the lights off. Joe was dying of sexual boredom. He was tired of having to cajole Sue into sex. Getting her to try something new wasn't worth all the coaxing, promising, and reassuring this required. But Joe couldn't wash his hands of the whole thing because he didn't want to have affairs, and he didn't want to go without sex for the rest of his life. As far as Sue was concerned, she was expressing legitimate feelings and concerns, and a good husband would be understanding if he was interested in more than just getting off.

For instance, Sue and Joe played out their dynamics the few times they experimented with rear-entry vaginal intercourse. Joe brought up the topic while they were having missionary-position sex in the dark. Sue acted like he hadn't said anything, hoping he'd drop the topic. When Joe persevered, Sue reluctantly agreed. But before she moved into position, she started talking about how embarrassed and insecure this made her feel. She wanted assurances from Joe that he would be thinking about her, and not just going off in his head or fantasizing about someone else. Sue said she felt degraded to be on her knees, and worried that Joe might secretly like that. She made it clear she was only doing it for Joe, and that he owed her for going out of her way for him like this.

Fifteen minutes later, they still hadn't started having intercourse in this position. Joe lost his erection and his patience. Sue castigated him for not being interested in her feelings and only wanting sex. She covered her own feelings of inadequacy by pointing out that Joe lost his erection, so he couldn't have been very interested in rear-entry intercourse anyway. Perhaps, Sue suggested, he had his own issues about doggie-style sex.

Sue felt entitled to talk about her fears and insecurities, whenever and wherever. She demanded that Joe put her feelings first and "support" her. Earlier we said people who can't regulate their own anxiety squeeze the lives out of the people around them. Sue was good at it. This is what her mother had done to her for decades.

Like many people, Sue felt entitled to demand safety, security, and reduced anxiety before she took a risk. She kept telling Joe, "You have to make me feel secure so I can feel safe enough to have sex or want you." This was more than just her narcissism talking. People like Sue who grow up with chronic anxiety hope and pray that in a *good* marriage they finally won't feel anxious, or insecure, or vulnerable.

• *The paradox of getting your security from your spouse*

Unfortunately, trying to get your security from your spouse leads to perpetual insecurity. The more you try, the more vulnerable and insecure you become. The ensuing clutching and grabbing for your partner encourages him to move away, creating a downward spiral that destroys many marriages. Ultimately, the only security you can really count on is your relationship with yourself. Your security lies in developing your Four Points of Balance.

## SAFETY AND SECURITY IN MARRIAGE

When we first discussed co-evolution, you may have envisioned partners nurturing, accepting, and parenting each other. As we've seen, however, people with weak Four Points of Balance (Solid Flexible Self, Quiet Mind–Calm Heart, Grounded Responding, Meaningful Endurance) don't have much nurturance or acceptance to offer others. Co-evolution happens differently.

Partners "help" each other grow in more ways than their deliberate efforts to support each other's growth. Your limitations and refusal to grow, your reflected sense of self, and your difficulty regulating your own anxiety continually *encourage* your partner to grow. He is stretched by his attempts to accept and accommodate you. But eventually he reaches his limits, and his *refusal*, in turn, stretches *you and him*. It forces him to define a "self" and take a stand. You are stretched by having to face his refusal to accommodate or validate you. Marriage attempts to bring out the best in you, but it doesn't count on you operating out of the best in yourself.

### • *Conflict and instability are not the same*

Conflict in love relationships is essential to human development. Arguments, confrontations, and refusals to compromise often result from the healthy processes of differentiation. The process of holding on to your sense of self in an intense emotional relationship develops your Four Points of Balance. Increasing your Four Points of Balance leads to stable long-term love relationships and preserves your sexual desire.

Conflict, in itself, doesn't automatically create instability, any more than it always reflects growth. High-conflict couples maintain stable forms of instability designed to forestall the need to change. Constant efforts to keep things safe and secure lead to long-term marital instability. But when instability is actually the result of battles of self-development, conflict and upheaval can lead to stability and peace. Conflicts arising from sexual desire problems are often a godsend if you focus on becoming more emotionally balanced within yourself.

### • *Why attachment doesn't improve marriage and kills sex*

Anxiety drives people into attachments. That is a basic way mammals respond to anxiety. Inability to regulate our own anxiety and maintain our own sense of self drives people into—and out of—relationships. That's because the anxiety-regulating mechanisms driving their attachments require keeping things stable at all times and accommodating each other's insecurities. Relationships invariably become stale, brittle, and gridlocked. Among other things, this makes partners unable to tolerate intense intimacy (Chapter 5) or to create sexual novelty (Chapter 7).

Poorly balanced people love when therapy emphasizes attachment needs. Their insecurities take precedence over their (or their partner's) self-exploration and self-development. According to this approach, secure attachment comes first. This sequence *is* true for infants, but is *not* true for adults. Often it's the other way around: Self-scrutiny and self-development provide the basis for stable attachments. The Four Points of Balance say, "First and foremost, hold on to your self!"

Couples usually need to become better balanced, not more attached. To the degree you and your partner manage your own anxiety, you can productively meet the self-confrontations and decisions required to resolve sexual desire problems. The more you prop each other up while making life-shaping decisions, the more likely your decisions and interactions will be misguided.

Attachment is about security. When you really look at it, attachment is about *not* wanting, *not* feeling vulnerable, *not* hungering. The ideal is to be satiated, like an infant sucking at a breast. Some people don't want to *want* because they know it causes pain all too well. Approaching adulthood through the lens of their childhood needs speaks to them (but not to the best in them) because it rationalizes not wanting to want. This framework makes it more difficult to move forward.

Though it's not safe to *want* until you can quiet your own heart, couples do this all the time. It is the triumph of the human spirit, Four Points of Balance in action, and co-evolution all in one.

## • *"I'll never forgive you!"*

Sue and Joe had another series of difficult interactions in bed. Afterward, Joe said he was starting to doubt the future of their marriage. He revealed he had sexual fantasies about a co-worker. This threw Sue into a resounding emotional crash. Two weeks later, she was still going on about how Joe had hurt her. He had shaken her faith in their marriage. She would never feel secure with him again. She would never forgive him. Men just can't be trusted. Sue worked him over good.

Joe complained he was prisoner of Sue's "database." Sue maintained a mental catalogue of Joe's transgressions. It went back to when they first met. New entries were made daily, but old "wounds" were never purged. Sue's "database" gave her the high ground in any argument. If she were wrong in the current situation, she would bring up the past and get upset all over again.

## • *Many couples can't accept and forgive*

Why didn't Joe and Sue just accept and forgive each other's bad behavior, instead of bringing things to a fever pitch? Joe and Sue wondered the same thing. They did try, but failed dismally. It was more than they could pull off. They lacked the necessary Four Points of Balance. You can't forgive or accept if you can't:

- Maintain a solid flexible self. (Instead you need your partner to be continually wrong and perpetually asking for forgiveness.)
- Have a quiet mind and calm heart. (You never get over your "emotional wounds.")
- Make grounded responses. (You're at your partner's throat when he points out your transgressions.)
- Endure meaningful pain. (You hold grudges and see your partner as the enemy.)

Poorly differentiated people can't practice acceptance and forgiveness because they lack these Four Points of Balance. There is nothing wrong with partners trying to accept and forgive each other. Try it, and if it works, your problem is over. If you can't, or it doesn't accomplish what you thought, buckle down and use the approach you're learning here.

Preaching acceptance and accommodation to poorly balanced couples isn't helpful, because they take their inability to do it as further proof of their inadequacy. Poorly balanced people fervently want forgiveness and acceptance *from their partner*. They believe in borrowed functioning—at least when they're on the receiving end. Acceptance and forgiveness by your partner briefly improves your functioning, but it doesn't last and further demoralizes you.

So where does "acceptance" come in? Acceptance—and the capacity to accept—comes *after* conflict, not before it or in the middle of it. Acceptance is not a solution to conflict; it follows the resolution of conflict. Acceptance involves your prefrontal neocortex telling your limbic brain to be quiet, and this involves your Four Points of Balance.

People who are dependent on a reflected sense of self have difficulty getting over things, because they lose their identity when their feelings change. They can't accept and forgive, because the worst in them controls their functioning. But sometimes the best in us refuses to accept and forgive, too. *Refusal* to accept is an important early stage in the co-evolutionary processes of emotionally fused couples. Sue and Joe were up against more than Sue's anxieties.

## BALANCING COMFORT, SAFETY, AND GROWTH

Think of relationships as having two distinct cycles. One is the comfort/safety cycle, where your relationship remains familiar and anxiety is low. The other is the growth cycle, where your relationship changes and anxiety is higher.[138]

All living things must balance stability and growth. This includes people and relationships. Without both, things fall apart.

When you're in the comfort/safety cycle, you stick with the same routine, your reflected sense of self is supported, and your anxiety is low because things are generally calm. Things feel warm and cozy between you and your partner, and there's lots of mutual reinforcement. In the comfort cycle, you don't want for much. It's where people who don't want to want hide out. They have little desire because they have what they want, and they don't want what they don't have. They restrict their lives to what exists within the comfort cycle.

Things are different in the growth cycle. It feels unstable because you are changing. Your self gets stretched to incorporate new facets of identity, new behaviors, and new ways of being. You feel like you don't know who you are. You're not sure you like the "new you." You're not sure how you and your partner will fit together in the future. You may want your partner's reassurance and soothing, but he has neither to offer. He's going through his own personal upheaval and struggles, and may be fully preoccupied maintaining his own precarious emotional balance.

This was completely antithetical to Sue's experience with relationships. What she learned could be summarized as *In an emergency, prop up the person driving the bus, because if she gets crazy we're all in trouble.* Because she'd done this with her mother, Sue wanted Joe to do this for her—in the name of love.

### • *Leaving the comfort cycle*

When Joe and Sue came to see me, Joe was leaving the comfort cycle. He was finally starting to confront himself about their lousy sex life. Sue could sense things were changing because Joe wasn't succumbing to her typical maneuvers. She felt she was losing control of the system, so she suggested they go for therapy.

Sue and Joe's pattern is not unusual. Sue promoted therapy to resolve their marital and sexual problems. In truth, however, her goal was to get Joe back into the comfort cycle. Sue planned to talk about her fears, enlist the therapist's aid in getting Joe more empathetically attuned, and extract commitments from Joe to make her feel more secure. She thought therapy would cool off their situation.

### • *The comfort cycle changes over time*

Over time the comfort cycle changes, festering discontent. Perpetually trying to keep things the same, and avoiding anything that makes us nervous, is a recipe for boring sex, superficial intimacy, and a rigid, sterile relationship. Your dependency makes you desperate to preserve your marriage's sameness, while you mask your overpowering urge to escape it.

The comfort/safety cycle gradually becomes the avoidance cycle. Dissatisfactions grow although you hide them from each other. Your self gets lost in repeatedly selling yourself out to accommodate and keep things peaceful. Your attempts to feel safe and secure eventually drive you into the growth cycle, because the comfort cycle stops being comfortable.

Balancing stability and growth in relationships is like balancing autonomy and attachment needs. One doesn't work without the other. No marriage can exist in the comfort/safety cycle forever (and keep sex and intimacy alive). No marriage and no person can remain in the growth cycle forever, either. You need time to consolidate your gains, do the laundry, put food in the refrigerator, and relax with a familiar partner who is a new stranger in some ways. The question is, where do you strike the balance?

The answer depends on your Four Points of Balance. The stronger your Four Points of Balance, the more willing and able you are to enter the growth cycle when it is time. But the more you depend on a reflected sense of self and can't regulate your anxiety, the more you cling to the comfort cycle, and the more anxiety-provoking the growth cycle seems. So, the weaker your Four Points of Balance, the more you need to be pushed into the growth cycle. That's exactly what your relationship is designed to do. Remember, your marriage operates differently depending on your Four Points of Balance.

## • Co-evolution: Shifting from comfort to growth

Shifting your relationship from the comfort cycle to the growth cycle is another form of co-evolution. When well-balanced couples enter the growth cycle, they soothe themselves and soothe each other. (However, self-soothing is the meat of the process, and soothing each other is the gravy.) The reason they're a well-balanced couple is because they are well-balanced individuals. Poorly balanced partners can't soothe themselves or each other when they hit the growth cycle.

A watershed experience occurs when you stop giving in to your (and your partner's) anxieties, fears, and insecurities, and you do what the best in you dictates. This requires validating and soothing yourself. This transition point is a step in personal development, which in turn triggers more of the same. This process has occurred since your earliest ancestors and has become part of the people-growing machinery of marriage.

### • Comfort and growth cycles and Four Points of Balance

When people won't enter the growth cycle this frequently results in dissolution of the relationship. Your Four Points of Balance determine how long you can keep the comfort cycle from collapsing like a black hole. Most of us can keep this going for four years to seven years. During this time the lust, infatuation, and attachment phases in your brain run their course, and emotional gridlock, two-choice dilemmas, and borrowed functioning build up.

The most poorly balanced couples bite the dust first. If partners suppress their functioning and live within each other's limitations, a couple can survive for decades. Sexual desire and intimacy (and their kids) are casualties of their collusion. Adultery is common in overly long comfort cycles. In many cases, your choices are to grow up (meaning enter the growth cycle) or divorce. The 50 percent divorce rate over the last century reflects what many of us choose.

### • Blackmail and ultimatums

Sue wasn't interested in co-evolution. She wanted to keep herself comfortable, even if that meant creating a ruckus. From the outset of therapy Sue positioned herself as the victim, but she was on the attack. "If I don't give Joe what he wants, he'll leave. That's blackmail. That's extortion. It's not fair. I'm not giving in to blackmail!"

It was my responsibility to take away Sue's high ground. "The fact that he will leave if he doesn't like the deal is not extortion; he'd be exercising his rights. Of the two of you, *you* are more the blackmailer and the extortionist."

Sue was incensed and refused to deal with me. She turned to Joe. *"Are you giving me an ultimatum?"*

Joe didn't say anything.

I said, "I think you're giving Joe an ultimatum right this moment."

"What ultimatum am I giving him?"

"You're saying to him, *I demand an answer right this moment. And if you don't don't give me one there will be hell to pay."*

Sue calmed down.

"I think you're asking him several difficult questions, while making it sound like a simple answer is required. You're asking him, *'Are you doing something serious here?'* And, *'Are you drawing a line in the sand between you and me?'* You are also asking, *'Are you going to back down or not? Do you dare defy my wrath?'* On top of this, you'd like him to respond with a simple yes or no."

Sue laughed. "How can you pull out all those meanings?"

I laughed. "How you can put *in* so many meanings? You are a marvelous communicator."

Sue's edginess evaporated. Joe watched her with a sharp eye because this was unusual. Sue gestured she wasn't comfortable with him watching her, so Joe turned to me. "What should we do about ultimatums and blackmail?"

"Don't give your partner ultimatums. And don't let your partner back you into thinking you're giving one."

### • When only one partner wants to grow

If the purpose of marriage is to make you feel secure, nobody bothered to tell Mother Nature. How come marriage didn't evolve to default to people's fears of abandonment? Marriage gives control to the person who wants to grow. Relationships only remain in the comfort cycle by consensus. One partner can drive it into the growth cycle. Attachment is not the core process guiding marriages and families. It is differentiation. This is why we, and our complex love relationships, have evolved the way we have.

Marriage (and therapy) bogs down when only one partner wants to grow, *if* it focuses on mobilizing the one who doesn't want to change. The one who wants change feels obligated to get their mate to go along. He acts as if changing the relationship requires permission or consensus.

We saw the same thing in our chapter on intimacy: the LDP (for intimacy) always controls the level of *other*-validated intimacy, which is why the HDP (for intimacy) tries to coerce her. But if the HDP holds on to himself and shifts to *self*-validated intimacy, the system gives control to the person who wants to change.

Joe thought he needed to drag Sue into the growth cycle. But when he finally let go of Sue and concentrated on confronting and controlling himself, suddenly his efforts lined up with how relationships and people work. As this happened, Joe had better control of himself and more leverage in his marriage.

When one partner holds on to himself in an emotionally fused relationship, the other feels controlled. Joe's controlling himself had an immediate impact on Sue. He was not only changing their relationship; he challenged her picture of reality. Moreover, when one partner starts to develop a solid flexible self, the options of the other shrink. They have just four alternatives: Dominate your partner, submit to your partner, withdraw (divorce or separate) from your partner, or grow.

You're in the crucible when you realize there's no way around your situation. The only solution lies in going *through* it. Some problems are not meant to be solved and forgotten. *Solutions to some problems only exist after we go through them, because our development is the solution.* In this way, marriage (and the marital bed) is the cradle of adult development.


• *"How could you!"*

Shortly thereafter, Joe and Sue had a pivotal interaction that brought things to a head. Sue said she was up for sex, but once they started, things quickly went wrong. Sue launched into a litany of *her* insecurities. Joe confronted himself and didn't give in to *his* own insecurities. He didn't back down and soothe Sue. She was shocked and tried to make him adapt to her. Joe managed not to fold.

In the following days Sue went into an agitated depression. She walked around the house ranting about abandonment and trashing Joe. She compared him to her father, which she knew he wouldn't like. Sue complained that both Joe and her father had abandoned her.

Maybe things wouldn't have hit the breaking point if Sue had stopped there. But Joe was doing a pretty good job of holding on to himself. She wasn't getting the response she typically got from him, and she needed it to quiet and calm herself down. So Sue decided to take a final emotional shot at Joe, and she wanted a knockout punch. She said, *"I'm giving up on this marriage. I'm getting a divorce!"*

This was the first time Sue had done this. This was a desperate move, hoping Joe would get scared, back down, and reassure her. Neither she nor Joe anticipated that it crossed a line for him that he didn't know he had. Joe became silent.

He waited a bit before he spoke. His voice was solemn. "Don't ever tell me that again unless you're on your way out the door!"

Finally, they had arrived at critical mass.

## CRITICAL MASS: THE POINT OF FUNDAMENTAL CHANGE

What does it takes to fundamentally change your relationship? How best to handle this? Growth generally occurs outside your comfort zone: Gridlock has to reach high intensity before someone does something productive. This point is known as *critical mass.*

Critical mass is the anxiety and pressure required to trigger fundamental change. Critical mass surfaces as an "uneasy quiet" rather than an emotional explosion. Volatile arguments stop. There are no threats, no screaming or yelling, no more ultimatums.

It's hard to understand this at first, because people think critical mass involves the worst argument of your life. *Critical mass is not the worst argument you've ever had, but it is the most important.* Critical mass isn't excoriating each other in brutal "honesty telling" and blood-letting. Critical mass doesn't leave you both so wounded that you decide to kiss and make up and never to do that again.

Shouting, accusations, and threats stop when you reach critical mass, because you sense you are on the verge of pivotal change. Self-preservation tells you this is not the time to do something stupid that will shape the rest of your life—like taunting or daring your partner.

All living entities (people, couples, families, organizations, and eco-systems) have a point of irrevocable change. Even as pressures for change mount, no fundamental change occurs short of this point. Then, like the proverbial straw that breaks the camel's back, a trigger event pro-vides the catalyst. Core change can result in short order. (The world wide economic downturn is an immediate unfortunate example. Let us hope global warming is not another.)

You can have lots of things needling you to change yourself or change your relationship, and still you do nothing. But when the situation de-clines to the point you can't ignore it anymore, then everything that has built up suddenly causes core change. Some couples reach critical mass over disclosure of an affair (but others don't). For others it's serious ill-ness, or the death of a child, parent, or friend.

For Sue and Joe, it occurred when Sue threatened to leave the mar-riage. Joe was stung Sue would throw that at him, especially when he knew she wasn't really thinking of leaving. How could she stoop that low to get him to back down? It triggered Joe's memories of his parents mishandling similar points in their marriage.

- *Weak Four Points of Balance create intense critical mass*

Your emotional balance determines how much anxiety and pressure it takes for you to reach critical mass. The lower your Four Points of Balance, the more anxiety and pressure it will take to mobilize you. Well-differentiated couples can reach critical mass in sobering conversations about difficult topics pretty much as they arise. Poorly differentiated couples require an atomic bomb.

Very poorly differentiated couples have a narrow "window of oppor-tunity" to resolve their issues: They don't budge until the last moment, when pressure and anxiety are intense, and they can't think straight or stay non-reactive. Unfortunately, the rules have been laid down through millions of years of human evolution. The weaker your Four Points of Balance, the higher the level needed for critical mass.

We touched on this earlier when we said the weaker your Four Points of Balance, the lower your level of integrity. However, when your integrity stands up and you can't buy your own bullshit anymore, things happen. For lots of couples, things don't have to get worse. All it takes is someone's integrity finally standing up. That's it. Suddenly, they've reached critical mass, because by this point they are already in over their heads.

You can't fake getting to this point, because your partner's radar is on full alert. Any inconsistencies tell him you're just pretending. That's why shouting, "I've had enough!" doesn't always create critical mass. No words inherently create critical mass (not even "I'm having an affair"). Your partner has to map your mind and see you're serious about not accepting the status quo.

### • *Why couples fail in therapy*

Sue and Joe's prior therapy hadn't made a significant difference for them. Their prior therapist admonished them to compromise and negotiate, accept and forgive, and give in for the good of the relationship. They both tried to behave better, acting like they thought couples were supposed to. Joe spent time being understanding and sympathetic, and Sue made a few overtures for sex. But once sex started, it was the same old thing.

This never helped them reach an irrevocable point in their relationship from which there was no turning back. Instead, their therapy had focused on making Sue feel more secure with Joe, presuming this would lead her to feel desire and passion. Joe listened and waited until Sue felt like initiating—or, more accurately, until Sue signaled she wanted Joe to initiate. Unfortunately, Sue never got to that point, and when she didn't, she blamed Joe for failing to make her feel secure enough. Not wanting to be blamed himself, the therapist sided with Sue. Your therapist's Four Points of Balance set the upper limits of his or her ability to help you.

• *Suggestions for going through critical mass*

Whether you're the HDP or the LDP, here are some suggestions for when you're approaching critical mass. These suggestions have different applications depending on which role you're in.

- *How you go through critical mass determines how you come out.* Your best bet is holding on to your Four Points of Balance (Solid Flexible Self, Quiet Mind–Calm Heart, Grounded Responding, Meaningful Endurance). Going through gridlock face-forward, facing your anxiety, will give you the best outcome. (Being dragged through gridlock gives you little gain for your pain.)
- *Quicker is better.* You don't want to bog down in the middle. The MFHC Intensive Therapy Program and Passionate Marriage® Couples Retreats help couples reach critical mass and get through gridlock as rapidly as possible in a productive manner. Acceleration and momentum are important.
- *Forget about your partner being there for you.* Partners are often a major source of anxiety, rather than a source of security. This is especially true when things reach critical mass. When this happens, your best move always involves maintaining your integrity, calling on your resilience, and operating from the best in you. In other words, being there for yourself.
- *Stop thinking marriage can't work when only one partner wants to grow.* Marriages and families cannot function effectively solely by consensus. I've said all along that relationship stability is maintained unilaterally. So is change.
- *Don't grab the high ground (and don't give it to your partner).* When things reach critical mass, there's no point in claiming to be the "real victim" or trying to grab the high ground. And if your partner (or you) can still get away with either one, you haven't reached critical mass yet.
- *Stop trying to change your partner.* Let marriage pressure your partner instead of you trying to do it directly.
- *Confront your self.* Self-confrontation keeps you from believing

your own nonsense and allows you to learn from your mistakes. The Four Points of Balance enable you to stand up to yourself! Instead of becoming defiant when you partner confronts you, things get *really* serious when you allow this to happen and you confront yourself.

• *Don't give your partner ultimatums or threats.* And don't let your partner back you into thinking you're giving one. When you issue an ultimatum, the only person it is binding for is you.

## MARRIAGE'S GRAND DESIGN

Why do things have to reach critical mass? According to William Brietbart, psychiatrist and psycho-oncologist at Sloan-Kettering Cancer Center, "If life is always smooth, we're never challenged. Suffering is probably necessary to make us grow. The need to find meaning is a primary force, but we may need to be confronted with our own mortality for that to occur."[139]

Cancer survivors, for instance, often use going through this crucible experience to reconstruct their lives. They don't return to their prior level of functioning, they go on to greater levels. According to one scientist who is also a cancer survivor, "Post-traumatic growth is above and beyond resilience. Life after cancer means finding a new normal, but for many the new normal is better than then old normal." The Office of Cancer Survivorship at the National Cancer Institute cites altered and enhanced relationships as one example.[140] Research indicates cancer survivors frequently come out of their crucible demonstrating the characteristics of increased Four Points of Balance: bravery, curiosity, fairness, forgiveness, gratitude, humor, kindness, and an enhanced sense of meaning.

Cancer survivors survive, in part, because they develop Meaningful Endurance. Meaningful Endurance can save your marriage and your life. It's about having hope when things don't look good. Meaningful Endurance is a sense of possibility, based on facing reality and accepting inherent risks, and being willing to work things out as best you can. According to one study, hope increases your chances of surviving cancer. It's not just a matter of faith. When you have hope you take action.[141]

So what's it like to reach critical mass? People who avoid things feel some measure of panic. But once they take the leap of faith they experience peace: Clients describe it like being inside the eye of a hurricane. They see the chaos of their lives from a quiet place and begin to understand it.

Joe finally looked at how he perpetually deferred to Sue's anxieties. Actually, to his own anxieties, really. He realized how his own insecurities made him adapt to Sue in ways he didn't respect. Against the backdrop of his life history, his actions took on the larger meaning needed to trigger his integrity. Would he always live within her limitations? Would he let her dominate their marriage by escalating beyond his comfort level? These soul-searching questions increased his resolve to deal with this.

"Eye of the hurricane" experiences happen when you take a leap of faith. But if your partner won't make the leap, it's not like that for her. You stepping up to daunting personal challenges puts your partner squarely *in* the hurricane, in which case she's probably anything but serene. Seemingly out of nowhere she's confronted with issues she's successfully avoided for years.

For Sue, this meant believing she could function at a higher level. Believing she could stop crippling herself and those she loved through her steadfast unwillingness to endure discomfort for growth. Believing she could be different than her mother. This, in turn, meant growing in places she had previously cauterized. It hurts to perpetually want and hope your parents are going to change.

### • Sue's leap of faith

I talked to Sue about using the people around her. She was borrowing function from her husband and her children, restricting their lives and suppressing their functioning. I noted how her pattern was similar to her mother. Sue tried to deflect this. It took a while for her to settle down and take a leap of faith.

Sue exploded at me. "You're not listening to me!"

"I'm *listening* to you. I'm just not *agreeing* with you. And I'm not reacting to you. Your truth doesn't become more correct when you yell, no matter how deeply you feel it."

"You're invalidating my feelings and making me feel insecure."

"I'm not here to validate your feelings. I'm here to help you cope with your feelings because they're running your life and the lives of the people around you."

"I'm not sure I feel secure enough to work with you."

"I agree. You don't feel secure with me. But if we wait until you feel secure with me, I won't be much help to you. If I only operate within your tolerance level, you won't develop more tolerance. And if I don't bring things up that make you nervous, I'm of no use to you."

"How can I work with you if you make me nervous rather than secure?"

"What use is there in working with me if I do what you want?"

"Well, I don't feel secure with you!"

"Well, I don't feel secure with you either." My response took Sue completely by surprise.

"Are you saying you're afraid of me?"

I paused for a moment to break cadence, and eased my voice. "I'm afraid *for* you. You're not an easy person to confront. I figure there's a reasonable likelihood you'll storm out of here and never come back. If I do my job, there's a good chance you're going to fire me."

Sue's response was instantaneous. "I'm not going to fire you. You're the only one who's not afraid of me." Sue switched tracks so quickly it was hard to keep up with her. I noted her ability to do that.

"Oh ...Well then, that makes me feel more secure."

"Why does that make you feel more secure?"

"That makes me less afraid for you and less afraid of being out of a job."

Sue laughed. "You're not afraid of being out of job. Your practice is full." She pulled herself together as quickly as she fell apart.

I smiled. "That's right. But it makes me less afraid for you when I watch you pull yourself together when you're losing your grip on yourself. Why are you afraid that I'm afraid of you?"

"I bully people and yell a lot. I could make you feel inadequate." Sue's acknowledgement was breathtaking.

"You see yourself do that?"

"In my better moments." This was indeed one of Sue's better moments. She was taking a leap of faith.

"Well, if this is one of your better moments, you're welcome to lose it whenever you like, because it's a pleasure to see you when you pull yourself together."

What made Sue settle down? I didn't let Sue run over me or get around me. I didn't tell her what to do, but I also didn't turn away from seeing what she did (and didn't) do. At first she was furious with me. I managed to stay with her and not react. Moreover, I offered her a collaborative alliance, which she never expected. I talked to Sue straight, and her functioning rose.

Until now it had been clear Sue's functioning could deteriorate rapidly, and she was often at her worst. But Sue had lots of strengths. There was something basically decent about her. This was more important than all of her limitations, fears, and weaknesses.

When Sue began to raise her Four Points of Balance, her talents and creativity could finally blossom. She was remarkably creative, inventive, and smart. When her overall functioning was poor, she was abrasive and demanding. When I didn't blow her off, and actually listened to her and talked to her— more closely and directly than she was comfortable with—Sue's functioning came right up. She felt, looked, and functioned better for several days.

When I helped Sue pull her functioning up to a higher level, she handled things quite well. But she couldn't maintain this on her own, and fairly quickly her functioning began to diminish. Her self-doubts and feelings of emptiness returned, and she was less able to quiet and calm her anxieties.

Two weeks later Sue and Joe were locked into familiar patterns. Only now Sue was more despondent about it than before. She'd had a glimpse of how life could be—how *she* could be—and now it was gone. She was winding herself up and drowning in despair. Minutes into our next session, Sue was raging.

"Everything is falling apart. This therapy isn't helping. I thought I was getting better. You're not helping me."

Backing away from Sue now would create a catastrophe. "Were you better?"

"This therapy isn't helping. I'm screaming at my children."

"Were you better?"

"I can't do this!"

"Were you better?"

"You're not helping me!"

"Were you better?"

Sue started sobbing. "Yes. I was better."

After a minute I spoke softly, "You've had a glimpse of who you can be. You couldn't have done that if you didn't have the raw ability. You just can't maintain this level of functioning by yourself—not yet. But if you pull yourself together and stop despairing every time you stumble, you'll get better at maintaining it."

Sue did exactly what I thought she would do. Only I didn't think she would do it so quickly. Sue's functioning improved on the spot. She still had snot running out of her nose, and her cheeks were wet. But she wasn't berating me as she spoke. She talked to me as if we had an alliance.

"I saw myself."

"What did you see?"

"I saw my mother. I watched myself manipulate my daughter into doing something I wanted her to do. When she resisted I started to yell at her. I frightened her, and she would have done anything to make me look less scary!" Sue sobbed, "I am a *monster*."

I gave Sue a minute to grieve. "At the risk of invalidating your feelings, that's not what I see. I see someone who has pulled herself together from a deep emotional crash in record time. Someone who has never pulled herself together this quickly in her life. I assume you were amazed at the improvement in your own functioning. You miss it. That's why you're crashing now."

Sue looked at me through tears and chuckled as she blew her nose. "You know, you really piss me off when you see me so clearly."

### • *Joe stands up*

Our interaction gave Sue something to hold on to when she finally confronted herself. Because how you go through gridlock determines how you get into it, Sue was in a good position. Joe had something going for him, too. He witnessed our interaction and saw her response. He saw her improvement with his own eyes. He applied to himself all the things that helped Sue.

Joe was adamant he did not want to get divorced. Instead of blocking his memories, Joe reviewed vignettes of his childhood, his parents' remarriage and two divorces. He remembered crying himself to sleep because his world was crashing around him. He watched his mother and father become disappointing failures as parents and as people. Joe became determined his children would not think of him the same way.

Joe decided he would do absolutely everything he could to keep his marriage together, short of violating his integrity. He had to stop selling himself out to his anxiety—or Sue's anxieties for that matter.

What were Sue and Joe thinking as they went through the crucible?

Sue was thinking, *Joe will never take care of me again. He'll have higher expectations for me. I won't be able to get away with as much. He'll expect me to handle my own anxiety. He won't give in to me. I'm afraid. I'm scared.*

Joe was thinking, *If I don't give in to Sue, she's going to turn up the heat until I fold. Maybe I should just give in now. Once I start this and I piss her off, there's no backing out. If I do Sue will eat me alive.*

This led to a conversation one night in bed. Joe said to Sue, "I will confront myself any way you ask. I will talk to you about anything and everything until we are blue in the face. I will do whatever I can do to keep our marriage together. But if you leave now, we're through. I will not do to my children what was done to me. So there will be no trial separations. I'm not saying this to threaten you or give you an ultimatum. And I don't want to do something stupid and make you angry. I want to say this so you can hear I'm not threatening, but dead serious: Either you stay and we work this out, or you can leave and we are through."

Sue said, "Do you love me?"

Joe thought for a moment and then proceeded slowly. "I'm … I'm not going to talk to you about that now."

Sue started to escalate. "What do you mean, you're not going to talk about whether you love me?!"

Joe felt the blood drain from his face. His stomach sank and his heart raced. His mouth went dry and his jaw trembled. The muscles in his face twitched as he fought to keep himself under control. With as much evenness as he could muster, Joe spoke slowly. "I'm not going to talk to you about whether I love you because that's not what we're discussing. We're discussing whether or not you're going to leave. Everything I could say to you, I have said. Look for yourself and decide whether I love you."

Sue felt a combination of anger, surprise, and respect. She didn't say anything, but the immediate de-escalation was striking. The tongue-lashing Joe expected didn't happen. A wave of compassion for Sue swept over Joe. He said, "If you would figure out how to love yourself, we would all be much happier."

Joe looked down and his hands were shaking. He held them out toward Sue. "This is the strangest damn thing. I'm shaking, my heart is pounding, and I'm terrified. I'm afraid we'll divorce, and you'll beat the crap out of me. And in this same instant, I have this profound sense I'm doing the right thing, and I've never felt more whole in my life!"

Sue was also having a unique experience. She saw Joe doing the most forceful thing she had ever seen him do. He had never stood up to her so boldly. But Joe wasn't talking to her like an adversary. He was relating to her like a partner going through a shared experience linking their fates. They were having a profound moment of meeting.

Sue knew her usual tendency was to trump any stand Joe took with a more forceful stand of her own. She could see herself flinging at Joe, *Well, we'll see about that! I'm leaving!!* She could imagine taking the air out of Joe's newfound sense of wholeness, and enjoying it. But Joe made it clear there was no turning back. Sue knew Joe pretty well, and her mind-mapping said he wasn't kidding.

Besides, their interaction made Sue less inclined to escalate. It was impressive watching Joe master himself. Sue was shocked and impressed.

Sue said, "Okay."

"Okay what?"

"Okay, we don't have to talk about whether you love me."

"Oh."

Things were quiet for a minute. Sue began to weep softly. "I don't want to leave. I get so desperate. I don't know what else to do."

"I don't want you to leave either. But I don't want you threatening to leave every time you don't know what else to do. I don't want to live with you having one foot out the door. I'm not living with that again, and neither will my children."

"I think that's fair."

Joe was surprised Sue didn't fight this to death. The tension went out of the air. It was like Sue finally stopped standing on tip-toes and put her heels on the ground. She was much more relaxed when she spoke. "I'll think about what you said about it being better for everyone if I could learn to love myself." Sue smiled at Joe, and he burst out laughing.

Sue said, "Why are you laughing?" She was starting to laugh, too.

Joe said, "I can't believe how nervous I am! I'm so relieved this isn't a disaster."

"I am too." Sue reached out to take Joe's hand and smiled at him. She was crying again.

"I feel incredibly alive!" Joe was ecstatic.

"I do too."

For a moment Joe thought about initiating sex. This was a terrific moment, and he suspected Sue would say yes. But he decided against it. Nothing was more important than sending Sue a clear message: *This is no longer business as usual.* Besides, he was already feeling better than he usually did.

### • Resolution requires Four Points of Balance

In the weeks that followed, there were noticeable changes between Joe and Sue and how each functioned individually. They were visibly more relaxed as they sat in my office. Sue was more solid and unequivocal as she spoke. "I can see the difference. We're still fighting, but not as much, and things don't flare as high. That's a huge difference. The big thing is I haven't talked about leaving one time. Neither has Joe. We're kinder to each other. I like the new Joe a lot."

"I like the new me, too," Joe chimed in.

Sue looked softer than I had seen her before. "We made love four times in two weeks, which is a record for us. I think we surprised ourselves."

Sue blushed. "We had rear-entry intercourse. I liked it. I need more prac-tice, but I think I could relax in that position."

Sue exposed her sexuality to me in a way she had not before. This rapid, dramatic improvement in Sue's functioning testified to her resources. Many poorly functioning people are capable of similar improvement once they finally apply their Four Points of Balance. They create a stable foundation upon which their other abilities and talents can build.

I admired Sue and Joe for a moment and gave thanks that I *could* ad-mire them. It's wonderful to watch people riddled with fear and anxiety finally make an abrupt about-face and function differently.

---

### IDEAS TO PONDER

- Attachment is about security. When you really look at it, attachment is about *not* wanting, *not* feeling vulnerable, *not* hungering. Constant attempts to stay safe and secure kill sexual desire.
- Marriage gives control to the person who wants to grow. Relationships only remain in the comfort cycle by consen-sus. One partner can drive it into the growth cycle.
- Critical mass is not the worst argument you've ever had, but it is the most important.

# PART FOUR

# Using Your Body, Rewiring Your Brain, and Co-Evolving in Bed

# 11

## A Collaborative Alliance Is More Important Than Perfect Technique

*T*hus far we've discussed lots of ideas about sexual desire problems and delved into the complex emotional situations that often surround them. But one thing we haven't touched on is actually having sex. Not to worry, I've been saving this for last.

There are lots of reasons to get your body involved in resolving your sexual desire problems. Holding on to your self during sex presents different challenges than learning to keep your mouth shut during arguments. You can only develop this in real time, while you're having physical contact with your partner. Moreover, lots of couples have problems during sex which need to be resolved in mid-process.

If you've been working on your Four Points of Balance (Solid Flexible Self, Quiet Mind–Calm Heart, Grounded Responding, Meaningful Endurance), your ability to hold on to your self, soothe your own heart, and make grounded responses may have already improved. However, to resolve sexual desire problems, you have to do these things during physical contact with your partner. Close physical and emotional proximity taxes your Four Points of Balance, and sex is about as close as it gets—especially if you do it right.

Part of sexual desire stems from your physical body. It is where your animal carnality and horniness come from. Your body allows self-expression through a million variations of snuggling, kissing, stroking—and anything else you can imagine! Your brain and mind appreciate luxurious motion, quivers of delight, sensuousness, wetness, tastes, scents, and licks. The feel of flesh on flesh. Palpitating membranes. Raw materials of sweet desire.

Previously we said human sexual desire is unique because of your ability to bring many meanings to sex. You can create new meanings with your partner through your physical senses. That's what "making love" is really about. Sensory experiences endowed with profound meaning, like more eroticism, deeper commitment, or greater self-mastery, tremendously impact your psyche. More aspects of your brain are activated, because your body as well as your mind is involved. Physical contact adds a whole new dimension in which to learn about yourself, your partner, and your relationship.

That's important because you want to activate your brain in as many ways as possible. And remember, your brain tracks your body all the time. What it's doing, how it's located in space, what's touching it, and more. So if you want to send your brain a wake-up call, in addition to all you've learned thus far, use your body to do it.

You increase your chances of solving sexual desire problems by getting your mind lined up with your body. That's why you need to know what's going through your mind while you have sex. Your best bet involves approaching this from the physical *and* mental side. What is your experience of sex really like? What are you typically thinking and feeling while you're having it? You have to map your own mind in the midst of it. These things drastically affect sexual desire before, during, and after sex. They also probably affect the neural pathways your brain forms as a result of these experiences.

### • *Creating positive plastic events*

The day isn't far off when sex education courses will teach teenagers that sexual encounters are "head-wiring" experiences—profound moments of meeting that shape the neural traces laid down in your brain while it is particularly malleable and subject to change (i.e., "plastic events").

It turns out your brain is altogether more "plastic" throughout your life than scientists ever imagined, more like soft clay than carved stone. Far from being just a product of your genes or environment, it's a highly adaptable structure that undergoes constant change throughout your life. Your brain is capable of remarkable positive changes through "neuroplastic training," which essentially strengthens your brain through repetition, just like a weak muscle. There's also increasing evidence your brain can rewire itself, even in the face of catastrophic brain damage and emotional trauma.[142] It even wires itself interpersonally in response to your experiences with other people, creating neural maps of your interactions with others.[143] Mind-mapping plays an important role.[144]

Emotional learning is a good example of brain plasticity.[145] Emotional learning comes primarily through your body and personal experience rather than your intellect. If your childhood environment greatly impacted you, it was because of plasticity in the neural circuitry underlying your emotions.[146] Research indicates plasticity extends down to the level of your genes. Whether or not your genes get to express themselves is directly linked to your environment and personal experiences.[147]

Chronic stress and anxiety create profound physical and neurochemical changes in the emotional centers of your brain that give rise to your emotions. These include your prefrontal cortex, amygdala, and hippocampus.[148] Your amygdala and hippocampus are involved in emotional learning and both are extremely plastic. So much so, scientists speak of "plastic events."

Plastic events can be positive or negative. Negative plastic events are like one-trial learning experiences triggered by aversive events that create subsequent difficulty with long-term memory.[149] Sexual abuse, rape, accidents, and near-death experiences are powerful neuroplastic events. So is discovering your father or mother is having an affair. Learning by associating feelings with experiences is a plastic event that brings together sensory stimuli with biologically and psychologically relevant (survival) information.[150] Plastic events happen in your amygdala and hippocampus when upsetting things happen in your life.[151]

People exposed to severe stress tend to have a smaller hippocampus (which regulates memory). The volume of the hippocampuses of twenty-two women reporting repeated childhood sexual abuse was 5 percent smaller than women who had not been sexually abused.[152] A study of seven Vietnam combat veterans with post-traumatic stress disorder (PTSD) found they had 24 percent smaller hippocampus size than non-traumatized active-duty soldiers. In the PTSD group, those with the most severe combat experiences had the smallest hippocampus size.[153] A long-term study of fifteen children with PTSD symptoms found they also had reduced hippocampus size.[154]

Unlike your hippocampus, which becomes *less* plastic under stress, your amygdala becomes *more* plastic. Emotionally intense experiences such as fear conditioning heighten its synaptic transmissions and long-term reactivity. Rats exposed to a cat (predator threat) for five minutes showed reduced neural plasticity in the hippocampus and enhanced plasticity in the amygdala. Strong or constant stress impacts your brain in complex negative ways.[155]

However, it doesn't take something this dramatic. Rats who had four brief encounters with a more aggressive rat over a ten-day period (social defeat stress) were particularly hyper-reactive when injected with amphetamine two weeks and ten weeks later. Episodes of repeated social defeat stress may create long-lasting neural changes that sensitize your amygdala and ventral tagmental area and increase your potential for psychostimulant drug dependency.[156] High-arousal experiences produce more durable memory traces than emotionally neutral ones.[157] Traumatic emotional experiences generate pathologically strong memories, which can trigger depression and anxiety disorders.[158]

That's the bad news about neural plasticity. Here's the good news: Important brain regions remain plastic throughout your life in good ways. New findings reveal nerve growth in the hippocampus of adults. Scientists believe this can be harnessed by psychotherapy and pharmacology to create therapeutic change. Research on plasticity provides new information and realistic hope for shaping the emotional circuitry in your brain and promoting well-being.[159]

The four chapters of Part Four offer time-tested ways to use your body to create sex worth wanting, broaden your sexual repertoire, become a better lover, and improve your relationship. They offer nonverbal as well as verbal modes of resolution. These aren't "sexual techniques" in the traditional sense. For one thing, they develop your Four Points of Balance. For another, they allow you to apply the fast-growing fields of neuroplasticity and interpersonal neurobiology. It doesn't hurt to use physical interactions with your partner to create circumstances that facilitate positive brain change.

In this chapter I'll show you three ways you and your partner can physically get together that help couples resolve their sexual desire problems. But before we do that, we need to establish the mental framework on which these activities greatly depend. Physical involvement deepens the emotional impact of working things out with your partner. But understanding of what you're trying to accomplish emotionally is as important as knowing what to do with your body.

## COLLABORATIVE ALLIANCES

To start with, you need to establish a collaborative emotional alliance with your partner. Then you need to maintain it while you're having physical contact. Unfortunately, couples with desire problems usually drop their alliance during sex—if they had one to begin with.

### • *What is a resilient collaborative alliance?*

Many couples don't have sex. Lots more don't have a collaborative alliance. Some may copulate four times a week and have multiple orgasms, but they don't have a collaborative alliance during sex (or before or after, either).

A collaborative alliance is an informal agreement based on mutual interest, an unwritten treaty of union, coalition, and friendship that brings out the best in both of you. In moments when you and your mate have a collaborative alliance, your partnership is conveyed through your actions and not just words. Collaborative alliances involve working together toward mutual goals and benefits, *even when this is difficult, anxiety-provoking, or painful.* In resolving desire problems, a collaborative alliance is far more important than perfect sexual technique.

There's a difference between a collaborative alliance and a good relationship. A collaborative alliance can be made or lost in a split second. (A good relationship involves a longer time frame.) It can seem like you're getting along great one moment, and the next moment it's gone. That feeling is the sudden breakdown of the alliance. Partners in good relationships don't maintain collaborative alliances every second. But if you're generally able to maintain a collaborative alliance with your partner over a period of months and years—especially during difficult times of stress or crisis—you'll feel like you have a good relationship. As in marriage, collaborative alliances play an important role in psychotherapy and parenting. Anywhere you look, collaborative alliances are incredibly important.

As soon as couples learn about collaborative alliances, they start tracking the coming and going of their alliance (unfortunately, mostly going at first). Collaborative alliances shift quickly because they rise and fall on your emotional stability, your ability to self-soothe, and your willingness to sacrifice for a cause. Collaborative alliances hinge on your (and your partner's) Four Points of Balance. They involve your moment-to-moment ability to *hold on to your self, remain focused on your joint effort, and make yourself do what needs to be done.*

That last part is important: *Collaborative alliances focus on what needs to be done,* not just interpreting what's going wrong or nursing your own feelings.

## • *Collusive alliances*

Not all alliances are collaborative. Some couples have no alliance at all, but others form collusive alliances. *Collusive alliances* appeal to the worst in people, rather than bringing out the best, and they are common in marriages and families. Whereas *collaborative* alliances involve working together for mutual benefit, *collusive* alliances allow people to dodge their responsibilities or avoid difficult issues. Spouses often maintain collusive alliances around their respective limitations. Parents and children develop collusive alliances to deny the truth of what's happening in the family. The weaker your Four Points of Balance, the more likely your alliances are collusive.

A warm, stable, *collaborative* alliance gives your brain optimal conditions to develop during childhood.[160] Moreover, a stable collaborative alliance with your partner now can help you get over difficult experiences earlier in your life. Successfully processing your emotions facilitates brain change (brain plasticity) by (a) increasing excitability and activation of neurons, (b) facilitating the growth of synaptic connections, and (c) better integrating widely distributed regions of your brain, all of which promote better self-regulation.[161] The three forms of physical contact I'll describe shortly are time-tested forms of physical and emotional collaborative alliances that may facilitate this process. They have the additional advantage of producing seven conditions believed to encourage positive brain change.

### • *Larry and Juanita*

Let me tell you about a couple who put this system to good use. Larry and Juanita hadn't had much sex during their nineteen-year marriage. During their first year together they had sex several times a week. Things were always a little rocky whenever they got started, but they got through it and most encounters went okay. But by their second year, sex dropped off to once a month and their foreplay went to hell.

Juanita usually got anxious and jumpy as foreplay progressed. As they approached what Juanita called "put up or shut up time" (i.e., intercourse), she felt obligated to take Larry inside her. It was hard for her to calm down and see it any other way. Juanita worried that Larry would get angry if she wasn't ready, no matter how many times he reassured her. They had been going through this for years. As foreplay continued, Juanita was increasingly cut off from Larry, drowning in her own mind. Her reflected sense of self crashed, as did any alliance she had with him. By the time Larry started to insert his penis, there were no thoughts of love or partnership. In Juanita's mind, *she* was on the firing line, all by herself. She was the one who was failing. She was the screwed up one from being sexually abused as a child.

Juanita and Larry sought therapy after an emotional blow-up. Larry had made his periodic overture for sex. Juanita pretended not to notice and continued reading her book. Larry persisted, and Juanita hesitated and then agreed because they hadn't had sex in almost two months. They were both nervous as they started making love. Just before intercourse Juanita called it off, saying she was feeling nervous and pressured. This was their typical pattern. Larry rolled over and went to sleep, leaving Juanita crying in the darkness. Two days later Larry told Juanita he was finally fed up and seriously thinking about divorce.

In our initial meeting, Juanita told me she was a sexual abuse survivor. She described herself as having been nervous all her life. Father fondled her through her underwear multiple times when she was between the ages of eight and twelve. She felt obligated to let him do it. Mother had a hard time keeping herself emotionally together, and Juanita thought Mother would come unglued if she found out. Juanita became sexually promiscuous during adolescence. Now she had difficulty getting relaxed and aroused during sex with Larry.

Juanita and Larry described themselves as having "a good relationship, but with problems in the sex department." Actually, they had difficulty maintaining a collaborative alliance in lots of circumstances. Juanita dropped her alliance with Larry whenever she felt threatened or frightened. On the other hand, Larry was no better at maintaining their alliance, which is common in couples. Larry's version of dropping their alliance was stomping off after she'd "pulled back."

Each time Larry or Juanita dropped their alliance, the other felt hurt. A single sentence like "Do I really have to?" or "Are you sure you really want to?" was all it took. After almost twenty years, Larry felt humiliated when he initiated and was rejected again. He was often depressed for days afterward. Juanita alternated between rage and despair; Larry became frustrated and hopeless. The combination demoralized them for months on end.

Juanita never realized she usually dropped their alliance first. It happened every time she started to have difficulty and envisioned Larry about to get frustrated. In response to her own anxieties, she dropped her side of the alliance by telling Larry, "Now, don't be angry." This in turn upset Larry, which increased her anxiety and decreased her arousal, at which point she simultaneously pulled away and felt "abandoned."

Maintaining an alliance involves emotional resilience. If you drop your end of the alliance every time your partner drops his, you can't have a *resilient* collaborative alliance. That's why your ability to maintain a collaborative alliance hinges on your Four Points of Balance. You need to stay clear about your commitments by holding on to your self, and meeting those commitments by quieting your mind, calming your heart, and soothing your emotions when you're anxious or upset. You have to stay grounded and not overreact when your partner drops his alliance with you. A resilient collaborative alliance requires meaningful endurance when times are rough.

## SOME FAMILIES NEVER HAVE COLLABORATIVE ALLIANCES

Many of us have been shaped by our parents' inability to maintain a collaborative alliance, either with us, or with each other, or both. This shapes your brain and your behavior, especially when it comes to controlling your emotions. Your brain responds to your interactions with others, for instance, through changes in neurochemicals and neuron wiring, and controlling the expression of your genes (called *epigenetics*).[162]

Some people have genes that produce lower amounts of neurochemicals that reduce the impact of stress and trauma (like serotonin and MAOA). This reduces their resilience and makes them particularly prone to depression and suicidal thoughts when they encounter stressful life events.[163] Childhood maltreatment increases children's chances of developing antisocial personality disorders and committing violent crimes as adults.[164] However, there is a strong interaction between genes and environment (G x E interaction) in the etiology of antisocial behavior.[165] Here's where your life experiences make a huge difference. Having problem-predisposing genetics makes no difference if you're not exposed to stress or maltreatment (i.e., your genetic predisposition is not "expressed").

In Juanita's case, although physical sexual abuse happened rarely (three or four times), collaborative alliances crashed all the time when she was growing up. The daily breaking of alliances, which often happens in families where sexual abuse occurs, can have greater negative impact on children than episodic sexual abuse per se.

Juanita was her parents' "perfect daughter." From early on they wanted harmony in the house, at all times and at all costs. Her parents sent her to prestigious schools and bragged about her accomplishments to their friends. They often talked with Juanita, but hardly listened. Juanita gave her parents the daughter they wanted to see, but she knew she was invisible to them. She always said she was fine, even when she wasn't, because that's what they wanted to hear.

Juanita never mentioned her childhood sexual experiences with her father. When your father touches you sexually, you know there's no collaborative alliance. Knowing your mother won't believe you or intercede does the same. You could say Juanita was being loyal to her parents even though they weren't loyal to her. But in reality they had a *collusive* alliance.

Juanita's parents had no alliance with each other: Her mother had walked in on her father screwing the maid, and her mother never missed an opportunity to remind him of it. She would often bring this up at the dinner table. Sometimes her father encouraged Juanita to appeal to her mother on his behalf in the name of "peace." In turn, Juanita's mother used her to "work out her feelings" about things Juanita's father had done.

When Juanita's parents talked about getting a divorce, her standing as a perfect child became even more important. Juanita's grandfather was a prominent person in town, and he had expected his son to keep up appearances and stay married even if he was unhappy. From an early age, Juanita knew her extended family was untrustworthy.

Larry's family history of collaborative alliances wasn't much better. Larry's father and uncle had sued each other over a failed business. They had started the venture to get back at Larry's grandfather. Grandfather had kept them working for decades with promises that they'd eventually inherit the business. Instead, one day he told them he planned to sell it.

Larry's father and uncle tried to steal the company's clients and start their own business. They weren't successful. Things worsened when Grandfather sold the business and kept all the proceeds.

Larry's father talked big, and he expected Larry to relate to him like he was a big important man. In reality, Larry's father was a little man who needed to look bigger than he was. His approach to parenting could be summarized as: "Let me be your rubber crutch."

Repeatedly, Larry's father cooked up plans that involved Larry. Invariably, this meant Larry had to make himself vulnerable by depending on his father in some way. Ten years ago Larry co-signed a car loan for his father. His father didn't pay it off, and the bank demanded payment from Larry. Two years ago, his father owed money to several people and Larry paid seven thousand dollars to keep him from going to jail. Dad promised to repay him, but Larry never saw a nickel. This hurt Larry and Juanita financially, because they didn't have gobs of money. But the real pain came from watching his father repeatedly drop the collaborative alliance Larry kept offering him.

Given their histories with their respective parents, it wasn't surprising that Juanita and Larry maintained a collusive alliance to avoid their sexual problems for over fifteen years.

## • Collaborative alliances in marriage

Your ability to maintain a collaborative alliance is rooted in human evolution and culture.[166] But forget the notion that marriage is inherently "till death do us part." Nothing could be farther from the truth. Anthropologist Helen Fisher notes most animals don't pair-bond, and those who do have two things in common: They give birth to helpless babies, and parents don't stay together for life, only long enough to co-parent their babies through infancy.[167] From this, Fisher realized kinship, rather than marriage, has been the steward of human evolution over the ages.[168] When couples broke up, mothers turned to kin for help. Junior had more contact with Auntie, Uncle, and Grandma than with Dad.

Kinship ties often outlast marriages because kinship relationships tend to be less intense. They involve fewer two-choice dilemmas, more degrees of freedom, and more emotional and physical space in which to interact. They don't tap your Four Points of Balance as much as marriage (although this isn't true in highly emotionally fused families). The more kinship relationships approach the intensity of monogamous marriages, the more collaborative alliances in extended families tend to break down. So if kinship rather than a two-parent household is the bedrock of civilization, you'd better be particularly good at maintaining a collaborative alliance if you want a stable long-term marriage.

You're not destined for one if you count on mammalian bonding to keep the two of you together. Alliances based on lust, romantic love, and attachment are short-lived. Collaborative alliances based on loyalty and integrity last longer. But loyalty in the face of adversity requires a fairly sophisticated "self." *Wanting* your marriage, and keeping it together by maintaining a collaborative alliance, is another way we humans evolve. So if you want a marriage based on a resilient collaborative alliance, you better get your Four Points of Balance involved, and keep your prefrontal neocortex in gear.

### • *Mind-mapping in collaborative alliances*

Mind-mapping plays a huge role in collaborative alliances. Collaborative alliances involve:

- Being honest even when it's personally disadvantageous or difficult.
- Not tampering with or withholding information to manipulate your partner.
- Confronting yourself, and letting your partner mind-map you and read you accurately.

As I said, collaborative alliances require working on mutual goals, even when they are anxiety-provoking or personally disadvantageous. When you misrepresent yourself, you've dropped your alliance. When you mask your mind from accurately being mapped, you've done it again. Some of us couldn't carry a collaborative alliance if it was given to us wrapped up in a box.

# MAINTAIN A RESILIENT COLLABORATIVE ALLIANCE

People drop their alliance for many reasons. Some do it because they aren't personally invested or they have limited capacity to invest in other people to begin with. Others drop the alliance because they want to get even. Some feel *entitled* to crash their alliance once things start going downhill. When you're struggling with "selfhood" issues like "who do you belong to," alliances usually evaporate. If you don't have much of a solid flexible self, collaborative alliances come and go as circumstance and convenience dictate.

Collaborative alliances frequently get dropped in the midst of emotional gridlock and two-choice dilemmas. At the first sign of trouble, Juanita bailed out. Every time she and Larry started having sex, she demanded his patience and acceptance. If he showed the slightest negative personal reaction or frustration, she ended the encounter.

### • *Eight key points about collaborative alliances*

Marriage is the Olympic training camp for collaborative alliances. Only your solid flexible sense of self can maintain a collaborative alliance when things get tough. In a collaborative alliance, the first person you confront is yourself. It's your primary responsibility. Self-confrontation is critical to maintaining a collaborative alliance, because that's how you check to see if you're doing your part. Resilient collaborative alliances require staying clear about your goals and values. Soothing your own heart keeps you from overreacting when your partner drops his alliance with you. You don't bail out, and you don't get all bent out of shape when he does. Your Four Points of Balance, the basis of human resilience, let you re-establish a collaborative alliance and move on. This is how collaborative alliances are sustained in the face of anxiety. If you want a collaborative alliance with your partner, here are eight key points to keep in mind:

#1. First and foremost, *collaborative alliances focus on what needs to be done.* Listening to your partner and speaking up for yourself are

276 INTIMACY & DESIRE

important in a collaborative alliance. But at the end of the day, collaborative alliances don't float on feelings, particularly when they're not backed up with behavior.

#2. *Re-establishing a collaborative alliance with your partner is more important than the fact that your alliance crashed.* Relationship repair is the most important thing. Keeping your marriage going is more important than your fears that your marriage is sinking.

#3. *Pay attention to when **you** drop your alliance.* The more supersensitive we are to others dropping their alliance with us, the more oblivious we may be to ourselves doing it. The first, hardest, and most important step in rebuilding a collaborative alliance involves being aware and acknowledging when you drop your side of it. Getting clear how *you* (not your partner) repeatedly drop your alliance improves things quickly. (It often echoes your prior life history, so you can anticipate where you're prone to do this.)

#4. *How you feel isn't the main issue.* Getting nervous doesn't entitle you to drop your end of things. The key issue in collaborative alliances is living up to your responsibilities. The fact that your feelings are understandable, given your circumstances, doesn't change your responsibility to hold on to your self and do what's right.

#5. *In a collaborative alliance your responsibilities are unilateral, not mutual or reciprocal.* A collaborative alliance involves unilaterally keeping up your end of the deal when your partner has temporarily dropped his (or hers). Your partner's bad behavior doesn't excuse your own. Rather than leaving your responsibilities unfulfilled and letting the lowest common denominator run your relationship, confront your partner about dropping his part of the bargain *after* you are sure you have fulfilled yours.

#6. *Collaborative alliances don't always feel good.* Sometimes collaborative alliances require confronting, challenging, and refusing to accommodate. This can be hard. Likewise a collaborative alliance does *not* mean always making your partner feel good about himself, or validated or accepted, or safe and secure. Collaborative alliances are defined by function, rather than feeling. (*Collusive* alliances revolve around making people feel particular ways.)

#7. *Collaborative alliances never involve blinding yourself* about your partner, or yourself, or what's going on between you. In a collaborative alliance everyone keeps their eyes open and their minds alert. Mind-mapping plays an important role. Don't shield your mind from being read accurately. (Asking someone to overlook your shortcomings, and offering to overlook his or hers, is a collusive alliance.)

#8. *Collaborative alliances test your integrity.* Ultimately, people keep their end of good-faith bargains to maintain their own integrity. It's always easier to drop your alliance and "look out for yourself" in the narrow sense. But as you become better differentiated, you do what you know to be right, in order to be at peace with your self in your own mind. An alliance formed of convenience may look collaborative, but when things get difficult it will fall apart.

### • *Don't presume you have a collaborative alliance*

Don't assume you have a collaborative alliance with your partner. Normal couples with desire problems (and/or sexual dysfunctions) often don't. Even if this didn't cause your desire problem, it usually is the result. If you realize you're dropping your alliance with your partner, there's actually cause for optimism: Things don't have to stay that way— *if* you strengthen your Four Points of Balance.

When couples say they have issues about "trust," they're really struggling with repeated breakdown or absence of a collaborative alliance. I've never found calling it a trust issue helps much, because this involves having faith in your partner's efforts. Things go better when approached as a lack of collaborative alliance. It shifts the focus from belief to performance.

## METHODS FOR BUILDING A PHYSICAL COLLABORATIVE ALLIANCE

Collaborative alliances provide the necessary framework for the activities I promised to share with you. You need to create a collaborative alliance in tangible physical form by you and your partner using your bodies. This means creating physical interactions that embody your collaborative alliance. You need to do this repeatedly and in different ways. I'm going to show you three ways do this in and out of bed. They are ways to use your body to change your mind, and quite possibly change your brain. This may be why they are so effective.

Keep a broad perspective as you learn about these tools. Don't simply focus on physical technique. Your goal is to focus your attention on a large number of important dimensions at once, creating a rich and meaningful multi-layered experience.

### • *Hugging till relaxed*

Your first major tool is *hugging till relaxed*.[169] Hugging till relaxed is elegant and simple. It has sophisticated uses, but its basics are easy. Here's all you do:

1. Stand on your own two feet.
2. Put your arms around your partner.
3. Focus on yourself.
4. Quiet yourself down. *Way* down.

With practice, anyone can take *hugging till relaxed* to profound levels. It doesn't require nudity or genital contact. You're probably better off doing it with your clothes on at first.[170] (Take your shoes off.) If you're emotionally estranged and not ready for full-blown sex, even if you don't want to arouse your partner or make her feel good, *hugging till relaxed* gets you started working with something physical. It's about centering yourself, physically and emotionally, while you and your partner have your arms around each other. It's simple enough to be worth a try, and it helps a wide range of desire problems and sexual dysfunctions.

Notice I didn't describe this as holding each other. That's a whole other mind-set that adds another degree of complexity. Allowing your partner to hold you, and holding your partner, triggers issues for most couples. I suggest you think about this as putting your arms around your partner, and holding on to your self. It points you in the right direction for what you need to do: Apply your Four Points of Balance as you stand there with your partner.

Initially, *hugging till relaxed* involves relaxing your body and mind by focusing on your body while you're in broad physical contact with your partner. Getting physically comfortable with your partner takes a while, both in a given encounter and over the course of time. Things can feel uncomfortable and awkward at first. It can take a month of frequent practice of five to ten minutes to get over this. Repetition is important.[171] If you're willing to endure meaningful discomfort for growth, *hugging till relaxed* eventually feels like you're melting into warm butter—but not losing yourself in the process.

You can use *hugging till relaxed* many different ways. At first, it is a mindfulness activity, a way of centering yourself, quieting your mind, and getting control of your emotions—while you're close to your partner. You could be great at meditating quietly by yourself, and still lose yourself when dealing with your mate. Holding on to your self (remaining mindful) becomes increasingly difficult as you become physical and emotionally engaged with your partner. *Hugging till relaxed* gives you a chance to practice this in real time, instead of just talking or thinking about it.

*Hugging till relaxed* lets emotionally and physically alienated couples re-establish comfortable physical contact, which their normal (brief) sexual pattern does not permit. You need time to cool things down inside you, and with your partner. *Hugging till relaxed* is a great way to do it.

Sooner or later (for many couples it's sooner), *hugging till relaxed* heats things up. The issues in your relationship will surface in your hugging. Who has difficulty letting herself be held? Who's leaning on whom? Who's making whom adapt? What happens when one loses her balance? Who wants to let go first? How is this communicated? What does the other do? Who initiates more of the time? The issues and dynamics are incredible.

This is your chance to work out these emotion-laden issues, physically and emotionally, as they arise (and to think and talk about them afterward). If dealing with issues like this is usually a disaster, here's your real-time opportunity to hold on to your self and handle this better. If you normally drop your collaborative alliance with your partner when something upsetting occurs, practice maintaining it here. I explain how to do this below.

You may need to stop hugging for a moment to straighten things out with your partner. This taps your ability to speak up for yourself and gives you practice taking feedback you might normally reject or feel is hurtful. If you hold on to your self, maintain your alliance with your partner, and validate yourself to say or hear something new, you should be able to return to *hugging till relaxed* and re-establish a mindful emotionally quiet and physically stable connection.

*Hugging till relaxed* can increase your Four Points of Balance. It's a tangible way to teach yourself how to stand on your own two feet, physically and emotionally, while you're close to your partner. You can use it to calm yourself down when you and your partner are both nervous. It improves your ability to quiet and calm yourself down without having to pull away from your partner. This last point is important. You can quiet yourself when your partner floods with anxiety. You don't have to move away from her, or calm her down to calm your own emotions. This is critical if you have sex and intimacy problems, because couples pass anxiety back and forth like a virus.

You have to learn to settle yourself down, even when (and especially when) your partner is unsettled, uncomfortable, or upset. That's where your Four Points of Balance come in.

- *How to handle things that surface while hugging till relaxed*

  1. Sooner or later, one partner loses her physical balance. If this starts to happen, let go of your partner, regain your balance, and re-engage. Emotionally fused couples sway back and forth, struggling to regain their balance while rigidly holding on to each other. If your stability comes from your partner, you have to control her to stabilize yourself. Physical and emotional balance works the same: The best thing to do when your partner starts to lose herself is hold on to *your* self, maintain your own balance, and quiet down.

2. If your partner pulls or pushes you off balance, or leans on you, move as is necessary to keep your own balance. *Just don't drop your alliance.* It can be as simple as whispering, "You're pulling me off balance. I need to readjust my position," and shifting your feet to regain your balance. If need be, you can bring your arms down while you remain in place. Let your partner know you need to momentarily disengage before you do it. If your partner is really leaning on you or pulling you off balance, step back if need be. Keep your purpose collaborative. Step forward to your partner. Re-center yourself. Reach out your arms and resume *hugging till relaxed.*

3. If you're not used to a relaxed physical connection, you may feel stiff and awkward when you start. When you finally start to relax, you'll probably have to readjust your body's position. What initially suited you no longer feels balanced. You need to move to get more comfortable on your feet *and* to better "fit" your partner. Couples feel constrained to move, fearing this will rupture their alliance. They fear their partner will misinterpret this as a signal they want to stop. They end up increasingly tense and uncomfortable in a misguided gesture. It's difficult to move in a hug—or a relationship—when partners take each other's readjustments as personal rejection.

   It works best to gently say, "I'm shifting position to get more comfortable. I don't want to stop." A collaborative alliance requires doing what is necessary to keep your balance. Remember this when your partner wants to adjust her position.

4. A two-minute hug often seems like eternity at first. Ten seconds is a long time for some couples. I recommend ten minutes to start. You may need fifteen minutes or more to finally relax your body, quiet your brain, and reach a deep, relaxed connection. Once you can do it, it will happen more quickly, and you'll do it longer because it feels good.

5. Start by focusing on your body sensations and slowing your breathing until you are emotionally and physically quiet. If you can't quiet down, focus on the emotions, perceptions, and memories from your past ("autobiographical memories") that occupy your mind. You don't have to concentrate on breathing or relaxing your body, particularly if that's not working for you. If you can't relax, pay attention

to what's getting in the way. If the pictures are upsetting, once you see what they are, try calming your mind by counting breaths.[172] You don't have to worry if you're not relaxing. There is always something to focus your attention on that can help you.

6. As you get better at doing *hugging till relaxed*, you can add new layers of attention: What's happening between you and your partner? Is your partner able to relax? What happens when you deliberately try to change your position? How do you make sense of your partner's response?

7. When *hugging till relaxed* becomes warm, comfortable, and reliable, use it to work through prior negative experiences. Briefly focus on mental images and memories of bad times that haunt you. Then return to focusing on your body, your solid relationship with your partner, and the feel of her body and the smell of her hair.

This multilayered focus of attention produces new associations in your mind and possibly new information-processing configurations in your brain.

### • *Juanita's process*

Juanita couldn't calm down the first three times she and Larry tried *hugging till relaxed*. But she was determined to keep up her end of their alliance. They kept at it, and she got to the point where she wasn't so tense. Then they started doing it more often. After doing it five or six times in a week, for ten minutes at a time, Juanita felt "good" while doing it. After three weeks, Juanita finally *relaxed*.

Shortly thereafter, there was a time where Juanita adjusted her position to get more comfortable. She smelled Larry's hair. She breathed deep to fill herself with his scent. Her brain recognized this as "home." She felt balanced within herself, and balanced with Larry. She could feel he felt the same. Juanita realized she was finally with Larry in the midst of an embrace. The impact was staggering.

Juanita's mind flashed to her parents. She couldn't imagine feeling this ease with either one of them. Father was a weak man who sexually exploited her and had affairs, and Mother was a empty bitter woman who loved to spread misery. Juanita swayed just a bit as she thought this, and Larry instinctively tightened his arms around her. It was just a tiny adjustment, but enough to register in Juanita's mind. She realized Larry was holding her. Juanita relaxed her body and her mind, and let herself be held. It wasn't so much a change in body position, it was more of a state of mind. She took a deep breath and exhaled a long, deep sigh of relief from the bottom of her soul.

• *Right brain–left brain integration*

Use *hugging till relaxed* to get the two sides of your brain better integrated. Your left brain thinks methodically, like a serial processor in a computer. It thinks in language and operates by logic. Your left hemisphere is dominant for drawing cause–effect relationships (syllogistic reasoning), linear thinking, and language semantics. It stores your autobiographical memories (your life history) in "explicit memory," meaning you can recall events by consciously thinking about them.

Your right brain has a distinctly different personality. It focuses on this present moment right now. It thinks in pictures rather than words. It operates like a parallel processor, taking in information from your five senses (your entire body) and producing an explosive integration that makes you conscious of the world around you and the people in it. Your right hemisphere connects you with other people by how they taste, smell, feel, sound, and look.

Your left brain takes the collage of activity in your right hemisphere, pulls out huge numbers of details, associates them with past learning, and projects the present out into future possibilities. This is where your inner voice ("I am!") and your calculating cunning intelligence reside.[173]

Your right hemisphere is "online" from birth. (Your left brain and explicit memories come online later). It grows markedly in your first three years, and its development is impacted by relationships with parents and other caregivers. The right side of your brain is dominant in tracking and regulating your body, and learns through body movement. It is more involved in perceiving and processing emotion, including facial displays of emotion and nonverbal aspects of language like gestures and tone of voice. It is especially involved in intense emotional experiences, retrieval of autobiographical memories, and mapping other people's minds.

Your right brain is also where your implicit memory is located.[174] Implicit memory records, among other things, early (pre-verbal) events you were too young to remember, but which impacted you nonetheless. Implicit memory can influence your current reactions even though you can't explicitly recall what triggers your feelings. If you have negative reactions to sex that you don't understand, or painful childhood experiences that may be getting in your way, you definitely want to get your body and right brain involved in creating new solutions.

Now let me explain what you're trying to do with *hugging till relaxed*: You want to get both sides of your brain talking to each other. Your right and left brains communicate through a nerve bundle, but otherwise, the two sides operate relatively independently.[175] As we'll discuss in the next chapter, trauma further isolates the hemispheres from each other. But whether or not you have been traumatized or abused, getting both sides working together facilitates neural growth, boosts your functioning, and increases your likelihood of resolving sexual desire problems.

If you want a coherent personal life story based on accurate autobiographical memory, your right and left hemispheres have to exchange information. Your ability to see yourself in the past, present, and future (known as "mental time travel") predominantly comes from your right hemisphere. Mind-mapping mostly occurs there as well. Your left hemisphere tries to interpret this using autobiographical memories retrieved by your right hemisphere, searching out cause-and-effect relationships through linear logical deductive thinking. If there are holes in your autobiographical memory, or your left and right hemispheres don't communicate, *your brain will readily construct a picture of your life that's inaccurate enough to keep your anxiety down, and accurate enough to keep your mind's deception-detector from going off.*

All this comes into play during *hugging till relaxed*. Your right brain detects that you and your partner are physically and emotionally relaxed with each other (or not). Your left brain infers what this means and where things are headed. *Hugging till relaxed* can get both sides talking to each other. Our next activity does this too.

### • *Heads on pillows*

*Hugging till relaxed* sets the stage for *heads on pillows*.[176] *Heads on pillows* puts you right where couples often have trouble, and lets you do something new about it. Here's how you do *heads on pillows*:

You and your partner lie on your sides, facing each other. Put your heads on your own pillows. Get your heads far enough apart so your partner doesn't look like a Cyclops. Then, quiet your mind and calm your heart. *Heads on pillows* is much like *hugging till relaxed* only lying down. They differ in that you'll be gazing directly into your partner's eyes and reclining together. If your intimacy tolerance isn't challenged by *hugging till relaxed*, *heads on pillows* may do that.

In *heads on pillows*, neither partner lies underneath or on top of the other. Both of you have one arm free. If you want to touch, touch each other's hand or face. With your mind and eyes, try to touch your partner's heart. You may feel awkward at first, but if you settle down and give yourself a chance, results can be dramatic.

You may not be comfortable with this level of intimacy. You become acutely aware of yourself, your partner, and the connection (or lack of it) between you. If during sex you tune out your partner and focus only on your physical sensations, *heads on pillows* can be challenging and productive. *Heads on pillows* lets you establish and maintain a collaborative alliance physically, in real time. For many couples, it's a godsend.

Remember, the closer Juanita and Larry got to intercourse, the more Juanita got nervous. No matter how much Juanita relaxed during *hugging till relaxed*, she got nervous when they lay down and intercourse became more likely. *Heads on pillows* allowed them to calm themselves down and re-establish their collaborative alliance once they were in bed. This was the optimal point to catch Juanita's downward emotional slide, the point where Juanita began to lose herself.

Building on the benefits of *hugging till relaxed*, Larry and Juanita put *heads on pillows* to good use. Instead of getting lost in mental pictures of things going wrong, Juanita focused on Larry. What she saw in his face showed her that the pictures in her mind were wrong. Rather than her fears and anticipations coming between them, *heads on pillows* made Larry her ally in dealing with them.

Thoughts and feelings of being pressured were still in her mind, but Juanita realized they were coming from her brain rather than from Larry. Larry didn't expect her to turn herself over to him. Larry wasn't being like her father. Larry wanted her to get a grip on herself. Thinking this made it easier to settle down and relax again.

After several repetitions, Juanita said, "Hey! Forget intercourse. Just give me *this*. If you want more of this, that's fine with me." The warmth of her voice said she wasn't dodging intercourse. She was invested. She *wanted* to do this with him.

This wasn't simply because Juanita's emotional needs were being met. Non-verbal aspects of *hugging till relaxed* and *heads on pillows* probably create "right-hemisphere-to-right-hemisphere brain attunement." That's where your right hemisphere can directly connect with your partner's right hemisphere. The right hemisphere is dominant in regulating your body and emotional states and social and emotional communication, especially nonverbal messages from facial expression, gestures, and tone of voice. It appraises the emotional meaning of things. Getting all these aspects aligned within both of you and between the two of you creates a powerful emotional connection. Your next tool does all of this as well.

### • *Feeling while touching*

Your third tool is *feeling while touching*. After years of living numbed emotional lives, you feel no one and no one feels you. Lots of partners stop feeling each other when they have sex, too. One touches the other, but they have mentally left the room.

Touching without feeling is pretty common, if not the norm. You can avoid feeling your partner during kissing, foreplay, and intercourse. (Imagine deep-kissing when your partner has bad breath, and you'll feel yourself do it.) You can also make it hard for your partner to feel you. In theory, sex is a good way to connect with your partner, but, in practice, it's where many people disconnect.

*Feeling while touching* doesn't have to involve drastic changes in behavior. One partner touches the other, while both of you mentally follow your point of physical connection as it moves. Instead of focusing on your sexual technique (or on your physical sensations) focus on *feeling* each other.

*Feeling while touching* requires a renewed collaborative alliance rather than new physical positions. You can start with any way you can feel each other. I suggest starting with hands, face, and arms rather than with each other's breasts, buttocks, and genitals. Once you recognize what feeling your partner (and being felt) is like, "follow the connection" as the two of you expand your range of touch. Let that feeling be your guide as to what to do next. When you can't feel your partner, stop briefly and return to what you were doing when you could. Discipline yourself to stick with what works and stay in the moment with your partner. That's your collaborative alliance. There's no technique or sequence to follow. It's just you and your partner, and what's happening between you.

Talking is appropriate. Smiling helps. Crying is allowed. Tears often flow as partners rediscover old friends. Slow-paced touch usually works better. Candles, incense, and music help create a soft, inviting mood. However, they can also feel artificial and contrived. Sometimes it's best to keep things simple to keep the focus on the two of you. Profound silence can be perfect, too.

Bridging from *heads on pillows* to *feeling while touching* went relatively smoothly for Juanita and Larry. All it took was Larry tenderly touching Juanita's arm. Juanita let her mind follow Larry's touch, and Larry felt her opening to his caress. Juanita and Larry did *feeling while touching* all over each other's body. Juanita settled down, and they enjoyed being together in whole new ways. The experience was an end in itself, completely satisfying.

This led to a common situation: Juanita encouraged Larry to insert his penis and have intercourse. As she said this, Larry's ability to feel Juanita completely evaporated. He hadn't even moved a muscle. Larry said, "I don't know if it's you or it's me, but I suddenly can't feel you. Let's stay with what we're doing until we can be together when we do that."

Juanita smiled. "I felt it leave too, but since I offered, I felt I couldn't say anything. I offered intercourse thinking that's what you wanted."

Larry laughed. "Please, no more favors like that." His tone was light but serious. Juanita nodded and they went back to stroking each other's bodies.

"Hmmmmmmm." Juanita sighed.

"I know," Larry said, "I can feel you again too."

- *The big three tools vs. intercourse*

*Hugging till relaxed, heads on pillows*, and *feeling while touching* have many things in common. They build a collaborative alliance with your partner. They are physical forms of collaborative alliances. They make your alliance with your partner more resilient. And they tangibly demonstrate your progress.

Each tool quiets your brain. Each one is a window into your mind. Each one is shaped by you, your partner, and your relationship. No two couples see, say, and do the exact same thing. You can use these tools early in rebuilding a collaborative alliance.

*Hugging till relaxed, heads on pillows*, and *feeling while touching* are better than intercourse for jump-starting a collaborative alliance (especially if you've stopped having sex). The gymnastics and gyrations of coitus don't promote emotional contact and renewed friendship, and make it easier to fool yourself that you're together.

You go through different stages of comfort and relaxation with each activity. First, you just try to get through it. (Some people can barely contain their twitching.) Then you relax and start to enjoy it. When you stop anticipating something's going to go wrong, you can be a little playful. Eventually your breathing is unlabored, your heart slows, and your shoulders relax. You can get so relaxed and quiet, your jaw goes slack, you're breathing from the back of your throat, and your eyelids are heavy. You can *hear* the quiet, not as an absence of sound, but as the presence of *peace*.

This can take weeks or months, but you can get there by methodically using your collaborative alliance with your partner. Once you've learned how to establish this deep level of contact, you can extend it into intercourse.

*Hugging till relaxed, heads on pillows*, and *feeling while touching* have something else in common. All three create seven conditions scientists believe facilitate brain change. These include:

1. A strong and resilient collaborative alliance.
2. Moderate levels of stress and emotional arousal, alternating with calm.
3. Intense and profound intersubjective moments of meeting.
4. Information and experiences gathered across multiple dimensions of cognition, emotion, sensation, and behavior.
5. Activating brain neural networks involved in processing and regulating thoughts, feelings, sensations, and behaviors.
6. New conceptual knowledge integrating emotional and bodily experiences.
7. Organizing experiences in ways that foster continued growth and integration.[177]

Whether or not these conditions permanently change your brain's chemistry or structure, *hugging till relaxed, heads on pillows*, and *feeling while touching* offer other benefits, including more control over yourself and a more stable and rewarding relationship.

### • *Larry and Juanita take their alliance seriously*

In the midst of all this progress, Larry's father approached him with another sure-fire scheme. Larry told him he wasn't interested. To make the point, Larry did something he never imagined he'd do. He told his father to forget about repaying the seven thousand dollars he'd spent keeping him out of jail. Larry figured he'd never see the money anyway, so instead he decided to increase his Four Points of Balance. Larry unhooked from his father. It was a self-preserving move. He stopped being tortured about whether his father would repay him or not.

Larry looked his father in the eye and added, "Dad, if you want to keep a relationship with me, don't come for money or another deal ever again. Do you understand?"

Dad didn't say anything for a minute. Then he laughed it off, saying, "Well, I guess I'll just have to keep my millions to myself." But his message was *Okay. I hear you.*

That didn't mean Dad wouldn't try something in the future. But he saw Larry was solid and decided not to mess with him. Juanita was bowled over by what she observed. Later that night she told Larry, "I loved the way you told your father you weren't going to climb out on a limb for him, knowing he would cut it off."

Larry's eyes were warm and smiling, "Thanks," he said and paused, looking Juanita in the eye. "I also want that to stop between you and me. I'm not having any more sex the way we usually do it. You don't want to feel pressured, and I don't want you mentally absent when we have sex. Either we stay together and keep our alliance, regardless of what we do, or I'm not interested."

Juanita looked inside herself for a moment. Then she met his gaze and nodded.

## PUT YOUR COLLABORATIVE ALLIANCE TO GOOD USE

A collaborative alliance is a major part of resolving sexual desire problems.[178] Things went differently when Larry and Juanita attended to it during sex. They focused on their emotional connection even before they started kissing and stroking. First and foremost, they paid attention to each other. It became a standard part of their collaborative alliance. They began to notice when their attention drifted off. They mentioned it (instead of masking it), and brought themselves back.

One time Larry stopped as they stroked each other. "You may not want to hear this, but I just went off in my head … I was thinking about my father. I know that's not romantic. He called me today. He hinted he was short on cash. I told him I was sorry to hear that but I had to get off the phone . . . I was proud of myself, but disappointed in him . . . I'm telling you this because I don't want to live afraid of the people I love."

"Me neither." Juanita thought about her parents and her relationship with Larry. They held each other's gaze for a long, bittersweet moment.

Larry said. "In the interest of full disclosure . . . I've lost my erection."

"Don't worry about it," purred Juanita. "Just look at me . . . " Larry didn't look.

"Hey. Look at me." Juanita shook him gently and caught his eye. "Don't take away the best teammate I've ever had."

Larry looked at Juanita. They were instantly in tears. Juanita said, "Come. Let me hold you. Let's lie down and just be together."

Thirty minutes later, things felt warm and cozy. Juanita reached down and touched Larry's penis. It quickly rose from the dead.

"Come inside me. I'm ready for company. Don't try to make me come. I just want to feel you in me." Larry hesitated for a moment and nodded.

Juanita got on her back. Larry got between her legs to insert himself. She spread her labia. "Here. Let me help you come inside me."

As Larry leaned forward, Juanita said, "Wait a second, Let me scoot up a little! You'll have a better angle. It will be easier for you to get in."

Larry looked at Juanita. They had the same thought: *"Collaborative alliance!"* and broke out laughing.

---

### IDEAS TO PONDER

- Partners drop alliances when sexual desire problems surface.
- Collaborative alliances involve (1) being honest even when it's difficult, (2) not tampering with the truth, (3) confronting yourself and letting your partner confront you and read you, and (4) operating from the best in you.
- *Hugging till relaxed, heads on pillows,* and *feeling while touching* are powerful tools for resolving sexual desire problems because they involve collaborative alliances.

# 12

# Curing Ticklishness
# and
# Noxious Touch

*A*re you ticklish? How about your partner? Odds are that one of you is. Ticklishness is a bigger problem than you may realize. Ticklish touch can directly interfere with sexual desire. I routinely ask my clients if they are ticklish for an additional reason: Taking care of ticklishness can really help desire problems and put a sexual charge in your love life.

There are many common forms of ticklishness. Do you have difficulty settling down when it's time for sex or snuggling? Do you feel twitchy or jumpy when your partner touches you? Does your partner's touch feel noxious or irritating? You can cure these feelings. Even if you're not ticklish and don't have any of these problems, understanding ticklishness teaches you a lot about sexual desire problems and collaborative alliances.

## WHAT IS TICKLISHNESS?

Ticklishness is a disagreeable tingling sensation, distinct from itching or pressure. It is often accompanied by nervousness, involuntary squirming, twitching, and laughter. Genetics may determine how ticklish you are; however, the majority of people are ticklish.[179]

I began studying ticklishness decades ago, when I realized many of my clients struggled with it. I paid close attention to how and why people became ticklish, and how this operated between partners. For example, laughter accompanying ticklishness can confuse you *and* your partner because it's reflexive and not a sign of pleasure. This creates mind-mapping errors and kills collaborative alliances.

To my surprise, curing ticklishness turned out to be a wonderful way to resolve desire problems because it increases your Four Points of Balance, improves your relationship, and enhances your love-making. Best of all, many couples finally experience *peace* lying relaxed in each other's arms.


• *Anthony and Colleen*

Anthony and Colleen weren't familiar with peace. After three years of celibacy, they sought my help restarting their sexual relationship.[180] They had been married seven years and had two children, a boy and a girl, age six and four. When they met in college, Colleen liked having sex with Anthony. It felt great to be with him, and she had orgasms when they made love. In my office, Colleen said she didn't know what her problem was now, but she had no desire for sex. She didn't think this had anything to do with her feelings for Anthony, or a dozen other things she'd considered and rejected.

Anthony brought up Colleen's ticklishness, with obvious exasperation. At that point in our session they both became defensive and their alliance cratered. According to Anthony, Colleen was too ticklish and she didn't like sex. According to Colleen, Anthony was too impatient and he wouldn't listen to what she needed. She explained, "When Anthony touches me, my skin starts crawling. I have to fight with myself just to let him touch me. I get angry at him for touching me that way, and angry at myself for being this way. Believe me, Doctor, at that point I'm not the least bit interested in sex."

Colleen had traits that predispose ticklishness. In general, she was shy, easily frightened, prickly, and easily upset. Her overall demeanor said, *I am someone who needs special handling. I am delicate. Be careful with me.*

Talking about sex was a touchy situation. Colleen was clearly on the defensive. Anthony was embarrassed about being celibate. Their alliance crashed at the first sign of either partner's displeasure with the other.

There are couples for whom tickling is a delightful game of "gotcha!" But not couples like Colleen and Anthony. They couldn't see that resolving ticklishness could create a stronger relationship. Colleen complained, "Anthony was tickling me last night, and I am extremely ticklish. He barely touched me, and I was laughing hysterically."

Anthony's reply was condescending. "You need to stop acting so hysterical. Just calm down."

Colleen's voice rose. "I can't! When you're tickling me, I panic. I get into a kind of fear-driven frenzied state. I feel like I'm freaking out." Turning to me for support, she said plaintively, "I get annoyed when Anthony tries to tickle me. If I'm in the right mood I can handle it, but not for very long. I get defensive. It makes my skin crawl. One time I tried to show him how bad it feels to be tickled, but I got nowhere. Tickling Anthony is like tickling a rock."

"I was extremely ticklish until I was thirteen," Anthony replied with derision. "Then I made up my mind I wouldn't be ticklish anymore. It worked. I just decided. That's the same way I developed good pain tolerance, too. If I can do it, she can do it. I know she has lots of strength. She just doesn't show it."

I asked Anthony, "What made you decide to not be ticklish anymore?"

"My family took turns holding each other down and tickling the victim until he peed in his pants. They helped my mother, who was the ringleader, because she only had one arm. My dad frequently joined in. I was the youngest of three brothers and a sister, so this happened to me a lot." I wondered if Anthony's life script was *You're not going to get to me!*

"Your wife has difficulty with ticklishness and you come from a family of ticklers."

Colleen interjected, "I think tickling is pretty common. I've been getting tickled in my family for as long as I can remember, and I still can't stand it. I'm ticklish all over my body."

"Well then, you and your husband have at least two things in common."

"Let me guess." Colleen's flat tone said we didn't have a collaborative alliance. "Both our families are into tickling. What's the other?"

"You both drop your alliance at the first sign of trouble." Colleen sat up and gave me a curious look.

Anthony asked, "You think we don't have sex because people in our families tickle each other?" His face said, *What on earth are you talking about? Why are we talking about this?*

"I'm not sure the reason you don't have sex has anything to do with ticklishness. But if it does, then dropping your alliance with your spouse is probably an important part of your problem."

"This is why we don't have sex?"

"That's been the case for some of my clients."

"Does this approach work?" Anthony sounded doubtful.

"In terms of solving ticklishness, it's never failed."

Anthony took a hard look at me. "It's never failed?"

"It's never failed."

Colleen perked up. Anthony still looked skeptical.

"Let me put it this way: You may be the first."


## CURING TICKLISHNESS

I discovered a note I wrote to myself in 1994. In it I detailed the cure for ticklishness I use today, including treating it as a co-constructed interpersonal system. (I'll explain in a moment.) According to the note, I had treated ticklishness for over a decade, and the approach had been "so efficient and reliable that every one of my clients who received the treatment showed marked improvement. Since then I have worked with hundreds of couples and it has never failed." That was in 1994, and this unbroken record (knock on wood) continues to this day.

• *Ticklishness and your brain*

Neurobiologists, social psychologists, and people who like bondage and "tickle torture" have also studied tickling. State-of-the-art brain scanners now document how this happens in our nervous system. Your brain tracks your body's position and movements because mammals developed brains that enhanced their own response. Your brain produces a "map" of commands sent to your muscles, and "subtracts" this from all other sensations to detect when you're being touched by someone else.

Your brain makes important distinctions between "self" and "other" when it comes to touch. This difference lies at the root of ticklishness.[181] Your ancestors' ability to rapidly detect being touched by an animal, bug, or object increased their chances of survival. Body parts that are crucial when damaged are among the most ticklish (feet, chest, and armpits).

Your brain's organization around "self" and "other" doesn't permit you to tickle yourself. It's not simply because you know you're doing it and you can't "attack" yourself. It's because, neurologically speaking, your brain keeps track. Scientists have discovered your brain "cancels out" self-produced movements, and the more a given touch registers as "that's not me touching me," the more your ticklish reflex is triggered. Generally speaking, it takes two to tickle.

However, ticklishness involves more than an involuntary neurological response. Your prefrontal cortex adds another layer of complexity. That's where different flavors of ticklishness, from noxious and intolerable to fun or even hot, come from. Research indicates that ticklishness coincides with activity in portions of your brain involved in thoughts, emotions, pain, action, and mapping other people's minds.[182]

"Where your partner is coming from" hugely determines whether or not you become ticklish. Tickling can be pleasure, and it can be used as punishment. It's how we play out power relationships, like all other primates. Chimpanzees, in particular, love to tickle.

Ticklishness "protects" us from unwanted touch, but tickling also satisfies our basic need for touch. Tickling is probably evolutionary human social and sexual behavior. Parents tickle children, lovers tickle each other, but you don't tickle strangers. You're more likely to be ticklish when touched by someone of the opposite sex. This is because we are meaning-making animals.

Ticklishness illustrates how the human prefrontal cortex hijacked archaic physiological self-protection brain mechanisms and harnessed them for more sophisticated struggles of "self" protection. Many aspects of selfhood include tracking your body. Your core sense of self in past, present, and future, and mind-mapping all occur in the same brain circuitry.[183]

### • *Ticklish laughter*

The laughter accompanying ticklishness confuses lots of people. This was certainly Anthony's situation. "Look, Doctor, what am I supposed to do?" he started off. "Sometimes she likes it, and sometimes she doesn't. She was laughing, and I thought she was having a good time. I was laughing along with her. How am I supposed to know she's having a bad time? I always think we're just playing with each other!"

Anthony didn't know laughter tends to occur with tickling because they are much alike: Laughter is part neurological reflex and part socially induced by close physical contact with another person (co-constructed).[184] When your brain detects laughter (your own or someone else's), this triggers other neural circuits in your head, larynx, and chest that generate more laughter. This is why laughter is contagious.

Your ticklish reflex and your laughter reflex are connected by nerve cells in your brain.[185] The tickle-laughter reflex arc has physical, emotional, and cognitive components, and any one can trigger the others.[186] Research indicates that your tendency to feel ticklish is related to your propensity for other reflexes, like laughing, giggling, smiling, blushing, crying, and goose bumps.

### • *Benefits of addressing ticklishness*

Most people find ticklishness interferes with orgasms, but for some it truly enhances them. One person wrote, "If God never endowed humans with ticklishness, I'd be bored to death and I'd be stripped of one of the most exciting sources of eroticism … I love to be tickled, even though it is pure torture sometimes, and it makes me horny as hell. I like to tickle women, too. There is nothing like a helpless, bound, ticklish woman."[187]

For the rest of us, there are many reasons to consider curing ticklishness:

1. Ticklishness can usually be cured relatively quickly.
2. When ticklishness diminishes it is often replaced by an intense erotic experience. Resolving ticklishness can produce hot sex that reveals untapped eroticism and meaning lying dormant in your bedroom.
3. Resolving ticklishness often increases sexual desire.

Do I have your attention? Do these perk your interest? You can accomplish other important things at the same time:

1. You can learn to quiet the limbic system of your brain, which handles emotional reactivity and startle responses.
2. You can deliberately use mind-mapping to quiet things down.
3. You and your partner can get better at maintaining a collaborative alliance.
4. Overall, you and your partner can get better at holding on to your selves, period.
5. You can change core dynamics of your relationship and create a deeper and more positive emotional connection.

### • Dynamics of ticklishness outside the bedroom

Ticklishness in the bedroom often goes hand in hand with a sense of losing control of yourself elsewhere in your life. In Anthony and Colleen's case, this happened because Anthony "took up too much space in the relationship," and Colleen's weak Four Points of Balance made her perpetually accommodate. When Colleen did speak up for herself, Anthony took this as criticism. There wasn't much room for her to disagree or say she didn't like something he was doing—in or out of bed.

For instance, Anthony wanted to open another store in their furniture business. Colleen wanted to stick with one store because she was afraid of losing what they had. Anthony was determined to go ahead nonetheless. Although all their personal property was owned conjointly, and technically Colleen owned half their business, Anthony took out a business loan that Colleen reluctantly co-signed.

Colleen felt vulnerable because she couldn't protect herself. But she went along because Anthony was saying clearly, *If you love me, have confidence in me. Bet on me. Didn't I get us this far? Trust me.*

The same dynamics played out in bed. Colleen felt like she lost control of herself during sex. It seemed like Anthony expected her to turn herself over to him. It felt like Anthony was going to touch her wherever and whenever he wanted, whether she liked it or not. Her job was to get over her ticklishness and like it.

## OTHER WAYS OF UNDERSTANDING TICKLISHNESS

Deliberately co-constructing ticklishness reveals how you do it spontaneously. To do that you and your partner need to play "I'm going to tickle you!"

The central dynamics of tickling are control and powerlessness. It breaks down to two essential roles: The tickler tries to touch the ticklee in ways the ticklee can't avoid or control. And the ticklee tries to regain control over what will be done to him or her. Even if you know you're doing this to learn, you'll probably trigger someone's tickle reflex if you really go at it.

Couples unknowingly create this dynamic—and struggle with ticklishness—when they have sex using what I call the "giver-in-control" mind-set. The "giver" (usually the man in heterosexual couples) is responsible for knowing how to please the "receiver." The receiver is responsible for reassuring the giver that his sexual performance is superlative. The receiver feels obligated to "oooh" and "aaaaah" and express no dissatisfaction. The giver's reflected sense of self monitors the receiver like a hawk. If you have any predisposition to ticklishness, the "giver-in-control" approach will trigger it, because it maximizes the likelihood you'll feel like you're losing control of yourself.

Charles Darwin thought ticklishness occurs when you can't predict or control the precise point of touch. Scientists have proven he was right: When using a remote-control robot to administer the touch, if the robot doesn't do exactly what you tell it to do, you *can* tickle yourself. This happens neurologically on a level that bypasses the thinking part of your brain. But couples don't need a robot to learn this is true, because they have each other.

•

- *"You're under attack! I'm going to get you and you can't stop me!"*

Ticklishness involves a perceived attack combined with a perceived *lack* of real bodily threat. You're being physically attacked; it's a fake attack, but it's an attack nonetheless. If you don't experience the touch as a violation or attack, you'll be much less ticklish. At the other extreme, you can easily become ticklish before your partner even touches you. All that you need to do is perceive an attack is imminent.

Mind-mapping plays a huge role in co-constructing ticklishness. The "tickle game" involves your partner thinking, *I'm going to get you and you can't stop me.* The more your sense of self-control hinges on your partner's state of mind, and the more your partner's attitude is *You must let me do to you whatever I want if you love me,* the greater your tendency to feel ticklish.

Ticklish people are not control freaks. (Ticklish people *and* their partners often make this mistake.) Ticklish people don't necessarily want to control everything. They just want to control what is done to *them.* There's nothing freakish about that. My clients do better when they think of themselves this way. It falls under the theorem stated earlier: *People who cannot control themselves (regulate their own anxiety) will control everyone and everything around them.*

- *Ticklishness as bondage and torture*

"Good" tickling and "bad" tickling probably involve similar receptors in your brain. One difference is how the thinking parts of your brain interpret the signal. Likewise, positive and negative tickling involve the same basic "out of control" dynamic. The significance of "being out of control" at the time determines whether it's fun or not.

Here's where personal experience and family history come into play. Remember, Anthony's family often ganged up and tickled someone until he lost bladder control. This kind of tickling involves something darker than our "tickle game." In this case the attack is real. You can cause enormous amounts of anguish by repeatedly tickling someone until he loses physical control and soils himself. This is normal family sadism in some households.

People drawn to tickling as stylized torture often refer to "the bond" between the tickler and the ticklee. Perhaps they have an alliance, but in my experience it's not collaborative: Erotic stories written by and for people who engage in tickling emphasize revenge, finding and exploiting weak spots, and tickling someone "until they can't take it anymore."

Some families enjoy inflicting pain and watching each other suffer. You owe it to yourself and your partner to confront yourself: Is this is what you're doing?

- *Do you guard your mind from being mapped?*

Another impact of Anthony's childhood was that he was hard to read. He developed this in his home growing up. Unfortunately, it was one more thing encouraging Colleen's ticklishness and low desire. She mapped his attempts to ward her off, and it set off her deception detector.

Emotionally abusive families produce people with several characteristics: They have well-developed radar and constantly scan other people for signs of trouble. They also constantly mask their mind to keep from being mapped. And they are so constantly anxious, they often have no idea how anxious they are. Their radar is on high all the time—even (and especially) when they look as though they are oblivious to their surroundings. But they're also blind to themselves because their incredible radar is all turned outward.

Anthony offered little information about himself and batted away my probing questions. This made it difficult for me to develop a collaborative alliance with him, although he kept insisting we had one. At least he had one with me, he assured me, implying he wasn't sure of my motivations. When I pursued this, Anthony said he trusted me.

Anthony said he couldn't remember much about his childhood. When I asked him to tell me what little he remembered, Anthony changed the subject. When I brought him back to it, he said he couldn't remember anything. I pointed out a moment ago he said he didn't remember *much*, which meant he *could* remember some things.

Before he answered, I backed off this point. I already had some information I needed: Anthony had remarkable ability to avoid being pinned down. And the only way he could do that was by tracking where I was headed. If I plunged ahead anyway and cornered him, we'd replicate the same "Trust me" out-of-control dynamics he had with Colleen.

I shifted our focus to the fencing happening between us. I said, "You know, a person can't develop the level of ability you have to mask your mind without lots of practice fending off emotional or physical attacks." Anthony looked at me warily. "You are remarkably skilled."

Anthony's face went blank and impassive, like a mask. I pointed to it. "That's what I mean." He kept it up for several seconds. Then he nodded ruefully, and began to talk about a childhood spent fending off his mother.

"My mother lost an arm operating a machine in the factory where she worked. After that, things went to hell. Not being able to physically do things made her control us kids like we were her missing hand. We had to do what she needed. She kept us in line with her switch. My father stayed out of her way, and left us to deal with her. She bad-mouthed our girlfriends, she feared losing her extra hands. It was the same when my brothers and I got old enough to leave home."

"Do I have this right?" I said, leaning forward toward Anthony. "You have a one-armed mother who liked to tickle you until you were immobilized. As you got older, she tried to play *I've got you* in other ways?"

Anthony nodded. "And at best your father left you to her and didn't intervene, and at worst, he joined in?" Another nod. "Then I'd guess your notion of love doesn't involve a collaborative alliance."

Anthony winced and swallowed. He had a large lump in his throat.

### • *Create a multilayered solution*

Studies show abused children have smaller brains overall and an impaired ability to transfer information between the right and left halves of their brain.[188] Traumatic experiences interfere with integrating your mind into a coherent whole, due in part to altered synaptic connections and breakdown between right and left hemispheres. Trauma impedes your mind's need for internal and interpersonal integration.

It's important to have your right and left brains working together if you're interested in resolving trauma. Your goal is to activate each hemisphere's dominant processes, and remove all constraints on what your brain has to process. This strengthens connections among neural circuits in different parts of your brain, especially those involved in processing emotions.

You also need to focus your attention on many important levels at the same time, including images, emotions, body sensations, perceptions, and autobiographical memories. A collaborative alliance with your partner and *hugging till relaxed, heads on pillows* or *feeling while touching* really help. This multilayered focus usually yields new memories and new ways of seeing events, which helps resolve trauma by reintegrating things you've previously missed, mislabeled, or misunderstood. This multilayered focus produces new associations in your mind and, presumably, new configurations in your brain.

## COLLABORATIVE ALLIANCE: THE KEY TO RESOLVING TICKLISHNESS IN THE MOMENT

If you're interested in resolving ticklishness, you need a collaborative alliance with your partner. You have to interact physically and emotionally so that the ticklish person feels in control of herself. The partner provides predictable methodical touch while acting in a calm, soothing way. The ticklish person calms herself down and focuses on her partner's touch instead of pulling away. Start with body parts that tend to be the least ticklish, which are your back, arms, neck, and head (excluding your face).

This isn't borrowed functioning. It doesn't suppress one's functioning while enhancing the other's. Both people have to function at their best. The giver has to hold on to himself, and participate voluntarily and generously without being passive-aggressive, petulant, or reluctant. There's no room for jokes, gestures, or teasing, no *I'm going to get you, and you can't stop me!* The giver follows the ticklish person's wishes, not as a robot or servant, but as a collaborator co-creating a "receiver in control" mindset. *Feeling with touching* works great.

Once Colleen could relax while Anthony touched her arms, she asked him to touch her breasts. Anthony placed his whole hand over her breast and pressed firmly but gently, instead of playing with her nipples as he usually did. Colleen leaned into his touch and calmed herself down. She didn't pull away from Anthony as she usually did. As Colleen relaxed, Anthony was able to touch her breast without triggering ticklishness.

Next, Colleen asked Anthony to touch her on her ribs, where she was usually more ticklish. She relaxed before he touched her there, and she made sure she kept breathing. Anthony moved his hand slowly but firmly across her ribcage, so his touch was predictable and easy to track. He only used one hand so Colleen could focus her attention on just one place and lean into his touch, physically and emotionally. All of this gave Colleen the sense she could control what happened to her. To their surprise and pleasure, her ticklishness disappeared within minutes.

• *What if you're extremely ticklish?*

I suggest starting with the receiver lying faceup in bed, facing the giver. Highly ticklish people try to get around their problem by lying facedown. The meaning of a "back rub" doesn't trigger them, and they don't feel vulnerable because their chest is guarded. But there's a limit to how much progress they can make in that position.

Don't start facedown unless you're *extremely* ticklish and find it impossible to calm down. If you need to, keep your arms by your sides so your ribs aren't exposed. Once you relax and your ticklishness passes, turn over to be faceup. Do this sooner rather than later (but not too soon) to reduce defensiveness between you and your partner. By the time you reach more sensitive areas, like your legs, chest, ribs, and abdomen, you'll be better at relaxing and leaning into your partner's touch.

If your partner increases the predictability and firmness of touch, this decreases your sense of losing control of yourself and reduces ticklishness. You know where his hands are and where they are going. By firm I don't mean "massage." I mean firmer than the touch that usually triggers ticklishness. Back or foot massages, or back-scratches, don't provide the stimulus needed to master ticklishness.

Work as a team. Ask your partner to use a methodical pattern you can follow in your mind. Lean into your partner's touch. Pulling away makes his touch less definite and predictable, and triggers your own ticklishness.

If you have incapacitating ticklishness, put your hand on his to guide his pressure and movement. Your goal is to increase pleasure from his touch, rather than to stop him from doing things you don't like. If you have a collaborative alliance while you do this, several repetitions are usually sufficient to make your hand on his unnecessary.

You're much better off keeping your eyes open. Watch where you're being touched. Closing your eyes decreases your mind-mapping ability and lets your negative anticipations take over. Don't do things that increase your anticipatory nervousness and physical tension because this fuels ticklishness.

- *Get control of yourself without dropping your alliance with your partner*[189]

What do you do when this doesn't work and you *really* can't control your ticklishness? Stop trying to master yourself while leaning into your partner's touch. This is easier to do if you're not fighting against yourself or your mate. Have your partner stop touching you while you get yourself under control. Have a clear agreement that you won't be touched until you're ready: No jokes or "pretend" attacks from the giver, and all touching stops. When you're quiet (usually in a minute or two), ask your partner to resume touching you. Shifting from "giver-in-control" to "receiver-in-control" is critical: The neurological basis of ticklishness is a signal that your physical integrity or your body's natural order has been violated.

Pulling back from your partner's touch is a common but self-defeating way of trying to get control of yourself. It is a losing strategy that makes ticklishness more likely. It breaks contact with your partner, physically and emotionally, and makes his touch less definite and predictable. You need the exact opposite: You need to feel that you can control where you'll be touched. You can't do that if you're "protecting" yourself. It's hard to turn off your emotional radar and come down from "red alert," but you can do this in a collaborative alliance.

If you remain ticklish to predictable, firm touch, your mind and body are probably really tense. Your tension level changes your subjective experience and can make your partner's touch noxious, no matter what he does. So take a deep breath and relax your stomach and buttocks. Tension creates shallow, rapid breathing that leaves you feeling "sucked in"—withdrawn into yourself, suffocated, and afraid to breathe. Stretch out your body. Remind yourself that you are not being attacked, and that your personal space has not been invaded.

Tensing up offers no protection, increases your reactivity, and makes your partner more likely to overreact. Take more time to calm yourself down, even if you don't want to or don't feel you need it. Calm your mind and relax your body, but don't shut your partner out. You'll need a collaborative alliance when you resume in a minute, and he's more likely to be patient if you don't withdraw from him.

If you do what I'm suggesting, you won't be ticklish when your partner touches you firmly. As you relax more and your ticklishness wanes, ask him to lighten his touch, so that you can work through another layer of ticklishness.

## • *Map your partner's mind*

Your brain is great at detecting deception and discrepancies, and discrepancies increase ticklishness. You want to experience your partner's touch as coming from an "insider" rather than an "outsider." To do this, track your partner and map his mind.

Once you read that his feelings and intentions are positive, your limbic system can relax. You can better control the perceived magnitude of things if they don't catch you unaware. Your prefrontal neocortex can kick in "executive functions" to regulate your emotions, reactivity, and startle-response. That's how you turn off your anticipatory negative reaction and decrease your ticklishness. It may sound like scientific gibberish, but lots of people need this, including those who don't consider themselves to be ticklish.

### • *Giver: Use the palm of your hand*

Colleen became ticklish when Anthony's hand simply moved toward her genitals. This was caused by a hardwired mechanism in her brain: Anticipation of noxious stimuli activates the same part of your brain as the tactile stimulation itself.[190] Anthony didn't understand this. He complained when Colleen pulled away before he even touched her.

Colleen was extremely ticklish when Anthony touched her between her legs, particularly when he touched her labia or played with her pubic hair. She usually stopped him at some point, if she let him do it at all. By that point, if they continued to have sex, Colleen had no sexual desire. She had hard feelings and no alliance with Anthony. She knew how Anthony's mind worked while they lay there in silence. Innumerable similar sexual encounters killed any desire when she thought about having sex.

To dampen Colleen's anticipation of noxious touch and give her something new to map out in Anthony's mind, they used a method I developed called *palm over groin*. A person's touch always communicates where his mind is (or isn't). Particular styles of touch convey different messages. You can reverse this to signal to your partner that you've changed your mind. I knew that the mind-frame Colleen needed to see in Anthony could be conveyed with a particular kind of tactile stimulation.

When Colleen was ready, Anthony placed his palm *covering* her genitals, with his fingers on her pubic hair. His pressure was definite and gently firm. He wasn't trying to stimulate her pubic area by pressing down (at this point). He was telling Colleen that she didn't have to worry about him trying to open her labia or putting a finger inside her. When touching a man, cupping his penis with one or both hands accomplishes the same thing. *Palm over groin* has been indispensable in helping women and men who have noxious sensations when their genitals are touched.

At the outset, Colleen didn't believe this would work. Maybe she wouldn't be ticklish when Anthony touched her stomach, but she was certain it would start when they got to her crotch. The first time they tried it (Colleen did it to prove me wrong), it still worked! Colleen's ticklishness didn't surface at all. Anthony took his time, focusing on not triggering her ticklishness rather than on bringing her to orgasm. Colleen pressed her pelvis into Anthony's hand. They kept their collaborative alliance throughout the interaction.

Afterwards, Colleen asked Anthony, "So what's it like to have a collaborative alliance in the palm of your hand? I never thought of having one in my vagina."

Bemused, Anthony said, "I'm not sure. I've never had one before." The shift in Colleen's state of mind stunned him.

*Palm over groin* gave Colleen the feeling of being in control of herself. Anthony made it clear he would move forward only when she was ready. He was focusing on what he was doing, but even more so, he was focusing on Colleen. He wasn't doing this because I told him to; this was between the two of them. Colleen didn't push him away, and Anthony tried to be with her. He let her map his mind so she would know he *wanted* her. Colleen started to believe she might get over being ticklish.

*Palm over groin* made it easy for Colleen to map Anthony's mind. The style of touch broadcasted his intent. She could see his intent lined up with his behavior. He wasn't just being patient; he seemed invested, satisfied with what they were doing, and genuinely happy. Had she detected the slightest discontinuity among his words, his emotional demeanor, and his behavior, Colleen's brain would have gone on red-alert. This would have categorized Anthony as an "intruder" and increased her ticklishness.

## RESOLVING TICKLISHNESS FOR THE LONG TERM

In our next session, Colleen said, "I'm actually surprised I can stop my ticklishness when it happens. I didn't think I ever could. I'm more hopeful it will get better. I don't expect perfection, but will it ever stop?"

"Resolving ticklishness in the moment has a cumulative benefit. But facing issues that keep you chronically tense and anxious also reduces your predisposition."

"Can you help me with this?"

"Maybe. For instance, what do you think about when Anthony touches you and you're ticklish?"

Without moving a muscle, Colleen suddenly became unreadable. "I don't know what I think when I'm being tickled."

"I think you know what you're thinking when you're ticklish. And I don't think you're thinking about being with Anthony. I'd guess you're not with him at all."

Colleen was wary. I hadn't seen this cold, hard side of her before. "You mean I'm thinking about something else? Or I'm fantasizing about someone else?"

"I don't know. But I'm pretty sure you're not thinking of you and Anthony as a team. You're not thinking of the two of you as a unit."

"I get pretty hysterical sometimes. Maybe I'm not thinking anything."

"Colleen, you have being tickled many times by your family. You probably thought about it between times. So when it happened repeatedly—or when it's happening with Anthony—it's not completely unfamiliar to you. You're having lots of feelings about what's happening. I'll bet you think the same things with Anthony that you thought with your family. You don't have to tell me, but let's not treat you like you're brain-damaged or screwed up."

Colleen's shot me a discerning look. Anthony interjected, "Doc, maybe she really doesn't know."

"Colleen, you can have control of this situation. Just do it openly. Just say you don't want to talk about it."

Colleen looked down at the floor. Then she looked over at Anthony and bit her lip. Then she looked at me. It looked like she was about to take a leap of faith.

"I'm thinking, *You're doing this to me again, aren't you? You are so selfish. You don't care about me. You only care about yourself!* I've thought it so often it's a litany in my mind."

Colleen's disclosure hit Anthony like a bombshell. In the aftershock, Anthony's first reaction was embarrassment for being so stupid. Colleen could play his game and beat him at it. He hadn't recognized she was covering up and keeping her mind from being mapped. Although Anthony had screwed his share of women, he had no first-hand experience of *being with* a woman in bed. Because he had so little experience of positive emotional connection, he didn't realize something was missing. Anthony looked at Colleen. He was clearly unsettled but not out of control. Ruefully, he said, "I should have guessed. When we have sex, I'm an attacker doing something to you and you're fighting me off."

Colleen didn't say anything. Anthony paused long enough to clarify this was her response. "I guess that captures how I feel too. I feel like you're constantly fighting me off. I never let myself really think this through . . . I guess you see me the same way I saw my family." Anthony slumped in his chair, staring at the carpet.

## • *Colleen takes the hit*

"I *do* feel like I'm fighting you off, but I've been afraid to say it." Anthony nodded in woeful agreement, still staring at the floor.

I said, "You're having these feelings about Anthony. But these are *your* thoughts and feelings, so maybe they are about *you*."

"What do you mean?" The woman who had taken the leap of faith and spoken up vanished and the *I am someone who needs careful handling, I am delicate, be careful with me* Colleen reappeared.

I spoke slowly and gently. "I said before that your thoughts with Anthony were probably the same as when your family tickled you and you hated it. Back then did you ever think, *You're doing this to me again. You are so selfish. You don't care about me. You only care about yourself!*?"

After several seconds Colleen said, "Well, yes."

"How often?"

"Often."

"Pick a number."

Tears ran down Colleen's face. "A hundred. Hundreds! I lost count!" Finally, thankfully, she relaxed and convulsed into sobs.

After a few minutes I said, "Those were moments of great anxiety and meaning. The kinds where, scientists think, your brain wires itself interpersonally. They're called 'moments of meeting.'"

"Are you saying those thoughts are wired into my brain?"

"I don't know. Maybe not those thoughts exactly, but maybe those themes. We don't really know exactly how it works. But you were having powerful emotional and physical interactions—powerful enough to trigger involuntary reactions in your brain."

Colleen nodded. "Does this mean my thoughts and feelings about Anthony have nothing to do with him?"

"No. He's doing things that trigger those kinds of thoughts and feelings. When you have these reactions toward him, it's personal. But maybe that's not the only reason these thoughts and feelings come up. Maybe your mind is predisposed to go this way, like a groove in your brain."

Colleen was predisposed to see Anthony and their relationship in ways that triggered her own ticklishness and pushing away. Now she feared he would be angry to learn her family dynamics set him up to be the bad guy. But Anthony's dominant reaction was relief. He thought back to times he felt Colleen was seeing him as trying to control her when he wasn't.

Colleen went into a slump after our session as she considered her past and the possibility that it had affected how her brain functioned. It took several days for her to pull herself out. When she was functioning better she suggested they make love. This was a pretty big move because they hadn't had sex in three years. This time Anthony and Colleen made sure they were together, and dealing with Colleen's ticklishness was their first priority. They did *hugging till relaxed* and *heads on pillows* for a long time and reached a deeper, quieter connection then ever before.

- *You're more anxious than you realize*

If you've never experienced sex without anxiety, you don't know the difference. You assume whatever you've felt is inherent in the act. Only when your anxiety drops *below* your baseline do you realize, in retro-spect, how anxious you were.

Colleen had difficulty recognizing how truly anxious she was because she didn't *feel* nervous. You can carry a whole level of anxiety you don't even know is there. You can't see your anxiety because it's what you grew up with. When you're wondering who's going to be the family's next tickle victim, you get accustomed to constant anxiety. You're nervous when you see it coming—and when you don't. This kind of anxious home environ-ment shapes how your brain lays down its neural connections. Colleen repeatedly had anxious thoughts and physical anxiety when her family tickled her.

The same was true for Anthony. He didn't like thinking about how his parents had tickle-tortured him, or his disappointment in them, but both existed in the previously existing holes in his autobiographical memory, things he "sort of knew but never really thought about." On the surface, Anthony didn't look at things analytically *or* emotionally. His view was that he just didn't think or feel much about these things. In truth, he avoided making meaning of his past experiences.

However, working on ticklishness brought up a wealth of vivid mem-ories, perceptions, and feelings that fleshed out both their childhoods. As we worked back and forth between reducing ticklishness in real time and reprocessing prior experiences, Colleen and Anthony were able to relax together physically and emotionally. Their lives made more sense to them in ways that grounded them, and they felt more in touch with themselves. It was as if their minds no longer needed to be organized around *not* remembering things. They recalled a host of events as vivid images and visceral reactions (right brain autobiographical memory re-trieval), sifted through the details (left brain analytical thinking), and then integrated this into a fuller picture.

Relaxing physically and mentally, with their bodies touching, was a major accomplishment for both Colleen and Anthony. Getting their bod-ies and minds working together took some effort, but it paid off. In my experience, this may be more important in resolving trauma than verbal-izing feelings or having insights or new memories. What seems to be im-portant is creating new levels of integration, whether it's (a) developing more coherent autobiographical life narratives, (b) passing information across brain hemispheres (left-right hemisphere integration), or (c) maintaining a collaborative alliance. Getting your body involved adds another level of integration that increases the benefits of all the others.

- *The sexual jolt in ticklishness*

Tickling may be a standard part of some people's sexual repertoire because they get a powerful jolt of arousal from it. A good game of *I'm gonna get you!* gets these folks' adrenalin going, heart pumping, and juices flowing. It comes from anxiety-based general physical arousal that cascades into sexual arousal.

Families around the world enjoy tickling (in moderation) when their children are young. But when kids reach puberty, tickling becomes a form of flirtation. Most families know it's time to stop. They can feel the child's sexuality needs a wider birth.

This didn't happen in Colleen's family. Her brothers, sisters, and parents played out their sexual impulses and hostility through eroticized torturous tickling. No one talked about it, but everyone could feel it as they mapped each other's minds. These highly anxious sex-tinged interactions occurred throughout Colleen's adolescence. Anthony's family's tickling was more sadistic than sexual, but the imprint was just as powerful. These high-voltage moments of meeting shaped both of their lives, their marriage, and, in all likelihood, their brains. In my experience, people who grow up in high-anxiety households (with or without tickling) frequently develop dominant anxiety arousal / sexual arousal patterns in later life.[191]

# IMPACTS OF TICKLISHNESS ON SEXUAL DESIRE

Colleen reacted the way most clients do: She went through a difficult experience and came out the better for it. At first this raised her anxiety, and then it settled her down. She got on top of her emotions instead of letting them control her. She had to call upon her Four Points of Balance to do this. She had to confront herself about her life experiences, quiet her mind and calm her heart, and endure painful but meaningful realizations without avoiding or overreacting. Her time in the crucible left her quieter, more grounded, and more solid.

Colleen looked terrific at our next session. She was brighter, more alive, more at peace, and less fragile. Sex had dramatically improved. Along with no longer hiding her mind from being mapped, Colleen let her eroticism show in full for the first time. From their description, it was pretty impressive.

### • *Sexual charge beneath ticklishness*

Resolving ticklishness can create some pretty hot sex. Most clients are surprised by the electric sex that typically follows. Some say this falls under the heading of "wall-socket sex." Once you cure noxious ticklishness, the same touch that previously triggered ticklishness often produces a sexual response. Or maybe it's that some highly erotic people are prone to ticklishness, and when they finally get their ticklishness under control, their sexuality blossoms. Both interpretations fit what I've seen clinically.

You resolve ticklishness the same way you submerge into wild sexual abandon. You can surrender to your impulses and sensations when you have control of yourself. When you're in control of what will be done to you, you can relax and allow yourself to receive it. When Colleen got over her ticklishness and delved into her eroticism, the results were explosive!

Over the course of three weeks, Colleen and Anthony did *palm over groin* a dozen times. Although occasionally she was ticklish, it quickly subsided. When it happened, it wasn't a tremendous impediment as it had been in the past. They knew they could get through it and it wouldn't destroy their alliance.

One particular time Anthony did *palm over groin* until Colleen wasn't ticklish. Then, at her request, he touched her labia with his fingertips. When this didn't tickle her, instead of sticking a finger inside her, Anthony slowly opened her labia. Colleen said this was one of her most memorable sexual experiences.

After a while, much to his surprise, Colleen rolled Anthony onto his back. She straddled his hips with his penis in her hand, and lowered herself until the shaft of his penis was against her labia. Then she rolled her hips and brushed herself against his penis, holding it with one hand while she steadied herself with the other. Anthony thought he was going to go out of his mind. This was the most erotic and intimate moment of his life!

Then, POW! Colleen's body bucked as an orgasm rippled through her body.

Colleen and Anthony were momentarily stunned. Then they laughed until their eyes had filled with tears. Afterward, Colleen lay like warm butter on top of Anthony's chest. Anthony groaned. He was emotionally "done," but he still hadn't come. Colleen gathered herself up, took him inside her, and rode him until he reached orgasm.

Ticklishness is one of marriage's cosmic jokes. Ticklish people, who may seem like erotic duds, often turn out to be high-powered sex pistols. Anthony was dazed by the shift in Colleen. He had a new understanding of their prior sexual encounters. It was a lesson in humility. The impact was pretty powerful.

### • *Other sexual ticklishness*

Many women and men become ticklish to genital stimulation immediately after orgasm. They are hyper-sensitive at that moment, and further stimulation causes irritation, pain, or numbness. They laugh a lot and push their partner's hand away. After several minutes, this reaction fades.

If you want to get over this form of noxious ticklishness—and maybe have some of the best sex of your life—you have to tolerate very intense stimulation while you make yourself relax. It doesn't work if you're fighting against your partner, nor does worrying that your partner is going to touch you whether you like it or not. You have to work as a team. This teamwork involves meaningful endurance for growth in the most delicious ways. It's a form of human resilience you may not have considered. It lets you walk the fine line between pleasure and pain that humans seem to relish.

## DOING THE SEEMINGLY IMPOSSIBLE

Curing ticklishness is great for couples who are celibate, or who have aversive sexual interactions. You can work on ticklishness with your clothes on if need be. Because it usually occurs early in a sexual encounter (and when restarting a stalled relationship), you can resolve ticklishness in your relationship long before you're ready for intercourse. It will increase your desire, intimacy, and personal development.

Ticklishness carries loads of meaning and emotion. When you become ticklish, even if it is rare, pay attention to what's going on inside you and between you and your partner. You'll learn about yourself and your relationship.

- *Yes, it's differentiation!*

As we've seen in previous chapters, everything I'm describing involves your Four Points of Balance. It takes two people stretching their Four Points of Balance to establish and maintain a collaborative alliance. When one partner becomes ticklish, both partners have to hold on to themselves, which involves a further step in personal growth. The process and outcome of resolving ticklishness is a further step in both partners' Four Points of Balance. I'm describing differentiation triggering differentiation triggering further differentiation. Co-evolution through resolving co-constructed ticklishness. One self encounters another self, and in the process, each self develops more self.

The cure for ticklishness I've outlined changes your brain function. It involves using your mind to quiet your brain, to change how you think and feel. It uses your prefrontal neocortex "executive functions" to regulate your limbic system. That is why your ticklishness goes away in real time. This is an example of positive brain plasticity.

This time-proven strategy creates seven conditions thought to facilitate positive brain change. These are the same seven conditions *hugging till relaxed*, *heads on pillows*, and *feeling while touching* create too (Chapter 11). These may be the reason this way of curing ticklishness is so effective. It creates:

1. A strong and resilient collaborative alliance.
2. Moderate levels of stress and emotional arousal, alternating with calm.
3. Intense and profound intersubjective moments of meeting.
4. Information and experiences gathered across multiple dimensions of cognition, emotion, sensation, and behavior.
5. Activity in brain neural networks involved in processing and regulating thoughts, feelings, sensations, and behaviors.
6. New conceptual knowledge integrating emotional and bodily experiences.
7. Organizing experiences in ways that foster continued growth and integration.

These seven conditions create a deep coherence that enables your mind to resume its natural integrative processes. This helps you develop autobiographical narratives that make better sense of your past and its impact on your present functioning. This can help you regain hope for the future.

We can learn a lot about ticklishness from neuroscience and anthropology. But the best lessons come from banishing noxious ticklishness from your bedroom. Odds are you'll get to the point that when your partner is tickled during sex, it means he or she is pleased, gratified, amused, and delighted.

## • *Looking ahead*

If you're like the 15 percent of people who took the 2006 Marriage and Family Health Center Dateline-NBC survey who said their sex was dead, this chapter and the prior one are exactly what you need. If your sex is alive but needs rejuvenating, this is still a good place to start.

However, most couples need something more: 53 percent said their sex was either comatose and in danger of dying, or asleep and needing a wake-up call. If you fall into this category, the next two chapters are for you.

Our two final chapters are more sexually explicit. They graphically describe things you can do to make sex more interesting, passionate,

erotic, and intimate. They address styles of sex and particular sexual behaviors many people love. You'll encounter straightforward discussion
of sexual realities appropriate for mature adults. If you're faint of heart,
easily shocked, or just plain not interested, you may want to stop here.
Nonetheless, one out of every two couples needs the next two chapters,
and I hope I've just whetted your appetite.

——————————— IDEAS TO PONDER ———————————

- Ticklishness creates sexual desire problems. Resolving ticklishness involves getting a grip on yourself without dropping your alliance with your partner.
- Tickling can cause powerful emotional and physical interactions—powerful enough to trigger involuntary reactions
  in your brain.
- *Palm over groin* shows your partner you respect his or her
  physical and psychological integrity.

# 13

## Tender Loving Sex

What you're learning can change your sexual desire problems, and the rest of your life for that matter. Couples in treatment have a more intense and focused multi-level experience than you have by reading about them. But no doubt the *mirror neurons* in your prefrontal neocortex are firing away just the same. Seeing or imaging something happening to someone else produces the same reaction in your brain as if it was happening to you. Mapping the minds of the couples you're reading about produces the same feelings and reactions as if you were going through it.

By letting the couples come alive in your mind—and mapping out their minds—you've probably learned more than you ever dreamed you could know. When you put this into action, you'll realize you learned even more. You may also find it's not enough. Keep at it. Take a second pass through this book. You'll reap the benefits for years to come.

Independent research on my three-day Passionate Marriage® Couples

Enrichment Workshop indicates couples continued to make methodical incremental progress when they were re-evaluated four months later. Partners were interviewed together and individually, four months before and after attending the program. Their responses during a two-hour structured interview were coded into statistical data and analyzed. Results indicate virtually all couples increased their differentiation, sexual satisfaction, intimacy, and ability to handle conflict, and conflict itself decreased.[192] They learned the same things you are learning here. Put this into action, and several months from now, it's likely you'll have made significant progress too.

Let's take another methodical step forward. For many people, sex worth wanting has two characteristics: It's loving and it's hot. This chapter focuses on tender loving sex, and our final chapter will turn up the heat even more. However, tender loving sex doesn't have to be lukewarm sex. As you'll see, it can be powerful in unimagined ways.

To be clear, tender loving sex is not a type of sex. It is a meaning that permeates your sexual experience. Tender loving sex is not reducible to specific techniques. If you don't have much capacity to love, or you can't stand being tender, nothing you do creates tender loving sex.

You can, however, develop your capacity to love and be tender by using your sexual relationship. You can repair yourself emotionally, replenish your soul, invigorate your relationship, and tickle your toes. You can change the face you show the world, and get control of your emotions, especially your temper. Tender loving sex can make a new person out of you. It can probably rewire your brain.

## • *Kate and Paul*

Kate and Paul came to see me for their sexual desire problems. They had been married eight years. This was the second marriage for both. Both felt sexual problems were major factors in the breakups of their first marriages. In this marriage, Paul was frustrated with their lack of sex, which only happened once a month. Kate and Paul were highly emotionally fused, and their gridlock over sex was intense.

Kate had a long history of promiscuity during adolescence, but in this and her prior marriage, Kate quickly became sexually uninterested. She had intermittent difficulty having orgasms, and while she felt bad about this, she didn't feel this was why she didn't want sex. Kate felt Paul's difficulty with orgasms had much bigger impact on her.

Paul often had difficulty being able to have an orgasm. When he was able, it took thirty minutes or more. Everything focused on him getting off. Kate and Paul often felt exhausted by that time, so when he came they would stop altogether. When he couldn't climax, Paul rolled over to his side of the bed and broke off all contact. Either way, sex wasn't very rewarding, and afterward was worse. Kate learned it didn't pay to get aroused because she was going to be disappointed, one way or another.

Paul and Kate had other problems too: They both had difficulty regulating their emotions. Paul had "emotional eruptions," and Kate's episodes of "bottoming out" were frequent and precipitous. Kate was often severely depressed, with crushing low self-esteem and feelings of inadequacy. Both partners felt anxious much of the time. Paul had emotional eruptions throughout his life in which he became angry, defensive, and accusatory.

The tremendous tension between Kate and Paul was obvious from the outset. This made therapy more difficult. They were highly guarded people. Kate led off by clarifying why she wasn't willing to have sex with Paul: She was too angry at him, and she wasn't up for more repetitions of frustrating empty sex. She said they were more at the level of holding hands. Paul scoffed at the idea.

I said there might be great utility in holding hands, depending on how they did it. I asked if they were willing to hold hands right there and then. Kate thought this was odd and Paul thought it was juvenile—but they agreed.

First I let them hold hands without my saying anything. I noticed they held each other's hand in a wooden and mechanical way. It was as though they were trying not to notice they were touching each other. There was no positive emotional connection between them, or any attempt to create one. They weren't even paying attention to the sensation in their own hands. They just looked nervous and awkward. They let go of each other when I nodded.

I asked if they'd be willing to try holding hands a little differently. Kate and Paul agreed. I suggested that when they took each other's hand, they take a deep breath and focus on calming themselves down. They were awkward at first, but ultimately they were able to do this. As they started to relax, I directed their attention to the actual point of physical connection between their hands. Kate got nervous again and giggled, and Paul twitched, so we repeated the process of calming themselves down.

Kate and Paul commented that holding each other's hand felt much more pleasant once they calmed themselves down. I said this was a microcosm of what was probably happening during sex. They could make sex feel much better—and each have an easier time with orgasms—if they could learn to calm themselves down during sex.

This in-session application of the Four Points of Balance, especially Quiet Mind–Calm Heart, was a revelation to Kate and Paul. Rather than trying to have faith I could help them, they had their own tangible demonstration to go on. By the end of our first session, Kate and Paul were willing to try *hugging till relaxed*. This surprised Kate because Paul didn't like to hug. Paul agreed because he had liked holding hands, which he usually didn't.

Paul asked if this might help him with his orgasms. I said it could, but they could do a lot more if they really used their bodies, minds, and brains. Organizing things in terms of these three dimensions had the greatest likelihood of increasing Paul's ease of having orgasms and Kate's sexual desire. I added that, if handled properly, resolving their sexual problems could dramatically help Paul's emotional outbursts and Kate's bouts of anxiety and depression. Paul and Kate exchanged silent glances.

I suggested that a good dose of tender loving sex could help them. This needed to be sex endowed with great meaning, and they needed to map each other's minds in the midst of it. As it turned out, just allowing their minds to be mapped during *hugging till relaxed* and *heads on pillows* had tremendous meaning for both of them.

## NEW APPLICATION OF FAMILIAR TOOLS

Over the next several sessions Kate and Paul did *hugging till relaxed* several different ways. They started by focusing on quieting their mind and brain while they had their arms around each other. I suggested they visualize and focus on a spot inside their head, midway between their ears, in the emotional center of their brain.

After doing this a half dozen times, Kate and Paul calmed down and relaxed more quickly and deeply. They could feel the difference. Being in each other's presence and feeling the other calm down—instead of getting more wound up—was meaningful to them.

I encouraged them to build on this and take things further. They used *hugging till relaxed* to become aware of remaining tensions in their own bodies, to deliberately relax that particular part, and to become more relaxed together. I proposed that if Kate and Paul could relax and feel centered in their own bodies, they would become aware of their partner's breathing without losing awareness of themselves. If *this* happened, they'd have learned an important lesson about how relationships really worked.

Kate and Paul returned to say it happened several times. Kate said that since I had prepared her, she was able to focus deeper on herself. Several times she was aware of Paul and aware of herself at the same time. One time Paul was able to do it too. I labeled this their initial experience of developing a positive physical and emotional connection without losing their grip on themselves. It was a physically tangible demonstration of what they needed to do in their relationship. It was a testimony to their deepening collaborative alliance.

## • *Create moments of meeting*

Kate and Paul reported a special moment when they felt very aware of themselves, each other, and deliberately constructing an experience together. Each was aware the other was invested in making the moment happen, and the other was enjoying it. Both had their own subjective experience, and yet it was intensely shared.

I told Kate and Paul they were describing an "intersubjective experience," a *moment of meeting*. I said these experiences play a crucial role in human relationships from the moment of birth, and especially during sex. Kate and Paul agreed this was a qualitatively different experience, one they certainly had never had during sex.

Kate and Paul's bodies, minds, and brains had lined up in a peaceful and powerful way. During intercourse their minds were usually a million miles apart. Kate said she liked doing *hugging till relaxed* with Paul more than having intercourse. Paul wasn't sure how to take this. I proposed that if and when Kate looked forward to moments of meeting during intercourse, she would probably like intercourse, too.

We developed a new and more meaningful picture of what happened between and within them when they had sex. By the time Kate and Paul left, they had a more helpful and hopeful view of their difficulties. This picture tied all their experiences together and gave them physical acts they could do to make things better. Instead of feeling at the mercy of things, now they could apply their will.

The picture you develop is important. You have to *do* something to get your brain to think differently. It takes more than just mentally talking to yourself more positively and doing self-affirmations every morning. You have to make sense of your experiences—especially your successes. How you process and organize things makes a huge difference. Given the myriad psychological theories and approaches out there, you can pretty much organize your experience any way you like. Unfortunately, explanations that fit your subjective experience and make intuitive sense aren't necessarily accurate.

Understanding your successes organizes your subsequent efforts. Whatever you identify as the critical ingredient is what you go after next time. For instance, Kate and Paul could have interpreted their intersubjective moment as feeling safer and more secure with each other. It's a common interpretation, but it creates a common disaster. If next time they tried to feel "safe and secure" with each other, it would increase their emotional fusion and borrowed functioning, and create an unpleasant experience that would further demoralize them.

I reminded Kate and Paul about where they started from and how they got to where they wanted to go. I took them back to their own physical process. That's when they got it: The critical ingredient in their success was regulating themselves in close emotional and physical proximity to each other. This is what they set out to do better next time.[193]

When Kate and Paul felt ready for more emotional and physical contact, after *hugging till relaxed,* they added *heads on pillows.* Eye contact during *heads on pillows* facilitates more core "I to I" connection. It allowed them to develop the same profound connection people get through *eyes-open sex* (which I'll discuss later in this chapter), but without the distraction and anxiety of sex per se.

Mutual gaze is a psychological process involving joint attention in which two people have the feeling of a brief link between their minds. Eye gazing is an important part of social perception and interaction, and plays a central role in mind-mapping. Brain imaging studies indicate that mind-mapping and eye gaze processing engage similar regions of your brain.[194].

Gaze following seems to be hard-wired in your brain, which contains neurons that respond selectively to faces, bodies, and eye gaze. Specific cell assemblies in your cerebral cortex respond specifically to eye gazing. This part analyzes biological motion for signals about another individual's actions. It is activated by movements of someone's eyes, mouth, hands, and body, as well as static images of a face or body that imply motion.[195]

Newborns spend more time looking at a photograph of a face with the eyes open than at one with the eyes closed. They may have a special neural mechanism that detects eye-like stimuli and orients attention toward them.[196] Joint attention triggered by eye gaze increases and speeds up visual activity in their brains. This demonstrates how eye gaze can rapidly create a plastic moment that modifies visual information processing.[197]

Depending on whether you make eye contact or not, and your anticipation of what it will be like, dopamine-producing neurons are activated (especially in your right hemisphere) and engage your brain's central reward system. Making eye contact with a face you perceive as attractive increases dopamine production. Dopamine decreases when eye gaze is lost. The opposite pattern happens if you anticipate eye-contact being a negative experience.[198]

• *Create focal attention*

You need more than just a multi-level focus. You want a multi-level focus that creates *focal attention*. Someone who is focally aware is highly attentive and consciously focusing on something, and deliberately using their short-term memory (as opposed to automatic attention that occurs without conscious effort). When you focus your attention on something, you bring it into your "working memory." Focal attention is the mental chalkboard of your mind. Some measure of focal attention is also required for your brain to store information, so you can retrieve it if you want to think about it later. *Heads on pillows* rivets your attention on right brain and left brain processes during an intensely meaningful interpersonal encounter. Your focus of attention shifts to many things: what you see, mind-mapping your partner, your feelings, body sensations, and autobiographical memories that cross your mind. Focus your attention wherever you will, something comes to mind when you and your partner are up close, eye to eye.

- *Does increasing your desire require rocket (or brain) science?*

Developing an optimal framework is important. Could you successfully resolve sexual desire problems if you did *hugging till relaxed, heads on pillows*, or *feeling while touching* like simplistic behavioral techniques (e.g., "exercises")? Possibly you could. But why would you want to? Sexual desire problems are hard enough to change. An integrated, multifaceted, multi-level approach increases your likelihood of success.

My clients like seeing the many ways their therapy fits together and how all the different levels line up. It's more than intellectual curiosity. Understanding different things that are going on, and what you are trying to accomplish, helps you appreciate and fully harness the benefit of whatever you do. It increases your willingness to tolerate discomfort for growth.

Anyone can see how hugging and relaxing with your partner might improve your relationship and increase sexual desire. But *hugging till relaxed, heads on pillows, feeling while touching*, and curing ticklishness are also wonderful tools for quieting and regulating your brain. They use your prefrontal neocortex and your body to regulate your limbic system. They create the seven conditions thought to encourage brain change. They produce intense "moments of meeting." And they differ from meditation because they are *interpersonal experiences* and exploit the fact that your brain wires itself interpersonally.

I often work with clients' spontaneous sexual behavior. I did this with Kate and Paul's hand-holding. I also work with kissing. Kissing, holding hands, and other spontaneous behaviors, all create *interpersonal soma-tosensory experiences*. They stimulate parts of your brain that track your body's experience (e.g., physical sensations, location in "space," physical orientation) and parts that make meaning of them. This "cross-talk" permits learning across multiple dimensions of experience. Curing ticklishness does the same thing.

Brain research and thousands of years of Buddhist psychology indicate that focused purposeful attention is a powerful tool. You can use it to quiet your mind and calm your brain. But what happens when you use your mind and body simultaneously, bringing together the power of sex, the crucibles of marriage, the Four Points of Balance, and knowledge of brain function? I think you have a method of growth and change equivalent to an atom-smashing cyclotron.

## DESIRE, SEX, BRAIN, AND SELF

It's amazing how many levels we've covered, and how they all come together in something as simple (and complex) as a hug. We started by seeing how developing and maintaining a solid flexible self became a primary shaper of human sexual desire. From there, we discovered how natural differentiation processes make sexual desire problems inevitable for normal healthy couples. You learned about the Four Points of Balance. You've seen how these four abilities underlie your sense of self, and how they bolster your functioning, help you resolve gridlock, and directly or indirectly resolve sexual desire problems.

Well, simultaneously with these selfhood and differentiation issues, there's lots of brain activity going on. It's all part of one big package. The human self originally arose from changes in the brain. The human brain evolved through differentiation. Your Four Points of Balance play critical roles in your brain's moment-to-moment operations. Your Four Points of Balance determine if and when your brain becomes dysregulated and your mind falls apart. Focusing on your Four Points of Balance pulls your head back together. Doing this repeatedly strengthens your brain's ability to function under stress. And there are other ways you can pull everything together and help yourself, which I'll cover throughout this chapter.

• *Stronger sense of self*

Doing *heads on pillows* and *hugging till relaxed* challenged Kate and Paul's Four Points of Balance. *Hugging till relaxed* challenged Paul's sense of self. He was the high desire partner for sex, but the low desire partner for hugging. He was more uncomfortable with hugging than Kate. On the surface, the possibility that *hugging till relaxed* might help his difficulty reaching orgasm sounded great. But it put his problem on the table. Paul had to quiet his mind and calm his heart a lot when they finally did it.

Kate was challenged differently: She was brought face-to-face with her loss of sexual interest once relationships began. Doing *hugging till relaxed* involved greater emotional investment. Her typical pattern had been to disinvest when her desire waned. She had to soothe her fears of being obligated to have sex if Paul got turned on. They both had to keep themselves from overreacting to the other. Both had to put forth some meaningful endurance for growth.

• *Better emotional regulation*

As Kate and Paul progressed further with *heads on pillows,* they showed the kind of progress I've come to expect: Kate's emotional crashes subsided, and so did Paul's volatile eruptions.

The change in Kate was readily apparent to Paul. For the first time, she didn't berate him emotionally in the midst of one of her crashes. For example, Kate was already irritated about how her day was going when something happened in the house that totally frustrated her. Paul prepared for the worst when he saw Kate's tears. She looked overwhelmed. However, instead of ranting at Paul that he didn't really care about her, Kate stopped the conversation. She walked out of the house and around the block several times. As she left she managed to say, "This isn't your fault. I'll be okay. This is something I just have to handle for myself." While she was gone she raged out loud and cried. When she returned, she still felt low. But the important thing was that she didn't inflict herself on Paul *while* she felt terrible.

Kate's progress caught her own attention, as well. She felt proud of herself. Gradually her ability to ease and control her crashes improved. She was able to stop several times in mid-crash and pull herself out of it. At best this ability remained shaky, but it was obvious a core change was occurring. It wasn't just that Kate had more self-esteem. Her "self" was getting stronger. Paul also became less emotionally reactive and didn't get angry when he would have in the past. (I'll describe this shortly.)

### • *Brightening*

Kate and Paul even started to *look* different. Their faces changed as *brightening* became apparent. Brightening is a softening of facial features and an appearance of aliveness, vitality, energy, and healthy overall countenance. Women look like they've had Botox or a face lift, and men look softer and more handsome. It's no mystery why many couples resume having sex: They feel and look more attractive, and they are more attracted to each other. Other people find them more attractive and approachable, too.

People who show brightening find their own eyes look clearer and brighter, their mental acuity is sharper, and their general (and emotional) intelligence increases. Brightening often quickly follows difficult-but-collaborative confrontations in our sessions. This happens too rapidly and dramatically simply to be "learning." It is my belief that *brightening* reflects shifts in brain function.

Brightening is identifiable by untrained observers—that's how I first came upon it. Around day four of my nine-day Passionate Marriage® Couples Retreat, people start telling each other, *"You look different! You look terrific!"* Couples who demonstrate brightening early in the retreat are invariably the ones other couples felt sorry for on days one, two, and three because they were confronting their issues and looked like hell. On day four other couples are jealous of them, and anxiously eyeing their own mates. This pattern has held up consistently in ten years of Couples Retreats. Brightening is commonplace in my therapy practice as well.

Couples who show brightening also end up thinking differently and handling their emotions better. Their marriages become more stable and less anxiety-driven. Partners become softer, more considerate, and more direct with each other. Relationships with children, parents, or friends become richer, deeper, and more resilient. These changes are relatively resilient under stress, as one might expect if people's brains were functioning differently.

### • *Kate and Paul improve*

Kate became less volatile, and her emotional crashes diminished. She still had days where she was down, but she was better able to catch her emotional slides and she didn't bottom out as badly. As Kate's facial expression, emotional tone, and demeanor began to change, so did the reactions she got from the people around her. Paul said he was more relaxed with her and less worried about her next crash. Their teenage son even commented that they seemed to be getting along better. Paul and Kate were amazed. They realized he was tracking them closely, watching their behavior and mapping their minds. From his outward behavior, they'd never guessed he was paying attention.

Equally importantly, Kate's sexual desire changed. Getting their minds together when their bodies touched increased her desire for sex. Despite all the sex earlier in her life, this was something new. The shift in Kate's desire wasn't lost on Paul. Kate felt desire coming out of her that wasn't about being drawn to Paul. She felt some of that too, but there was more: Kate felt it was *her* desire coming out of her. She likened it to popping the cork on a champagne bottle.

Not coincidently, Kate began remembering more about her childhood. At the outset of our sessions, she said she didn't remember much, but from what she could remember, things were pretty normal. Her mother stayed home and raised the kids. Her father worked hard and was often gone from home. Her parents got along. She and her sister went to school. One time her father got steamed when he caught them smoking. She was active in Girl Scouts. Mother helped her sew her badges on her uniform. Nothing unusual, just typical stuff.

Kate's revised picture looked quiet different: Father was often gone but frequently drunk when he was home. Mother was unable or unwilling to take care of Kate and her older sister. Kate and her sister often ended up doing whatever was necessary to keep the house running and keep their mother stable. Mother would get overwrought about something and withdraw into her room for days. She also was a self-centered, brutal woman who enjoyed wiping the smiles off her children's faces. The one thing she could do well was sew. Things got worse when Kate's sister got married at eighteen and moved out. After that Kate stayed out of the house as much as possible, but Mother played cat-and-mouse mental games trying to keep her in. When Kate did get out, much of her time was spent partying and having sex.

How could Kate's picture shift so radically? Heretofore there were serious holes in her autobiographical memory. Gaps in autobiographical memory occur in traumatic events or overwhelming circumstances. The way Kate saw things before was the picture she'd constructed with the remaining pieces. With enough strategic pieces missing, Kate could put things together as she preferred. Everyone's life picture is inaccurate enough to keep their anxiety down, and accurate enough to keep their "bullshit detector" from going off. This was particularly true for Kate's large gaps in autobiographical memory.

### • Paul changes too

Paul went through his own transformation. He realized he was angry most of the time. It was an automatic response to almost everything in his life. Everything that disturbed Paul triggered a flood of anger. Seeing this pervasive response frightened him. All the years Kate had complained about his anger took on new meaning. Heretofore, Paul had stored this in his brain under the heading of *Kate's a crazy bitch.* Now Paul started worrying, *What the hell is the matter with me?*

Paul buckled down and started approaching his anger as his brain's de facto response to anxiety and stress. When he was emotionally overloaded (which didn't take much), out came his anger. The new Paul got less caught up in his thoughts and feelings when he got angry. He realized his emotions were out of control, and that the important thing was to pull himself together and get control of himself. Period. If he couldn't do that, intellectually understanding why a particular stimulus triggered him was useless. Rather than *express* his feelings, Paul needed to learn to *tolerate* them.

As with other clients, Paul gradually became better able to control his anger when he lost his grip on himself by applying his Four Points of Balance. He also got angry less often. His marriage became more stable and his alliance with Kate grew more resilient. Both Paul and Kate were better able to tolerate their own emotions without falling apart, to handle their feelings when they did fall apart, and to tolerate it when the other fell apart.

In one session Paul said, "Remember I told you I didn't remember my childhood? Now that I'm more aware of my anger, I remember my father had thunderous fits of rage. I sort of always knew it, but I didn't let myself know it. I'm aware now that I didn't want to know it. It's like I stored it under the wrong heading. It was right out in front of me, but I couldn't see it.

"In my memory my father worked long hours. That was the story in my family. My father worked long hours, he was an important executive, and we were supposed to understand the stress he was under. This was the explanation for everything. But he'd go into rages, and we would be standing there in shock. We hid this because your slightest indication he was acting like an asshole would make you his target. One time I watched my dad beat my brother up because he spoke back. It was like it was happening to me—to both of us at the same time. When my mother made excuses for my father, I was so frustrated and angry I thought I would explode.

"In retrospect, my picture of my childhood was the family line: 'Dad works for the family and we need to appreciate how hard he works. Yes, he has a problem with anger, but that's understandable given the stress he is under.' It really freaks me out that my family said about my Dad the same thing you said about my anger. But it's creepy how this gets used so differently. My family said this to *excuse* my dad's anger, and you're using it to help me *control* my anger."

## BENEFITS OF TENDER LOVING SEX

Paul and Kate made enough progress to make having sex appropriate and useful. They were more likely to succeed when they did. They had already accomplished the most difficult parts first: *Developing a resilient collaborative alliance and using physical contact in whole new ways.* They got to this place by exercising their Four Points of Balance. They were more willing to look at themselves, even if they didn't look good. They had less anxiety about letting themselves be held and seen. They didn't have shouting matches anymore. They had difficult—necessary—discussions they'd avoided in the past.

Your ability to have tender loving sex is linked to your Four Points of Balance. You have to hold on to your self to be *deeply* engaged with your partner. You have to confront yourself about who you are (sexually and otherwise) and decide whether or not that's okay. It can be hard to be known to this degree, especially in that way. It's harder to validate your eroticism with a long-term partner than a one-night stand. This makes tender loving sex with your spouse all the more worth doing.

Think of this in terms of the Four Points of Balance: Tender loving sex challenges, broadens, and solidifies your solid flexible self. Letting your self entwine with your partner, both emotionally and physically, challenges your grip on yourself, your self-worth, and your sense of personal agency. Any fears of engulfment or loss of autonomy you have get pushed to the surface.

Tender loving sex stretches your ability to quiet your mind and calm your heart. It's a big step to turn off your radar, drop your guard, trust yourself, relax—and then let your partner see you and be with you. This level of being known can be unnerving. Don't give in to your urge to back off when your anxiety starts to rise.

Tender loving sex requires grounded responding to your partner's reactivity. You get no guarantee your partner's response will be *"Yes! LET'S DO IT!!"* If he gets nervous or threatened, he's likely to overreact, get angry, put you down, and/or become condescending, dismissive, or belligerent. Tender loving sex involves your Four Points of Balance, whether you're having sex or fighting about it.

Tender loving sex requires meaningful endurance and tolerating discomfort for growth. (I don't mean painful intercourse.) Sometimes this means going through difficult discussions or disappointing sexual encounters to get to a better place. If you're not used to tender loving sex—particularly with your spouse—you may be awkward or nervous or even a little scared.

It takes courage to experiment with tender loving sex. You might be great at raunchy sex, but lack the courage to let someone hold you while you make love. The deeper your connection goes, the more likely any lingering unresolved issues will get triggered. Profound tender loving sex requires *self*-validated intimacy rather than validation from your partner. (That's why people dependent on their partner's validation don't deeply engage in it.)

Tender loving sex requires personal integrity, sometimes more than you may have. Once you realize the Four Points of Balance underlie all forms of personal integrity, it's easier to see how tender loving sex is part of the people-growing machinery of marriage.

Besides increasing desire, heating up your sex life, and improving your relationship and your disposition (as if this wasn't enough!), tender loving sex can do good things for your brain. Using your body this way creates the seven important conditions that facilitate brain change, just like *hugging till relaxed, heads on pillows, feeling while touching,* and resolving ticklishness:

1. A strong and resilient collaborative alliance.
2. Moderate levels of stress and emotional arousal, alternating with calm.
3. Intense and profound intersubjective moments of meeting.
4. Information and experiences gathered across multiple dimensions of cognition, emotion, sensation, and behavior.
5. Activity in brain neural networks involved in processing and regulating thoughts, feelings, sensations, and behaviors.
6. New conceptual knowledge integrating emotional and bodily experiences.
7. Organizing experiences in ways that foster continued growth and integration.

## EXPLORING YOUR SEXUAL POTENTIAL

If you have sexual desire problems, developing your capacity for tender loving sex may be your solution. Here are two specific ways you can do this:

- *Eyes-open sex*

Usually when they had sex, Kate followed Paul's lead. Paul liked having sex before they went to sleep. They always had sex lying down in bed, usually under the covers. Even when Kate opened her eyes, there wasn't much to see. The room was dark and silent. Paul's eyes were usually closed. They never looked at each other. In fact, they rarely kissed and hardly talked. Instead of the splash of waves or wind in the trees, like she had heard during her adolescent sexual escapades, Kate listened to the clock ticking the minutes away as Paul groped her and she tried to get aroused. They usually did it missionary-style. To Paul, doggy-style was pretty daring. This was a far cry from the eyes-open sex Kate dreamed about.[199]

Kate told me about a sexy dream she had. Without knowing it, she was envisioning eyes-open sex. Eyes-open sex creates a powerful intersubjective experience. It's possible to have sex with your eyes open during which you're staring at your partner while shielding your thoughts. However, the eyes-open sex Kate dreamed about involved actively taking someone in, letting him map her mind, and create an intersubjective state in which she knew him and she let herself being known, as he did the same.

You can use eyes-open sex even more effectively once you understand it involves learning about yourself in the process of letting yourself be known. *Effectively* doesn't mean without difficulty; eyes-open sex challenges your Four Points of Balance. *Effectively* means (a) understanding why and how eyes-open sex feels great or uncomfortable to you, and (b) using this knowledge to focus your attention when you deliberately have eyes-open sex again. You'll increase your pleasure, decrease your discomfort, and raise your Four Points of Balance more efficiently.

You can even have eyes-open sex without actually touching your partner. Just reach down and pleasure yourself while looking your partner in the eye! You'd be giving a clear picture of who you are, as well as challenging yourself, soothing yourself, not overreacting, and taking a *big* step toward sexual maturity.

Most of us have sex with our eyes closed and the lights off. Why? Not because it's more romantic. It's because we fear we wouldn't be loved if we were truly known. We break contact because we fear getting close enough to touch and map each other's minds. People who can't hold on to themselves don't let themselves be seen.

- *Do you have sex with your eyes open?*

Many people don't. Out of 10,500 people who completed a survey on passionatemarriage.com, 23 percent never made eye contact during sex because they or their partner always kept their eyes closed. Another 14 percent never made eye contact even though both partners opened their eyes. Only 52 percent sometimes made eye contact during sex. (The remaining 10 percent never had sex.)

People who have eyes-open sex don't have their eyes open every moment. (It is not a staring contest. You're allowed to blink or close your eyes.) They also don't always do it this way. Sometimes it's fun to lie back, close your eyes, and let your partner put you into orbit. But when they close their eyes, they're not avoiding their partner.

You can map out a person's mind by the way he or she *does* you. It creates a special bond. That's what tender loving sex is all about. But when your partner won't even open his eyes or doesn't want to see you, you know he isn't interested in intimacy with any real depth. He probably isn't interested in seeing himself either.

If this describes your situation, you can use eyes-open sex to get a better grip on your life. It will challenge who you are and make you nervous and prone to react. It will stretch you emotionally and help you grow. You may feel some initial awkwardness, but a little meaningful endurance will help you get over it. Eyes-open sex is a change in pace that prolongs sex, reduces anxiety, and increases emotional connection. It provides a place to take a breath and *relax*, instead of humping away like rabbits. Over time, having sex with your eyes open will become your norm rather than an exception.

Eyes-open sex (like *hugging till relaxed*) can revitalize your relationship with unnerving speed. Your style of sex (like your hugging) is connected to what's inside you. Changing how you have sex can change you.

Eyes-open sex broadens and deepens the meanings you can bring to sex. It's pretty electric when eye contact becomes "I to I" contact—the meeting of two selves. Judging from my clients, this moment of meeting with someone you love increases your brain's plasticity and facilitates positive change.

## • *Watch what goes on in your mind*

If you take the plunge and have eyes-open sex, keep this in mind: Couples' experiences differ, but they always fit the people involved. Some find it a great turn-on; for others it's a turn-off. Some find it profoundly meaningful and tender, while others find it disquieting, embarrassingly, or too revealing. Eyes-open sex is a collaborative alliance, and if you don't have one, that's going to show one way or another. Eyes-open sex invites your partner to look into your heart and soul and examine your relationship.

If you're not used to this kind of thing, I suggest you start off with *heads on pillows* (Chapter 11). This will help you get an emotional connection from the outset. With this in place, eyes-open sex involves nothing more than "following the connection" established during foreplay and keeping that going through whatever else you do. When your partner sees interest in your eyes and feels your intent, that's the start of *doing* him. Carry this into touching some (non-genital) part of your partner's body. *Feeling while touching* can make a big improvement. Look into your partner, let him look into you, and pair this with your caress. It's a lovely way to put the eye-gazing / mind-mapping circuitry in your brain to use.

When you're on the receiving end of things, you can start off by focusing your attention on your point of physical contact to tune in to your partner's touch. Focus "from the inside" by following the moving pattern of sensations with your mind. If you're having difficulty, some people find it helpful to focus from "outside," by watching their partner touch them. If you're easily distracted or your mind often drifts off during sex, just focus on maintaining protracted connection through the touch. You'll get to the point where you can follow your partner's touch "from inside" while making eye contact at the same time. Rather than diminishing your sensations, mapping his mind becomes another dimension of connection. Eventually your physical sensations and emotional connection combine in a grand symphony, rather than as a mix of chamber music and MTV. Being with your partner visually, emotionally, physically, sensorially, and cognitively become integrated parts of your total stimulation. This high-meaning, high-plasticity, somatosensory moment of meeting can do wonders for your sexual desire.

If eyes-open sex seems like too much, you and your partner can do *heads on pillows* where you both only open your left eye. This way you get to see your partner without feeling seen. Who knows, you might feel daring and open both eyes. Play "peek-a-boo" if you need to!

### • *Eyes-open orgasm*

Once you get comfortable with eyes-open sex, you can extend it to eyes-open orgasms. It's powerful to gaze into the eyes of someone you love before, during, and after your orgasm. Of all the intense moments of meeting you can have, this one ranks among the best.[200]

An eyes-open orgasm brings together everything we've talked about: *feeling while touching*, moments of meeting, being *seen*, *felt*, and *tasted*, letting your partner map your mind, and taking him into your core. It's one of the loveliest and most carnal demonstration of willfulness there is. It takes wanting to want and consciously chosen, freely undertaken desire, all at the same time.

Eyes-open orgasms are something like Dr. Spock's "Vulcan mind-meld" in *Star Trek*: a profound level of partner engagement and emotional transparency. Your partner's presence provides emotional meaning without distracting you from your physical sensations. For this to happen, you have to accept yourself as you are at that moment, because that's who your partner is going to see. You have to hold on to your self and invite your partner to look into you while you "pop!"

Don't feel bad if you can't reach orgasm with your eyes open just yet. Most people can't. Of the 10,500 people who participated in the passion atemarriage.com web site survey, only 13 percent said they or their partner had eyes-open orgasms. You could easily argue eyes-open orgasms are (statistically) abnormal—or maybe a miracle. However, you can learn to have eyes-open orgasms if you want to. The process is as reliable as curing ticklishness and much the same.

### • *Give it to me, baby!*

Paul started confronting himself about why he couldn't come. Why was he uncomfortable having tender loving sex with a woman who wanted it? It was his own wife, for crying out loud! How much more "permission" could he get? What was it going to take? Paul realized he wanted to unlock himself.

One day Paul found Kate as she was drying herself after a bath. Paul walked in the bathroom and, without a word, took the towel out of her hand as she stood there. Kate looked at him curiously, not understanding what was happening. Paul took her by the hand, led her over to the vanity, and had her sit with her back to the mirror. At that point Kate thought Paul wanted to talk about something important.

Paul leaned forward and put his hands on the inside of her thighs. Immediately, Kate mapped out what Paul was doing. She gave him a sideways glance of disbelief. Paul smiled and kept her gaze. Slowly, he parted her thighs. He stepped forward so he was standing over her. No part of his body touched her except for his hands. Paul stroked the inside of her thighs, never taking his eyes off her. Kate gave Paul a grin from ear to ear. Paul broke the silence.

"Is this what you want, you bad girl?"

Kate thought she had died and gone to heaven. "Yeah ... Are you a bad boy?"

"We're going to find out." Paul's response was immediate and determined. Kate giggled.

Paul took Kate's hand and led her to the soft carpet. Kate was thrilled that they weren't in bed. First they did *hugging till relaxed* with Kate laying upon Paul's chest.[201] Then they did *heads on pillows* using a stack of towels. After they were deeply engaged for a while, Paul licked two fingers of his hand and reached down and touched her labia. Kate smiled and gave him an appraising look.

Paul opened Kate's labia with his hand, licked two fingers on his other hand, and brought them to her clitoris. Paul never took his eyes off her. Kate was engrossed in mapping his mind. His *mind* was rubbing her clitoris, and looking her in the eye, simultaneously. Kate read Paul. He was serious!

Then Paul licked his fingers again and brought more saliva to her clitoris. Kate thought, "Oh, God. He is *really* serious!"

Paul kept his eyes on Kate while he rubbed her with his fingers. His jaw was set, he was determined, there was a twinkle in his eye. It wasn't so much how he moved his fingers; it was what was in his mind. *That* really turned Kate on. It wasn't just the clitoral sensations. The sexual vibes from Paul blew her away. There wasn't a sound in the room except for Kate's moans.

Moaning in pleasuring was new for them. Paul read her mind. As Kate approached orgasm, her eyes started to close. Paul laughed and said, "Stay with me." Kate looked at Paul, and her eyes were full of love.

Eyes-open orgasms involve more than keeping your eyelids apart. It's about lifting your "emotional shades," taking your partner in, and letting him inside your mind. Kate looked at Paul and drank him in. It was all she needed to put her over the edge. A look of awe appeared in her eyes. Her body bucked reflexively, and she exhaled, *"Uuuhhhhhhhhhh!"* Paul chuckled.

Kate laughed and Paul laughed with her.

"Oh God. I'm not only having an eyes-open orgasm, I'm laughing in the middle of my orgasm too!"

"Indeed you are." Paul attested.

Paul relaxed to give Kate a chance to catch her breath. Instead, she pulled herself on top of him.

"I thought you were dead," Paul said.

"I'm dead from being done. Now it's my turn to do you."

"Don't you want a minute to relax?"

In answer, Kate squatted over Paul's hips. She put her hands around the back of his neck and used her arms to take the weight off her thighs. She could move her hips up and down freely. Paul put a pillow under his head, making it effortless for him to see Kate as she pulled against him. Kate thought, *He's making himself comfortable and not pulling back. Here goes.* Kate readjusted her feet to position herself so it felt easy for her to move. Then she took his penis inside her and began moving. Rhythmically, slowly, up and down, up and down. On some down strokes, she bumped into him with a gentle thud. The impact resonated through her pelvis too.

Kate glanced around the room while she kept her rhythm. The room was light and airy. It looked like a still-life painting, a slice of life. Kate thought, *This is just like my fantasies. We're doing it as part of daily life.* Keeping her rhythm, Kate started humming softly to herself. She looked down at Paul, and they smiled.

"What are you doing?"

"I'm loving you!"

"Yes, I know. But you're *humming.*"

Kate smiled. She kept her rhythm and kept humming except to say, "Maybe I hum when I make love." Paul thought this was hilarious. He started humming, too. Kate thought this was hysterical.

Kate started emphasizing some down-strokes more than others. Each bump produced a blip in Paul's humming. She and Paul started laughing when he realized what she was doing. She was playing him like a kazoo. They were doing it together, actually. They were literally making beautiful music together. They were friends. Kate and Paul looked at each other and smiled.

Kate wasn't humping Paul's penis. She was going after his mind with all her energy and essence. In her mind Kate was clear: She wanted to watch Paul finally let himself be taken. She wanted to feel him shoot into her. She wanted to see him spent and exhausted. Paul kept looking at Kate as she drove her energy into him. The thought occurred to her, *I've got him in me both ways. In my body and in my mind. I'm taking him in. Absorbing him. Surrounding him. Cuddling him.*

Kate could feel Paul was not far from orgasm. They were wet and more revved up then ever before. Kate's accented down-thrusts turned Paul's humming into grunts. *Oh my God!* Kate thought, *We're really making love!*

Then Kate started doing Paul on the up-stroke. After she established her rhythm in his mind, Kate intermittently stopped at the top of her stroke. Then she'd restart the rhythmic up-and-down. Paul didn't know when Kate would pause, or how long the pause would last. One thing he knew for certain, though, was that Kate was playing with his mind. She was doing his penis *and* his brain. She had his undivided attention.

Kate and Paul were eye to eye. The gleam in her eyes intensified, and they began a dialogue repeated by lovers throughout time. It was a conversation of great meaning and few words.[202]

Kate said, "I love you!"

Paul responded, "*I* love you!"

"No, I love *you.*"

"No, *I* love *you.*"

"*I'm* making love to *you.*" Kate stopped at the top of her thrust to prove her point.

"Ohhhhhhh!" Paul gasped for air. Kate delighted in her new-found sense of power.

"*You're* loving *me!*"

"I *love* you!" The power in Kate's down stroke and voice increased. Her eyes were wide, riveted on Paul.

"*Yes!*" Paul's neck bulged as he brought his face within inches of her. His eyes were wide, and his nostrils flared. Kate liked seeing him strain to meet her.

"*Oh God, I'm coming!!*" Kate saw a look of shock came into his eyes. She brought her hips down on him with one last resounding thud. Paul's orgasm thundered through his mind and body.

"*Yeessssssss!!!*" The breath hissed out of Paul, as his arms locked around Kate's hips and convulsively pulled her to him. He was deep inside her. He felt completely contained, completely welcomed, completely at home and at peace. For what felt like several minutes, Paul's thoughts raced while time stood still. The room faded. He was acutely aware of himself as a finite being. And he was with another finite separate self, who was closer to him than he had ever let anyone. It was Kate, bringing him to this moment of self-awareness.

Paul had the distinct thought that Kate was holding him in her vagina the way a mother holds a child. Like she was holding him and rocking him. Kate's humming took on completely different meaning. All the while, Kate pushed down without letting up. He could feel her leaning into their connection. Paul's biceps ached but he kept pulling her against him. The intensity was right on the edge between pleasure and pain.

Paul suddenly realized he was back with Kate. It was like he'd never left. He was just less absorbed in his own thoughts. What seemed like a long time was only a minute. Paul realized he was crying. He was flooded with love and compassion for Kate. He wanted to tell her about his journey through his mind. As he started to talk, he realized her face was glowing. He didn't realize he was looking at positive brain plasticity.

## • *Going forward*

It's incredible how marriage works: Sexual desire problems provoke growth in people's Four Points of Balance. Could the bane of your existence be part of the Grand Design? Has Nature built a trauma-resolving mechanism into the guts of adult relationships? Is this how the human race has repaired (and developed) its brain since prehistoric times?

Will this happen for you? Everything depends on how you see it and how you use it. The doorway beckons. All you have to do is *truly* make love.

---

### IDEAS TO PONDER

- Tender loving sex can strengthen your Four Points of Balance, change your mind, and possibly change your brain.
- Mind-mapping plays a big role in tender loving sex.
- Tender loving sex involves things like letting yourself be held and engaging your partner through eyes-open sex. Eyes-open orgasms are like Dr. Spock's "Vulcan mind-meld" in *Star Trek:* a profound level of partner engagement and emotional transparency.

# 14

# Blow Your Mind!

*S*ome time ago I had lunch with one of sweetest and dearest people in my life. He is a man I hold in the highest regard. Someone whose impeccable integrity does not permit me to mention his name. He was my therapist. He became my friend. He's one of finest therapists I've ever known.

Now in his senior years, I went back to visit him as a peer. We spent an afternoon in a restaurant, talking frankly about our respective professional work, our lives, and ourselves. In the midst of our conversation my dear friend asked, *"Do you still fuck?"*

I convulsed into laughter and nearly fell out of my chair. It was hard to breathe! After several minutes, I managed to get out, "Yes. How about you?"

"No," my friend said. "Not like I used to. That's why I asked you. I'm taking too many medications, my medical problems have taken their toll, and I'm getting old. But I tell you, I miss it! You need to write another book—about fucking. That's where so many couples need help."

This whole thing was so precious and funny I couldn't stop laughing. "I'm not sure about a whole book about fucking, but I'm writing something now. Maybe I can work in a chapter."

"*Do that*," he said and smiled. "So many people don't know what they're missing. But I do!"

This was a small part of a wonderful lunch full of rich, meaningful, funny interchanges and the best crab au gratin I've ever tasted. As we said our good-byes, my friend brought the topic up again. With great seriousness, he implored, "Write about fucking. Write it for young couples. They waste so much time!"

Once again I was laughing. But this time my friend kept a straight face. "You're serious," I said.

"Indeed I am," he said forthrightly.

I became serious too. "I need you to clarify this. Do you mean write about sex, like making love, or do you really mean *fucking*?"

"I mean *fucking*! That's what I said. Fucking. That's the part I miss. It's too important to let just slip away."

"Okay. I'll see what I can do."

We knew this might be our last time together, which it turned out to be. We expressed our love for each other. He kissed my head. His last words as we parted were, "Couples waste so much time. Teach them about fucking. It will save so much heartache in so many marriages!"

This chapter is in his honor.

## • *Nicolle and Phillip*

My friend was referring to couples like Nicolle and Phillip, who came to see me for their sexual desire problems. Sex was down to once a month. Nicolle was the low desire partner. She said she wasn't interested in sex but she wasn't sure why. She thought she liked sex. Phillip was sure he liked sex, and his problem was he couldn't get enough.

In short order Nicolle revealed she couldn't stand the way they did it. Phillip got defensive. Nicolle went on to say she found their sex *boring*.

They always did the same old thing. It was predictable. It wasn't inter-esting. Phillip reached orgasm too quickly. It wasn't romantic. It wasn't satisfying. It wasn't worth doing. Nicolle acknowledged she was partly to blame. She was lazy, too. She didn't put the energy into sex that she knew she should.

Phillip squirmed during Nicolle's list of dissatisfactions. He managed to hold on to himself, but just barely. I could have asked Nicolle what she liked about their sex, to shore up his reflected sense of self. But she might not have anything really positive to say, and I didn't want to encourage her to prop him up.

Instead, I asked her to describe what kind of sex she liked. It was a better move for both of them. Nicolle hesitated and then answered my question. As she described what she wanted, her face lit up. Her descrip-tion was pretty detailed and graphic. When she finished and realized I was looking at her and smiling, she blushed.

"Why are you smiling at me?" She grinned.

"Do you like *fucking*?"

"I ... I don't know."

"That's what you just described."

"You mean do I like sex? Yes, I do."

"No. I mean, do you like to *fuck*? You just described you and your partner fucking. First you do him, and then he does you. Throughout your whole description you two are fucking. Apparently you know about fucking."

Nicolle agreed. "Apparently I do!" Phillip stopped squirming and paid attention to what was unfolding.

"You didn't answer my question. And you don't have to. But I'll ask you one more time: Do you know about fucking? Do you know what I mean?"

Nicolle glanced at Phillip, and then to me. Her hesitation was obvious. She took a deep breath and finally let her secret out. (It was already out.) "... Yes."

"How do you know about fucking? From your relationship with Phillip?"

"... No." Nicolle watched his reaction. I paused to let this happen.

"I see. Then you're in a box that's difficult to get out of. Particularly for women."

Nicolle watched me closely. "What do you mean?"

"It sounds like you like sex, but you're dying of frustration and boredom. You know what you like: You like to fuck. But you can't tell Phillip because he'll ask you how you know. Then you'll have to tell him you discovered this with someone else, and you're afraid he'll feel threatened. So you look like a sexual dud, who doesn't know what will please her, to keep your husband's reflected sense of self from taking a nose-dive."

Nicolle looked amazed. She was openly astonished. "How do you know all this?"

"Many women are in that box. Lots of them never get out—they just give up sex instead. Or have affairs."

"I think Phillip and I got close to fucking once or twice." Nicolle was trying to be supportive and optimistic, but it sounded hollow.

"Maybe so. But you haven't said whether or not what I described is accurate about you."

"About being in a box?" Nicolle was tracking Phillip's state of mind.

"Yes."

"… Yes. I'm in that box."

Phillip shook his head in disbelief. "When Nicolle first started talking, I thought I sounded like a dumb fuck. Now I'm learning I'm not even that."

I said, "Play your cards right, and you could turn out to be a great fuck."

After several seconds, Phillip nodded. "All right. I'm willing to learn."


• *Hidden Talent*

When Nicolle and Phillip had sex at the start of their relationship, she realized he didn't *do* her. Initially she attributed this to lack of experience. She was willing to be patient. She figured they'd work into it as she had with previous partners. Only this didn't happen. Nicolle subtly encouraged Phillip, but he didn't want to go there.

Nicolle tried to map out why Phillip pulled back from *doing* and *being done.* Over time she realized it wasn't just naïveté. Sometimes when Nicolle sensed things were heading in the right direction, Phillip did something to cool things down. At first she couldn't figure out why Phillip did this. She assumed anyone would want to fuck because it feels so great.

Then she though maybe Phillip was holding back to slow his rapid orgasms and prolong sex. She thought this for a long time. However, from mind-mapping over many sexual encounters, Nicolle realized there was something else: Phillip pulled back because he feared his own aggression. She encouraged Phillip, saying that she wasn't fragile or breakable, that she was built for action, but to no avail. Nicolle put two and two together as she got to know Phillip's out-of-control father.

By their third year of marriage, Nicolle gave up. They still had sex, but it was lackluster. Nicolle mostly went along with whatever Phillip wanted to do. She struggled with the urge to have an affair many times.

In many ways, Nicolle epitomized a common type of low desire partner: A fire-breathing momma who looks sexually uninterested, but who is frustrated, angry, and misses being *done.* Nicolle wanted Phillip to *do* her, and she wanted to experiment with *doing* him. She wanted Phillip to be the kind of man she would like to *do.* He had the right body, give or take a few pounds. The real question was, would he allow himself to be *fucked?*

Like many men, Phillip was intimidated by women's sexuality. His first intercourse occurred when his high school girlfriend proposed it. The next several times other women came on to him, Phillip demurred. Being with a sexually hungry (and presumably sexually knowledgeable) woman was daunting. The few times Nicolle had tried to *do* him, he got nervous, too. Phillip knew society and Nicolle expected him to be the high desire partner. But he didn't think he could fill this tall order with women who really like sex.

### • *Women's remnants of "heat"*

Perhaps the female anatomy simply doesn't encourage it, but terms depicting female sexual power don't really exist. It reflects how Western civilization plays down women's carnality.[203] But countless generations have known it existed. Remnants of your ancestral grandmother's sexuality have been trickling down for ages. Phillip didn't realize part of his feeling intimidated stemmed from millions of years of human breeding.

It's a common stereotype that men are more into fucking and women prefer making love. I would believe this too, if I didn't do the work I do. But in helping many female clients, they let me see them as they are. And having worked with lots of them, I have to say this isn't so.

Around the world, women are *at least* as interested in sex as men. Anthropologist Helen Fisher notes that although people commonly think men are supposed to take the sexual initiative, a 1970s survey of ninety-three societies found men and women in seventy-two societies believed both sexes had roughly equal sex drives.[204]

Actually, in my professional experience, women are *more* interested. Meaning many women want sex frequently—*if it is good*. Women are more concerned about the quality of their sex. Many are more sexually interested and knowledgeable than their husbands. Women are at least equally interested in, and often more knowledgeable about, fucking.

One aspect of sex is its strength and quality of *intention*. Intention is desire. Intention is crucial when you are courting someone to have sex for the first time. It's crucial when making love to your partner after several decades together. And a large part of what you fuck someone with is your focused carnal intentions.

Men and women look at sexually explicit photos differently. Men look first at faces, whereas normal cycling (non-contracepted) women look first at genitals, and women taking oral contraceptives look first at non-sexual contextual aspects.[205]

Studies of *intention cues* (one of five courting behaviors) indicate women exhibit more intent: The woman usually makes the first move by touching her suitor's body. Studies conducted in singles bars say women begin two-thirds of all pickups.[206] Women around the world frequently actively initiate their sexual encounters.

Contemporary wisdom holds that "good girls make love, and bad girls fuck." Many women rail at this double standard. The idea that women aren't supposed to fuck seems especially peculiar when you realize women's interest in fucking goes back to their ancestral grandmothers, who went into heat like other primates.

All female primates have a period of heat (estrus), human women being the only apparent exception. Female apes and monkeys have monthly menstrual cycles just like women, but they also go into heat in the middle of each cycle. The vast majority of copulations occur during this time. When the females cease having monthly menstrual cycles while they are breastfeeding, our ape brethren aren't as sexually frisky. (The same occurs when couples have a new baby, except the man's reflected sense of self declines for lack of attention. Male orangutans presumably handle this better because they don't have as much of a sense of self.)

Each month a woman's sexual desire peaks during some point in her menstrual cycle. Is this the remnants of our prehistoric grandmothers' heat? Very likely it is. But women's hereditary desire for sex goes farther then recurrent hormonal blips: Their brains are hard-wired to have sex for social regulation of anxiety. This is certainly true for Bonobo monkeys, the primates most sexually similar to humans.[207] Like people, Bonobos separate sex and reproduction. Sexual contacts are not confined to estrus.

Female Bonobos copulate during most of the year, because their heat extends through three-quarters of their menstrual cycle. But there's another powerful reason: Bonobo females initiate sex daily to ease tension, reaffirm friendships, and reduce stress in the group. They also use sex to bribe male and female friends for food. Sexuality is a primary way female Bonobos and women relate to the world.

Women's sexual desire is rooted in human evolution. This would be a lot of desire, if Bonobos and humans were sexually similar. But the similarity stops at a unique human quirk: We are the only primates whose females lost their heat!

Why would such a thing happen? Why did women lose their heat?

Is it possible women's heat intimidated men? Did men breed heat out of women through sexual selection? Man's emergent reflected sense of self may have demanded it. Perhaps he didn't want women making him feel sexually inadequate all the time.

Women's ability to have multiple orgasms may be a remnant of heat. Or maybe men bread multiple orgasms into women by sexual selection. Women's multiple orgasms may have been more ego-gratifying to prehistoric men than heat-driven sexual aggressiveness. Perhaps men liked women writhing in orgasmic bliss while they thrust in their mighty phalluses. Perhaps they preferred to play out this drama with women who came easily, and multiple times. Over millions of years, could men have bred women for multiple orgasms? Is this why 30 percent of women today can orgasm during intercourse? No one knows.

## PEOPLE DON'T FUCK WITH THEIR SUPPORT SYSTEM

Humans have another interesting sexual characteristic: Most long-term partners don't fuck their spouse. Why is this important? Because Mother Nature didn't spend millions of years building a capacity in your brain, and then tell you not to use it. *Fucking, doing,* and *being done* takes your primate animalness and smacks it up against your most evolved brain faculties. Your forebears evolved a prefrontal neocortex that created Tantric Buddhism. This means you are an animal who can use sex to achieve spiritual enlightenment and self-transcendence. As sexual potential goes in the animal kingdom, you are at the top.

Remember that when you're struggling with desire problems, because this is how your species got there.

### • *The hardest person to fuck is your spouse*

So why don't long-term couples fuck? For that matter, how come many young couples don't fuck either? Would you be surprised if I told you it has to do with differentiation?

People don't fuck with their support systems. Couples who fuck at the beginning of their relationship stop later on. Other couples copulate for years and still have no idea something else exists. Many couples are virgins when it comes to fucking.

Like Nicolle and Phillip, most couples don't fuck. Is this anything more than limited experience or sexual hang-ups? What if this involves ongoing human evolution that's as much a part of the saga as women losing their heat? I propose it does, that it has to do with Four Points of Balance (just like everything else you've read in this book): You can't *do* your spouse if you depend on each other for validation.

If there's a good place for wantonness, you'd think it would be your marriage. Wanton sex is the kind of sex lots of people want. Woody Allen says, "Sex *is* dirty, that's why you should save it for someone you love!" We laugh at the joke, but we don't believe it.

It's hard to fuck your spouse in the most wholesome, erotic sense. It's a lot easier to fuck a stranger, or a "fuck buddy,"[208] or someone *else's* wife or husband. This is the paradox of partner-swapping and affairs: You're dying to fuck someone whose mate doesn't want to. Letting your eroticism loose with these people doesn't challenge your sense of self as much as fucking your spouse.

It feels easier to validate fucking in an affair because (a) you're both there for sex, (b) your girlfriend or boyfriend is busy stroking your reflected sense of self, and (c) you're in a collusive alliance to not see or be seen by each other. That's why people who are a sexual dud in their marriage may be "swinging from the chandeliers" in an affair.

Nicolle wasn't having an affair, but sometimes she wished she was. In the meantime, her sex life revolved around Phillip's reflected sense of self. She knew he would have a hard time knowing she had fucked other men. When they first met, Nicolle felt her sexual past was none of his business. Once they started a sexual relationship and she began to care about him, Nicolle realized Phillip didn't know about fucking. She wondered if it actually involved not letting himself fuck. Nicolle didn't set out to plant a false picture in Phillip's mind about her past, but she didn't correct it when she realized he didn't know this part of her.

Fucking is wanton and naughty. Adding it to your repertoire demands greater acceptance of your sexuality. Fucking *your* spouse brings your conflicts about love, intimacy, carnality, and spirituality right to the surface. That's why you may be hiding the fact that you know anything about this.

## • *Mapping your erotic brain-mind*

Fucking involves nuances of meaning, particularly of the lusty, lascivious, desirous, carnal, and wanton variety. Fucking can't be reduced to particular behaviors or positions, just like intimacy isn't reducible to communication exercises. Mind-mapping plays a *big* role. Your brain is able to create these meanings, and detect and respond to them as they arise (or don't). For people who like to fuck, that's more important than having an orgasm. But given a choice, it's the way they want to reach orgasm too.

According to my informal research, fewer than one in four people know about fucking.[209] Do you? Has anyone ever fucked you? Not just brought you to orgasm—really *fucked* you. I can usually identify people who know: They reveal themselves with an instantaneous (and somewhat self-conscious) smile. (Are you smiling now?)

*Fucking* starts before physical foreplay: You send massive sexual vibes even before you get into the bedroom. The mind-mapping starts long before you hit the sheets. During sex, from foreplay to exhaustion, you follow the connection. Your physical movements remain deadly erotic whether they are slow or fast.

*Fucking* involves a sexual experience distinct from "making love" in the traditional sense, in that sexual aggression is front and center. People who like to fuck argue there's no finer form of love making. *Being fucked* involves surrender, union, and the power of receiving. Relaxing into it, opening up to it with no ticklishness and no pulling back. Just, *"Yeah! Do me!"* Why wouldn't you want to do this with someone you love?

## • *You can be both the low desire partner and a sex-starved wife*

*Fucking* and *being fucked* are positions in a relationship, just like being the high or low desire partner. They are roles in an erotic collaborative alliance that include a dose of healthy aggression and, sometimes, a sprinkling of competitiveness. It *isn't* true, however, that high desire partners are more into fucking and low desire partners only like to be fucked. Lots of high desire partners are *dying* to be fucked, but their partners won't oblige. They are more likely to be fighting to have sex at all.

Lots of women are low desire partners *and* sex-starved wives. You can be both, and many women are. It messes with your mind. Most people think the low desire partner doesn't have much desire for sex. But, as you see with Nicolle, that's not necessarily true. How can you have no desire for sex with your husband, and be starving for sex at the same time? Unfortunately, it's all too easy.

## • *Sexual aggression and being the center of attention*

Healthy aggression plays an important role in fucking the one you love. Not the raw, hurtful sadism partners inflict on each other. Healthy aggression comes from digesting your "dark" side through your Four Points of Balance, turning dirty aggression and normal marital sadism into something useful. Differentiation is about self-modulation, about not inflicting yourself on others. There's a place for using your partner *well* in the service of personal growth, intimacy, and love. That place opens up after several passes through emotional gridlock.

There's room for your partner to dislike one thing or another. In fucking, an "I don't care how we do this" attitude generally prevails. Fucking your partner requires being aggressive, passionate, playful, adventurous, and generous. You may be stroking her body, but you're aiming for her mind. You focus your intentions and let her map your mind. Your goal is to create an intense mind and body connection around a particular co-constructed, multi-dimensional, phenomenological, intersubjective moment of meeting (known as fucking).[210]

There are people who can't imagine fucking being loving, because they think aggression is never appropriate in sex. Sexual aggression in couples is a volatile issue. Under the tyranny of contemporary political correctness, all forms of aggression have been banished from the bedroom, ostensibly for women's benefit. This doesn't help women who would love to be ravished. They want to be the object of their partner's carnal intent.

If you've ever told your partner, *"Put more into this!"* you know a little aggression can be a good thing.

Lots of women and men prefer oral sex to intercourse. They know all about sexual aggression, and power and submission, and oral sex lets them play out both sides with abandon. They like the sense of power that comes with getting someone off. But sometimes they give oral sex from a submissive psychological position. Often they like giving oral sex both ways, and receiving both ways, too.

It's interesting that some people who love giving oral sex won't let themselves receive it. You'd think they'd love to have their partner's complete and undivided (sexual) attention. But these folks experience "being the center of attention" quite differently when they're on the receiving end. They are frightened to relax, turn off their defensive radar, and let someone take care of them this way. It makes no difference if they've given their partner head for over an hour.

Letting your self be fucked ("taken") is no simple matter. You have to hold on to your self with "a tight grip on a loose rein." This lays the groundwork for sexual surrender. You don't throw yourself away, violate your integrity, or abdicate personal responsibility (in the broad sense) when you let yourself be taken. It's about not giving in to your fears, so you can surrender to your sensations and play out archetypical relationships.

## ORAL SEX: FABULOUS FOR CHANGING YOUR BRAIN WITH YOUR BODY AND MIND

Fucking is brain-candy to us meaning-making animals. "Fucking your brains out" suggests you're damaging your brain, and "fucking someone's brains in" sounds like you're doing that to your partner. In both cases, nothing could be further from the truth. I'm going to show you how a blow job that drives you out of your mind may help reorganize your brain. At the very least, it'll put a smile on your face, a spring in your step, and leave you in a good state of mind.

Oral sex is great for creating a rich, multi-layered experience. It can simultaneous light up multiple circuits in your brain and curl your toes (actually and euphemistically). Oral sex hits you at many different levels. When you get them all in reinforcing harmony, you're playing with something powerful and helpful. You've got an intensely pleasurable intersubjective somatosensory moment of meeting, where your genitals are being licked (or you're licking someone's genitals) and your right brain and left brain are working overtime, talking to each other, trying to keep up with the action.[211]

My professional and personal experience indicates strategically pairing these bodily sensations with intense feelings and meanings create unique mind states that foster breakthroughs in information processing. (In other words, great blow jobs from a loving partner are good for your brain.)

### • Back to Nicolle and Phillip

When Nicolle and Phillip started focusing on oral sex, the results rippled through their relationship. The dynamics in their relationship changed. For one thing, Nicolle was less deferent without being belligerent.

Weeks of *hugging till relaxed* and *heads on pillows* dramatically reduced the physical and emotional tension between them. But years of worrying he'd orgasm too quickly made it difficult for Phillip to really relax when he was physically close to Nicolle. He was progressing a little slower than she was.

Nicolle's desire returned, but not so much out of desire for Phillip. Our conversation about fucking had her thinking about sex all the time. Her sexual fantasies came alive, her masturbation increased, and the pictures in her mind became more daring.

Nicolle started thinking her sexuality was neat. In fact, she started thinking she was a neat woman. She liked herself more. She had desire because she respected her efforts to be her own person. She felt desirable, in and of herself. This had nothing to do with Phillip. She felt like she had more integrity.

Nicolle asked, "I know this may sound funny, but if we wanted to experiment with *fucking*, do you have any recommendations?"

I paused for a moment to consider Nicolle's request. I could have said, *Nicolle, you know about fucking. That's what our last session was all about. Have the guts to show Phillip what you know.*

Instead I calmly said, "You might try oral sex."

"Why oral sex?" Nicolle was genuinely surprised.

"Yes, Doctor. Why oral sex in particular?" Phillip had expected me to recommend intercourse. "Why don't we take care of where I disappoint Nicolle? I come too quick when we have intercourse, and we do that far more often than we have oral sex. I like to go down on Nicolle, but she usually stops me. Shouldn't we have intercourse?"

"As for taking care of where you disappoint Nicolle, that's what I had in mind. And as for having intercourse more often than oral sex, you might want to change that. Oral sex lets you approach sex as equals. It reduces the pressure on you because you don't need an erection. You don't have to worry about coming quickly, because even if you do, you can still make sure Nicolle isn't disappointed. You can probably do a better job of pleasing her if you use your tongue instead of your penis. You'll probably be able to feel what you're doing better, too. You can afford to tune into Nicolle whether you're giving oral sex or receiving it, and stop distracting yourself to delay your orgasm."

"Okay, I see your point." Phillip sounded unconvinced.

"Oral sex won't automatically keep you from tuning out. I'll bet you distract yourself when receiving oral sex, too. But oral sex removes the explanation that you're doing this to delay your orgasm. If you still go off, it's because of something else. It's no different than Nicolle tuning out when it's her turn to receive. She does it, too. " Phillip looked at Nicolle. Nicolle hesitated for a moment and nodded in agreement.

"Oral sex lets you collaborate in several different ways: You can deliberately tune in to each other instead of tuning each other out. You each get a chance to let yourself be held, in the metaphorical sense."

Nicolle remarked, "Huh. I never would have thought that. But once you point it out, it's perfectly obvious. I never thought of oral sex that way … Phillip is right. I usually stop him when he's going down on me. I get to a point I'm uncomfortable with it. I never saw it as not letting Phillip hold me. I guess I'd be willing to give it a try. What do you think, Phillip?"

Phillip hesitated. "Doc, maybe we're not ready for this. What if we're not successful?"

"If you're not ready or not interested, don't do it. What you do with your body is up to you, and I don't get a vote. And I'm not suggesting you bring each other to orgasm. It's fine if that happens, but it's not the point. If you both pay attention, you'll have a useful experience whether you reach orgasm or not. Oral sex offers people like you more time to relax. You have more chance to settle down and get comfortable with each other."

"Okay, I get that." Phillip still wasn't convinced.

"If and when you try it, take the time to look inside yourself and see what you're thinking. If you're driving yourself nuts, it will be easier to see it than during intercourse. For example, oral sex, more than intercourse, confronts you with the issue of letting yourself be held. Do you have a firm enough grip on yourself to allow yourself to receive?"

"Okay. I get that too." Phillip sounded increasingly less interested.

"By the way, oral sex is a better way to develop control of your orgasms during intercourse. Intercourse itself isn't strong enough to do it."

"You're kidding!" Phillip didn't understand how this could be true, but I'd finally piqued his interest.

"It's easier to develop better control with oral sex and transfer it to intercourse."

"But I'll be lasting longer during oral sex. How will that help me during intercourse?" Phillip was trying to think this through with me.

"You need to learn to regulate your anxiety during sex, period. It's easier to learn to do that when you're just receiving. The physical stimulation you'll receive will also be more intense than intercourse. Developing more tolerance for intense stimulation, and getting better control of your anxiety, will give you more control of your orgasms during intercourse."

Phillip's demeanor changed. "Okay, Doc. Now you've got my attention. Keep talking."

## • More than a mouthful about oral sex

I don't assume you're comfortable with oral sex. If you want to change this, you can. But do yourself a favor and go further than getting over your squeamishness or awkwardness See Appendix B for suggestions on how to resolve. You can get to the point that it calms you down and blows your mind in a unique and delightful way. I've helped clients use it to digest very difficult childhoods. You can do it in ways that promote brain change.

I work with my clients around oral sex because the benefits are remarkable—even if they don't have problems with oral sex, but especially if they do. Some have never had oral sex in their lives. Some couldn't climax that way. It's the only way that worked for others. Some had strong gag reflexes, and others had olfactory-triggered flashbacks, which is serious stuff. What makes these people hang in and work with oral sex? Let me put it this way: Given the many things we've been able to wring out of *hugging till relaxed,* imagine what you can get from a good blow job.

Sucking is our first interpersonal experience. Your innate sucking response is a core part of human bonding, at work from your first moments of life. Oral sex also shoots your partner's pheromones into your brain through your nose and mouth.[212] In terms of interpersonal neurobiology, oral sex packs an olfactory wallop. Oral sex taps directly in to your brain's somatosensory cortex. Smelling and tasting your partner's genital fluids promotes bonding and stimulates the attachment neurochemistry of your brain. The reptilian parts of your brain probably light up too.

Later-evolving parts of your brain probably like it too. Oral sex has powerful interpersonal impacts. One of the best examples of right-brain-to-right-brain attunement occurs when you partner's genitals are in your mouth, you can taste him and smell him, and he's really letting you fuck him. When you're thinking, *Wow. This is the best sex we've ever had! I love the taste and feel of him in my mouth. It means so much that we are doing this,* it's hard to tell whether that's your right brain or your left brain talking. I think it's a sign of bilateral hemispherical integration.

Oral sex is a great way to create meaning. You can use it to fuck or to have tender loving sex. Both giver and receiver can be dominant or submissive. You can use it to finally make peace with your partner. You can use it to finally be at peace, period.

Oral sex is handier (and more fun) than a Swiss Army knife, and you don't have to worry about leaving it somewhere. This multipurpose tool doesn't involve particular techniques like "deep throat."[213] It involves approaching oral sex as a mindful activity, a conjoint mental practice, and a point of joint focal attention.

Mindfulness makes oral sex *hot*. Erotic. Sexy. Smart. Mind-mapping makes oral sex the main event, rather than a prelude to intercourse.

You can use oral sex as a window into who you are and where you came from. You can use it as a pathway to the person you want to be. The power of oral sex comes alive when you embed it in a new and more accurate picture of your past: Once you retrieve a new piece of your autobiographical memory, you can use it during oral sex to encourage your brain to reorganize itself. It's also possible to repair holes in your autobiographical memory during oral sex. I'll give you an example shortly.

I realize this sounds incredible. It's hard to think along these lines. The only reason I propose this—even think up something this fantastic—stems from seeing this happen with my clients. I had some professional skepticism, but when my clients fairly reliably used oral sex to resolve their past, repair the present, and reorganize the future in their minds, thinking this way got easier. Pairing oral sex with an accurate autobiographical memory seems to encourage your brain to function differently.

## • *Setting the stage for surrender*

Creative applications of oral sex can resolve many desire problems. As we've seen, it's a great way to create sex worth wanting that has nothing to do with having orgasms. But don't sneeze at the fact that oral sex is one of the easiest ways for women to climax. (This includes women who think they can *only* reach orgasm during intercourse.) And oral sex is great for solving sexual dysfunctions too. But our focus isn't about increasing your frequency, intensity, and ease of orgasms. (If that happens, live with it.) Oral sex confronts you at your core.

Phillip asked, "Why put so much emphasis on receiving? My problem is being the giver."

"You can do both with Nicolle during oral sex."

"But I already feel selfish because I come quickly. I'd be more selfish if I focused on receiving. I should be focusing on actively pleasing Nicole."

"If you're interested in pleasing her, take your turn receiving oral sex. That's how you'll develop more ejaculatory control, which we know Nicolle would like you to do."

"That's right, I would," Nicolle chimed in.

"When you won't let Nicolle fuck you with oral sex, you deprive her the way she deprives you: You like going down on her, but she stops you. You don't like that. That's about more than your reflected sense of self. Going down on her gratifies the part of you that genuinely cares for her. When you won't receive, you deprive Nicolle of the same satisfaction."

Phillip chuckled. "So I'm selfish for not letting Nicolle give me a blow job?"

"You like going down on Nicolle, but only you can be the oral sex virtuoso. Nicolle is smart and competent, but she doesn't reveal herself and show what she's got, at least not in sex, and probably not in other ways."

Nicolle spoke up as I hoped she would. "You're right, Dr. Schnarch, sometimes I *would* like to be the one doing the giving. And I don't always want my orgasm first because Phillip's worried about his ejaculation. Sometimes I would like to have my orgasm second. And, actually, I think I can give head just as good as Phillip. I'd go down on him more if he wasn't so anxious when we do it. It's no fun to blow a guy who's nervous."

All three of us looked at each other with expressions of amazement. This was quite a demonstration of Nicolle showing herself. Phillip was so surprised, he didn't get defensive. He really didn't know what to make of this. Nicolle had even surprised herself.

Phillip laughed. "Well, I'm willing to learn. I can't believe we're sitting here talking about blow jobs and fucking. This sort of makes me nervous."

I replied, "Since you've managed to calm yourself down during *hugging till relaxed* and *heads on pillows*, you'll probably succeed during oral sex too."

Phillip nodded seriously. "Thanks for the vote of confidence, Doctor. I wouldn't want to flunk oral sex." His delivery was funny and loaded with multiple meanings.

I asked, "So would you like to talk about something else, or do you want me to help you set the stage?"

Nicolle laughed, "Don't stop now! That would be *oral sex interuptus*."

Phillip added, "Nicolle's right, Doc. Don't stop now."

"So let's see what we've got: Phillip rapidly reaches orgasm during intercourse, and thinks intercourse is the only solution to the problem. Nicolle wants to be fucked, and she's pissed off and hasn't wanted sex since early in their marriage." They both nodded in agreement

"They could have oral sex, which gets around the problem for now, solves the guy's rapid orgasms over time, and lets them experiment with *fucking*. But the guy's not that interested. He likes to go down on her, but she won't let him. She likes to go down on him, but he won't let her. The guy's frustrated she won't let him do what he's good at, while he's depriving her of the same. Both are angry the other stops sex when they're receiving. And both are lousy receivers!"

"See, Doctor, I told you we were screwed up." Nicolle was signaling she got the picture. Phillip did the same. His impassive face accentuated his deadpan delivery. "Let me get this straight, Doc: I'm selfish because I won't let Nicolle blow me. Most guys complain their wives never give them oral sex, and their wives counter that that's all they want. And, moreover, I'm selfish because I want Nicolle to have her orgasm first? All along, I've been thinking I was noble. Thanks for clearing things up!"

I laughed, "You're welcome." I love when clients function better.

## RECEIVING CAN BE A SPECIAL FORM OF GIVING

When Nicolle and Phillip returned for their following session we had a lot to talk about. They had been busy since our last meeting. One afternoon Nicolle and Phillip had sex. There was a heightened sense of connection and purpose as they went into the bedroom. They did *heads on pillows* and things felt good between them. Then Phillip went down on Nicolle. She thought back to our discussion about who received first, but she didn't make an issue of it. She wanted this to be a good experience for both of them.

Nicolle tried to focus her mind and not let it wander off. She still had intrusive worries that she wouldn't reach orgasm anyway. She brought herself back into the present by opening her eyes and looking at Phillip. This was the first time in all their years together that Nicolle had watched him give her oral sex. It was sexy, and she felt very adult. Nicolle thought, *Phillip looks like he's really enjoying himself.* Right then, Phillip smiled at her. The impact was amazing.

As Nicolle described it, a jolt of energy went from Phillip's mind through his eyes to Nicolle's eyes and into her brain. Another jolt went through his tongue to her clitoris and up her spine to her brain. Nicolle was fully engrossed in their moment of meeting. She raised her head so she could see Phillip better. After a few minutes, she relaxed her neck and let her head hang back. Her neck was stretched and her throat was open. Phillip licked her clitoris and she thought, *By God, this is what collaborative alliances are all about!*

Nicolle was highly aroused. She let Phillip fuck her, and she loved it. She was proud of herself. This was her first real experience with being fucked during oral sex. This time she didn't stop Phillip. She would have preferred having an orgasm this way, but she couldn't quite organize all these new stimuli to make that happen. In some ways this was bigger. She knew what orgasms felt like. Being fucked was more exotic.

Phillip knew Nicolle was making progress because he really enjoyed giving her oral sex this time. *This* was what he wanted to feel with Nicolle all along. In retrospect Phillip realized that he wanted to fuck Nicolle, and he wanted to feel her allowing herself to be fucked. He wanted to see the eroticism she hid in the secret parts of her mind. He had vaguely known about Nicolle's prior promiscuity, and he'd always wondered what she was like in bed back then.

When it was Phillip's turn to receive, Nicolle expected to give to him the blow job of his life. She made moves to go down on him, but he stopped her and positioned her for intercourse. Nicolle said she wanted to give him oral sex, but Phillip said he wanted intercourse. Nicolle hesitated for a moment because she was mapping Phillip's mind: He was avoiding taking a turn receiving.

Rather than press the issue and upset Phillip, Nicolle went along. It never left her mind that Phillip was dodging. When he finished in less than a minute they were both disappointed, although Phillip told Nicolle he was happy with his turn.

The next morning Nicolle confronted Phillip about his lack of self-confrontation three times last evening: He controlled their order of receiving so that he did her first; he initiated intercourse instead of receiving oral sex; and he didn't let himself be brought to orgasm. Phillip became defensive, saying no one told him he had to confront his issues right then. However, having confronted herself in the wee hours of the morning, Nicolle wasn't about to back down. She said the issue wasn't that he didn't do what he was told, but rather his intent and his lack of Meaningful Endurance. She had stepped up to her issues and taken them on, and in the process Phillip got what he wanted. But instead of pushing himself in kind, Phillip chose to dodge his issues. Nicolle was disappointed.

Phillip countered that Nicolle had had a terrific orgasm. Nicolle stayed with her question: How come he hadn't confronted any of his anxieties? Was this going to be a real collaborative alliance, where they didn't dodge difficult issues? Phillip said he didn't have any answers.

• *The blow job blues*

Nicolle and Phillip didn't talk about this for the rest of the week. They unloaded their stories as soon as they walked in to my office. Nicolle said she felt pretty good about herself, but she feared what would happen in our session.

Phillip said he felt okay when he woke up that morning after sex. However, he got upset during their subsequent breakfast conversation and stayed that way for days. He felt ambushed because, as far as he was concerned, they'd had a wonderful time the night before. He described their encounter in glowing terms.

"When Nicolle let me do her, it was amazing. She was amazing. We were amazing. I amazed myself. I felt like a great lover. I thought we were really making progress!" Phillip's language was enthusiastic, but his face and mind were masked. I recognized what he was doing and noted his skill: Phillip was praising Nicolle to keep the focus off himself.

"I admire your ability to use true statements to manipulate the truth. You've got that down to an art form. To use the truth to implant false understanding, you have to be *incredibly* good at mapping other people's minds—and keep your own mind from being mapped."

"What do you mean?" Phillip's face was blank and his tone was suspicious.

"You're praising Nicolle for receiving and crowing about what you were able to do. In the process you completely avoid Nicolle's perception that you dodged receiving. She's asking you to confront the facts now and tell her what you make of it."

"I asked Nicolle to have sex with me in ways I thought I would like."

"Okay. Let's say that's true. You're still unable or unwilling to address the pieces Nicolle is pointing out."

"*I can't do that because I don't see it that way.*" Anything that remained of Phillip's collaborative alliance with Nicolle, or with me, was now gone. Phillip could see the mess in front of him, and he was trying to avoid it. I noted his method: Claiming he didn't see it at all.

Phillip was about to erupt, and signaling Nicolle and me that we had better back off. I had to find another way to engage him. I visualized them having sex that night. I paused to let Phillip's reactivity subside, and then I spoke slowly and softened my voice.

"You must have been *very* disappointed."

"What? What do you mean?" Phillip was on guard.

"When you came quickly. You must have been very disappointed."

"How do you know that?" Phillip wasn't denying or confirming anything. He was asking for my data.

I paused to take a breath. "I'm trying to help, but that doesn't include fencing with you. Here's my ante for our collaborative alliance: The issue is not how I know this; the question is, 'Is it true?'"

Phillip hesitated, deciding what to do. Then he let out a long, slow, "… Yesss!" I had laid our collaborative alliance on the line and he stepped up to accept it.

"Coming quickly after dodging receiving first, and dodging oral sex, must have really hurt."

"...Yes." Phillip was settling down. Our collaborative alliance was reestablished.

"Why did you dodge?"

"... I don't know."

"Come on. You dodged that night, and whatever motivated you was happening then and there. You understood the significance of what was happening. Why'd you back away?"

"I don't know." Phillip was emphatic but not defiant. There was room for me to help him try to access the information a different way.

"In your mind's eye, can you see Nicolle wanting to give you oral sex that night?"

"... Yeah. I can see it."

"Good. Can you see the two of you?"

"Yeah."

"Good. Can you see yourself in that moment?"

"Yeah."

"Good. Tell me what that guy is feeling and thinking."

Phillip was silent for a moment. "He's thinking ... this is going to sound weird ... he's thinking his wife is closing in on him ... like he doesn't have a choice ... like he has to do it, because she wants to do it. He's cornered, and he has to let her do what she wants ... because she can blackmail him with their therapy."

"Well, what do you make of that feeling? Do you think that is what Nicolle was intending?"

"... No."

"So what do you make of the fact this comes up when Nicolle offers you a blow job?"

"... That I'm a lunatic?" Phillip wasn't kidding. He was being collaborative and following the data. "I don't know, Doc. I've never seen this so clearly before. I don't know what to make of it. What do you make of it?"

"I'd guess you come from a place where people don't keep alliances ... A place where you felt manipulated and controlled—blackmailed, to use your term—... someplace where people aren't trustworthy ... where emotional extortion is common and it wouldn't be smart to relax. A place you wouldn't let someone hold you, even if you were dying for it."

Phillip buried his face in his hands. After several minutes of silence, he put his hands down and sighed. Phillip described growing up with his parents and his grandmother, who lived with them. His parents fought constantly. Oftentimes Grandma (his father's mother) joined in the ruckus. He remembered being in his room, trying to ignore their screaming arguments that traveled from one end of the house to the other. His mother was typically depressed or angry, and complained bitterly to Phillip about his grandmother. His mother used her depression to blackmail Phillip into listening to her bitch.

Phillip's gaze turned inward. "… I see how I manipulate and control Nicolle … I blackmail her into giving me what I want … or I fend her off from confronting me, by escalating things further than she will go. My father did that all the time!"

Phillip stared at the floor a long time, watching his past parade through his mind. When he looked up, the change in his face was remarkable.

"You should see your face at this moment," I said. "I don't know if it will still be there, but next time you go to the bathroom you ought to look in the mirror."

"Why?"

"Your face is softer. There's more softness to your facial muscles. You face is more readable and less impassive."

Nicolle nodded warmly, with tears in her eyes. "I see it too."

Phillip had developed a masked face as a child so his father couldn't read him. When his father mapped out what Phillip thought about him, it would set his father off. By the time Phillip was an adolescent (and his brain had gone through two wiring and rewiring epochs of childhood and adolescence), his face was like a mask.

### • *Don't confuse weakness with power*

People confuse weakness with power. Phillip made this mistake when it came to his father. Phillip's father was an alcoholic oil rig worker with a violent temper. When he wasn't off-shore, he was usually drunk and frequently vicious. Phillip spent his childhood staying out of his way. He described his father as a powerful man with a bad temper who overpowered anyone who challenged him.

More accurately, Phillip's father was a *weak* man. What Phillip had to fear was his father's *weakness*. Weak people are destructive; powerful people are constructive. Powerful people create, facilitate, and make things happen. Truly powerful people do this for the betterment of others. Weak people, like Phillip's father, spend their time depriving and controlling others. There are good reasons to fear weak people.

The difference between powerful and weak domineering people is important. The children of weak destructive parents often confuse the two. Like many men (and women) whose fathers lost their grip on themselves in fits of rage, Phillip paid the price: He backed away from his own sexual aggression, like lots of men searching for the part of themselves that can fuck. When your father is often raging, it's hard to keep straight the difference between being masculine and being intimidating. Learning to access, validate, and use that part—especially with their spouse—is a milestone in their lives.

I've worked with lots of couples where the man became the low desire partner when his wife made it clear she wanted to be fucked. It's fun to have that kind of sex when you're newly wed, but when you realize you're dealing with someone more erotically inclined than you, lots of men get intimidated and their reflected sense of self feels dominated.

## HOW TO USE YOUR MIND AND BODY WHEN GIVING OR RECEIVING HEAD

I looked at Phillip and Nicolle and nodded as I exhaled. They took a breath and relaxed too. I turned to Nicolle and in a slow, soft voice asked, "So, is Phillip the only one who needs to take off his mask?"

Nicolle immediately picked up my lead. "No indeed. I am fed up spending my life afraid of 'standing too tall.' We have a saying where I come from, 'The tall poppy always gets chopped down.' My father could be mean when he drank, but it was my mother who really came after us kids. Anything you did well or felt proud of, Mother would try to chop down. I stopped letting her know what was important to me. I stopped letting her read my mind. Then she started playing 'cat and mouse' with me. She tried to catch me lying or having sex with boys. I started doing both to say, *'Fuck you!'* I was smart, but I refused to get good grades in school, because I knew that's what she wanted."

I decided to focus on Nicolle's ability rather than her defiance. "So there's more to you, sexually and otherwise, then has surfaced to date?"

Nicolle closed her eyes as if taking mental inventory. Then she nodded affirmatively. "Yup."

"Then you and Phillip have everything to gain by taking yourselves on when you have sex. You'll be able to make your lives better now and resolve your past issues in the present."

Nicolle was never at peace when she went down on Phillip. Usually she didn't want to do it, and when she did, Phillip was such a bundle of nerves she couldn't enjoy it. She worried about setting him off, about him losing his erection or coming too quickly, or her doing it too well. Yes, doing it too well. Nicole never got to relax with Phillip and enjoy her own prowess or the physical sensations of sucking a man's penis. She'd given enough blow jobs to know guys liked receiving them, but some looked down on a woman who really enjoyed giving them. It had been many years since she felt the power and agency of sending a man off into nirvana.

"Sounds like you don't have experience standing tall in front of people you love. You could create a corrective experience for yourself by doing it with Phillip. You'd have to deliberately give him great oral sex and relax while you do it, quieting and centering yourself. If that isn't motivation enough, you might consider doing it for Phillip."

"How so?"

"Letting your competence shine will help Phillip confront himself. If it's obvious you like giving him head, he'll only have himself left to confront. Your ability to give good head positions him to confront his difficulty with being the receiver. You're enjoying what you're doing: fucking him. When he doesn't relax and let himself be fucked, it won't be attributable to you."

Nicolle giggled. "If I blow his brains out, can I clean out the cobwebs in his head?"

"Certainly figuratively, and perhaps literally. The more you *feel* him while you do him, the more you confront Phillip to receive what you're offering. The emotional and physical intensity will push his issues in spades." Phillip nodded.

"While you have him in your mouth, think about the issues he's facing right that moment. Before you start, let him know you'll be thinking this. This way Phillip will be better able to map your mind while you're sucking him. Let him read your mind. Use your head while you're giving Phillip head—if you want to leave his mind spinning."

Nicolle laughed and looked at Phillip. Her smile was carnal. "Sounds good!"

Phillip laughed nervously. "Am I obligated to receive oral sex to preserve my alliance with my wife?" His question sounded absurd, but it made perfect sense.

"You sure sound like someone whose automatic response is defiance when you feel your partner *wants* you. If you keep this possibility in mind while Nicolle sucks your brains out, you just might get your brain to think differently."

Phillip paused for a moment. "I see that now."

"When you last had sex you dropped your alliance with Nicolle. Nicolle was offering you more than a blow job. She reached out to you. She felt your alliance deteriorating as you withdrew into yourself. You could have declined oral sex and still maintained your alliance. You just needed to tell Nicolle you knew you weren't confronting your issues. Then she could have agreed to intercourse as a friend, rather than as someone colluding with you.

"I get it!" Phillip's eyes were solid in a way I hadn't seen before. His face was soft. His functioning increased as if he had gone from groggy to fully awake.

"Ever had a collaborative alliance with a woman through your penis?"

The picture dazed Phillip. "No. "

"Never had a collaborative alliance when your penis was in her mouth?"

"… Never."

• *Moment of meeting: Trackers meet*

Nicolle turned to Phillip. "I can handle you getting nervous during sex. I know what that's like. But I can't accept you breaking contact with me and expecting me to go on as if you're still present. I'm not going to do that anymore when I'm receiving, and I'm not doing it when I'm giving to you. The other night, I continued having sex when I knew you were gone, and I'm not doing that anymore. I want you to stop doing it too."

Phillip's reply was slow and thoughtful. "I think I finally get what happens for you when I run away from my issues. When I get nervous, I drop our alliance and withdraw. I tell myself I'm worried about disappointing you, while I'm already disappointing you by what I'm doing. But I'm blown away picturing myself doing that while you're sucking me. My penis is in your mouth, my mind is somewhere else, you know it, but you're carrying on as if I'm there, because you know that's what I want you to do. What an awful image. It's pathetic."

I said, "You're dead on. It's a pleasure watching your mind work."

Phillip's functioning was improving. I was tracking him. My comment made him realize I was mapping his mind. Phillip looked at me and we shared a moment of meeting. He looked at me full-on, and he was solid, without a trace of belligerence.

Tears ran down Nicolle's cheeks. She was tracking our interaction. Phillip was allowing much deeper intimacy in our session. This was a moment of shared attention for all three of us. The room was quiet and alive with possibilities. Nicolle told Phillip, "I really like you when you're like this." Then she turned to me. "Why don't we let our guards down and do this with each other?"

"You are both trackers. You *see* people. You map their minds. The trouble is you're hypervigilant about other people and blind to yourself. Your hypervigilance and blindness go hand in hand with the holes in your childhood memories and your difficulty regulating your emotions." Nicolle and Phillip looked at each other.

"Maybe you can stop using your radar to defend yourselves and use it to see and be with each other."

Phillip didn't hesitate. "Seeing the picture of us having sex that I just saw, really being with Nicolle doesn't sound so scary. *Not* being with her sounds *really* scary. You think if we really do this right, for the first time in my life I won't come so quick?"

Nicolle reached out for Phillip's hand. "Maybe we can find out when we leave here." There was a twinkle in her eye and sexual innuendo in her voice.

## IGNITE DESIRE IN YOUR BEDROOM

Phillip and Nicole went through gridlock, held on to themselves, and developed their Four Points of Balance. They came out with a clearer sense of who they were and who they wanted to be. They had confidence they could become those people. Their relationship was more important to them, they were more important to each other, and, last but not least, they were more important to themselves.

Innumerable couples grow through dealing with sexual desire problems. My professional and personal experience makes me believe a people-growing system exists within emotionally committed relationships. Sexual desire, intimacy, and differentiation are the primary (but not the only) drive wheels. Emotional gridlock is how they surface. Resolving gridlock is how you grow.

I believe this is how the human race evolved. How we became more human in the best sense, how "human nature" was shaped. It stretched our brains. I have no hard proof, but this view fits extensive information from many sciences. Whether or not it's true doesn't lessen the utility of applying what you've learned here.

The brain-changing impact of sex deserves healthy skepticism. I've worked marriage's differentiation system with couples for thirty years. I've only pursued brain-changing therapy for a decade. During that time, I saw people who were unable to make progress when they had focused on feelings, insights, and communication make changes when they tried these solutions. When therapy involved their bodies, more accurate autobiographical memory, new meanings for sex, and physical contact with their partner, many (but not all) made progress like Nicolle and Phillip.

Nicolle became stronger and less willing to automatically defer to everyone. She stopped playing down her abilities. She became alive and vivacious. Partly this came from feeling desirable within herself, and partly from deciding she really liked her carnal side. Through oral sex she and Phillip created the seven brain-change-facilitating conditions we've encountered in the last three chapters. This probably helped her, too.

Phillip went on to cure his rapid orgasms. Intense physical and emotional stimulation during oral sex had its predictable impact once he was able to let himself receive it. Phillip maintained his alliance and confronted his issues by straight-out asking Nicolle to give him head and fuck him. His Four Points of Balance and his penis got a workout. This did more than raise his ejaculatory threshold (which increased his control during intercourse too). His reflexive anger, reactivity, and belligerence declined. His control of his temper was so much better that Nicolle started calling him "Sweetie."

"Sweetie" was more than terribly touching. It was a measure of therapy outcome. All their struggles to hold on to themselves were summed up in that word. To go from emotional crashes and rage to "Sweetie" suggests these people had developed more than insight. Things like this make me think my clients are rewiring their brains. Perhaps my respect and admiration for them reduces my ability to be totally objective. But "Sweetie" sounds a lot like what Daniel Siegel, who coined the term "interpersonal neurobiology," specified as the criterion for effective treatment:

> One can deduce that the general approach to psychotherapy for individuals with unresolved trauma is to attempt to enhance the mind's innate tendency to move towards integration, both within the brain and within interpersonal relationships.
>
> The measure of efficacy for such an approach is an enhancement in self-regulation and emotional processing. In addition to the dissolution of the many and varied symptoms of PTSD, one could also predict numerous other fundamental changes in the individual's functioning. From a systems perspective, therapeutic improvement would be re-

vealed as a more adaptive and flexible mind capable of responding to changes in the internal and external environment. Mood stability would replace emotional liability. An increased capacity to experience a wider range and intensity of emotions would emerge, as would a greater tolerance for change. Resolution would also be indicated by the individual's movement toward more differentiated abilities while simultaneously participating in more joining experiences. This increased individual differentiation and interpersonal integration would reflect the mind's movement toward increasingly complex states. Overall, these changes would reflect not only the freedom from post-traumatic symptomatology but also the enhanced capacity of the individual to achieve integration (internal and interpersonal) and thus more adaptive and flexible self-regulation.

This enhanced integration would result in more coherent autobiographical narratives of specific traumatic events and the life of the individual as a whole.[214]

## • *Your future awaits*

When you started reading *Intimacy & Desire* you probably never thought you'd end up learning about your brain. Then again, when you're drowning in sexual desire problems, you never envision finding the divine in the middle of giving or getting oral sex. You never think of desire problems and oral sex as co-construction and co-evolution, either. But, like everything we've seen so far, there's a lot more going on than is apparent—until you learn about differentiation.

You've seen the incredible people-growing processes that come from simply falling in love, becoming a couple, and staying together. As a scientist, I see in this the self-organizing processes found in all ecological systems. Sexual desire is human evolution in action: We are both scientists and the experiment.

Working with couples has shown me how dark our dark side can truly be, especially when the worst in us hijacks our ability to map other people's minds. And yet, the more I see how desire, sex, intimacy, and love work together to produce the absolute worst and best of times, the more I think I'm seeing spirit in action. It has inspired my own personal spirituality. This is the Great Oneness embodied in daily life. This view of God is acceptable to the left side of my brain.

When I started doing therapy I never imagined I'd end up talking about Creation. I never thought of two-choice dilemmas, emotional gridlock, and fucking as blessed sacraments capable of embodying our highest abilities and aspirations. But then again, I never imagined that developing and preserving your self lies at the heart of sexual desire. Are sexuality, spirituality, and self-discovery a holy trinity that drives human evolution? As I've come to appreciate the Four Points of Balance, I am inclined think so.

If, as I propose, we're dealing with the Great Oneness, is it possible to condense everything down to one single point? Something simple and profound that captures the essence of differentiation? Something to keep you hopeful when you have the urge to quit? Something to reassure you that your struggles are worthwhile? Something to help you, humor you, pique your narcissism, and welcome you to the club?

I've pondered long and hard, and here's the best that I can do:

> You can work on your relationship all you want,
> but your relationship will be working on YOU!

---

## POINTS TO PONDER

- You can be the low desire partner and sex-starved too.
- Your spouse is the hardest person in the world to fuck (and sometimes the easiest to screw over). Fucking your partner requires being aggressive, passionate, playful, adventurous, and generous. You may be stroking her body, but you're aiming for her mind.
- Getting your body and mind quietly aligned with your partner may help you change your brain.

# APPENDIX A
## ADDITIONAL RESOURCES

ONE OF THE basic premises of this book is that normal healthy people in good relationships have sexual desire problems. Another is that emotionally committed relationships are people-growing machines. Everything in this book is designed to help you use your relationship to enhance your Four Points of Balance and resolve sexual desire problems.

However, you may want or need the help of a therapist to help you effectively harness the people-growing processes. The weaker your Four Points of Balance are, the more likely this will be the case. A good therapist can monitor important topics to keep you on track, help you observe your process, and assist in modulating and containing anxiety in your marriage to increase your differentiation. The less differentiated your relationship, the more differentiated the therapist needs to be. A therapist can't bring you to a higher level of differentiation than he or she has achieved, because when anxiety and pressure in your marriage exceeds his or her differentiation, he or she gets "infected" and treatment effectiveness declines. Nothing in therapists' training or licensing requirements ensures they are more differentiated, or know more about sex and intimacy, or have better marriages, than you. You may have to try several before you find one who can really help. Ask your friends for therapists they'd recommend, but ultimately, you'll have to assess their differentiation for yourself.

Find someone you respect, but don't pick someone you are totally comfortable with—that's usually someone who you're sure won't confront you. Find someone with whom you feel *productively* uncomfortable. A "good match" is not the same as your therapist "understanding" and "accepting" you the way you want to be seen; it's one in which you self-confront, self-soothe, and mobilize yourself to do what you need to do. On the other hand, therapists can be wrong—working with a therapist is not the same as turning yourself over to him or her. You'll need to hold on to your self, even with your therapist.

He or she should have postgraduate training in conducting psychotherapy and be licensed to practice psychotherapy or counseling in your state. Not all therapists are trained in couples therapy, so find one who is. If you're dealing with additional sexual dysfunctions (like problems with lubrication, erections, and orgasms), it's best to find a therapist who has specific training in sexual problems, preferably a *certified* sex therapist (who has met basic standards of preparation).

The approach outlined in this book is based on differentiation. Couple therapists are generally more familiar with attachment-based therapy (focused first and foremost on "safety and security") and teaching listening and communications skills. As the Crucible Approach has popularized differentiation-based therapy, some clinicians have tried to blend the two. This is usually not a good idea in theory or practice. It is my belief that a "first you have to get more attached before you can differentiate" strategy is neither accurate nor effective. In practice, interventions in differentiation-based therapy often go in the opposite direction from attachment-based treatment. Differentiation-based therapy generally operates at a higher level of intensity. And when things get difficult, anxious, or contentious, fears and insecurities run the show in attachment-based therapy, whereas differentiation-based therapy orients around people's strengths. Crucible® Therapy focuses on the Four Points of Balance™.

For almost twenty years, the Marriage & Family Health Center (MFHC) has offered the Crucible® Intensive Therapy Program, consisting of four or more consecutive days of closely spaced sessions in half-day blocks. This special sequence of sessions allows people outside

Colorado to benefit from Crucible Therapy, especially those who cannot make progress in the traditional one-hour-a-week treatment format. Rapidly accelerated therapy allows some couples to work through issues they would otherwise bog down in. Topics and focus of an Intensive are determined by each couple's unique needs. Couples fly in from across the United States and around the world.

MFHC also conducts programs for the general public. Passionate Marriage® Couples Enrichment Weekends (CEW) are weekend workshops held in major metropolitan cities, which address common but difficult problems in committed relationships. Passionate Marriage® Couples Retreats are nine-day programs held in retreat settings conducive to helping gridlocked couples get "unstuck." This longer duration provides opportunities for couples to work through their issues during the program. For further information about the Crucible Intensive Therapy Program, Passionate Marriage Couples Enrichment Weekends, and Couples Retreats, visit www.crucibletherapy.com

Additional audio, video, and printed materials are also available online. Visit www.cruciblepublishing.com

For speaking engagements for your organization related to this book, go to www.DesireBook.com

An online social community is now available to support your efforts. The Four Points of Balance Community is the first social community for couples and singles devoted to differentiation as a way of life. You can talk with other people who have faced similar problems with desire, intimacy, sex, affairs, parenting, or divorce. You can share your own experiences. New materials are released there periodically. Community members have several things in common: They want to be solid individuals, have fruitful relationships, live emotionally healthy lifestyles, and meet others who embrace this book's message. Singles can meet other like-minded singles.

Visit www.4pointsofbalance.com

Or contact:

Marriage & Family Health Center
2922 Evergreen Parkway, Suite 310
Evergreen, CO 80439
phone (303) 670-2630   fax (303) 674-9304
email: mfhc@crucibletherapy.com
web site: www.crucibletherapy.com

# APPENDIX B
## OVERCOMING DISCOMFORT WITH ORAL SEX

THE GOAL HERE is not to detail good technique, but rather to help you get over common sticking points if you're not comfortable giving or receiving oral sex. Most people can get past any and all of these issues if they are motivated to do so.

Chapter 14 is written for monogamous couples. If you're not in a monogamous relationship, or just starting into one, get yourselves tested for HIV and other sexually transmitted diseases (STDs). It will help you relax during sex and build "eyes open" (rather than blind) trust. STDs are readily transmitted through the exchange of bodily fluids inherent in oral sex. If need be—or if you just don't know—use condoms for fellatio and dental dams for cunnilingus. Granted, oral sex doesn't feel as good with a latex barrier. But putting yourself or your partner at risk eliminates the possibility of having the kind of oral sex experience described here. Soap and water and general cleanliness help as well.

It's hard to relax if you're fending off tasting or being tasted in ways you don't feel comfortable. This holds true whether you're giving or receiving oral sex. You need to become more than comfortable and at ease with it. If you're uncomfortable with oral sex, you need to do more than get over your hesitancies or squeamishness. You need to develop a sense of peace.

First you need to deal with any issues about smelling, tasting, or swallowing your partner's sexual fluids or your own. Besides the fact that you're not going to be an enthusiastic giver or receiver, you'll drop your alliance with your partner while you're having oral sex. You'll be pulling back from the experience, preoccupied with your own discomfort, and trying not to gag or be nauseous. You won't put much enthusiasm into pleasuring (or being pleasured by) your partner. But the real issue here isn't lousy technique. It's that you won't be able to produce a profoundly positive somatosensory moment of meeting with heightened, positive neuroplasticity.

Additionally you won't like anything you taste if you feel you're being forced, and you won't like being tasted if your partner feels forced. It's hard to relax and enjoy receiving oral sex when your partner is obviously ill at ease. Don't force your partner. Let him or her control going down on you. The giver's head must be free to move. Don't try to stick the penis down the giver's throat. Make sure both people are in a comfortable position. Take a breather and relax. Talk to each other. If your partner knows you're not avoiding or stopping, then both of you can relax. If you make it seem like a job, your partner will be turned off. If your jaw or tongue gets tired, shift to manual stimulation.

Do yourselves a favor: taste your partner's and your own flavor—when you're not having oral sex. When you're having it, there's no time to deal with any negative reactions or focus on really getting comfortable with it. So although it may seem a little odd at first, here's a logical solution that works.

Before you have sex, deliberately taste each other. A healthy vagina has a natural mild musky smell, but people can have a negative reaction to it, just like with ejaculate. Each of you should stick your finger in the vagina and take a taste. Do the same with ejaculate after the man reaches orgasm (e.g., from manual stimulation or intercourse).

It's hard to get comfortable with semen when it's coming at you fast. It's slightly salty or bitter with the texture of egg-whites, and sometimes has a slight chlorine bleach scent. Some people like the taste of it, many are neutral, and some don't like having it in their mouths. Dealing with ejaculate is an issue for many couples, and is best dealt with directly. Both partners' reflected sense of self issues can complicate matters. Some men feel rejected when their partner won't swallow their semen, and some partners feel demeaned if the man ejaculates in their mouth.

Talk openly in advance with your partner about how you plan do deal with his ejaculate so there are no surprises (unless it's a good one). Address this before you start. If he thinks he's going to be ejaculating in your mouth and you stop, it's hard to keep a collaborative alliance. Ask your partner to tell you when he's about to ejaculate so you can implement the plan. This way both of you can relax and stay together as he gets close to orgasm.

Here's how to do fellatio (oral sex on a man) without triggering your gag reflex by having the penis too far down your throat. You don't have to worry about gagging using this method, and your partner will still have the feeling of being fully contained. Place your hand around the base of the penis so the head sticks up like a lollipop. You can focus on sucking, and using your tongue; experiment with what the two of you like. Then, keeping your hand against your mouth, move your head up until the penis head stops in your hand. That is the height of your up-stroke. Your hand lets you control how much you take into your mouth on the down-stroke.

A man may want to ejaculate in his partner's mouth because stopping and pulling out interrupts the emotional connection, not to mention his orgasm. If you don't want the ejaculate actually in your mouth, one option is to use an unlubricated condom. Another is, by prior agreement, finishing him off with manual stimulation. If you're comfortable having him ejaculate in your mouth but you don't want to swallow, have a towel handy on the bed. Let it run out of your mouth and down his penis as you finish. If you like, have a glass of water nearby. A guy who needs his partner to swallow for him in order to "feel accepted" needs to deal with his reflected sense of self. And if your partner won't kiss you after he ejaculates in your mouth, you have something to talk about.

If you're new to giving a woman oral sex, brush back her pubic hair to either side of her labia so you don't end up with a hair down your throat. Many women are insecure about the taste and smell of their vagina, so don't act like you're putting your tongue someplace dangerous. If she's bathed recently, you don't have to worry about smelling or tasting something rank. Start slowly and gently. Don't just grind away on her clitoris at first. Women do like clitoral stimulation, especially as they become more highly aroused, but some find it too intense or irritating at first. Start with her outer labia, licking or taking one side or the other into your mouth. Then spread her labia with your fingers and stimulate her inner lips, gradually working your way up to her clitoris. You can thrust your tongue in and our of her vagina, but do *not* blow into it like you're trying to expand a balloon. As she becomes more aroused she will probably want increased speed and/or pressure from your tongue, but don't "get ahead" of her and try to make her have an orgasm by speeding up or pressing harder.

If you're new to oral sex, practice makes a big difference. You'll need lots of repetition beyond what it takes to get comfortable with the mechanics. It takes lots of collaboration to be at peace with your partner in the midst of a somatosensory moment of meeting endowed with high arousal and great meaning. Repetitive progressive engagement works much better than occasional high pressure "do or die" efforts.

# REFERENCES

Abu-Akel, A. (2003). A neurobiological mapping of theory of mind. *Brain Research Reviews*, 43(1), 29–40.

Adolphs, R. Damasio, H., Tranel, D. Cooper, G., & Damasio, A. R. (2000). A role for somatosensory cortices in the visual recognition of emotion as revealed by three-dimensional lesion mapping. *Journal of Neuroscience*, 20(7), 2683–2690).

Alexander, R. D. (1974). The evolution of social behavior. *Annual Review of Ecology and Systematics*, 5, 325–383.

Allison, T., Puce, A., & McCarthy, G. (2000). Social perception from visual cues: Role of the STS region. *Trends in Cognitive Sciences*, 4(7), 267-278.

American Psychiatric Association (1987). *Diagnostic and statistical manual of mental disorders.* (3rd edition-revised.) Washington, DC: American Psychiatric Association.

Amsterdam, B. (1972). Mirror self-image reactions before age two. *Developmental Psychobiology*, 5, 297–305.

Arnow, B. A., Desmond, J. E., Banner, L. L., Glover, G. H., Solomon, A., Polan, M. L., et al. (2002). Brain activation and sexual arousal in healthy heterosexual males. *Brain*, 125(5), 1014–1023.

Arsenijevic, Y., & Tribollet, E. (1998). Region-specific effect of testosterone on oxytocin receptor binding in the brain of the aged rat. *Brain Research*, 78, 167–170.

Aspinwall, L. G., & Staudinger, U. M. (Eds.) (2003). *A psychology of human strengths: Fundamental questions and future directions for a positive psychology.* Washington, D. C.: American Psychological Association.

Bach, L. J., Happe, F., Felminger, S., & Powell, J. (2000). Theory of mind: Independence of executive function and the role of frontal cortex in acquired brain injury. *Cognitive Neuropsychiatry,* 5, 175–192.

Baldwin, D. A., & Moses, L. J. (1994). In C. Lewis and P. Mitchell (Eds), *Children's Early Understanding of Mind*, (pp. 133–156). New York: Psychology Press.

Baron-Cohen, S. (1991). Precursors to a theory of mind: Understanding attention in others. In A. Whiten, (Ed.), *Natural Theories of Mind* (pp. 233–251). Oxford: Blackwell.

Baron-Cohen, S., & Ring, H.A. (1994). A model of the mindreading: neuropsychological and neurobiological perspectives. In P. Mitchell and C. Lewis (Eds.), *Children's Early Understanding of Mind* (pp. 183–207). Hillsdale, N.J.: Erlbaum.

Baron-Cohen, S., O'Riordan, M., Stone, V., Jones, R., & Plaisted, K. (1999). Recognition of faux pas by normally developing children with asperger syndrome or high-functioning autism. *Journal of Autism and Developmental Disorders,* 29, 407–418.

Bartels, A., & Zeki, S. (2000). The neural basis of romantic love. *NeuroReport,* 11(17), 3829-3834.

Bartels, A., & Zeki, S. (2004). The neural correlates of maternal and romantic love. *NeuroImage,* 21(3), 1155-1166.

Bartsch, K., & Wellman, H. (1995). *Children Talk about the Mind.* New York: Oxford University Press.

Batki, A., Baron-Cohen, S., Wheelwright, S., Connellan, J., & Ahluwalia, J. (2000). Is there an innate gaze module? Evidence from human neonates. *Infant Behavior and Development,* 23(2), 223-229.

Begley, S. (2007a). *Train Your Mind, Change Your Brain: How a New Science Reveals our Extraordinary Potential to Transform Ourselves.* New York: Ballantine Books.

Begley, S. (2007b, March 19). Beyond Stones and Bones. *Newsweek,* http://www.newsweek.com/id/36309.

Bekoff, M. & Pierce, J. (2009). *Wild Justice: The Moral Lives of Animals.* Chicago: University of Chicago Press.

Benes, F. M. (1998). Human brain growth spans decades. *American Journal of Psychiatry,* 155, 1489.

Berg, A. M. (2000). Qualitative evaluation of the Passionate Marriage® couple enrichment weekend. Doctoral dissertation, University of Minnesota, Department of Family Social Science.

Berg, S. J., & Wynne-Edwards, K. E. (2001). Changes in testosterone, cortisol, and estradiol levels in men becoming fathers. *Mayo Clinic Proceedings,* 76(6), 582–92.

Berretta, S. (2005). Cortico-amygdala circuits: Role in the conditioned stress response.

Bierce, A. (1911). *The Devil's Dictionary.* New York: Doubleday, Page and Company.

Blakemore, S., Frith, C., & Wolpert, D. (1999). Spatio-temporal prediction modulates the perception of self-produced stimuli. *Journal of Cognitive Neuroscience,* 11:5, 551–559.

Booth, A., & Dabbs, J. M. (1993). Testosterone and men's marriages. *Social Forces,* 72(2), 463–477.

Bower, B. (1996, May 18). Exploring trauma's cerebral side. *Science News,* 149(20), 315.

Brothers, L. (1990). The social brain: A project for integrating primate behavior and neurophysiology in a new domain. *Concepts in Neuroscience,* 1, 27–51.

Brothers, L. (1997). *Friday's Footprint: How Society Shapes the Human Mind.* New York: Oxford University Press.

Buber, M. (1958). *I and Thou.* (R. G. Smith. Trans.) New York: Charles Scribner's Sons. (Original work published in German, 1923.)

Butterworth, G. & Jarrett, N. (1991). What minds have in common is space: Spatial mechanisms serving joint visual attention in infancy. *British Journal of Developmental Psychology,* 9, 55–72.

Butterworth, G. (1991). The ontogeny and phylogeny of joint visual attention. In A. Whiten, (Ed.), *Natural Theories of Mind* (pp. 223–232). Oxford: Blackwell.

Byrne, R. W., & Whiten, A. (1991). Computation and mindreading in primate tactical deception. In Whiten, A. (Ed.), *Natural Theories of Mind.* Oxford: Blackwell.

Byrne, R. W., & Whitten, A. (Eds.) (1988). *Machiavellian Intelligence: Social Expertise and the Evolution of Intellect in Monkeys, Apes, and Humans.* Oxford: Clarendon Press.

Cahill, L. (2000). Neurobiological mechanisms of emotionally influenced, long-term memory. *Progressive Brain Research,* 126, 29–37.

Calter, A.J., Lawrence, A.D., Kean, J., Scott, S.K., Owen, A.M., Christoffels, I., et al. (2002). Reading the mind from eye gaze. *Neuropsychologica,* 40, 1129-1138.

Carrion, V. G., Weems, C. F., & Reiss, A. L. (2007). Stress predicts brain changes in children: A pilot longitudinal study on youth stress, posttraumatic stress disorder and the hippocampus. *Pediatrics,* 119(3), 509–516.

Carruthers, P. (1996). Simulation and self-knowledge: A defense of the theory-theory. In P. Carruthers & P.K. Smith (Eds.), *Theories of Theories of Mind.* Cambridge: Cambridge University Press.

Caspi, A., McClay, J., Moffitt, T. E., Mill, J., Martin, J., Craig, I. W., et al. (2002). Role of genotype in the cycle of violence in maltreated children. *Science,* 297, 851–853.

Caspi, A., Sugden, K., Moffitt, T.E., Taylor, A., Craig, I.W., Harrington, H., et al. (2003). Influence of life stress on depression: Moderation by a polymorphism in the 5-HTT gene. *Science*, 301, 386-389.

Castelli, F., Happe, F., Frith, U., & Frith, C.D. (2000). Movement and mind: A functional imaging study of perception and interpretation of complex intentional movement patterns. *Neuroimage* 12, 314–325.

Coleman, C. C., Cunningham, L. A., Foster, V. J., Batey, S. R., Donahue, R. M., Houser, T. L., et al. (1999). Sexual dysfunction associated with the treatment of depression: A placebo-controlled comparison of bupropion sustained release with sertraline treatment. *Annals of Clinical Psychiatry*, 11(4), 205–215.

Cook, S. C., & Wellman, C. L. (2004). Chronic stress alters dendritic morphology in rat medial prefrontal cortex. *Journal of Neurobiology*, 60(2), 236–248.

Coontz, S. (2006). *Marriage, a History: How Love Conquered Marriage.* New York: Penguin.

Cosmides, L. M., & Tooby, J. (1991). Cognitive adaptations for social exchange. In J. H. Barkow, L. Cosmides, and J. Tooby (Eds.), *The Adapted Mind* (pp. 163–228). New York: Oxford University Press.

Cozolino, L. (2002). *The Neuroscience of Psychotherapy: Building and Rebuilding the Human Brain.* New York: W. W. Norton & Co.

Czeh, B., Simon, M., van der Hart, M., Schmelting, B., Hesselink, M. B., Fuchs, E. (2005). Chronic stress decreases the number of parvalbumin-immuno-reactive interneurons in the hippocampus: Prevention by treatment with a substance P receptor (NK1) antagonist. *Neuropsychopharmacology*, 30(1), 67–79.

Damasio, A. (1999). *The Feeling of What Happens: Emotion and the Body in the Making of Consciousness.* New York: Harcourt, Brace.

Damasio, A. (2003, May 15). Mental self: The person within. *Nature*, 423, 227.

Davidson, R. J. (1994). Asymmetric brain function, affective style and psychopathology: The role of early experience and plasticity. *Development & Psychopathology*, 6, 741–758.

Davidson, R. J., Jackson, D. C., & Kalin, N. H. (2000). Emotion, plasticity, context and regulation: Perspectives from affective neuroscience. *Psychological Bulletin*, 126(6), 890–909.

De Bellis, M. D., Keshavan, M. S., Clark, D. B., Casey, B. J., Giedd, J., Boring, N., et al. (1999). Developmental traumatology, Part II: Brain development. *Biological Psychiatry*, 45, 1259–1270.

De Quervain, D. J., Fischbacher, U., Treyer, V., Schellhammer, M., Schnyder, U., Buck, A. & Fehr, E. (2004). The neural basis of altruistic punishment. *Science*; 305(5688), 1254–1258.

De Rougemenont, D. (1983). *Love in the Western World.* (M. Belgion, Trans.). Princeton, N.J.: Princeton University Press.

de Waal, F. B. (1995). Bonobo sex and society. *Scientific American,* 272, 82–88.

Deville, Y., Mansour, K. M., & Ferris, C. F. (1996). Testosterone facilitates aggression by modulating vasopressin receptors in the hypothalamus. *Physiology and Behavior,* 60(1), 25–29.

Diamond, J. (1992). *The Third Chimpanzee: The Evolution and Future of the Human Animal.* New York: Harper Collins:

Diamond, L.M. (2004). Emerging perspectives on the difference between romantic love and sexual desire. *Current Perspectives in Psychological Science,* 13(3), 116–119

Diamond, L.M.(2003). What does sexual orientation orient? A biobehavioral model distinguishing romantic love and sexual desire. *Psychological Review,* 10(1), 173–192.

Doidge, N. (2007). *The Brain that Changes Itself: Stories of Personal Triumph from the Frontiers of Brain Science.* New York: Viking Adult.

Edelman, G. M. (2004). *Wider Than the Sky: The Phenomenal Gift of Consciousness.* New Haven: Yale University Press.

Eisenberg, L. (1995). The social construction of the human brain. *American Journal of Psychiatry,* 152(11), 1563–1575.

Ellis, H. (1933). *Studies in the Psychology of Sex,* Volume II. Digital version available on the Internet at Project Gutenberg. (http://www.gutenberg.org/ebooks/13611).

Emery, N.J. (2000). The eyes have it: The neuroethology, function and evolution of social gaze. *Neuroscience and Biobehavior Reviews,* 24, 581-604.

Fabre-Nys, C. (1998). Steriod control of monoamines in relation to sexual behavior. *Reviews of Reproduction,* 3(1), 31–41.

Fanselow, M. S., & Poulos, A. M. (2005). The neuroscience of mammalian associative learning. *Annual Review Psychology,* 56, 207–234.

Fisher, H.E. (1992). *Anatomy of Love: The Natural History of Monogamy, Adultery, and Divorce.* New York: W. W. Norton & Co.

Fisher, H.E. (1998). Lust, Attraction, and Attachment in Mammalian Reproduction. *Human Nature,* 9, 23–52.

Fisher, H.E. (2004). *Why We Love: The Nature and Chemistry of Romantic Love.* New York: Henry Holt & Company.

Flavell, J. H. (1999). Cognitive development: Children's knowledge about the mind. *Annual Review Psychology,* 50, 21–45.

Flavell, J. H., Green, F. L., & Flavell, E. R. (1995). Young children's knowledge about thinking. *Monographs of the Society for Research in Child Development,* series no. 243.

Ford, C. S., & Beach, F. A. (1951). *Patterns of Sexual Behavior.* New York: Harper & Brothers.

Fox, R. (1972). Alliance and constraint: Sexual selection in the evolution of human kinship systems. In B. Campbell (Ed.) *Sexual Selection and the Descent of Man* (pp. 282–323). Chicago: Adline.

Fridlund, A. J., & Loftis, J. M. (1990). Relations between tickling and humorous laughter. *Biological Psychology,* 30:141–150.

Frith, C. D., & Frith, U. (1999). Interacting minds: A biological basis. *Science,* 26, 1692–1695.

Frith, U., & Frith, C. D. (2001). The biological basis of social interaction. *Current Directions in Psychological Science* 10(1), 151–155.

Frith, U., Morton, J., & Leslie, A. M. (1991). The cognitive basis for a biological disorder: Autism. *Trends in Neurosciences,* 14(19), 433–438.

Galfi, M., Janaky, T., Toth, R., Prohaszka, G., Juhasz, A., Varga, C., et al. (2001). Effects of dopamine and dopamine-active compounds on oxytocin and vasopressin production in rat neurohypophyseal tissue cultures. *Regulatory Peptides,* 98(1), 49–54.

Gianino, A., & Tronick, E. Z. (1998). The mutual regulation model: The infant's self and interactive regulation coping and defense. In T. Field, P. McCabe, and N. Schneiderman (Eds.), *Stress and Coping* (pp. 47–68). Hillsdale, N.J.: Erlbaum.

Gonzaga, G.C., Turner, R.A., Keltner, D., Campos, B., & Altemus, M. (2006). Romantic love and sexual desire in close relationships. *Emotion,* 6(2), 163–179.

Gopnick, A., & Astington, J. W. (1988). Children's understanding of representational changes and its relation to the understanding of false belief and the appearance-reality distinction. *Child Development,* 59, 26–37.

Gopnik, A., & Meltzoff, A. (1997). *Words, Thoughts and Theories.* Cambridge, Mass: MIT Press.

Gopnik, A., & Wellman, H. (1992). Why the child's theory of mind is a theory. *Mind & Language,* 7, 145–171.

Gordon, R. M. (2004). Folk psychology as mental simulation. In E. N. Zalta (Ed.), *The Stanford Encyclopedia of Philosophy* (Fall 2004). Stanford, CA: Stanford University.

Greenfieldboyce, N. (2009, June 5). Parrots join humans on the dance floor. *National Public Radio.*

Grèzes, J., Costes, N., & Decety, J. (1999). The effects of learning and intention on the neural network involved in the perception of meaningless actions. *Brain,* 122, 1875–1887.

Gurvits, T. V., Shenton, M. E., Hokama, H., Ohta, H., Lasko, N. B., Gilbertson, M. W. et.al. (1996). Magnetic resonance imaging study of hippocampal volume in chronic combat-related posttraumatic stress disorder. *Biological Psychiatry*, 40, 1091–1099.

Hamann, S., Herman, R.A., Nolan, C.I., & Wallen, K. (2004). Men and women differ in amygdala response to visual sexual stimuli. *Nature Neuroscience*, 7(4), 411-416.

Hammack, J. K. (2007). *Women in ancient Mesopotamia: The mothers of female subordination.* Doctoral dissertation, Jackson State University, Department of History.

Harris, C. R., & Christenfeld, N. (1997). Humour, tickle, and the Darwin-Hecker hypothesis. *Cognition and Emotion*, 11, 103–110.

Harris, P. L. (1990). The child's theory of mind and its cultural context. In G. Butterworth and P. Bryant (Eds.), *Causes of Development*, (pp.215–237). New York: Erlbaum.

Harris, P. L. (1992). From simulation to folk psychology: the case for development. *Mind Language,* 7, 120–144.

Heaton, J. P. (2000). Central neuropharmacological agents and mechanisms in erectile dysfunction: The role of dopamine. *Neuroscience Biobehavioral Reviews,* 24(5), 561–569.

Herbert, J. (1996). Sexuality, stress and the chemical architecture of the brain. *Annual Review of Sex Research,* 7, 1–44.

Homeida, A. M., & Khalafalla, A. E. (1990). Effects of oxytocin and an oxytocin-antagonist on testosterone secretion during the oestrous cycle of the goat (Capra hircus). *Journal of Reproduction and Fertility,* 89, 347–350.

Huang, Y.Y., Cate, S.P., Battistuzzi, C., Oquendo, M.A., Brent, D., & Mann, J.J. (2004). An association between a functional polymorphism in the monoamine oxidase A gene promoter, impulsive traits and early abuse experiences. *Neuropsychopharmacology*, 29, 1498–1505.

Hull, E. M., Lorrain, D .S., Du, J., Matuszewich, L., Lumley, L. A., Putnam, S.K., et al. (1999). Hormone-neurotransmitter interactions in the control of sexual behavior. *Behavioral Brain Research,* 105(1), 105–116.

Humphrey, N. K. (1976). The social function of intellect. In P. P. G. Bateson & R. A. Hinde (Eds.), *Growing Points in Ethnology,* (pp. 303–318). Cambridge: Cambridge University Press.

Hunt, M. M. (1974). *Sexual Behavior in the 1970s.* Chicago: Playboy Press.

Hurley, S., & Noe, A. (2003). Neural plasticity and consciousness. *Biology & Philosophy,* 18(1), 131–168.

Iacaboni, M. (2000). Mapping human cognition: thinking, numerical abilities, theory of mind, consciousness. In A. W. Toga and J. C. Mazziotta (Eds.), *Brain Mapping: The Systems* (pp. 523–534). San Diego: Academic Press.

Iacoboni, M., Molnar-Szakacs, I., Gallese, V., Buccino, G., & Mazziotta, J. C. (2005). Grasping the intentions of others with one's own mirror neuron system. *PLoS Biology*, 3(3), 529–535.

Jaffee, S.R., Caspi, A., Moffitt, T.E., Dodge, K., Rutter, M., Taylor, A., et al. (2005). Nature X nurture: Genetic vulnerabilities interact with physical maltreatment to promote behavior problems. *Development and Psychopathology*, 17, 67-84.

Jankowiak, W. R., & Fisher, E. F. (1992). A cross-cultural perspective on romantic love. *Ethnology*, 31(2), 149.

Johnson, E. (2002). The biology of . . . humor. *Discover*, 23(5), 24–25.

Jones, T. J., Dunphy, G., Milsted, A., & Ely, D. (1998). Testosterone effects on renal norepinephrine content and release in rats with different Y chromosomes. *Hypertension*, 32(5), 880–885.

Kagan, J. (1981). *The Second Year: The Emergence of Self-Awareness*. Boston: Harvard University Press.

Karama, S., Lecours, A. R., Leroux, J. M., Beaudoin, G., Joubert, S., & Beauregard, T. 2002. Areas of brain activation in males and females during viewing of erotic film excerpts. *Human Brain Mapping*, 16(1), 1–13.

Kinsey, A. C., Pomeroy, W. B., & Martin, C. E. (1948). *Sexual Behavior in the Buman Male*. Philadelphia: W. B. Saunders Co.

Kinsey, A. C., Pomeroy, W. B., and Martin, C. E. (1953). *Sexual Behavior in the Human Female*. Philadelphia: W. B. Saunders Co.

Knut, K., Kampe, W., Frith, C.D., Dolan, R.J., & Frith, U. (2001). Reward value of attractiveness and gaze. *Nature*, 413(11), 589-602.

Kohl, J. V., & Francoeur, R. T. (2002). *The scent of eros: Mysteries of odor in human sexuality*. Internet: Iuniverse (http://www.iuniverse.com) ISBN 059523.

Komisaruk, B.R., Beyer-Flores, C., & Whipple, B. (2006). *The Science of Orgasm*. Baltimore: Johns Hopkins University Press.

Kovacs, G. L., Sarnyai, L. Z., Barbarczi, E., Szabo, G., & Telegdy, G. (1990). The role of oxytocin-dopamine interactions in cocaine induced locomotor hypteractivity. *Neuropharmacology*, 29(4), 365–368.

Laland, K. N., Odling-Smee, J., & Feldman, M. W. (2000). Niche construction, biological evolution and cultural change. *Behavioral and Brain Sciences*, 23(1), 131–146.

LeDoux, J. (1996). *The Emotional Brain: The Mysterious Underpinnings of Emotional Life*. New York: Simon and Schuster.

LeDoux, J. (2003). The emotional brain, fear, and the amygdala. *Cellular and Molecular Neurobiology*, 23(4–5), 727–738.

Leslie, A. M. (1987). Pretence and representation: The origins of "theory of mind". *Psychological Review*, 94(4), 412–426.

Lewis, T., Amini, F., & Lannon, R. (2000). *A General Theory of Love*. New York: Vintage Books.

Lopez, S. J., & Snyder, C. R. (Eds.) (2003). *Positive psychological assessment: A handbook of models and measures.* Washington, D. C.: American Psychological Association.

MacLean, P. D. (1990). *The Triune Brain in Evolution: Role in Paleocerebral Functions.* New York: Plenum Press.

MacPhee, D. (1995). *The effect of marital therapy on inhibited sexual desire: An outcome study.* Doctoral dissertation. University of Ottawa, Department of Psychology.

Marcus, G. (2004). *The Birth of the Mind: How a Tiny Number of Genes Creates the Complexities of Human Thought.* New York: Basic Books.

McDougall, W. (1922). Why Do We Laugh? *Scribners,* 71, 359—363.

Meaney, M. J., Bhatnagar, S., Larocque, S., McCormick, C., Shanks, N., Sharma, S., et al. (1996). Early environment and the development of individual differences in the hypothalamic-pituitary-adrenal stress response. In C. R. Pfeffer (Ed.), *Severe stress and mental disturbance in children* (pp. 85–127). Washington DC: American Psychiatric Press.

Meltzoff, A. N., & Gopnik, A. (1993). The role of imitation in understanding persons and developing a theory of mind. In S. Baron-Cohen & H. Tager-Flusberg (Eds.), *Understanding other minds: Perspectives from autism.* Oxford: Oxford University Press.

Moffitt, T.E. (2005). Genetic and environmental influences on antisocial behavior: Evidence from behavioral-genetic research. *Advances in Genetics,* 55, 41-104.

Murdock, G. P. (1949). *Social Structure.* New York: MacMillan Company.

Murdock, G. P. (1967). *Ethnographic Atlas: A Summary.* Pittsburgh: University of Pittsburgh Press.

Newman, B., O'Grady, M. A., Ryan, C. S., & Hemmes, N. S. (1993). Pavlovian conditioning of the tickle response of human subjects: Temporal and delay conditioning. *Perceptual Motor Skills,* 77, 779–785.

Nikulina, E. M., Covington III, H. E., Ganschow, L., Hammer Jr., R. P., & Miczek, K. A. (2004). Long-term behavioral and neuronal cross-sensitization to amphetamine induced by repeated brief social defeat stress: Fos in the ventral tagmental area and amygdala. *Neuroscience,* 123(4), 857–866.

Ovid (A.D. 8). The Art of Love. In R. T. Tripp (Ed.), *International Thesaurus of Quotations,* (p. 386). New York: Harper & Row, Perennial Library.

Patel, A. D., Iversen, J. R., Bregman, M. R., & Schulz, I. (2009), Experimental Evidence for Synchronization to a Musical Beat in a Nonhuman Animal. *Current Biology,* 19(10), 827–830.

Perper, T. (1985). *Sex Signals: The Biology of Love.* Philadelphia: ISI Press.

Perper, T., & Weis, D.L. (1987). Proceptive and rejective strategies of U.S. and Canadian college women. Journal of Sex Research; 23(4), 455–480.

Perrett, D.I., Harries, M. H., Bevan, R., Thomas, S., Benson, P. J., Mistlin, A. J., et al. (1989). Frameworks of analysis for the neural representation of animate objects and action. *Journal of Experimental Biology,* 146, 87–114.

Peterson, J. (2002). *Sexual Revolutions: Gender and Labor at the Dawn of Agriculture.* Walnut Creek, Calif: AltaMira Press.

Pfaff, D. W. (1999). *Drive: Neurobiological and Molecular Mechanisms of Sexual Motivation.* Cambridge, Mass.: The MIT Press.

Povinelli, D. J ., & Preuss, T. M. (1995). Theory of mind: evolutionary history of a cognitive specialization. *Trends in Neurosciences* 18(9), 418–424.

Puce, A., Allison, T., Bentin, S., Gore, J. C., & McCarthy, G. (1998). Temporal cortex activation in humans viewing eye and mouth movement. *Journal of Neuroscience,* 18, 188–199.

Quevedo, J., Sant' Anna, M. K., Madruga, M., Lovato, I., de Paris, F., Kapczinski, F., et.al. (2003). Differential effects of emotional arousal in short- and long-term memory in healthy adults. *Neurobiology of Learning and Memory,* 79, 132–135.

Quindlen, A. (2009). The End of an Error. *Newsweek,* April 13, 2009.

Ravenscroft, I. (2003). Simulation, collapse and human motivation. *Mind & Language,* 18, 162–174.

Ravenscroft, I. (2004). Folk Psychology as a Theory. In E. N. Zalta (Ed.), *Stanford Encyclopedia of Philosophy* (Fall 2004 Edition). Stanford, CA: Stanford University. http://plato.stanford.edu/entries/folkpsych-theory/.

Ravenscroft, I. (2004). Folk Psychology as Mental Simulation. In E. N. Zalta (Ed.), *Stanford Encyclopedia of Philosophy* (Fall 2004 Edition). Stanford, CA: Stanford University. http://plato.stanford.edu/entries/folkpsych-simulation/.

Ridley, M. (1993). *The Red Queen: Sex and the Evolution of Human Nature.* New York: Harper Collins.

Rizzolatti, G., & Craighero, L. (2004). The mirror-neuron system. *Annual Review of Neuroscience,* 27, 169–192.

Rogers, S. J., & Pennington, B. F. (1991). A theoretical approach to the deficits in infantile autism. *Development and Psychopathology,* 3, 137–162.

Rutter, M. (2006). Implications of resilience concepts for scientific understanding. *Annals of the New York Academy of Sciences,* 1094(1), 1–12.

Rutter, M., Moffitt, T.E., & Caspi, A. (2006). Gene-environment interplay and psychopathology: Multiple varieties but real effects. *Journal of Child Psychology and Psychiatry,* 47(3), 226–261.

Sapolsky, R. (1999). Stress and your shrinking brain. *Discover,* 20(3) p. 116.

Schnarch, D. M. (1991). *Constructing the Sexual Crucible: An Integration of Sex and Marital Therapy.* New York: W.W. Norton & Co.

Schnarch, D. M. (1997, 2009). *Passionate Marriage: Keeping love and Intimacy Alive in Committed Relationships.* New York: W.W. Norton & Co.

Schnarch, D. M. (2001). The therapist in the crucible: Early developments in a new paradigm of sexual and marital therapy. In S. McDaniel, D. D. Lusterman, & L. C. Philpot (Eds.), *Casebook for integrating family therapy: An ecosystemic approach.* American Psychological Association, 2001.

Schnarch, D. M. (2002). *Resurrecting Sex: Resolving Sexual Problems and Rejuvenating Your Relationship.* New York: Harper Collins.

Schore, A. N. (1994). *Affect Regulation and the Origin of the Self: The Neurobiology of Emotional Development.* Hillsdale, N.J.: Erlbaum.

Schore, A. N. (1996). The experience-dependent maturation of a regulatory system in the orbital prefrontal cortex and the origin of developmental psychopathology. *Development and Psychopathology,* 8, 59–87.

Schover, L., & Lopicollo, J. (1982). Effectiveness of treatment of dysfunctions of sexual desire. *Journal of Sex & Marital Therapy,* 8(3), 179–197.

Schuller, A.M., & Rossion, B. (2001). Spatial attention triggered by eye gaze increases and speeds up early visual activity. *Cognitive Neuroscience,* 12(11), 2381-2386.

Siegel, D. J. (2001). *The Developing Mind: How Relationships and the Brain Interact to Shape Who We Are.* New York: Guilford Press.

Siegel, D. J. (2002). The developing mind and the resolution of Trauma, In F. Shapiro (Ed.), *EMDR as an integrative psychotherapy approach* (pp. 85–121). Washington, D.C.: American Psychological Association.

Singer-Kaplan, H. (1979). *Disorders of Sexual Desire and Other New Concepts and Techniques in Sex Therapy.* New York: Simon and Schuster.

Slutske, W.S. (2001). The genetics of antisocial behavior. *Current Psychiatry Reports,* 3(2), 158-162.

Sodian, B. (1991). The development of deception in young children. *British Journal of Developmental Psychology,* 9, 173–188.

Stearns, F. R. (1972). *Laughing.* Springfield, IL: Charles C. Thomas.

Stern, D. N. (1985). *The Interpersonal World of the Infant: A View from Psychoanalysis and Developmental Psychology.* New York: Basic Books.

Stern, D. N. (2004). *The Present Moment in Psychotherapy and Everyday Life.* New York: W. W. Norton & Co.

Stich, S., & Nichols, S. (1993). Folk psychology: Simulation or tacit theory. *Mind & Language* 7, 35–71.

Svoboda, E., McKinnon, M. C., & Levine, B. (2006). The functional neuroanatomy of autobiographical memory: A meta-analysis. *Neuropsychologia,* 44(12), 2189–2208.

Tannahill, R. (1980). *Sex in History.* New York: Stein & Day.

Tavris, C., & Sadd, S. (1977). *The Redbook Report on Female Sexuality.* New York: Delacorte.

Taylor, J. B. (2008). *My Stroke of Insight: A Brain Scientist's Personal Journey.* New York: Viking Adult.

Taylor, J. B. (2009, January 6). Stroke of Insight. Lecture (video) on TED.com. http://www.ted.com/talks/jill_bolte_taylor_s_powerful_stroke_of_insight. html.

Taylor, T. (1996). *The Prehistory of Sex: Four Million Years of Human Sexual Culture.* New York: Bantam Books.

Thomas, A, N., Kim, N. B., & Amico, J. A. (1996a). Differential regulation of oxytocin and vasopressin messenger ribonucleic acid levels by gonaldal steroids in postpartum rats. *Brain Research,* 738(1), 48–52.

Thomas, A, N., Kim, N. B., & Amico, J. A. (1996b). Sequential exposure to estrogen and testosterone (T) and subsequent withdrawal of T increases the level of arginine vasopressin messenger ribonucleic acid in the hypothamalic paraventricular nucleaus of the female rat. *Journal of Neuroendocrinology,* 8(10), 793–800.

Tripp, R. T. (1970). *The International Thesaurus of Quotations.* New York: Harper & Row.

Tronick, E. Z. (1989). Emotions and emotional communication in infants. *American Psychologist,* 44(2), 112–119.

Udwin, O., Boyle, S., Yule, W., Bolton, D., O'Ryan, D. (2000). Risk factors for long-term psychological effects of a disaster experienced in adolescence: Predictors of post traumatic stress disorder. *Journal of Child Psycholology & Psychiatry,* 41, 969–979.

Vogeley, K., Bussfeld, P., Newen, A., Herrmann, S., Happe, F., Falkai, P., et al. (2001). Mind reading: Neural mechanism of theory of mind and self-perspective. *Neuroimage,* 14, 170–181.

Vouimbai, R. M., Oz, C. M., & Diamond, D. M. (2006). Differential effects of predator stress and the antidepressant tianeptine on physiological plasticity in the hippocampus and basolateral amygdala. *Stress,* 9(1), 29–40.

Wallen, K. (2009). Intimate gaze: Hormones and sex differences in response to sexual images. Paper presented at the *19th WAS World Congress for Sexual Health,* Goteborg Sweden, June 21-25, 2009.

Weintraub, P. (2009). The new survivors. *Psychology Today,* 42(4), 87-93.

Weise, E. (June 17, 2004). Report: Rodents may offer insight to monogamy. *USA Today.* http://www.usatoday.com/news/science/2004-06-16-voles-usat_x. htm

Wellman, H. M, & Bartsch, K. (1988). Young children's reasoning about beliefs. *Cognition,* 30, 239–277.

Whelihan, W. A. (2000). Changes in couples' perception of intimacy and sexuality and meanings of sex: Evaluation of a couple enrichment program. Doctoral dissertation, University of Minnesota, Department of Family Social Science.

Whythe, M. K. (1978). *The Status of Women in Preindustrial Societies.* Princeton: Princeton University Press.

Wicker, B., Michel, F., Henaff, M.A., & Decety, J. (1998). Brain regions involved in the perception of gaze: A PET study. *NeuroImage*, 8(2), 221-227.

Willi, J. (1982). *Couples in Collusion.* New York: Jason Aronson.

Wolfe, L. (1981). *The Cosmo Report.* New York: Arbor House.

# END NOTES

1  See my textbook, *Constructing the Sexual Crucible* (Schnarch, 1991).

2  People who had sexual desire problems previously are not included in these figures. Including them would greatly increase these numbers.

3  This was called *bypassing*, developed by Dr. Singer-Kaplan. See Singer-Kaplan (1979).

4  Schover & Lopicollo (1982).

5  When I was trained, clinicians referred to the *low-desire partner* and the *asymptomatic partner*. In this framework, you were either the partner with an obvious problem, or the one who was equally screwed-up but didn't show it. Although therapists tried to avoid labeling one sick and one healthy, they were operating from a pathological viewpoint.

6  If the high desire partner controls the frequency of sex, it's probably a situation of rape, psychological torture, or extreme cultural bias against women. Polygamy is man's attempt to "beat the system" that the LDP always controls sex, by shifting his sexual attention from a low desire wife to a different wife, one who may be sexually receptive because it shifts her position in the household.

7  See Aspinwall & Staudinger (2003) and Lopez & Snyder (2003).

8  See Fisher's wonderful book, *Why We Love: The Nature and Chemistry of Romantic Love* (2004).

9  The caudate nucleus.

10  This general region directs bodily movement. The caudate nucleus, in particular, is involved in detecting, perceiving, and discriminating in ways that allow you to anticipate and mobilize yourself to obtain a reward.

11  Fisher, *Why We Love*, p. 69.

12  This part, the ventral tegmental area (VTA), has long dopamine-distributing branches into the caudate nucleus and other brain regions.

13  *A General Theory of Love* (Lewis, Amini & Lannon, 2000) is also about the neuroscience of love. The authors argue that love is as fit a subject for scientific discourse as cucumbers or chemistry. They note love involves the emotional centers of the brain (as Helen Fisher found), but people erroneously assume every part of their brain should be logical since as a species we are more aware of the verbal, rational part of our brains.

14  Researchers made naturally promiscuous meadow voles (mouse-like rodents) become monogamous by implanting a single gene in the pleasure center of their brains. When they examined how this remarkable behavior change was actually accomplished, they found dopamine and vasopressin receptors normally located apart in the brain had grown together (Weise, 2004).

15  Dopamine and norepinephrine, two natural brain stimulants (*neurochemicals*) found in mammals and birds, may underlie romantic love. Research shows that sexual behavior and elevated dopamine and norepinephrine go hand in hand among many animals. Both neurotransmitters produce exhilaration, increased energy and activity, increased focused attention, prolonged motivation, and goal-oriented behavior (like pursuit of a mating partner). Lovers' obsessive thoughts may be due to decreased brain levels of serotonin. See Fisher, *Why We Love*, p. 55.

16  This is not the same as mature adult love. Mature adult love is also focused on the partner as a separate person, but involves caring in ways that benefit the loved one.

17  The anterior cingulate cortex and insular cortex are where your emotions, attention, and working memory interact. They enable you to become aware of your own emotional states, such as happy feelings. They are also where you assess other people's feelings during social interactions. You make split-second assessments about what things mean. Your insular cortex collects data about your body, both external (touch and temperature), and internal (pain, gut reactions, and viscera). It's involved in the cognitive and visceral aspects of processing your emotions, such as "butterflies in the stomach," or your heart pounding. See Fisher, *Why We Love*, p. 73.

18  Bartels & Zeki (2004). Romantic love and friendship both activate the medial insula, anterior cingulate cortex, caudate nucleus, and putamen. Gazing at pictures of lovers and friends deactivates your posterior cingulated gyrus, amygdala, right prefrontal, parietal and middle temporal cortices, posterior cingulate gyrus, and medial prefrontal cortex. Your amygdala is more active when viewing friends than a loved partner. Men and women have the same activation and deactivation patterns. Deactivation of the amygdala is noteworthy because

it mediates emotional learning, and activity in it correlates with fear, sadness, and aggression. Other research suggests happiness correlates with deactivations in the right prefrontal and bilateral parietal and temporal cortices. Romantic love and friendship involve a unique network of interconnected areas, a functionally specialized brain system underlying two of humankind's richest experiences. Studies of sexual arousal find different patterns of activation in adjacent regions. See Bartels & Zeki (2000).

19 Drives have several distinct characteristics: They are tenacious and difficult to control, they focus on a specific reward, and they aren't associated with a particular facial expression (as are emotions). They may also be associated with elevated brain dopamine levels (Pfaff, 1999).

20 Fisher, *Why We Love*, p. xiii.

21 A survey of 168 cultures found direct evidence of romantic love in 87 percent of them. See Jankowiak & Fisher (1992).

22 See Fisher (1998) and Diamond (2003, 2004) for elaboration of sexual desire, romantic love, and attachment as three separate but interactive systems. This conceptualization, and the extensive research behind it, has far-reaching implications. First, it explains why romantic love and attachment don't necessarily produce sexual desire, and conversely, why sexual desire may not involve romantic love or lead to attachment. Second, this suggests attachment-based psychotherapy is likely to be ineffective at increasing sexual desire, which is consistent with research findings of MacPhee (1995). Third, it provides a non-pathological explanation of same-sex attraction and gay and lesbian relationships. Also see Gonzaga et al. (2006).

23 Scientists have identified the areas of the brain involved when you look at erotic video material. These include your anterior cingulate, medial prefrontal cortex, orbitofrontal cortex, insula and occipitotemporal cortices, as well as your amygdala, ventral striatum and hypothalamus. See Arnow et al. (2002) and Karama et al. (2002).

24 Romance also promotes sexual desire because dopamine and norepinephrine can trigger increased testosterone. Increased testosterone can increase dopamine and norepinephrine and suppress serotonin. See Fabre-Nys (1998), Hull et al. (1999), and Jones, Dunphy, Milsted, & Ely (1998). As in many other species, elevated dopamine increases sexual arousal and sexual behavior in men and women. See Coleman et al. (1999), Heaton (2000), and Herbert (1996).

25 The complex relationships between hormones and neurotransmitters are still being discovered. Dopamine and norepinephrine can contribute to attachment by increasing oxytocin and vasopressin. But increased oxytocin (found in both men and women) can also reduce dopamine and norepinephrine. See Galfi et al. (2001) and Kovacs et al. (1990). Men with high testosterone marry

less frequently, divorce more often, and have more affairs. Moreover, a man's testosterone levels rise as his marriage unravels, and further increases with divorce. Conversely, his testosterone declines as he becomes more attached, especially with the birth of a child, and even from just holding a baby. See Berg & Wynne-Edwards (2001); also Booth & Dabbs (1993). Increased testosterone reduces vasopressin and oxytocin, and vasopressin can decrease levels of testosterone. However, under some circumstances, testosterone elevates vasopressin and oxytocin and increases attachment behaviors. Likewise, oxytocin and vasopressin can increase testosterone production. See Arsenijevic & Tribollet (1998); Deville, Mansour, & Ferris (1996); Homeida & Khalafalla (1990); Thomas, Kim, & Amico (1996a); and Thomas, Kim, & Amico (1996b).

26  Fisher, *Why We Love*, p. 92.

27  Your testosterone, oxytocin, vasopressin, sexual desire, and "self" are all mutually interactive.

28  See Denis de Rougemont's *Love in the Western World* (1983) for an elegant analysis.

29  Paul MacLean, evolutionary neuroanatomist and senior research scientist at the National Institute of Mental Health, proposed that your brain is comprised of three distinct sub-brains, each a product of a different stage in human evolution. The oldest is your *reptilian* brain (top portion of your spinal cord at the base of your brain), which controls breathing, swallowing, heartbeat, visual tracking, and startle response. The second part is your *limbic* brain, which sits on top of your spinal cord in the center of your skull (it includes your hippocampus, fornix, amygdala, septum, cingulate gyrus, perirhinal, and parahippocampal regions). You share the first part in common with reptiles, and the second with other mammals. Your *neocortex* is the last part of the human brain to evolve; it's the largest of the three, and it surrounds the other two parts. Other mammals like dogs, cats, and monkeys have a neocortex, but yours is huge by comparison. All three parts of your brain interact, and are not as distinct or functionally separate as this "triune brain" sounds. Murray Bowen, who created differentiation theory, knew MacLean personally and was greatly influenced by his work. From the outset, differentiation theory looked at emotions as physical processes that affect the brain and not just as subjective experiences. This is why the Crucible® Approach, developed thirty years ago, fits well with emerging neuroscience and lends itself to neuroplastic training, which I discuss in Part Four. See MacLean (1990).

30  The left inferior frontal cortex and anterior cingulate.

31  The medial prefrontal cortex.

32  Just to be clear, your "self" is not in a single location in your brain. The physical underpinnings of your self involve an ever-changing cascade of physical processes distributed throughout diverse portions of brain matter.

33 In *Wider Than the Sky*, Nobel laureate Gerald Edelman proposes our conscious "self" is dynamically and continually constructed from bodily cues. (Scientists refer to this as our "immunological self," what our immune system identifies as belonging to our own body.) See Edelman (2004).

34 Edelman writes: "The dynamic core [self], whose activities are enriched though learning, continues throughout life to be influenced by new processes of categorization, connected to what might be termed the bodily self" (p. 74). See p. 79 for depiction of causal chains between the world, your body, and your brain that affect your dynamic core self (primary consciousness and primitive sense of self).

35 "Primary consciousness is the state of being mentally aware of things in the world, of having mental images in the present. It is possessed not only by humans, but also by animals lacking semantic or linguistic capabilities, whose brain organization is nevertheless similar to ours. Primary consciousness is not accompanied by any sense of a socially defined self with a concept of a past or future. It exists primarily in the remembered present" (Edelman, p. 9).

36 Do dogs and birds have higher-order consciousness? Edelman (2004) believes primary consciousness appeared in vertebrates at the transition between reptiles and birds and the transition between reptiles and mammals. In *Wild Justice*, Bekoff and Pierce (2009) argue that animals feel empathy for each other, treat one another fairly, cooperate toward common goals, help each other out of trouble, and have morality. Now that we know parrots can dance, they obviously have rhythm, but do they have soul? (Patel et al., 2009.)

37 Brain researcher Antonio Damasio hypothesizes how your mental self builds on your brain mapping the state of your body. "This machinery included pathways that transmit chemical signals from the internal milieu, through bloodstream, directly to brain regions such as the area postrema [which controls vomiting] or the hypothalamus; and the neural signal from the viscera and muscles that are conveyed by nerve fibres to the brain regions in the spinal cord and bloodstream. Within the brain itself, dedicated pathways signal this body-related information to certain sectors of the thalamus (a nucleus known as VMPo), and to the cerebral cortex (a sector of the insula). The integration of such signals constructs composite and dynamic maps of the body's state from moment to moment." See Damasio (2003), p. 227.

38 According to Eldeman, "Through the complex shifting states of the dynamic core [self], these interactions underlie the unitary property of conscious states, as well as the shifting diversity of these states over time. Because the earliest interactions involve bodily inputs from centers of the brain concerned with value systems, motor areas, and regions involved in emotional responses, the core process are always centered around a self that serves as a reference for memory.

In primary consciousness, this self exists in a remembered present, reflecting the integration of a scene around a small interval of time" (Edelman, p. 77).

39 "… higher-order consciousness involves the ability to be conscious of being conscious, and it allows the recognition by a thinking subject of his or her own acts and affections. It is accompanied by the ability in the waking state explicitly to create past episodes and to form future intentions. At a minimal level, it requires semantic ability, that is, the assignment of meaning to a symbol. In its most developed form, it requires linguistic ability, that is, the mastery of a whole system of symbols, and a grammar. Higher primates, to some minimal degree, are assumed to have it, and in its most developed form it is distinctive of humans. Both cases require an internal ability to deal with tokens or symbols" (Edelman, p. 9).

40 To understand how consciousness is *not* reducible to simple neural correlates, see Hurley & Noe (2003). Gerald Edelman says it simply: "No two socially defined selves (necessarily socially defined in a speech community) will ever have identical brain states" (Edelman, p. 137).

41 Stern (1985) and Siegel, D. J. (2001).

42 Your self is "the genetic and immunological identity of an individual… [that] refers to characteristic inputs from an individual body related to its history and value systems. In its most developed form, seen in higher-order consciousness, it is a social self related to interactions within a speech community" (Edelman, p. 175).

43 Hurley & Noe (2003).

44 As humans differentiated from other primates, each step brought us closer to the complex sense of self that infuses human sexual desire and shapes human evolution. This is evident in major differences between sexual habits of humans and gorillas. First, the hallmark of human sexuality is private couplings, whereas gorillas copulate in public. Secondly, female gorillas readily join a harem, but human women rarely do. Power struggles commonly surface within human harems. Finally, human pair-bonds are more short-lived than those of gorillas. Gorillas mate for life; people tend to switch partners.

45 According to archeologist Richard Klein of Stanford University, representational art, figurines, and jewelry (reflecting more advanced language and working memory) didn't appear until 50,000 year ago. But representational art is probably not a good marker for the earliest emergence of the complex human self. Complex consciousness (something above primary consciousness) emerged much earlier than that. See Begley (2007b).

46 It's probably not accurate to talk about emergence of the complex human self as if it popped out at one point in history and then remained from then on. Scientists believe evolutionary advances showed up at different points in time but then died out and reappeared again at some point in the future. It's likely some

individuals lived out their existence being the only ones in their community who had a complex self. This occurred at different times in the dim past until complex consciousness became a dominant trait.

47  Begley (2007b).

48  In *The Birth of the Mind,* Gary Marcus gives a remarkable explanation of how a relatively small number of highly communicative genes produced the complex human brain with staggering innate powers of self-organization and reorganization. However, archeologist Timothy Taylor fleshes out the other side of the story in *The Prehistory of Sex.* He writes: "The human ability to learn presupposes a mind that can be changed, a mind that can make certain choices. The development of such a mind, to be sure, may have been enabled by the development of particular genes...But the emergence of that mind put an end to most of the determinism of the other genes. That is, although one may have 'an instinct' to do something, one may choose to do the opposite." Taylor (1996), p. 85. See also Marcus (2004).

49  In *Anatomy of Love,* Fisher (1992) proposes jealousy had taken its current form by the time "Lucy" lived 3.5 million years ago. But jealousy is not simply that "I want what she has," which is common to primates. It is also, "I want to have what she has so I can be happy like she is. I want to feel what she feels. She is happier than me. And if I have what she has I'll be happy like her." This involves symbolic thinking, the ability to apply an abstract concept in the concrete world, which probably emerged millions of years later. Burials, religious practices and belief in an afterlife, and humanitarian acts reflect some level of symbolic thinking, early manifestations of the human self. When your ancestors created symbols for thoughts, ideas, and concepts, and manipulated these symbols to express themselves, the human complex self emerged.

50  For a review of empirical data suggesting culture is a non-genetic "knowledge-carrying" inheritance system that influenced human genetic evolution, see Laland et al. (2000).

51  Anthropologist Timothy Taylor (1996) says contraception, homosexuality, transsexuality, and prostitution show how sexual choices made by your ancestors shaped human evolution, which is not reducible to genetic determinism.

52  A niche is an area in which an organism can survive.

53  In Europe, Dr. Jürg Willi is known as the father of ecological psychology. See Willi (1982).

54  Co-evolution is the evolution of two or more interdependent species or people, each adapting to changes in the other. It occurs, for example, between predators and prey and between insects and the flowers they pollinate. Co-evolution goes on between partners in a love relationship. Niche construction is a form of co-evolution.

55  Eisenberg (1995).

56  "Working on your relationship" is nothing more that niche construction. Some of us construct our niche by refusing to work on our relationship.

57  There is nothing wrong with wanting other people's acceptance and validation. But problems arise when we are *dependent* on this. When this occurs, a host of other problems ensue, including feeling controlled by other people, even when they are not trying to do so. Our own overpowering needs for approval also make us easy targets for manipulation.

58  Buber (1958).

59  Common preoccupation with clothes, sexy bodies, and perpetual youth stems, in part, from our penchant for validating ourselves by eliciting desire in others (reflected sense of self). When people constantly focus on how they look, it is because they need someone to want them. Getting your sense of self from your body is inevitably self-defeating, given how humans age.

60  Scientists have studied mind-mapping for many years under the heading of "theory of mind" (ToM). The link between theory of mind, reflected sense of self, and differentiation, discussed here, is new.

61  See Abu-Akel (2003) for a review and synthesis of voluminous research on mind-mapping. The three brain structures of mind-mapping are *posterior regions* (temporal and parietal) (which include the inferior parietal lobe and superior temporal sulcus); *limbic–paralimbic regions* (which include the amygdala, orbitofrontal cortex, the ventral medial prefrontal cortex, and anterior cingulated girus), and *prefrontal regions* (which include the dorsal medial prefrontal cortex and infrolateral frontal cortex). Also see Frith & Frith (2001) and Baron-Cohen & Ring (1994).

62  We discussed this in the last chapter as primary consciousness: a basic "body self" derived from discriminating "me" from "not me." Even a crocodile has primary consciousness.

63  Brothers (1997) and Flavell (1999).

64  Scientists discovered cells in the reptilian part of the human brain that do nothing but track another person's mouth. Others track just their eyes, and they only track human eyes. From similar cells, reptiles track what other animals are eating, or wanting, or likely to do. Mind-mapping probably developed out of these primitive abilities. Social intelligence makes mind-mapping much more powerful. See Frith & Frith (1999) and Castelli et al. (2000).

65  My emphasis here is that rudimentary mind-mapping ability is hard-wired in your brain. It is relatively automatic, much of it occurs below conscious awareness, and does not primary rely on your prefrontal neocortex. See Bach et al. (2000).

66  Your anterior cingulate gyrus and insular cortex, respectively. A study looked at brain function when predicting other people's behavior in order to distinguish between developing a theory of their mind vs. making inferences by

projecting your own mental states. The "theory" method produces activity in your anterior cingulated cortex and left temporopolar cortex. Projecting your own mental states involves your anterior cingulated cortex and your right temproprarietal juncture. See Vogeley et al. (2001).

67 Alexander (1974) and Humphrey (1976).

68 Matt Ridley writes: "We are obsessed with one another's minds. Our intuitive commonsense psychology far surpasses any scientific psychology in scope and accuracy.... Horace Barlow points out that great literary minds are, almost by definition, great mind-reading minds. Shakespeare was a far better psychologist than Freud, and Jane Austen a far better sociologist than Durkheim. We are clever because we are—to the extent that we are—natural psychologists." Ridley (1993), p. 333.

69 Byrne & Whitten (1988).

70 Cosimedes & Tooby (1991).

71 In *The Present Moment*, psychiatrist Daniel Stern proposes that the rudiments of mind-mapping are present from birth (Stern, 2004). Also see *The Interpersonal World of the Infant* (Stern, 1985) for further discussion of mind-mapping.

72 Butterworth (1991) and Baron-Cohen (1991).

73 Butterworth & Jarrett (1991).

74 Baldwin & Moses (1994).

75 Rogers & Pennington (1991).

76 Bartsch & Wellman (1995), Amsterdam (1972), and Leslie (1987).

77 Frith, Morton, & Leslie (1991).

78 Povinelli & Preuss (1995).

79 Wellman & Bartsch (1988) and Harris (1990).

80 Flavell, Green, & Flavell (1995) and Gopnik & Astington (1988).

81 False beliefs illustrate mind-mapping because you have to track the way someone's mind diverges from the real world, demonstrating that you can track both. (It usually takes years of marriage to finally understand how many false beliefs exist in your own mind.)

82 Sodian (1991).

83 Baron-Cohen (1991).

84 Some say theory-based mind-mapping is largely learned by a child gradually developing a picture of how his parents' minds work from his experiences with them, much as a scientist develops a theory. See Gopnik & Wellman (1992) and Gopnik & Meltzoff (1997). Others believe theory-based mind-mapping is largely innate. See Carruthers (1996). For two excellent reviews of "theory" aspects of mind-mapping, see Gordon (2004) and Ravenscroft (2004).

85 For an overview of "simulation" aspects of mind-mapping, see Raven-scroft (2004) and Stich & Nichols (1993).

86 Meltzoff and Gopnik propose that innate mechanisms allow infants to attribute emotional states to others from birth, by the infant automatically activating her own bodily emotional states by imitating adults' facial expressions. They say imitation-generated affect states play a crucial role in developing mind-mapping ability. "Imitation of behavior provides the bridge that allows the internal mental state of another to 'cross-over' to and become one's own experienced mental state." Meltzoff and Gopnik (1993), p. 358.

When you see someone express an emotion, you feel the visceral part of your own corresponding emotion as when it originates in you. Recognition of facially-expressed emotion relies on your own gut reactions. If the part of your brain that reads your own visceral responses is damaged, your ability to recognize emotions in someone else's face is impaired. See Adolphs et al. 2000.

87 Mirror neurons in your premotor cortex may be involved in understanding other people's actions and experiences. However, only a narrow range of actions trigger mirror neurons. They seem to involve purposive behavior such as reaching for an apple, grasping it, bringing it to your mouth, and eating it. Purposive behavior reflects an intent, desire, or decision. See Iacoboni et al. (2005) and Rizzolatti & Craighero (2004).

88 The distinction between simulation and theory models gets muddier as knowledge of mind-mapping expands. For example, Gopnik and Meltzoff (1997) developed a learned theory model based on infants' innate visceral responses from imitating parents' faces. Ravenscroft (2003) says simulation models may simply "collapse" into an internal theory framework.

89 Some of these sensations come from the reptilian part of your brain (Allison, Puce, & McCarthy, 2000). The posterior part of the superior temporal sulcus, STS, is involved in tracking other people's eye gaze and mouth movement. This may be functionally related to adjacent superior temporal regions, which track others' hands and body movements. See Grèzes, Costes, & Decety (1999) and Puce et al. (1998). Moreover, the STS responds selectively to observing goal-directed actions like reaching, grasping, holding, and tearing, but not to movements lacking such intentions. See Perrett et al. (1989).

90 Brothers (1997) and Byrne & Whiten (1992).

91 Daniel Stern distinguishes three types of consciousness: *phenomenological* consciousness (perception-based awareness of things happening in the moment, which exist only in short-term memory), *introspective* consciousness (verbal-based awareness of things stored symbolically or visual images in your brain retrieved by introspection), and *intersubjective* consciousness (social-based co-

created experiences involving overlapping phenomenological consciousness with a partner). Stern (2004), pp. 129–132.

92 Ovid wrote *The Art of Love* in the year 8 A.D.

93 Oscar Wilde, see www.brainyquote.com/quotes/quotes/o/oscarwilde131549 .html.

94 My approach developed out of treating couples who had previously failed in marital therapy or sex therapy and thereafter refused to do traditional therapy activities. For another case example, see Schnarch (2001).

95 My book *Resurrecting Sex* is written entirely in terms of "holding on to yourself." The term "differentiation" isn't introduced until the final chapter. I did this so readers would learn about differentiation as a real-life process rather than as a concept. The Four Points of Balance™ program is designed to help you develop differentiation in daily practice.

96 Bierce (1911).

97 Many people with amputations, congenital deformities, and paralyses "stand on their own two feet" better than those with two good legs.

98 This review is detailed in hundred of references in *Constructing the Sexual Crucible* (Schnarch, 1991).

99 In your reptilian brain, the inferior parietal lobule (IPL) of your right posterior parietal system is involved in mapping your mind. Your superior temporal sulcus (STS) helps you map other people's minds. See Abu-Akel (2003).

100 Mapping someone else's mind involves medial frontal activation (anterior cingulated cortex and left superior temporal cortex). Mapping your own mind involves the right temproparietal junction and superior parietal lobe (in addition to the anterior cingulated cortex). Discriminations requiring both self and other frames of reference are resolved in the right prefrontal cortex. See Vogeley et al. (2001) and Iacaboni (2000).

101 It takes two people to create intimacy because the salience of the experience is determined in part by your partner's importance to you. However, when two people are being intimate, only one partner may experience it. Self-validated intimacy is co-created, but not necessarily a shared experience. Confronting and disclosing yourself in front of your partner may be acutely intimate for you, but if you partner is not doing likewise (or dodging), he or she may not experience it as intimacy.

102 Birth control, artificial insemination, neonatal gender selection, and epigenetics are examples of how we increasingly control our biology.

103 Helen Fisher provides a nice summary of relevant research in *Anatomy of Love* (1992).

104 During the time babies and mothers are out of sync, the self-soothing and regulation comes from the infant (e.g., thumb sucking), not from the

mother. Moreover, infants in sync with their mother deliberately break contact several times a minute to soothe and regulate themselves. See Tronick (1989) and Gianino & Tronick (1988).

105  Fisher, *Anatomy of Love*, p. 141. Fisher suggests women weren't monogamous since they were in fewer numbers. Other anthropologists argue it was the men who had multiple partners (e.g., Tannahill, 1980). The odds are neither sex was monogamous.

106  Murdock (1967).

107  Murdock (1949).

108  Fisher, *Anatomy of Love*, p. 64.

109  For statistics on men and women's sexual behavior, see Kinsey, Pomeroy, & Martin (1948 and 1953).

110  Hunt (1974).

111  Tavris & Sadd (1977).

112  Wolfe (1981).

113  This is differentiation: balancing attachment and pair-bonding with autonomy and self-direction.

114  Whythe (1978).

115  The ancient Mesopotamian societies of Sumer, Babylon, and Assyria (about 1100 B.C.) formalized the subordination of women in the ancient world. Religions and laws prevented them from controlling reproduction. Social institutions further diminished women's social power and reduced them to chattel and men's possessions. See Hammack (2007) and Peterson (2002).

116  In 1694, Nicolas Hartsoeker, a Dutch mathematician and physicist, discovered sperm in men and animals' semen. The discovery led to the medieval theory that men's semen contained a "homunculus"—a fully formed little man which matured when planted in a woman's womb. This became another prohibition against masturbation (besides all the religious ones) on the grounds that you were killing your already-existing child.

117  Tannahill (1980) says something *big* must have happened during the seven thousand years of the Neolithic period to change men from being equal partners with women to being acknowledged despots. Men's growing control over food production and domesticated animals may have been part of it. But Tannahill proposes men made their move based on some blinding revelation beyond argument or question. She proposes it was when men discovered their own crucial role in reproduction: That was the end of woman's sexual freedom.

118  This doesn't mean everyone who wants monogamy is poorly differentiated.

119  Sexual expectations don't have the same impact in the animal world. For example, a female gorilla mates willingly with the group's alpha male, who clearly expects her to have sex whenever he wants. Why didn't gorillas evolve so

that females respond negatively to the male's expectations for sex, the same way humans do? Perhaps if they had, they would have a more advanced brain.

120 In Catholicism, the obligation to have sex goes both ways. In Judaism, the man owes the woman sex, but not the other way around.

121 Fox (1972). Also see Fisher (1992), *Anatomy of Love,* and Tannahill (1980), *Sex in History.*

122 People derive satisfaction from punishing norm violators, in part, because this activates their caudate nucleus, which releases dopamine in their brain. The caudate nucleus plays a decisive role in "altruistic punishment." It is generally involved in making decisions or taking actions motivated by anticipated rewards. See De Quervain et al. (2004).

123 Are you entitled to your sexual preferences? For a complete discussion of this question, see Chapter Seven in *Passionate Marriage.*

124 Helen Fisher writes, "Man the natural playboy, women the doting spouse—Americans already believed it. Because of our agrarian background and sexual double standard it became acceptable to view men as would-be Don Juans and women as the more virtuous of the genders. So when Symons presented an evolutionary explanation for men's philandering nature, many scholars bought it like a better chocolate bar." Fisher, *Anatomy of Love,* p. 89.

125 Fisher, *Anatomy of Love,* p.93.

126 Ford & Beach (1951).

127 This is why your partner can have an affair with someone else and the sex can indeed be better. He doesn't care about the other person as much as he cares about you, so he can "let it all hang out." It is not a good thing to become more important to a partner who can't hold on to himself or herself.

128 Other primates show some capacity to *want* in the sense I'm using here. Primates who learn sign language from human trainers indicate they wish and long for someone with whom they've established an attachment. Apparently dogs and elephants can *want* too. Perhaps dolphins *want,* but how do they show it?

129 Issues about *wanting* often get mixed up with issues about exclusivity. Wanting to be your partner's "one and only" is another quagmire of reflected sense of self. See *Passionate Marriage,* p. 242, for further discussion.

130 Ovulation is obvious in all other species from changes in females' behavior and appearance of their genitals. Fisher speculates that women's shift to unobtrusive, "silent" ovulation gave them a powerful payoff: *choice.* Women had the ability to *choose* their mates more carefully. (Fisher, *Anatomy of Love,* p. 186–187.) In *The Third Chimpanzee,* Jared Diamond summarizes six theories from anthropologists and sociobiologists about why humans developed concealed ovulation. These include (1) enhancing cooperation and reducing aggression among male hunters, (2) cementing bonds between a particular

couple, thus laying the groundwork for the evolution of the human family, (3) insuring constant food supply from men, (4) forcing men into a permanent marriage bond, (5) manipulating men by confusing paternity, and (6) giving women the opportunity to control conception and avoid the pain of childbirth. He thinks the core drive for silent ovulation was the second theory: inducement for pair-bonding and defining that pair-bond as a couple in a community. This coincides with Fisher's ideas about kinship. See Diamond (1992).

131  An ape has a two-inch penis but three times the body mass of a man. An ape's penis is also thinner. Given that female chimps have a much larger clitoris than women do, it's not as simple as humans having larger genitals because it encourages sex. Beyond whatever pleasure female chimps derive from their larger clitoris, it offers a larger signal and target for mating when they are into heat.

132  "Making things official" is an important developmental step that is currently available only to heterosexual couples in the United States. Gay and lesbian couples cannot legally marry in most states in America, though same-sex couples have this (equal) right in more enlightened countries. Debate over the legal definition of marriage overlooks the fact that Nature has already defined it. Future generations in the United States will look back and wonder what the fuss was all about. See Quindlen (2009).

133  Quote from *The Inquiry* by Ugo Betti, cited in Tripp (1970) p. 383.

134  I've met celibate couples who live without rancor and find that celibacy comes easily. Others find it more difficult, but do so out of love. Like some couples I've seen cope with serious illness or disability, celibacy truly comes from the best in them. There's lightness in their interactions, they still touch each other with affection, and they may share other kinds of sensual experiences. Such partners do exist and they are well-differentiated people. However, don't kid yourself that this is the norm. In many situations, celibacy comes out of (much) less than the best in us.

135  American Psychiatric Association (1987).

136  Bullying, hate crimes, domestic violence, and mass shootings at schools are everyday examples of people wreaking havoc on the people with whom they are emotionally fused. The 1999 Columbine High School massacre in Colorado and the 2007 Virginia Tech shootings are particularly sad examples.

137  For highly fused couples, their torturous relationship continues well beyond divorce. Some remained locked in emotional combat for the rest of their lives. Time, distance, property settlement, and remarriage to new partners doesn't diminish their emotional fusion and reflected sense of self, which surfaces as financial disputes, jealousy, lying, and manipulation.

138  *Passionate Marriage* contains a detailed discussion of the comfort/safety cycle and the growth cycle, together with an illustration showing details of each cycle and how the two fit together. See Chapter 9.

139  Weintraub (2009) p. 89. William Brietbart, chief of psychiatry at Sloan-Kettering Cancer Center, and other cancer treatment specialists, see this as a question of whether or not people take advantage of having had cancer.

140  Weintraub (2009) p. 92.

141  According to a study of cancer survivors, the hopeful ones managed their treatment instead of letting doctors and medical staff run things, and often chose the most aggressive treatments. Hope was not a given for these people, it was something they wrestled from despair. See Weintraub (2009).

142  The neuroplasticity of the human brain is amazing. Scientists have discovered the visual cortex of blind people's brains gets converted to auditory processing. Blind people hear better because they have twice as much brain space devoted to processing sounds. The visual cortex seems to be so plastic it can be used for anything. By using a photo-sensitive device attached to their *backs*, blind people have been able to see. Stroke victims have recovered from neurological damage, Jill Bolte Taylor being one remarkable example (Taylor, 2008 and 2009). Through massed repetitive neuroplastic training, brain-damaged children can regain functions presumed lost due to the site of their injury. For an uplifting view of neuroplasticity and human resilience, see Doidge (2007). Begley (2007a) documents how psychotherapy and personal development can change your brain for the better, which Doidge calls "positive plasticity."

143  Your corpus callosum, orbitofrontal cortex, cerebellum, anterior cingulate, and hippocampus can be positively as well as negatively affected by interpersonal experiences. See Damasio (1999) and Benes (1998).

144  Stern (1985).

145  LeDoux (1996).

146  Meaney et al. (1996).

147  This falls under the new science of *epigenetics*—how personal experience modifies gene expression. See Caspi et al. (2002).

148  Cook & Wellman (2004) and Czeh et al. (2005).

149  Barretta (2005).

150  Fanselow & Poulos (2005).

151  See LeDoux (2003) for a thorough review.

152  Bower (1996).

153  Gurvits et al. (1996).

154  For further evidence of stress damage to the hippocampus, see Carrion, Weems, & Reiss (2007) and Sampolsky (1999).

155  Although rats exposed to a cat (predator threat) showed reduced neural plasticity in the hippocampus and enhanced plasticity in the amygdala, but Tianeptine, an antidepressant (e.g., Stablon, Coaxil, Tatinol), enhanced synaptic plasticity by increasing general excitability of the hippocampus and reducing it

in the amygdala. Tianeptine is a selective serotonin reuptake enhancer (SSRE). Unlike conventional SSRE tricyclic antidepressants (Torfanil, Norpramin), Tianeptine enhances serotonin reuptake instead of inhibiting it. This increases the effects of serotonin in your limbic system and pre-frontal cortex, which elevates your mood. See Vouimbai et al. (2006), p. 32–33.

156  Nikulina et al. (2004).

157  Cahill (2000) and Quevedo et al. (2003).

158  Udwin et al. (2000).

159  Davidson (2000) and (1994).

160  Schore (1994 and 1996) and Stern (1985).

161  Siegel (2002).

162  Whereas genetics focuses on how traits are inherited through the genes in your DNA, epigenetics refers to changes in how your genes express themselves that don't actually alter your DNA. (Changes occur in the protein wrapper surrounding your DNA.) Epigenetic effects show up in embryonic cell development, maternal effects, gene silencing, X chromosome inactivation, gene position effect, cell regeneration and normal turnover, cell mutation, the progress of tumors, the effects of carcinogens, bookmarking, imprinting, reprogramming, parthenogenesis and cloning. See Rutter, Moffitt, & Caspi (2006) and Rutter (2006).

163  A long-term study of over a thousand people in one New Zealand town discovered a strong link between how people responded to multiple episodes of stress, and "short" and "long" forms (called an allele) of a serotonin transporter gene. Those with the "short" allele produced less serotonin and had fewer serotonin reuptake transporter molecules in their brains. If these people had three or four severe life stressors in a five-year period, they were more likely to develop depressive symptoms, diagnosable depression, and suicide. People with the "long" allele (which produces and transports more serotonin) were much more depression resistant under similar episodes of severe life stress. See Caspi et al. (2003).

164  Caspi et al. (2002). Another study found maltreatment was more likely to produce conduct disorder symptoms in children at high genetic risk. Maltreatment produced a 24 percent increase in antisocial behavior among these children, but just a 2 percent increase among other children. In other words, if a child with a "short" allele was mistreated, he or she was twelve times more likely to get into trouble. But if he wasn't maltreated, he was no more likely to engage in antisocial behavior than other children. See Jaffee et al. (2005).

165  There are "short" and "long" alleles of a gene for MAOA, which metabolizes (neutralizes) neurotransmitters produced when children are mistreated and exposed to aggressive behavior. Mistreated boys with the "short" MAOA allele were more likely to develop adolescent conduct disorders, adult antisocial and aggressive personality traits, and be convicted of a violent crime by

age twenty-six. In one study, 85 percent of them had some antisocial history. Although they constituted only 12 percent of the sample, they accounted for 44 percent of violent convictions, because they offended at a higher average rate than other violent offenders. See Moffitt (2005) and Slutske (2001). Another study found that men with the low MAOA-producing allele who reported early childhood abuse before age fifteen, were more impulsive. See Huang (2004).

166  Even our primate relatives display primitive collaborative alliances. See Povinelli & Preuss (1995).

167  Fisher realized the length of human infancy and the length of many marriages is about four years. She proposes that pair-bonding originally evolved to only last long enough for a couple to raise a child through infancy and weaning. If a second infant wasn't conceived, couples tended to separate and form another pair-bond with a different partner. This differs from the picture that life-long pair-bonding is the norm for adult "attachment" relationships. Fisher, *Anatomy of Love*, p.154.

168  This coincides with Stephanie Coontz's thesis. See Coontz (2006).

169  Chapter Six of *Passionate Marriage* is devoted to background and practical advise on *hugging till relaxed.*

170  You'll be easily distracted, so start off doing *hugging till relaxed* someplace where you won't be disturbed, especially if you have kids. And if you do have children, get good at doing *hugging till relaxed* in private, and then do it in your living room (with your clothes on). It will lower the anxiety and tension in your house and help everyone calm down. It reduces the ambient stress level, creating an environment that promotes healthy brain function.

171  Repetition is critical for success with all the activities I describe in Part Four. Clients who do *hugging till relaxed* frequently (almost daily) for at least ten minutes obtain better results. When you're starting out, several times a day works best. Frequent repetition and massed practice appears to be important in neuroplastic training (Doidge, 2007).

172  You can quiet your mind and calm your heart by counting breaths: Take a deep breath in and count "1." Exhale deeply and count "2." Slow your breathing and keep counting "1—2—1—2." This focuses your attention and synchronizes your mind and body. When your mind drifts off and you've lost count, start over.

173  Taylor (2009).

174  Svoboda, McKinnon, & Levine (2006).

175  Your right and left hemispheres communicate through your corpus callosum.

176  Some couples start off working with *heads on pillows* and then add *hugging till relaxed.* These two activities are not hierarchical. It's a matter of how

best to use them in your particular situation. For instance, one couple started with *heads on pillows* because they needed to confront years of deception between them. They did *heads on pillows* with clothes on, looking eye to eye. Out of bed, they began to deal with how they lied to each other, face to face, day after day. This laid the groundwork for doing *hugging till relaxed*. For more details on *heads on pillows*, see Chapter 11 in *Resurrecting Sex*.

177  Cozolino's (2002) book on psychotherapy and neuroplastic changes has six of the seven items listed here. To this I have added "intense and profound intersubjective moments of meeting" based on the work of Stern (1985 and 1994), Schore (1996), and others.

178  Sexual dysfunctions and low desire often go hand in hand. Sexual desire is an important component of your total level of stimulation in a sexual encounter, and thus greatly determines whether or not your body responds and you become aroused and reach orgasm. If you have low sexual desire, you're more likely to have difficulty getting aroused, staying lubricated or erect, or having an orgasm. *Resurrecting Sex* contains a complete system, called the *Quantum Model*, for resolving sexual dysfunctions, including arousal problems like lack of interest, difficulties with lubrication or erections, and orgasms that are too fast, too slow, or no-show. See pp. 31–36 and 170–171.

Basically, your total level of stimulation has to reach your body's physical response thresholds for genital response and orgasm. When your total level of stimulation reaches or exceeds your response thresholds, your genitals do what they're suppose to do. Your total level of stimulation has three components: (1) your body's ability to respond physically, (2) stimulation you receive in all sensory modalities, and (3) your emotions, thoughts, and feelings while you're having sex. Increased desire adds directly and indirectly to your total stimulation. It enhances your sensations and optimizes your thoughts and feelings. By applying the *Quantum Model*'s three dimensions, you can systematically analyze your sexual dysfunctions and resolve them.

179  See www.misterpoll.com/polls/3256/results.

180  This discussion of restarting your sexual relationship also applies to relationships that are not necessarily completely celibate.

181  "First, externally produced stimuli normally carry more biological significance than self-produced stimuli, and self-produced stimuli need not be picked out as important. An animal must be attuned to sensory events that indicate the actions of other animals, and this can only be achieved by being able to ignore the sensory events that arise as a consequence of the animal's own actions. This allows unexpected stimulation to be selectively detected. The attenuation of self-produced tactile stimuli might distinguish them from biologically more important (externally produced) stimuli . . . As the tactile stimulus diverges

temporally or spatially from the motor command producing it, the efference copy is less able to predict and cancel the sensation, which is therefore perceived as more tickly." See Blakemore et al. (1999), p. 556.

182 The medial frontal regions of the brain. See Frith & Frith (1999).

183 Damasio (1999).

184 Fridlund & Loftis (1990) and Harris & Christenfeld (1997).

185 Stearns (1972) discusses the neural pathways of the tickle-laughter reflex arc in Chapter 1.

186 See Johnson (2002) and Ellis (2007). Havelock Ellis, a famous sexologist of the early 1900s, speculated about a neural connection between tickling and laughter mediated by a common cognitive component.

187 Posted by Ron on July 25, 1999, in the "Tickle Torture Forum." Also see www.ticklingforum.com and www.ticklingemporium.com.

188 The corpus callosum. See De Bellis et al. (1999).

189 How does "getting control of yourself without dropping your alliance with your partner" fit with focusing on being able to hold on to your self by yourself? Holding on to your self independently is always the bottom line. It's a fall-back position that lets you relax. You can temporarily stop the activity at any time if you need to get control of your self by yourself.

But "holding on to your self independently" doesn't mean away from your partner. Differentiation is about holding on to your self while you're emotionally and physically *close* to your partner. If your Four Points of Balance are weak, you maintain your emotional balance by keeping people either more distant or closer then they want to be. This strategy for overcoming ticklishness will challenge your Four Points of Balance and stretch your ability to maintain a collaborative alliance with your partner. If you do have a true collaborative alliance and your partner isn't pressuring you to conform, your brain may still say he is. If it does, show yourself the difference between what's happening in your mind and what's actually happening between the two of you. Repeatedly comparing the two, right then and in subsequent sessions, will quiet your brain's hyperreactive emotional centers.

190 Subjects in one study reported ticklish sensations when the examiner's hand approached but did not touch their bodies. See Newman et al. (1991).

191 Anxiety arousal / sexual arousal is sexual arousal triggered by the physiological side effects of anxiety. As your body becomes more physiologically activated, it can trigger sexual arousal. This is a naturally occurring response. However, people raised in highly anxious households often develop this into their dominant sexual arousal pattern. As children and adolescents they are sexually aroused or masturbate in highly anxious surroundings. Masturbation isn't the problem, it's the negative plasticity, emotional learning, and context it occurs in.

This combination makes developing a dominant anxiety arousal / sexual arousal pattern more likely. It's why many people like to have extramarital affairs and lie. A little anxiety makes them hot.

Highly anxious, stressful houses involve constant arguments, or things being thrown or broken, or corporal punishment, or days of "nobody speaking to each other" and emotionally freezing someone out. Sometimes one or both parents are alcoholics, or the family breadwinner keeps loosing his job or becomes seriously ill. The more acute the anxiety and stress, and the more poorly differentiated the family, the more likely you are to develop a powerful anxiety arousal / sexual arousal pattern. For the physiology behind anxiety arousal / sexual arousal, and a case example of how to deal with it, see *Resurrecting Sex*.

192  Whelihan (2000) and Berg (2000).

193  You could argue that Kate and Paul *did* feel more safe and secure with each other while going into the experience. They established a collaborative alliance through hand-holding, and each saw the other was motivated to go forward. However, this overlooks how they got there: It came by regulating themselves and not trying to "get what they needed" from each other.

194  Calter et al. (2002). Your posterior superior temporal sulcus (STS) and medial prefrontal cortex.

195  Subsequent analysis is carried out in the amygdala and orbitofrontal cortex, in a three—structure system. See Allison, Puce, & McCarthy (2000). The evolutionary role of social gaze in vertebrates apparently changed substantially for primates compared to other animals. This may have been driven by changes in primate faces and eyes that facilitated communicating about the environment, and emotional and mental states. Eyes communicate different messages depending on the status, disposition, and emotional state of the sender and receiver of such signals. See Emery (2000).

196  Batki et al. (2000).

197  Schuller & Rossion (2001).

198  Knut et al. (2001). Averted gaze and mutual gaze also trigger blood flow responses in similar areas which differ from those involved in face processing. These areas include the occipital part of your fusiform gyrus, the right parietal lobule, the right inferior temporal gyrus, and the middle temporal gyrus in both hemispheres. See Wicker et al. (1998).

199  You can read more about eyes-open sex in Chapter 8 of *Passionate Marriage*. The origin of eyes-open sex as a clinical tool is covered in *Constructing the Sexual Crucible*.

200  Eyes-open sex and orgasm described here involves partner engagement and bonding, and not just visual stimuli per se. It is usually of equal interest to men and women. This is different than looking at photos of sexual activity.

Men are generally more interested in and responsive to sexually arousing pictures than women (although plenty of women like this too). Men and women show similar activation patterns across multiple brain regions, including ventral striatal regions in the brain's reward circuitry. But men's amygdala and hypothalamus are more strongly activated, even when women report greater sexual arousal, and differences show up more in the left amygdala than the right. See Hamann et. al. (2004).

201 I don't recommend starting off with *hugging till relaxed* with one partner lying one on top of the other, or sitting in the other's lap. It triggers too many other issues. If Paul and Kate had tried this earlier in therapy, it probably would not have worked out as well. Paul offered to hug lying down with Kate on his chest, but it would have been a dodge for him letting himself be held. He would have been holding Kate rather than her holding him. He also wouldn't have learned to stand on his own two feet—literally and emotionally—while letting himself be held.

202 I've said couples always communicate, even if they think they don't. If you analyze automatic talking just before orgasm, you'll often find it's not the gibberish it appears to be. It requires extensive mind-mapping to fill in the blanks. But context and emotional learning through your body usually makes this fairly easy, if you know the person. If you have a collaborative alliance, most people can do it on the spot. This very positive circumstance increases positive plasticity.

203 Eastern cultures make many references to female sexual power. There's a Hindu myth that the gods *Shiva* (male) and *Parvati* (female) competed to see who could create a better race of people without the participation of the other. Parvati's well-shaped, well-mannered, and attractive *Yonijas* beat the stupid, feeble, misshapen *Lingajas* of Shiva in battle.

204 Fisher, *Anatomy of Love*, p.32.

205 A woman's ovulatory cycle also plays a big role in her response to sexual stimuli. Her hormonal state when first exposed affects her subsequent response as well. If she is ovulating during her first exposure, her interest is high and remains high on subsequent exposures. But if her first view occurs in her postovulatory phase, her sexual interest is lower and remains lower later, even when she's ovulating again. See Wallen (2009).

206 Perper & Weis (1987) and Perper (1985).

207 Bonobos have 98 percent of our genetic profile, making them a very close relative. Bonobos are among the smartest apes, they have similar physical traits, and their sexual behavior is most similar to ours. See de Waal (1995).

208 A "fuck buddy" is someone with whom you share sex and friendship ("friendship with benefits"), with the clear understanding that it's not about love or a future together.

209 Of 150 marriage and family therapists attending my 1993 Networker Symposium presentation, less then a dozen (8 percent) acknowledged personal experience with fucking. At the Louisiana Association for Marriage and Family Therapy Annual Conference, the figure was 15 percent. This means you can easily end up seeing a therapist whose sole knowledge of fucking comes from reading this book.

210 Think of this as harnessing the sexual energy in your union—*yin* and *yang* in Eastern terms. Tantric sex utilizes the "energy loop" formed during sex. It's no surprise that fucking, doing your partner, and being done create desire and growth. According to Tantra, self-awareness and self-transcendence are part of your sexual potential and the sacred goal of sex.

211 The neurophysiology and neurochemistry of orgasm has also been documented. The same kind of dopamine pathway involved in romantic love is also activated during orgasm from women's nucleus accumbens and men's ventral tagmental area. Oxytocin is released at orgasm in both men and women, together with sympathetic autonomic activation (increased blood pressure, heart rate, and pupil diameter of the eye). Brain components involved in orgasm are the nucleus accumbens, cingulate cortex, insular cortex, amygdala, hippocampus, paraventricular nucleus (PVN) of the hypothalamus, basal ganglia, and cerebellum. After orgasm the amygdala is also deactivated. See *The Science of Orgasm* (Komisaruk, Beyer-Flores, & Whipple, 2006) for an excellent review.

212 Kohl & Francoeur (2002).

213 "Deep throat" is oral sex on a man in which the giver suppresses her (or his) gag reflex and takes the penis deep into the back of the throat.

214 Siegel, (2002) pp. 105–106.

# INDEX

**NOTE:** An '*n*' in the page number indicates a note; '*nn*' indicates multiple notes. For example, 397*n*6 is page 397, note 6; 412*nn*164-165 is page 412, note 165 and note 166.